The Latest, the Best, the Cheapest.

McGUFFEY'S NEW CLASS BOOKS.

McGUFFEY'S NEW PRIMARY SCHOOL CHARTS, complete in six numbers: 2½ feet wide and 3 feet long. printed on large, bold, type: to be placed on the wall of the school room.

McGUFFEY'S NEWLY REVISED ECLECTIC SPELLING BOOK, containing more than 12,000 words, mostly *primitive*, with rules and examples for the formation of *derivatives.*

McGUFFEY'S NEW FIRST ECLECTIC READER; containing the alphabet and lessons, simple and easy, for little learners.

McGUFFEY'S NEW SECOND ECLECTIC READER; easy lessons in reading and spelling, for young pupils.

McGUFFEY'S NEW THIRD ECLECTIC READER; interesting and instructive primary lessons, for young pupils.

McGUFFEY'S NEW FOURTH ECLECTIC READER; chaste and instructive lessons in prose and poetry. for the young.

McGUFFEY'S NEW FIFTH ECLECTIC READER; choice extracts in prose and verse, for middle classes.

McGUFFEY'S NEW SIXTH ECLECTIC READER; a rhetorical reading book, for the more advanced classes.

Auxiliary Books—Just Published.

McGUFFEY'S NEW HIGH SCHOOL READER: copious classic exercises, for the highest classes in schools and academies

McGUFFEY'S NEW ECLECTIC SPEAKER; comprising three hundred exercises for reading or declamation.

This book may be used as a reader or speaker; the selections being peculiarly adapted to the *double* purpose of declamation and reading in High Schools.

McGUFFEY'S NEW JUVENILE SPEAKER, for Common Schools: choice and animating exercises in speaking or reading, designed for young pupils. *Preparing for publication.*

PUBLISHED BY

CLARK, AUSTIN & SMITH,—NEW YORK:

JOSHUA B. LIPPINCOTT & CO.,—PHILADELPHIA:

W. B. SMITH & CO.,—CINCINNATI.

Simple, Comprehensive, Practical, Thorough.

RAY'S NEW ARITHMETIC—ALGEBRAS.

Each Book *of the Arithmetical Course, as well as the Algebraic, is Complete in itself, and is sold separately.*

PRIMARY ARITHMETIC.—RAY'S ARITHMETIC, FIRST BOOK; simple Mental Lessons and tables for little learners.

INTELLECTUAL ARITHMETIC.—RAY'S ARITHMETIC, SECOND BOOK: the most interesting Intellectual Arithmetic extant.

PRACTICAL ARITHMETIC.—RAY'S ARITHMETIC, THIRD BOOK: for schools and academies; a full and complete treatise, on the inductive and analytical methods of instruction.

KEY TO RAY'S ARITHMETIC, containing solutions to the questions; also an Appendix of test Examples for the Slate and Blackboard.

RAY'S NEW HIGHER ARITHMETIC.—The Principles of Arithmetic, analyzed and practically applied. For advanced classes.

KEY TO RAY'S HIGHER ARITHMETIC, containing full and lucid solutions to examples in that work.

ELEMENTARY ALGEBRA.—RAY'S ALGEBRA, FIRST BOOK; for common schools and academies; simple, thorough, progressive.

HIGHER ALGEBRA.—RAY'S ALGEBRA, SECOND BOOK; for advanced students in academies, and for colleges; a progressive, lucid, and comprehensive work.

KEY TO RAY'S ALGEBRA, 1st and 2d BOOKS, in one vol., 12 mo.

Preparing for Publication.

I.—THE ELEMENTS OF GEOMETRY, embracing plane and solid geometry, with numerous practical exercises. **II.—TRIGONOMETRY AND MENSURATION,** containing logarithmic computations, plane and spherical trigonometry, with their applications, mensuration of planes and solids, with logarithmic and other tables. **III.—SURVEYING AND NAVIGATION;** surveying and leveling, navigation, barometric hights, etc.

To be followed by others, forming a complete Mathematical Course for schools and colleges.

PUBLISHED BY

CLARK, AUSTIN & SMITH,—NEW YORK:
JOSHUA B. LIPPINCOTT & CO.,—PHILADELPHIA:
W. B. SMITH & CO.,—CINCINNATI.

Preferred by the best Teachers.

PINNEO'S SERIES OF GRAMMARS.

PINNEO'S PRIMARY GRAMMAR: a simple and thorough elementary work for common schools.

PINNEO'S ANALYTICAL GRAMMAR: a complete treatise for schools and academies.

PINNEO'S ENGLISH TEACHER: a simple, practical, and thorough work on the Analysis of English sentences.

PECULIARITIES OF THIS SERIES.

1. Simplicity of arrangement, definitions, rules, exercises and illustrations.

2. Variety and attractive nature of the exercises, which are varied and full.

3. Minute and extensive analysis—introduced early and continued to the close.

4. Composition is taught in all its elementary principles.

THEIR POPULARITY.

Probably no series of grammars published, ever attained so firm an introduction into the best schools of the country.

This is owing to their rare and unquestioned merit, as numerous testimonials from leading educators show.

They are commended as "works of the highest merit,—clear, comprehensive, practical and thorough, embodying the true system of teaching the principles of the English language."

"Their philosophical plan and simplicity of arrangement, the progressive character of the lessons, the abundance, variety and excellence of the exercises, and their admirable adaptation to the wants of both pupil and instructor, leave little need of further improvement.'

PUBLISHED BY

CLARK, AUSTIN & SMITH,—NEW YORK:
JOSHUA B. LIPPINCOTT & CO.,—PHILADELPHIA:
W. B. SMITH & CO.,—CINCINNATI.

THE ECLECTIC EDUCATIONAL SERIES

EMBRACES,

McGUFFEY'S PRIMARY SCHOOL CHARTS,. . 6 No's.

McGUFFEY'S ECLECTIC SPELLER, ... 1 Book.

McGUFFEY'S NEW ECLECTIC READERS, . . 8 Books.

RAY'S SERIES OF ARITHMETICS, ... 4 Books.

RAY'S SERIES OF ALGEBRAS, ... 2 Books.

PINNEO'S SERIES OF GRAMMARS, ... 3 Books.

These School Books possess the highest merit, are more widely introduced than any other series published, and have received the cordial indorsement of the most intelligent and successful teachers, throughout the Union.

ECONOMY TO PARENTS.—They combine the rare advantages of superior intrinsic merit, typographical beauty, **CHEAPNESS,** and extensive uniformity of adoption and use.

Approved and adopted in many Schools in the **NEW ENGLAND STATES,** in **NEW YORK CITY** Public Schools,—in the Public Schools of **PENNSYLVANIA,**—and in nearly every other State where liberal attention is given to public instruction.

This Series has been Officially Recommended

BY THE OHIO STATE SUPERINTENDENT OF PUB. INSTRUCTION,
INDIANA STATE SUPTS. OF PUBLIC INSTRUCTION,
INDIANA STATE BOARD OF EDUCATION,
ILLINOIS STATE SUPT. OF PUBLIC INSTRUCTION,
ILLINOIS STATE BOARD OF EDUCATION,
IOWA STATE SUPTS. OF PUBLIC INSTRUCTION,
WISCONSIN STATE SUPT. OF PUBLIC INSTRUCTION,
MICHIGAN STATE SUPT. OF PUBLIC INSTRUCTION,
AND BY MORE THAN **10,000** SCHOOL BOARDS.

PUBLISHED BY
CLARK, AUSTIN & SMITH,—NEW YORK:
JOSHUA B. LIPPINCOTT & CO.,—PHILADELPHIA:
W. B. SMITH & CO.,—CINCINNATI.

ECLECTIC EDUCATIONAL SERIES.

McGUFFEY'S

NEW

HIGH SCHOOL READER:

FOR ADVANCED CLASSES.

EMBRACING ABOUT

Two Hundred Classic Exercises.

STEREOTYPE EDITION.

PUBLISHERS:

CINCINNATI—WINTHROP B. SMITH & CO.,

NEW YORK—CLARK, AUSTIN & SMITH.

PUBLISHERS' NOTICE.

THE widely extended approval and patronage bestowed upon the Eclectic Educational Series for several years past, have given to them a constantly increasing demand.

Their sale is NOT EQUALED *by any other similar School Books in the United States.*

Such approval renders it the *duty* and PRIVILEGE of the Publishers to sustain and increase their usefulness by such improvements as are demanded by judicious educational progress. With that view,

McGUFFEY'S ECLECTIC READERS

Have been entirely remodeled. Such lessons as discriminating practical teachers had found the least interesting have been removed, and others, with large additions—especially of primary matter—have been introduced into the series.

A careful attention to progression, by which the learner is led forward, step by step, by an easy gradation — a pure moral and religious sentiment inculcated in interesting and instructive lessons—a neat typography and handsome style of publication, render them the best class-books for reading in the English language; and, at their very low prices, the cheapest.

☞ To secure accuracy in those who order books, these volumes (six in number), are entitled

McGUFFEY'S NEW ECLECTIC READERS,

That they may not be confounded with the former editions, which are still continued in publication.

Stereotyped by C. F. O'Driscoll & Co.

PREFACE.

THIS volume is designed for advanced classes in reading.

It is adapted to this purpose by the following characteristics:

1. There is great *variety* in style and subjects.

2. The exercises are of a highly *elevated* character.

3. There is an *exclusion* of all *collateral matter*, such as Rhetorical Rules and Notation, Exercises in Articulation, Definition, &c., &c., which have been so extensively treated of in the other volumes of this series as to render further instruction unnecessary.

This book is thus adapted to *general practice* in reading, and with the preceding volumes of this series or any other of similar character, will furnish an abundant amount of matter for a thorough course in this department.

It is presented to the public with the hope, that it may receive that favor which has been so liberally awarded to the other volumes of the ECLECTIC SERIES.

CONTENTS.

EXERCISES IN PROSE.

(9)

CONTENTS. 11

EXERCISES IN POETRY.

EXERCISE I. — THE CONTRAST.

6. ZIﾱﾱERﾱANN; a German writer.
11. CLEP'-SY-DRA; a contrivance used by the ancients for meas-
uring time by the running of water.

1. SOME years since, a German prince, making a tour of
Europe, stopped at Venice for a short period. It was the
close of summer; the Adriatic was calm, the nights were
lovely, and the Venetian women in the full enjoyment of
those delicious spirits, that, in their climate, rise and fall
with the coming and the departure of the finest season of
the year. Every day was given by the illustrious stranger
to research among the records and antiquities of this
singular city, and every night to amusement on the river
Brenta. When the morning was nigh, it was the custom
to return to sup at some of the palaces of the nobility.

2. In the commencement of his intercourse, all national
distinctions were carefully suppressed; but, as his intimacy
increased, he was forced to see the lurking vanity of the
Italians breaking out. One of its most frequent exhibitions
was in the little dramas that wound up these stately fes-
tivals. The wit was constantly sharpened by some contrast
of the Italian and the German, some slight aspersions on

To TEACHERS.—Rules for Reading, Rhetorical Notation, etc., are
dispensed with in this volume, as the student, if he has been properly
taught, has received abundant instruction on this subject from the
New Fifth and Sixth Eclectic Readers of this Series, and should
now be left to his own judgment, with such suggestions as the
Instructor may see fit to make.

Teutonic rudeness, some remark on the history of a people untouched by the elegance of southern manners. The sarcasm was conveyed with Italian grace, and the offense softened by its humor. It was obvious that the only re-taliation must be humorous.

3. At length, the prince, on point of taking leave, invited his entertainers to a farewell supper. He drew the con-versation to the infinite superiority of the Italians, and, above all, of the Venetians, acknowledged the darkness in which Germany had been destined to remain so long, and looked forward with infinite sorrow to the comparative opinion of posterity upon the country to which so little of its gratitude must be due. "But, my lords," said he, "we are an emulous people, and an example like yours cannot be lost, even upon a German. I have been charmed with your dramas, and have contrived a little arrangement to give one of our country, if you will follow me to the great hall." The company rose and followed him through the splendid suite of Venetian apartments to the hall, which was fitted up as a German barn.

4. The aspect of the room produced first surprise, and next a universal smile. It had no resemblance to their own gilded, sculptured, and sumptuous little saloons. However, it was only so much the more Teutonic. The curtain drew up. The surprise rose into loud laughter, even among the Venetians, who have been seldom betrayed into any thing beyond a smile, for generations together.

5. The stage was a temporary erection, rude and uneven. The scene represented a wretched and irregular street, scarcely lighted by a few twinkling lamps, and looking the fit haunt of robbery and assassination. On a closer view, some of the noble spectators began to think it had some resemblance to an Italian street, and actually discovered in it one of the leading streets of their own famous city. But the play was on a German story; they were under a German roof: the street was, notwithstanding its ill-omened similitude, of course, German. The street was solitary. At length, a traveler, a German, with pistols in a belt round his waist, and apparently exhausted by his journey.

came pacing along. He knocked at several doors, but could obtain no admission. He then wrapped himself up in his cloak, sat down on a fragment of a monument, and soliloquized.

6. "Well, here have I come; and this is my reception. All palaces; no inns; all nobles, and not a man to tell me where I can lie down in comfort or in safety. Well, it can not be helped. A German does not much care; campaigning has hardened us. Hunger and thirst, heat and cold, dangers of war and the roads, are not very formidable, after what we have had to work through from father to son. Loneliness, however, is not so well, unless a man can labor or read. Read! That's true; come out, Zimmermann." He took a volume from his pocket, moved nearer to the decaying lamp, and soon seemed absorbed.

7. Another form soon attracted the eyes of the spectators. A long, light figure came with a kind of visionary movement, from behind the monument, surveyed the traveler with keen curiosity, listened with apparent astonishment to his words, and in another moment had fixed itself gazing over his shoulder on the volume. The eyes of this singular being wandered rapidly over the page, and when it was turned, they were lifted to heaven with the strongest expression of wonder. The German was weary; his head soon drooped over his study, and he closed the book.

8. "What," said he, rising and stretching his limbs, "is there no one stirring in this comfortless place? Is it not near day?" He took out his repeater, and touched the pendant; it struck four. His mysterious attendant had watched him narrowly; the repeater was traversed over with an eager gaze; but when it struck, delight was mingled with the wonder that had till then filled its pale, intelligent countenance. "Four o'clock," said the German; "in my country, half the world would be thinking of going to their day's work by this time. In another hour, it will be sunrise. Well, then, I'll do you a service, you nation of sleepers, and make you open your eyes." He drew out one of his pistols, and fired it. The attendant form, still hovering behind him, had looked curiously upon the pistol,

H. S. R.—2

but on its going off, started back in terror, and with a loud cry that made the traveler turn.

9. "Who are you?" was his greeting to this strange intruder. "I will not hurt you," was the answer. "Who cares about that?" was the German's retort; and he pulled out the other pistol. "My friend," said the figure, "even that weapon of thunder and lightning cannot reach me now; but if you would know who I am, let me entreat you to satisfy my curiosity a moment; you seem a man of extraordinary powers." "Well, then," said the German, in a gentle voice, "if you come as a friend, I shall be glad to give you information; it is the custom of our country to deny nothing to those who love to learn."

10. The former sighed deeply, and murmured, "And yet you are a Teuton. But you were just reading a little case of strange, and yet most interesting figures; was it a manuscript?" "No, it was a printed book." "Printed? What is printing? I never heard but of writing." "It is an art by which one man can give to the world, in one day, as much as three hundred could give by writing, and in a character of superior clearness, correctness, and beauty; one by which books are made universal, and literature eternal." "Admirable, glorious art!" said the inquirer; "who was its illustrious inventor?" "A GERMAN."

11. "But another question. I saw you look at a most curious instrument, traced with figures; it sparkled with diamonds; but its greatest wonder was its sound. It gave the hour with miraculous exactness, and the strokes were followed by tones superior to the sweetest music of my day." "That was a repeater." "How? When I had the luxuries of the earth at my command, I had nothing to tell the hour better than the clepsydra and the sun-dial. But this must be incomparable, from its facility of being carried about, from its suitableness to all hours, and from its exactness. It must be an admirable guide even to a higher knowledge. All depends upon the exactness of time. It may assist navigation and astronomy. What an invention! Whose was it? He must be more than man." "He was a GERMAN."

12. "What, still a barbarian? I remember his nation.

I once saw an auxiliary legion of them marching toward Rome. They were a bold, and brave, blue-eyed troop. The whole city poured out to see those northern warriors; but we looked on them only as savages. I have one more question, the most interesting of all. I saw you raise your hand with a small truncheon in it; in a moment, something rushed out that seemed a portion of the fire of the clouds. . Were they thunder and lightning that I saw? Did they obey your command? Was that truncheon a talisman? And are you a mighty magician? Was that truncheon a scepter commanding the elements? Are you a god?"

13. The strange inquirer had drawn back gradually as his feelings rose. Curiosity was now solemn wonder, and he stood gazing in an attitude that mingled awe with devotion. The German felt the sensation of a superior presence growing on himself, as he looked on the fixed countenance of this mysterious being. It was in that misty blending of light and darkness which the moon leaves as it sinks just before morn. There was a single hue of pale gray in the east, that touched its visage with a chill light; the moon, resting broadly on the horizon, was setting behind; the figure seemed as if it were standing in the orb. Its arms were lifted toward heaven, and the light came through its drapery with the mild splendor of a vision; but the German, habituated to the vicissitudes of " perils by flood and field," shook off his brief alarm, and proceeded calmly to explain the source of this miracle. He gave a slight detail of the machinery of the pistol, and alluded to the history of gunpowder.

14. " It must be an effective instrument in the hands of man for either good or ill," said the former. " How much it must change the nature of war! How much it must influence the fate of nations! By whom was this wondrous secret revealed to the inhabitants of earth?" " A GERMAN."

15. The form seemed suddenly to enlarge; its feebleness of voice was gone; its attitude was irresistibly noble. Before it uttered a word, it looked as if it were made to

persuade and command. Its outer robe had been flung away; it stood with an antique dress of brilliant white, gathered in many folds, and edged with a deep border of purple; a slight wreath of laurel, of dazzling green, was on its brow. It looked like the genius of eloquence. "Stranger," it said, pointing to the Apennines, which were then beginning to be marked by the twilight, "eighteen hundred years have passed, since I was the glory of all beyond those mountains. Eighteen hundred years have passed into the great flood of eternity, since I entered Rome in triumph, and was honored as the leading mind of the great intellectual empire of the world. But I knew nothing of those things. I was a child to you; we were all children to the discoverers of those glorious potencies. But has Italy not been still the mistress of mind? She was then the first of the first; has she not kept her superiority? Show me her noble inventions. I must soon sink from the earth: let me learn still to love my country."

16. The listener started back : "Who, what are you?" " I am a spirit; I was Cicero. Show me, by the love of a patriot, what Italy now sends out to enlighten mankind!" The German looked embarrassed; but in a moment after, he heard the sound of a pipe and a tabor. He pointed in silence to the narrow street from which the interruption came. A ragged figure tottered out with a barrel organ at his back, a frame of puppets in his hand, a hurdy-gurdy round his neck, and a string of dancing dogs in his train. Cicero uttered but one sigh; "Is this Italy?" The German bowed his head.

17. The organ struck up, the dogs danced, the Italian capered round them. Cicero raised his broad gaze to heaven. "These, the men of my country! These, the orators, the poets, the patriots of mankind! What scorn and curse of Providence can have fallen upon them?" As he gazed, tears suddenly suffused his eyes; the first sunbeam struck across the spot where he stood; a purple mist rose around him, and he was gone.

18. The Venetians, with one accord, started from their seats and rushed out of the hall. The prince and his suite

had previously arranged every thing for leaving the city, and they were beyond the Venetian territory by sunrise. Another night in Venice, they would have been on their way to the other world.

EX. II. — THE OLD CLOCK.

FROM LONGFELLOW.

H. W. LONGFELLOW is one of the most distinguished living Poets of America. He is a native of Portland, Maine, a graduate of Bowdoin College, and was, for some years, a Professor there. Many of his best pieces are contained in this work, and in former volumes of this Series.

8. HOROLOGE; a time-piece.

1. SOMEWHAT back from the village street
   Stands the old-fashion'd country-seat.
   Across its antique portico
   Tall poplar-trees their shadows throw;
   And from its station in the hall
   An ancient time-piece says to all:
       "Forever, never! Never, forever!"

2. Half-way up the stairs it stands,
   And points and beckons with its hands
   From its case of massive oak,
   Like a monk, who, under his cloak,
   Crosses himself, and sighs, alas!,
   With sorrowful voice to all who pass:
       "Forever, never! Never, forever!"

3. Through days of sorrow and of mirth,
   Through days of death and days of birth,
   Through every swift vicissitude
   Of changeful time, unchanged it stood;
   As if, like God, it all things saw,
   It calmly repeats those words of awe:
       "Forever, never! Never, forever!"

4. In that mansion used to be
   Free hearted hospitality;
   His great fires up the chimney roar'd;
   The stranger feasted at his board;
   But, the skeleton at the feast,
   That warning time-piece never ceased:
       "Forever, never! Never, forever!"

5. There groups of merry children play'd;
   There youths and maidens, dreaming, stray'd.
   O precious hours! O golden prime
   And affluence of love and time!
   Even as a miser counts his gold,
   Those hours the ancient time-piece told.
       "Forever, never! Never, forever!"

6. From that chamber, clothed in white,
   The bride came forth on her wedding-night.
   There, in that silent room below,
   The dead lay in its shroud of snow!
   And in the hush that follow'd the prayer,
   Was heard the old clock on the stair:
       "Forever, never! Never, forever!"

7. All are scatter'd now and fled,
   Some are married, some are dead;
   And when I ask, with throbs of pain,
   Ah! when shall they all meet again,
   As in the days long since gone by?
   The ancient time-piece makes reply:
       "Forever, never! Never, forever!"

8. Never here, forever there,
   Where all parting, pain, and care,
   And death, and time shall disappear!
   Forever there, but never here!
   The horologe of eternity
   Sayeth this incessantly:
       "Forever, never! Never, forever!"

III. — THE SLIDE OF ALPNACH.

MOUNT PILATUS is a mountain near Lucerne in Switzerland, which derives its name from a tradition that Pontius Pilate died there, by throwing himself from one of its peaks.

The following is a description of the plan by which timber was obtained from that mountain.

1. FOR many centuries the rugged flanks and deep gorges of Mount Pilatus were covered with impenetrable forests. Lofty precipices encircled them on all sides. Even the daring hunters were scarcely able to reach them; and the inhabitants of the valley had never conceived the idea of disturbing them with the ax. These immense forests were, therefore, permitted to grow and to perish without being of the least utility to man, till a foreigner, conducted into their wild recesses in the pursuit of the chamois, was struck with wonder at the sight, and directed the attention of several Swiss gentlemen to the extent and superiority of the timber. The most intelligent and skillful individuals, however, considered it quite impracticable to avail themselves of such inaccessible stores.

2. It was not till November, 1816, that Mr. Rupp and three Swiss gentlemen, entertaining more sanguine hopes, drew up a plan of a slide, founded on trigonometrical measurements. Having purchased a certain extent of the forests from the commune of Alpnach for six thousand crowns, they began the construction of the slide, and completed it in the spring of 1818. The slide of Alpnach is formed entirely of about twenty-five thousand large pine trees, deprived of their bark, and united together in a very ingenious manner, without the aid of iron. It occupied about one hundred and sixty workmen during eighteen months, and cost nearly one hundred thousand francs, or about twenty thousand dollars. It is about three leagues, or forty-four thousand English feet long, and terminates in the Lake of Lucerne. It has the form of a trough, about six feet broad, and from three to six feet deep. Its bottom is formed of three trees, the middle one of which has a groove cut out in the direction

of its length, for receiving small rills of water, which are conducted into it from various places, for the purpose of diminishing the friction. The whole of the slide is sustained by about two thousand supports; and in many places it is attached, in a very ingenious manner, to the rugged precipices of granite.

3. It is often carried along the sides of hills and the flanks of precipitous rocks, and sometimes passes over their summits. Occasionally it goes under ground, and at other times it is conducted over the deep gorges by scaffoldings one hundred and twenty feet in hight. The boldness which characterizes this work, the sagacity displayed in all its arrangements, and the skill of the engineer, have excited the wonder of every person who has seen it.

4. Mr. Rupp was himself obliged, more than once, to be suspended by cords, in order to descend precipices many hundred feet high; and in the first months of the under-taking, he was attacked with a violent fever, which deprived him of the power of superintending his workmen. Nothing, however, could diminish his invincible perseverance. He was carried every day to the mountain in a barrow, to direct the labors of the workmen, which was absolutely necessary, as he had scarcely two good carpenters among them all; the rest having been hired by accident, without any knowledge which such an undertaking required. Mr. Rupp had also to contend against the prejudices of the peasantry. He was supposed to have communion with the devil. All these difficulties, however, were surmounted, and he had at last the satisfaction of observing the trees descend from the mountain with the rapidity of lightning. The larger pines, which were about a hundred feet long, and ten inches thick at their smaller extremity, ran through the space of three leagues, or nearly nine miles, in *two minutes and a half*, and during their descent they appeared to be only a few feet in length.

5. The arrangements for this part of the operation were extremely simple. From the lower end of the slide to the upper end, where the trees were introduced, workmen were posted at regular distances, and as soon as every

thing was ready, the workman at the lower end of the slide cried out to the one above him, "Let go." The cry was repeated from one to another, and reached the top in *three minutes.* The workmen at the top of the slide then cried out to the one below him, "It comes," and the tree was launched down the slide, preceded by the cry, which was repeated from post to post. As soon as the tree had reached the bottom, and plunged into the lake, the cry was repeated as before, and a new tree launched in a similar manner. By these means a tree descended every five or six minutes, provided no accident happened to the slide, which sometimes took place, but which was instantly repaired when it did.

6. In order to show the enormous force which the trees acquired from the great velocity of their descent, Mr. Rupp made arrangements for causing some of the trees to spring from the slide. They penetrated by their thickest extremities no less than from eighteen to twenty-four feet in the earth, and one of the trees having by accident struck against the other, it instantly cleft it through its whole length, as if it had been struck by lightning. After the trees had descended the slide, they were collected into rafts upon the lake, and conducted to Lucerne. From thence they descended the river Reuss, then the Aar, to near Brugg, afterwards to Waldshut by the Rhine, then to Basle, and even to the sea, when it was necessary.

IV. — THE LAUNCHING OF THE SHIP.

FROM LONGFELLOW.

1. ALL is finish'd! and at length
   Has come the bridal day
   Of beauty and of strength.
   To-day, the vessel shall be launch'd!
   With fleecy clouds the sky is blanch'd,
   And o'er the bay,
   Slowly, in all his splendors dight,
   The great sun rises to behold the sight.

2. The ocean old,
   Centuries old,
   Strong as youth, and as uncontroll'd,
   Paces restlessly to and fro,
   Up and down the sands of gold.
   His beating heart is not at rest;
   And far and wide,
   With ceaseless flow,
   His beard of snow
   Heaves with the heaving of his breast.

3. He waits impatient for his bride.
   There she stands,
   With her foot upon the sands,
   Deck'd with flags and streamers gay,
   In honor of her marriage day,
   Her snow-white signals fluttering, blending,
   Round her like a vail descending,
   Ready to be
   The bride of the gay, old sea.

4. Then the Master,
   With a gesture of command,
   Waved his hand;
   And at the word,
   Loud and sudden there was heard,
   All around them and below,
   The sound of hammers, blow on blow,
   Knocking away the shores and spurs.
   And see! she stirs!
   She starts! she moves! she seems to feel
   The thrill of life along her keel,
   And, spurning with her foot the ground,
   With one exulting, joyous bound,
   She leaps into the ocean's arms!

5. And lo! from the assembled crowd
   There rose a shout, prolong'd and loud,
   That to the ocean seem'd to say,
   "Take her, O bridegroom, old and gray;

Take her to thy protecting arms,
With all her youth and all her charms."

6. How beautiful she is! how fair
She lies within those arms, that press
Her form with many a soft caress
Of tenderness and watchful care!
Sail forth into the sea, O ship!
Through wind and wave, right onward steer!
The moisten'd eye, the trembling lip,
Are not the signs of doubt or fear.

7. Sail forth into the sea of life,
O gentle, loving, trusting wife,
And safe from all adversity,
Upon the bosom of that sea
Thy comings and thy goings be!
For gentleness, and love, and trust,
Prevail o'er angry wave and gust;
And in the wreck of noble lives,
Something immortal still survives!

8. Thou, too, sail on, O ship of state!
Sail on, O Union, strong and great!
Humanity, with all its fears,
With all the hopes of future years,
Is hanging breathless on thy fate!
· We know what Master · laid thy keel,
What workmen wrought thy ribs of steel,
Who made each mast, and sail, and rope,
What anvils rang, what hammers beat,
In what a forge, and what a heat,
Were shaped the anchors of thy hope.

9. Fear not each sudden sound and shock;
'Tis of the wave, and not the rock;
'Tis but the flapping of the sail
And not a rent made by the gale.

In spite of rock and tempest roar,
In spite of false lights on the shore,
Sail on, nor fear to breast the sea:
Our hearts, our hopes, are all with thee.
Our hearts, our hopes, our prayers, our tears,
Our faith triumphant o'er our fears,
Are all with thee, are all with thee.

V. — RHYME OF THE RAIL.

FROM SAXE.

JOHN G. SAXE is a living American poet, distinguished for his wit and humor. Like many other poets of our country, he has spent most of his life as a newspaper editor.

1. SINGING through the forests,
    Rattling over ridges,
Shooting under arches,
    Rumbling over bridges,
Whizzing through the mountains,
    Buzzing o'er the vale,
Bless me! this is pleasant,
    Riding on the rail!

2. Men of different stations,
    In the eye of Fame,
Here are very quickly
    Coming to the same;
High and lowly people,
    Birds of every feather,
On a common level,
    Traveling together!

3. Gentlemen in shorts,
    Looming very tall;
Gentlemen at large,
    Talking very small;
Gentlemen in tights,
    With a loose-ish mien;
Gentlemen in gray,
    Looking rather green!

4. Gentlemen quite old,
    Asking for the news;
Gentlemen in black,
    In a fit of blues;
Gentlemen in claret,
    Sober as a vicar;
Gentlemen in tweed,
    Dreadfully in liquor!

5. Stranger on the right,
    Looking very sunny,
Obviously reading
    Something rather funny.
Now the smiles are thicker,
    Wonder what they mean?
Faith, he's got the Knicker-
    Bocker Magazine!

6. Stranger on the left,
    Closing up his peepers;
Now he snores amain,
    Like the seven sleepers;
At his feet a volume
    Gives the explanation,
How the man grew stupid
    From " association!"

7. Ancient maiden lady
    Anxiously remarks,
That there must be peril
    'Mong so many sparks;
Roguish-looking fellow,
    Turning to the stranger,
Says 'tis his opinion,
    She is out of danger!

8. Woman with her baby,
    Sitting vis-à-vis;
Baby keeps a-squalling,
    Woman looks at me;

Asks about the distance;
  Says 'tis tiresome talking;
Noises of the cars
  Are so very shocking!

9. Market woman, careful
    Of the precious casket,
  Knowing eggs are eggs,
    Tightly holds her basket;
  Feeling that a smash,
    If it came, would surely
  Send her eggs to pot,
    Rather prematurely!

10. Singing through the forests,
     Rattling over ridges,
   Shooting under arches,
     Rumbling over bridges,
   Whizzing through the mountains,
     Buzzing o'er the vale,
   Bless me! this is pleasant,
     Riding on the rail!

VI.—A FLOWER FOR THE WINDOW.

FROM LEIGH HUNT.

LEIGH HUNT is an English author, born in 1784. He has written poetry and prose of a lively and interesting character, and is popular, both in England and America. The following is in his best style, and is not only interesting, but has a valuable moral.

1. WHY does not every one (who can afford it) have a geranium in his window, or some other flower? It is very cheap; its cheapness is next to nothing, if you raise it from seed, or from a slip; and it is a beauty and a companion. It sweetens the air, rejoices the eye, links you with nature and innocence, and is something to love. And if it can not love you in return, it can not hate you;

it can not utter a hateful thing even for your neglecting it; for, though it is all beauty, it has no vanity; and such being the ease, and living as it does purely to do you good and afford pleasure, how will you be able to neglect it?

2. But, pray, if you choose a geranium, or possess but a few of them, let us persuade you to choose the scarlet kind, the "old original" geranium, and not a variety of it, not one of the numerous diversities of red and white, blue and white, ivy-leaved, etc. Those are all beautiful, and very fit to vary a large collection; but to prefer them to the originals of the race, is to run the hazard of preferring the curious to the beautiful, and costliness to sound taste. It may be taken as a good general rule, that the most popular plants are the best; for otherwise they would not have become such. And what the painters call "pure colors" are preferable to mixed ones, for reasons which Nature herself has given when she painted the sky of one color, and the fields of another, and divided the rainbow itself into a few distinct colors, and made the red rose the queen of flowers.

3. Every thing is handsome about the geranium, not excepting its name; which can not be said of all flowers, though we get to love ugly words when associated with pleasing ideas. The word "geranium" is soft and pleasant; the meaning is poor, for it comes from a Greek word which signifies a crane, the fruit having the form of a crane's head or bill. Cranesbill is the English name for geranium, though the learned appellation has superseded the vernacular. But what a reason for naming the flower! as if the fruit were any thing in comparison, or any one cared about it. Such distinctions, it is true, are useful to botanists; but as a plenty of learned names are sure to be reserved for the freemasonry of the science, it would be well for the world at large to invent joyous and beautiful names for these images of joy and beauty. In some instances we have them; such as heartsease, honeysuckle, marigold, mignonette, (little darling,) daisy, (day's eye,) etc. And many flowers are so lovely, and have associated

names, otherwise unmeaning, so pleasantly with one's memory, that no new ones would sound so well, or seem even to have such proper significations.

4. In pronouncing the words lilies, roses, tulips, pinks, jonquils, we see the things themselves, and seem to taste all their beauty and sweetness. Pink is a harsh, petty word in itself, and yet assuredly it does not seem so; for in the word we have the flower. It would be difficult to persuade ourselves, that the word rose is not very beautiful. Pea is a poor, Chinese-like monosyllable; and brier is rough and fierce, as it ought to be; but when we think of sweet-pea and sweet-brier, the words appear quite worthy of their epithets. The poor monosyllable becomes rich in sweetness and appropriation; the rougher dissyllable also; and the sweeter for its contrast.

5. The names of flowers, in general, among the polite, are neither pretty in themselves, nor give us information. The country people are apt to do them more justice. Goldylocks, ladies' fingers, rose-a-ruby, shepherd's clock, shepherd's purse, sauce-alone, scarlet runners, sops-in-wine, sweet-william, etc., give us some ideas, either useful or pleasant. But from the peasantry come many uncongenial names, as bad as those of the botanist. It is a pity that all fruits and flowers, and animals too, except those with good names, could not be passed in review before somebody with a genius for christening, as the creatures did before Adam in paradise, and so have new names given them, worthy of their creation.

6. Suppose flowers themselves were new! Suppose they had just come into the world, a sweet reward for some new goodness, and that we had not yet seen them quite developed; that they were in the act of growing; had just issued, with their green stalks, out of the ground, and engaged the attention of the curious. Imagine what we should feel when we saw the first lateral stem bearing off from the main one, or putting forth a leaf. How we should watch the leaf gradually unfolding its little graceful hand; then another, then another; then the main stalk rising and producing more; then one of them giving indications of

astonishing novelty — a bud! then this mysterious bud gradually unfolding, like the leaf, amazing us, enchanting us, almost alarming us with delight, as if we knew not what enchantment were to ensue, till at length, in all its fairy beauty, and odorous voluptuousness, and mysterious elaboration of tender and living sculpture, shone forth

"The bright consummate flower!"

7. Yet this phenomenon, to a person of any thought and lovingness, is what may be said to take place every day; for the commonest objects are wonders at which habit has made us cease to wonder, and the marvelousness of which we may renew at pleasure, by taking thought. Last spring, walking near some cultivated grounds, and seeing a multitude of green stalks peeping forth, we amused ourselves with imagining them the plumes or other head gear of fairies, and wondered what faces might ensue: and from this exercise of the fancy, we fell to considering how true, and not merely fanciful, those speculations were; what a perpetual reproduction of the marvelous was carried on by Nature; how utterly ignorant we were of the causes of the least and most disesteemed of the commonest vegetables, and what a quantity of life, and beauty, and mystery, and use, and enjoyment, was to be found in them, composed of all sorts of elements, and shaped as if by the hands of fairies. What workmanship with no apparent workman! A tree grows up, and at the tips of his rugged, dark fingers he puts forth, — round, smooth, and shining delicately, — the golden apple, or the cheek-like beauty of the peach.

8. The other day we were in a garden where Indian corn was growing, and some of the ears were plucked to show us. First, one leaf or sheath was picked off, then another, a third, a fourth, and so on, as if a fruit seller were unpacking his papers; and at last we came, in the inside, to the grains of corn, packed into cucumber shapes of pale gold, and each of them pressed and flattened against each other, as if some human hand had been doing it in the caverns of the earth. BUT WHAT HAND?

9. The same that made the poor, yet rich hand (for is

it not his workmanship also?) that is tracing these mar-
veling lines; and if it does not tremble to say, so, it is
because love sustains, and because the heart also is a flower
which has a right to be tranquil in the garden of the
All-wise.

VII. — THE USE OF FLOWERS.

From Howitt.

Mary Howitt is a living English authoress. She is distinguished
for the beauty of her ballads, and of her translations from the
Swedish of Miss Bredter's Tales. Her husband is also distinguished
as an author. This worthy pair belong to the Society of Friends.

1. God might have bade the earth bring forth
       Enough for great and small;
    The oak-tree and the cedar-tree,
       Without a flower at all.

2. We might have had enough, enough
       For every want of ours,
    For luxury, medicine, and toil,
       And yet have had no flowers.

3. The ore within the mountain mine
       Requireth none to grow;
    Nor doth it need the lotus-flower
       To make the river flow.

4. The clouds might give abundant rain,
       The nightly dews might fall,
    And the herb that keepeth life in man
       Might yet have drunk them all.

5. Then wherefore, wherefore were they made,
       All dyed with rainbow light,
    All fashion'd with supremest grace,
       Upspringing day and night;

6. Springing in valleys green and low,
    And on the mountains high,
And in the silent wilderness,
    Where no man passes by?

7. Our outward life requires them not,
    Then wherefore had they birth?
To minister delight to man,
    To beautify the earth;

8. To comfort man, to whisper hope,
    Whene'er his faith is dim;
For whoso careth for the flowers,
    Will much more care for him.

VIII. — AUTUMN FLOWERS.

FROM MRS. SOUTHEY.

MRS. SOUTHEY was the wife of Robert Southey, who is known as the Poet Laureate of England, and as the author of a greater variety and quantity of poetry, than almost any other poet. Mrs. Southey, still living, is also a poetess of distinction, and the following is among her sweetest occasional pieces.

1. THOSE few pale Autumn flowers,
    How beautiful they are!
Than all that went before,
Than all the summer store,
    How lovelier far!

2. And why? They are the last!
    The last! the last! the last!
O, by that little word
How many thoughts are stirr'd;
    That sister of the past!

3. Pale flowers! Pale perishing flowers!
    Ye're types of precious things:

Types of those bitter moments,
That flit like life's enjoyments,
   On rapid, rapid wiugs.

4. Last hours with parting dear ones
   (That time the fastest spends,)
Last tears iu silence shed,
Last words half utter-ed,
   Last looks of dying friends.

5. Who but would fain compress
   A life into a day,
The last day spent with one
Who, ere the morrow's sun,
   Must leave us, and for aye?

6. O, precious, precious moments!
   Pale flowers! ye 're types of those,
The saddest, sweetest, dearest,
Because, like those, the nearest
   To an eternal close.

7. Pale flowers! Pale perishing flowers!
   I woo your gentle breath;
I leave the summer rose
For younger, blither brows:
   Tell *me* of change and death! -

IX. — OUR OLD GRANDMOTHER.

1. THERE is an old kitchen somewhere in the past, and an old-fashioned fire-place therein, with its smooth old jambs of stone; smooth with many knives that have been sharpened there; smooth with many little fingers that have clung there. There are andirons with rings in the top, wherein many temples of flame have been builded with spires and turrets of crimson. There is a broad, worn hearth; broad enough for three generations to cluster on;

worn by feet that have been torn and bleeding by the way, or been made "beautiful," and walked upon floors of tesselated gold. There are tongs in the corner, wherewith we grasped a coal, and "blowing for a little life," lighted our first candle; there is a shovel, wherewith were drawn forth the glowing embers, in which we saw our first fancies and dreamed our first dreams; the shovel with which we stirred the logs, until the sparks rushed up the chimney as if a forge was in blast below, and wished we had so many lambs, or so many marbles, or so many somethings that we coveted; and so it was that we wished our first wishes.

2. There is a chair; a low, rush-bottomed chair; there is a little wheel in the corner, a big wheel in the garret, a loom in the chamber. There are chestsful of linen and yarn, and quilts of rare patterns and samplers in frames.

3. And every-where and always, is the dear old wrinkled face of her whose firm, elastic step mocks the feeble saunter of her children's children, the old-fashioned grandmother of twenty years ago; she, the very Providence of the old homestead; she who loved us all and said she wished there were more of us to love, and took all the school in the hollow for grandchildren besides. A great expansive heart was hers, beneath the woolen gown, or that more stately bombazine, or that sole heir-loom of silken texture.

4. We can see her to-day, those mild, blue eyes, with more of beauty in them than time could touch, or death could do more than hide; those eyes that held both smiles and tears within the faintest call of every one of us, and soft reproof that seemed not passion but regret. A white tress has escaped from beneath her snowy cap; she lengthened the tether of a vine that was straying over a window, as she came in, and plucked a four-leaved clover for Ellen. She sits down by the little wheel; a tress is running through her fingers from the distaff's disheveled head, when a small voice cries, "Grandma," from the old red cradle, and "Grandma," Tommy shouts from the top of the stairs. Gently she lets go the thread, for her patience is almost as beautiful as her charity, and she touches the

little red bark a moment, till the young voyager is in a dream again, and then directs Tommy's unavailing attempts to harness the cat.

5. The tick of the clock runs fast and low, and she opens the mysterious door and proceeds to wind it up. We are all on tip-toe, and we beg in a breath, to be lifted up, one by one, and look in, the hundreth time, upon the tin cases of the weights, and the poor lonely pendulum, which goes to and fro by its little dim windows; and our petitions are all granted, and we are all lifted up, and we all touch with the finger the wonderful weights, and the music of the wheel is resumed.

6. Was Mary to be married, or Jane to be wrapped in a shroud? So meekly did she fold the white hands of the one upon her still bosom, that there seemed to be a prayer in them there; and so sweetly did she wreath the white rose in the hair of the other, that one would not have wondered had more roses budded for company. How she stood between us and apprehended harm; how the rudest of us softened beneath the gentle pressure of her faded and tremulous hand! From her capacious pocket, that hand was ever withdrawn closed, only to be opened in our own with the nuts she had gathered, with the cherries she had plucked, the little egg she had found, the "turn-over" she had baked, the trinkets she had purchased for us as the products of her spinning, the blessings she had stored for us, the offspring of her heart.

7. What treasures of story fell from those old lips of good fairies and evil; of the old times when she was a girl; but we wonder if ever she *was* a girl; but then she couldn't be handsomer or dearer; she was ever little. And then, when we begged her to sing: "Sing us one of the old songs you used to sing for mother, grandma."

8. "Children, I can't sing," she always said, and mother used always to lay her knitting softly down, and the kitten stopped playing with the yarn on the floor, and the clock ticked lower in the corner, and the fire died down to a glow, like an old heart that is neither chilled nor dead, and grandmother sang. To be sure, it would not do for

the parlor and concert room now-a-days; but then it was the old kitchen and the old-fashioned grandmother, and the old ballad, in the dear old times, and we can hardly see to write for the memory of them, though it is a hand's breadth to the sunset.

9. Well, she sang. Her voice was feeble and wavering, like a fountain just ready to fail; but then how sweet toned it was, and it became deeper and stronger; but it could not grow sweeter. What "joy of grief" it was to sit there around the fire, all of us, excepting Jane, and her we thought we saw when the door was opened a moment by the wind; but then we were not afraid, for was not it her old smile she wore? to sit there around the fire, and weep over the woes of the babes in the woods, who laid down side by side in the great solemn shadows! and how strangely glad we felt, when the robin redbreast covered them with leaves, and last of all, when the angel took them out of night into day everlasting!

10. We may think what we will of it now, but the song and the story, heard around the kitchen fire, have colored the thoughts and the lives of most of us, have given the germs of whatever poetry blesses our hearts, whatever of memory blooms in our yesterdays. Attribute whatever we may to the school and the schoolmaster, the rays which make that little day we call life, radiate from the God-swept circle of the hearthstone.

11. Then she sings an old lullaby, the song of her mother, her mother sang it to her; but she does not sing it through, and falters ere it is done. She rests her head upon her hands, and is silent in the old kitchen. Something glitters down between her fingers in the firelight, and it looks like rain in the soft sunshine. The old grandmother is thinking when she first heard the song, and of the voices that sang it, when, a light-haired and light-hearted girl, she hung round that mother's chair, nor saw the shadows of the years to come. Oh! the days that are no more! What words unsay, what deeds undo, to set back just this once the ancient clock of time?

12. So our little hands were forever clinging to her

garments, and staying her as if from dying; for long ago she had done living for herself, and lived alone in us.

13. How she used to welcome us when we were grown, and came back once more to the homestead! We thought we were men and women, but we were children there; the old-fashioned grandmother was blind in her eyes, but she saw with her heart, as she always did. We threw out long shadows through the open door, and she felt them as they fell over her form, and she looked dimly up, and she said: " Edward I know, and Lucy's voice I can hear, but whose is that other? It must be Jane's," for she had almost forgotten the folded hands. "Oh, no! not Jane's, for she, let me see, she is waiting for me, isn't she?" and the old grandmother wandered and wept.

14. "It is another daughter, grandmother, that Edward has brought," says some one, "for your blessing." "Has she blue eyes, my son? Put her hands in mine, for she is my late-born, the child of my old age. Shall I sing you a song, children?" and she is idly fumbling for a toy, a welcome gift for the children that have come again.

15. One of us, men as we thought we were, is weeping; she hears the half-suppressed sobs, and she says, as she extends her feeble hand, "Here, my poor child, rest upon your grandmother's shoulder; she will protect you from all harm." "Come, my children, sit around the fire again. Shall I sing you a song or tell you a story? Stir the fire, for it is cold; the nights are growing colder."

16. The clock in the corner struck nine, the bedtime of those old days. The song of life was indeed sung, the story told. It was bedtime at last. Good-night to thee, grandmother. The old-fashioned grandmother is no more, and we shall miss her forever. The old kitchen wants a presence to-day, and the rush-bottomed chair is tenant-less. But we will set up .a tablet in the midst of the heart, and write on it only this;

SACRED TO THE MEMORY
OF THE
GOOD OLD-FASHIONED GRANDMOTHER.
GOD BLESS HER FOREVER.

X. — ANNABEL LEE.

FROM POE.

EDGAR A. POE, an American Poet of great power and beauty, died in 1849, at the age of 38. His poems are few, but they exhibit a high order of talent.

1. IT was many and many a year ago,
    In a kingdom by the sea,
  That a maiden there liv'd whom you may know
    By the name of Annabel Lee.
  And this maiden she liv'd with no other thought
    Than to love and be lov'd by me.

2. I was a child and *she* was a child,
    In this kingdom by the sea;
  But we lov'd with a love that was more than love,
    I and my Annabel Lee;
  With a love that the winged seraphs of heaven
    Coveted her and me.

3. And this was the reason that, long ago,
    In this kingdom by the sea,
  A wind blew out of a cloud, chilling
    My beautiful Annabel Lee;
  So that her high-born kinsmen came
    And bore her away from me,
  To shut her up in a sepulcher
    In this kingdom by the sea.

4. Our love it was stronger by far than the love
    Of those who were older than we,
    Of many far wiser than we;
  And neither the angels in heaven above,
    Nor the demons down under the sea,
  Can ever dissever my soul from the soul
    Of the beautiful Annabel Lee.

5. For the moon never beams without bringing me dreams
    Of this beautiful Annabel Lee;
  II. S. R.—4

And the stars never rise, but I feel the bright eyes
  Of the beautiful Annabel Lee :
And so all the night-tide, I lie down by the side
Of my darling, my darling, my life and my bride,
  In the sepulcher there by the sea,
  In her tomb by the sounding sea.

XI. — FERDINAND AND ISABELLA.

FROM IRVING.

FERDINAND AND ISABELLA were the King and Queen of Spain who supplied Columbus with ships and men to prosecute his voyage of discovery.

WASHINGTON IRVING, from whose works this extract is taken, is a living American author of distinction. He is one of the best and most popular of modern authors in America or England.

2. PAL'-A-DIN; a knight errant.

1. IT has been well observed of Ferdinand and Isabella, that they lived together, not like man and wife, whose estates are in common, under the orders of the husband, but like two monarchs, strictly allied. They had separate claims to sovereignty, in virtue of their separate kingdoms, and held separate councils. Yet they were so happily united by common views, common interests, and a great deference for each other, that this double administration never prevented a unity of purpose and action. All acts of sovereignty were executed in both their names; all public writings subscribed with both their signatures; their likenesses were stamped together on the public coin; and the royal seal displayed the united arms of Castile and Arragon.

2. Ferdinand possessed a clear and comprehensive genius, and great penetration. He was equable in temper, indefatigable in business, a great observer of men, and is extolled by Spanish writers as unparalleled in the science of the cabinet. It has been maintained by writers of other nations, however, and apparently with reason, that he was bigoted in religion, and craving rather than mag-

nanimous in his ambition; that he made war less like a paladin than a prince, less for glory than for mere dominion; and that his policy was cold, selfish, and artful. He was called the wise and prudent, in Spain; in Italy, the pious; in France and England, the ambitious and perfidious.

3. Contemporary writers have been enthusiastic in their descriptions of Isabella; but time has sanctioned their eulogies. She was of the middle size, and well formed; with a fair complexion, auburn hair, and clear blue eyes. There was a mingled gravity and sweetness in her countenance, and a singular modesty in her mien, gracing, as it did, great firmness of purpose and earnestness of spirit. Though strongly attached to her husband, and studious of his fame, yet she always maintained her distinct rights as an allied prince. She exceeded him in beauty, personal dignity, acuteness of genius, and grandeur of soul. Combining the active, the resolute qualities of man, with the softer charities of woman, she mingled in the warlike councils of her husband, and, being inspired with a truer idea of glory, infused a more lofty and generous temper into his subtle and calculating policy.

4. It is in the civil history of their reign, however, that the character of Isabella shines most illustrious. Her fostering and maternal care was continually directed to reform the laws, and heal the ills engendered by a long course of civil wars. She assembled round her the ablest men in literature and science, and directed herself by their councils in encouraging literature and the arts. She promoted the distribution of honors and rewards for the promulgation of knowledge, fostered the recently-invented art of printing; and, through her patronage, Salamanea rose to that eminence which it assumed among the learned institutions of the age. Such was the noble woman, who was destined to acquire immortal renown by her spirited patronage of the discovery of the New World.

XII. — QUEEN ISABELLA'S RESOLVE.

FROM VINET.

QUEEN ISABELLA OF SPAIN, DON GOMEZ, AND COLUMBUS.

Isabella. And so, Don Gomez, it is your conclusion that we ought to dismiss the proposition of this worthy Genoese.

Don Gomez. His scheme, your majesty, seems to me fanciful in the extreme; but I am a plain matter-of-fact man, and do not see visions and dreams, like some.

Isa. And yet Columbus has given us cogent reasons for believing that it is practicable to reach the eastern coast of India by sailing in a westerly direction.

Don G. Admitting that his theory is correct, namely, that the earth is a sphere, how would it be possible for him to return, if he once descended that sphere in the direction he proposes? Would not the coming back be all up hill? Could a ship accomplish it with even the most favorable wind?

Columbus. Will your majesty allow me to suggest that if the earth is a sphere, the same laws of adhesion and motion must operate at every point on its surface; and the objection of Don Gomez would be quite as valid against our being able to return from crossing the Strait of Gibraltar.

Don G. This gentleman, then, would have us believe the monstrous absurdity, that there are people on the earth who are our antipodes; who walk with their heads down, like flies on the ceiling.

Col. But, your majesty, if there is a law of attraction which makes matter gravitate to the earth, and prevents its flying off into space, may not this law operate at every point on the round earth's surface?

Isa. Truly, it so seems to me; and I perceive nothing absurd in the notion that this earth is a globe floating or revolving in space.

Don G. May it please your majesty, the ladies are privileged to give credence to many wild tales which we

plain matter-of-faet men can not admit. Every step I take, confutes this visionary idea of the earth's rotundity. Would not the blood run into my head, if I were standing upside down? Were I not fearful of offending your majesty, I would quote what the great Lactantius says.

Isa. We are not vain of our science, Don Gomez; so let us have the quotation.

Don G. "Is there any one so foolish," he asks, "as to believe that there are antipodes with their feet opposite to ours; that there is a part of the world in which all things are topsy-turvy, where the trees grow with their branches downward, and where it rains, hails, and snows, upward?"

Col. I have already answered this objection. If there are people on the earth who are our antipodes, it should be remembered that we are theirs also.

Don G. Really, that is the very point wherein we matter-of-fact men abide by the assurance of our own senses. We know that we are not walking with our heads down.

Isa. To cut short the discussion, you think that the enterprise which the Genoese proposes is one unworthy of our serious consideration; and that his theory of an unknown shore to the westward of us is a fallacy.

Don G. As a plain matter-of-fact man, I must confess that I so regard it. Has your majesty ever seen an ambassador from this unknown coast?

Isa. Do you, Don Gomez, believe in the existence of a world of spirits?

Don G. I accept what the church says.

Isa. But have you ever seen an ambassador from that unknown world?

Don G. Certainly not. By faith we look forward to it.

Isa. Even so by faith does the Genoese look forward, far over the misty ocean, to an undiscovered shore.

Col. Your majesty is right; but let it be added that I have reasons, O! most potent and resistless reasons, for the faith that is in me: the testimony of many navigators who have picked up articles that must have drifted from this distant coast: the nature of things,

admitting that the earth is round; the reports current among the people of one of the northern nations, that many years ago their mariners had sailed many leagues westward till they reached a shore where the grape grew abundantly; these and other considerations have made it (next to faith in my Savior) the fixed persuasion of my mind, that there is a great discovery reserved for the man who will sail patiently westward, trusting in God's good providence, and turning not back till he has achieved his purpose.

Don G. Then truly we should never hear of him again. Speculation! mere speculation, your majesty! When this gentleman can bring forward some solid facts that will induce us plain matter-of-fact men to risk money in forwarding his enterprise, it will then be time enough for royalty to give it heed. Why, your majesty, the very boys in the street point at their foreheads as he passes along.

Isa. And so you bring forward the frivolity of boys jeering at what they do not comprehend, as an argument why Isabella should not give heed to this great and glorious scheme; ay, sir, though it should fail, still great and glorious; urged in language so intelligent and convincing, by this grave and earnest man, whom you think to undervalue by calling him an adventurer? Know, Don Gomez, that the "absurdity," as you style it, shall be tested, and that forthwith.

Don G. Your majesty will excuse me if I remark that I have from your royal consort himself the assurance that the finances are so exhausted by the late wars, that he cannot consent to advance the necessary funds for fitting out an expedition of the kind proposed.

Isa. Be mine, then, the privilege! I have jewels, by the pledging of which I can raise the amount required; and I have resolved that they shall be pledged to this enterprise, without any more delay.

Col. Your majesty shall not repent your heroic resolve. I will return, your majesty; be sure I will return, and lay at your feet such a jewel as never queen wore yet, an imperishable fame, a fame that shall couple with your

memory the benedictions of millions yet unborn in climes yet unknown to civilized man. There is an uplifting presentiment in my mind, a conviction that your majesty will live to bless the hour you came to this decision.

Don G. A presentiment? A plain matter-of-fact man, like myself, must take leave of your majesty, if his practical common sense is to be met and superseded by presentiments! An ounce of fact, your majesty, is worth a ton of presentiment.

Isa. That depends altogether upon the source of the presentiment, Don Gomez. If it come from the Fountain of all truth, shall it not be good?

Don G. I humbly take my leave of your majesty.

XIII. — THE RETURN OF COLUMBUS.

DON GOMEZ AND HIS SECRETARY.

Don Gomez. What! What is this you tell me? Columbus returned? A new world discovered? Impossible!

Secretary. It is even so, sir. A courier arrived at the palace but an hour since with the intelligence. Columbus was driven by stress of weather to anchor in the Tagus. All Portugal is in a ferment of enthusiasm, and all Spain will be equally excited soon. The sensation is prodigious.

Don G. O! it is a trick! It must be a trick!

Sec. But he has brought home the proofs of his visit: gold and precious stones, strange plants and animals; and, above all, specimens of a new race of men, copper-colored, with straight hair.

Don G. Still I say, a trick! He has been coasting along the African shore, and there collected a few curiosities, which he is passing off for proofs of his pretended discovery.

Sec. It is a little singular that all his men should be leagued with him in keeping up so unprofitable a falsehood

Don G. But 't is against reason, against common sense, that such a discovery should be made.

Sec. King John of Portugal has received him with royal magnificence, has listened to his accounts, and is persuaded that they are true.

Don G. We shall see, we shall see. Look you, sir, a plain matter-of-fact man, such as I, is not to be taken in by any such preposterous story. This vaunted discovery will turn out no discovery at all.

Sec. The king and queen have given orders for preparations on the most magnificent scale for the reception of Columbus.

Don G. What delusion! Her majesty is so credulous! A practical, common-sense man, like myself, can find no points of sympathy in her nature.

Sec. The Indians on board the returned vessels are said to be unlike any known race of men.

Don G. Very unreliable all that! I take the common-sense view of the thing. I am a matter-of-fact man; and do you remember what I say, it will all turn out a trick! The crews may have been deceived. Columbus may have steered a southerly course, instead of a westerly. Any thing is probable, rather than that a coast to the westward of us has been discovered.

Sec. I saw the courier, who told me he had conversed with all the sailors; and they laughed at the suspicion that there could be any mistake about the discovery, or that any other than a westerly course had been steered.

Don G. Still I say a trick! An unknown coast reached by steering west? Impossible! The earth a globe, and men standing with their heads down in space? Folly! An ignorant sailor from Genoa in the right, and all our learned doctors and philosophers in the wrong? Nonsense! I 'm a matter-of-fact man, sir. I will believe what I can see, and handle, and understand. But as for believing in the antipodes, or that the earth is round, or that Columbus has discovered land to the west—— Ring the bell, sir; call my carriage; I will go to the palace and undeceive the king.

XIV. — COLUMBUS IN SPAIN.

FROM IRVING.

1. THE fame of the discoverer of the new world, had resounded throughout Spain; and, as the route of Columbus lay through several of the finest and most populous provinces, his journey appeared like the progress of a sovereign. Wherever he passed, the surrounding country poured forth its inhabitants, who lined the road, and thronged the villages. In the large towns, the streets, windows, and balconies, were filled with eager spectators, who rent the air with acclamations. His journey was continually impeded by the multitude, pressing to gain a sight of him, and of the Indians, who were regarded with as much admiration as if they had been natives of another planet. It was impossible to satisfy the craving curiosity, which assailed himself and his companions, at every stage, with innumerable questions. Popular rumor, as usual, had exaggerated the truth, and had filled the newly found country with all kinds of wonders.

2. It was about the middle of April, that Columbus arrived at Barcelona, where every preparation had been made to give him a solemn and magnificent reception. The beauty and serenity of the weather, in that genial season and favored climate, contributed to give splendor to this memorable ceremony. As he drew near the place, many of the more youthful courtiers and hidalgos of gallant bearing, together with a vast concourse of the populace, came forth to greet and welcome him.

3. First, were paraded the Indians, painted according to their savage fashion, and decorated with tropical feathers and with their national ornaments of gold; after these, were borne various kinds of live parrots, together with stuffed birds, and animals of unknown species, and rare plants, supposed to be of precious qualities; while great care was taken to make a conspicuous display of Indian coronets, bracelets, and other decorations of gold, which might give an idea of the wealth of the newly-discovered

regions. After these, followed Columbus, on horseback, surrounded by a brilliant cavalcade of Spanish chivalry.

4. The streets were almost impassable from the countless multitude; the windows and balconies were lined with the fair; the very roofs were covered with spectators. It seemed as if the public eye could not be sated with gazing on these trophies of an unknown world, or on the remarkable man by whom it had been discovered. There was a sublimity in the event, that mingled a solemn feeling with the public joy. It was looked upon as a vast and signal dispensation of Providence, in reward for the piety of the monarchs; and the majestic and venerable appearance of the discoverer, so different from the youth and buoyancy which are generally expected from roaming enterprise, seemed in harmony with the grandeur and dignity of his achievement.

5. To receive him with suitable pomp and distinction, the sovereigns had ordered their thrones to be placed in public, under a rich canopy of brocade of gold, in a vast and splendid saloon. Here, the king and queen awaited his arrival, seated in state, with the prince Juan beside them, and attended by the dignitaries of their court and the principal nobility of Spain, all impatient to behold the man who had conferred so incalculable a benefit upon the nation.

6. At length, Columbus entered the hall, surrounded by a brilliant crowd of cavaliers; among whom he was conspicuous for his stately and commanding person, which, with his countenance rendered venerable by his gray hairs, gave him the august appearance of a senator of Rome. A modest smile lighted up his features, showing that he enjoyed the state and glory in which he came; and certainly nothing could be more deeply moving, to a mind inflamed by a noble ambition, and conscious of having greatly deserved, than the testimonials of the admiration and gratitude of a nation, or rather a world. As Columbus approached, the sovereigns rose, as if receiving a person of the highest rank. Bending his knees. he requested to kiss their hands; but there was some

hesitation on the part of their majesties to permit this act of vassalage. Raising him in the most gracious manner, they ordered him to seat himself in their presence; a rare honor in this proud and punctilious court.

7. At the request of their majesties, Columbus now gave an account of the most striking events of his voyage, and a description of the islands which he had discovered. He displayed the specimens he had brought of unknown birds and other animals; of rare plants of medicinal and aromatic virtue; of native gold, in dust, in crude masses, or labored into barbaric ornaments; and, above all, the natives of these countries, who were objects of intense and inexhaustible interest; since there is nothing to man so curious as the varieties of his own species. All these he pronounced mere harbingers of great discoveries he had yet to make, which would add realms of incalculable wealth to the dominions of their majesties, and whole nations of proselytes to the true faith.

8. The words of Columbus were listened to with profound emotion by the sovereigns. When he had finished, they sunk on their knees, and raising their clasped hands to heaven, their eyes filled with tears of joy and gratitude, they poured forth thanks and praise to God for so great a providence; all present followed their example; a deep and solemn enthusiasm pervaded that splendid assembly, and prevented all common acclamations of triumph. The anthem of *Te Deum laudamus*, chanted by the choir of the royal chapel, with the melodious accompaniments of the instruments, rose up from the midst, in a full body of sacred harmony, bearing up, as it were, the feelings and thoughts of the auditors to heaven; "so that," says the venerable Las Casas, the historian of the occasion, "it seemed as if, in that hour, they communicated with celestial delights." Such was the solemn and pious manner in which the brilliant court of Spain, celebrated this sublime event; offering up a grateful tribute of melody and praise; and giving glory to God for the discovery of another world.

9. When Columbus retired from the royal presence, he

was attended to his residence by all the court, and followed by the shouting populace. For many days, he was the object of universal curiosity, and whenever he appeared, he was surrounded by an admiring multitude.

XV. — THE SEA.

1. The sea! the sea! the open sea!
   The blue, the fresh, the ever free!
   Without a mark, without a bound,
   It runneth the earth's wide regions round;
   It plays with the clouds; it mocks the skies;
   Or like a cradled creature lies.

2. I'm on the sea! I'm on the sea!
   I am where I would ever be;
   With the blue above, and the blue below,
   And silence wheresoe'er I go;
   If a storm should come and wake the deep,
   What matter? I shall ride and sleep.

3. I love (O, *how* I love) to ride
   On the fierce, foaming, bursting tide,
   When every mad wave drowns the moon,
   Or whistles aloft his tempest tune,
   And tells how goeth the world below,
   And why the south-west blasts do blow.

4. I never was on the dull, tame shore,
   But I lov'd the great sea more and more,
   And backward flew to her billowy breast,
   Like a bird that seeketh its mother's nest;
   And a mother she *was*, and *is* to me;
   For I was born on the open sea!

5. The waves were white, and red the morn,
   In the noisy hour when I was born;
   And the whale it whistled, the porpoise rolled,
   And the dolphins bared their backs of gold;

And never was heard such an outcry wild
As welcom'd to life the ocean child!

6. I've liv'd since then, in calm and strife,
Full fifty summers, a sailor's life,
With wealth to spend and a power to range,
But never have sought, nor sigh'd for change;
And Death, whenever he comes to me,
Shall come on the wild unbounded sea!

XVI. — MARINER'S HYMN.

FROM MRS. SOUTHEY.

1. LAUNCH thy bark, mariner!
   Christian, God speed thee;
   Let loose the rudder bands,
   Good angels lead thee!
   Set thy sails warily,
   Tempests will come;
   Steer thy course steadily,
   Christian, steer home!

2. Look to the weather bow,
   Breakers are round thee;
   Let fall the plummet now,
   Shallows may ground thee.
   Reef in the foresail, there!
   Hold the helm fast!
   So, let the vessel wear,
   There swept the blast.

3. What of the night, watchman?
   What of the night?
   "Cloudy, all quiet,
   No land yet, all's right."
   Be wakeful, be vigilant,
   Danger may be
   At an hour when all seemeth
   Securest to thee.

4. How! gains the leak so fast?
　　Clear out the hold,
　Hoist up thy merchandise,
　　Heave out thy gold;
　There, let the ingots go;
　　Now the ship rights;
　Hurrah! the harbor's near,
　　Lo! the red lights.

5. Slacken not sail yet
　　At inlet or island;
　Straight for the beacon steer,
　　Straight for the high land;
　Crowd all thy canvas on,
　　Cut through the foam;
　Christian! cast anchor now,
　　Heaven is thy home!

XVII. — THE CONQUEROR'S GRAVE.

FROM BRYANT.

WM. C. BRYANT, one of the best poets that America has ever produced, is still living, and widely known, not only for the exquisite beauty and elevated character of his poetry, but also as the able editor of the New York Evening Post.

1. WITHIN this lowly grave a conqueror lies;
　　And yet the monument proclaims it not,
　　Nor round the sleeper's name hath chisel wrought
　The emblems of a fame that never dies,
　　Ivy and amaranth in a graceful sheaf
　　Twined with the laurel's fair, imperial leaf.
　　　　A simple name alone,
　　　　To the great world unknown,
　Is graven here, and wild flowers rising round,
　Meek meadow-sweet and violets of the ground
　　Lean lovingly against the humble stone.

2. Here, in the quiet earth, they laid apart
   No man of iron mold and bloody hands,
   Who sought to wreak upon the cowering lands
   The passions that consumed his restless heart;
   But one of tender spirit and delicate frame,
      Gentlest in mien and mind
      Of gentle womankind,
   Timidly shrinking from the breath of blame;
   One in whose eyes the smile of kindness made
   Its haunt, like flowers by sunny brooks in May;
   Yet at the thought of others' pain, a shade
   Of sweeter sadness chased the smile away.

3. Nor deem that when the hand that molders here
   Was rais'd in menace, realms were chill'd with fear,
   And armies muster'd at the sign as when
   Clouds rise on clouds before the rainy east,
   Gray captains leading bands of veteran men
   And fiery youths to be the vultures' feast.
   Not thus were waged the mighty wars that gave
   The victory to her who fills that grave;
      Alone her task was wrought;
      Alone the battle fought;
   Through that long strife her constant hope was staid
   On God alone, nor look'd for other aid.

4. She met the hosts of sorrow with a look
   That alter'd not beneath the frown they wore;
   And soon the lowering brood were tamed, and took
   Meekly her gentle rule, and frown'd no more.
   Her soft hand put aside the assaults of wrath,
      And calmly broke in twain
      The fiery shafts of pain,
   And rent the nets of passion from her path.
   By that victorious hand despair was slain.
   With love she vanquish'd hate, and overcame
   Evil with good in her great Master's name.

5. Her glory is not of this shadowy state,
   Glory that with the fleeting season dies;

But when she enter'd at the sapphire gate,
   What joy was radiant in celestial eyes!
How heaven's bright depths with sounding welcomes
         rung,
And flowers of heaven by shining hands were flung!
      And He, who, long before,
      Pain, scorn, and sorrow bore,
The mighty Sufferer, with aspect sweet,
Smiled on the timid stranger from his seat;
He, who, returning glorious from the grave,
Dragg'd Death, disarm'd, in chains, a crouching slave.

6. See, as I linger here, the sun grows low;
   Cool airs are murmuring that the night is near.
O gentle sleeper, from thy grave I go
   Consoled, though sad, in hope, and yet in fear.
      Brief is the time, I know,
      The warfare scarce begun;
Yet all may win the triumphs thou hast won;
Still flows the fount whose waters strengthen'd thee.
   The victors' names are yet too few to fill
Heaven's mighty roll; the glorious armory,
   That minister'd to thee, is open still.

XVIII. — ANECDOTE OF WILLIAM WIRT.

1. THE distinguished William Wirt, within six or eight
months after his first marriage, became addicted to intem-
perance, the effect of which operated strongly on the mind
and health of his wife; and in a few months more she was
numbered with the dead. Her death led him to leave the
country where he resided; and he removed to Richmond,
where he soon rose to distinction. But his habits hung
about him, and occasionally he was found with jolly and
frolicsome companions in bacchanalian revelry. His true
friends expostulated with him, to convince him of the
injury he was doing himself. But he still persisted. His
practice began to fall off, and many looked on him as on

the sure road to ruin. He was advised to get married, with a view of correcting his habits. This he consented to do, if the right person offered.

2. He accordingly paid his addresses to Miss Gamble. After some months' attention, he asked her hand in marriage. She replied: "Mr. Wirt, I have been aware of your intentions, for some time back, and should have given you to understand that your visits and attentions were not acceptable, had I not reciprocated the affection which you evinced for me. But I can not yield my assent until you make me a pledge never to taste, touch, or handle, any intoxicating liquors." This reply to Mr. Wirt was as unexpected as it was novel. His reply was, that he regarded the proposition as a bar to all further consideration on the subject, and left her. Her course to him was the same as ever; his, resentment and neglect. In the course of a few weeks he went again, and again solicited her hand. But her reply was, that her mind was made up. He became indignant; and regarded the terms she proposed as insulting to his honor, and vowed it should be the last meeting they should have. He took to drinking worse and worse, and seemed to run headlong to ruin.

3. One day, while lying in the outskirts of the city, near a little grocery or grog shop, dead drunk, a young lady, whom it is not necessary to name, was passing that way to her home not far off, and beheld him with his face upturned to the rays of the scorching sun. She took her handkerchief, with her own name marked upon it, and placed it over his face. After he had remained in that way some hours, he was awakened; and his thirst being so great, he went into the little grocery or grog shop to get a drink, when he discovered the handkerchief, at which he looked, and seeing the name, exclaimed, "Who has left this with me? Who placed this on my face?" No one knew. He dropped the glass, exclaiming, "Enough, enough." He retired instantly from the store, forgetting his thirst, but not the debauch, the handkerchief, or the lady, vowing, if God gave him strength, never again to touch, taste, or handle intoxicating drinks.

4. To meet Miss G. again, was the hardest effort of his life. If he met her in carriage or on foot, he would dodge around the nearest corner. She at last addressed him a note under her own hand, inviting him to her house, which he finally gathered courage enough to accept. He told her if she bore affection for him, he would agree to her own terms. Her reply was: "My conditions are now what they have ever been." "Then," said the disenthralled Wirt, " I accept them." They were soon married ; and from that day he kept his word, and his affairs brightened, while honors and glories gathered thick upon his brow. His name has been enrolled high on the temple of fame, while his deeds, his patriotism, and renown, live after him with imperishable luster. How many noble minds might the young ladies save, if they would follow the example of the heroine-hearted Miss Gamble, the friend of humanity, of her country, and the relation of Lafayette.

XIX. — INTEMPERANCE.

FROM WIRT.

THIS is an Extract from a letter written in 1831. William Wirt, having been, in early life, a dissipated man, became a lawyer of distinction, a writer of great pathos and beauty, the author of the " British Spy," which contains his description of the Blind Preacher, of the " Life of Patrick Henry," and of " The Old Bachelor." He was, at one time, a candidate for the presidency of the United States. He died in 1834.

1. INTEMPERANCE paralyzes the arm, the brain, the heart. All the best affections, all the energies of the mind, wither under its influence. The man becomes a maniac, and is locked up in the hospital ; or imbrues his hand in the blood of his wife and children, and is sent to the gallows or doomed to the penitentiary ; or, if he escapes these consequences, he becomes a walking pestilence on the earth, miserable in himself and loathsome to all who behold him.

2. How often do we see, too, whole families contaminated by the vicious example of their parents; husbands, wives, daughters, and sons, all drunkards and furies; sometimes, wives murdering husbands; at others, husbands their wives; and, worst of all, if worse can be in such a group of horrors, children murdering their parents. But below this grade of crime, how much is there of unseen and untold misery throughout our otherwise happy land, proceeding from this fatal cause alone.

3. I am persuaded that if we could have a statistical survey and report of the affairs of unhappy families and individuals, with the causes of their misery annexed, we should find nine cases out of ten, if not a still greater proportion, resulting from the use of ardent spirits alone. With this conviction, which seems to have become universal among reflecting men, the apathy shown to the continuance of the evil can only be ascribed to the circumstance that the mischief, though verbally admitted, is not seen and felt in all its enormity.

4. If some fatal plague of a contagious character, were imported into our country, and had commenced its ravages in our cities, we should see the most prompt and vigorous measures at once adopted to repress and extinguish it; but what are the most fearful plagues that ever carried death and havoc in their train through the eastern countries, compared with this? They are only occasional, this is perennial.

5. They are confined by climate or place; this malady is of all climates and all times and places. They kill the body at once; this consumes body and soul by a lingering and dreadful death, involving the dearest connections in the vortex of ruin. What parent, however exemplary himself, can ever feel that his son is safe while this living fountain of poison is within his reach. God grant that it may soon become a fountain sealed, in our country at least.

6. What a relief, how delightful would it be, to turn from the awful and horrid past, to the pure, peaceful, and happy future! to see the springs of life, and feeling, and

intelligence renewed on every.hand; health, industry, and
prosperity glowing around us; the altars of domestic peace
and love rekindled in every family; and the religion of the
Savior presented with a fair field for its celestial action.

XX. — THE COLD-WATER MAN.

FROM SAXE.

1. THERE liv'd an honest fisherman,
    I knew him passing well;
    Who dwelt hard by a little pond,
    Within a little dell.

2. A grave and quiet man was he,
    Who lov'd his hook and rod;
    So *even* ran his *line* of life,
    His neighbors thought it *odd*.

3. For science and for books, he said,
    He never had a wish;
    No school to him was worth a fig,
    Except a "school" of fish.

4. This single-minded fisherman
    A double calling had,
    To tend his flocks in winter-time,
    In summer, fish for shad.

5. In short, this honest fisherman
    All other toils forsook;
    And though no vagrant man was he,
    He liv'd by "*hook* and *crook*."

6. All day the fisherman would sit
    Upon an ancient log,
    And gaze into the water, like
    Some sedentary frog.

7. A cunning fisherman was he;
     His *angle*s all were *right;*
   And, when he scratch'd his aged *poll,*
     You'd know he got a *bite.*

8. To charm the fish he never spoke,
     Although his voice was fine;
   He found the most convenient way
     Was, just to *"drop a line."*

9. And many a "gudgeon" of that pond,
     If made to speak to-day,
   Would own with grief this angler had
     A mighty *"taking way."*

10. One day, while fishing on the log,
      He mourn'd his want of luck,
    When, suddenly, he felt a bite,
      And jerking, caught a *duck!*

11. Alas! that day, the fisherman
      Had taken too much grog;
    And being but a landsman, too,
      He couldn't *keep the log."*

12. In vain he strove with all his might,
      And tried to gain the shore;
    Down, down he went to feed the fish
      He'd *baited* oft before!

13. The moral of this mournful tale
      To all is plain and clear:
    A single "drop too much" of rum,
      May make a watery *bier.*

14. And he who will not "sign the pledge,"
      And keep his promise fast,
    May be, in spite of fate, a *stark,*
      Cold-water man, at last.

XXI. — HIGHLAND SNOW STORM.

FROM WILSON.

John Wilson, born in 1788, and recently deceased, was, for many years, a professor in the university at Edinburgh, Scotland, the principal editor, under the name of Christopher North, of "Blackwood's Magazine," the author of "Lights and Shadows of Scottish Life," etc., and of many exquisite fugitive pieces in prose and poetry. He is remarkable for depth of pathos, beauty of imagery, keenness of wit, and his genial sympathies with all the finer feelings.

1. One family lived in Glencreran, and another in Glenco, the families of two brothers, seldom visiting each other on working days, seldom meeting even on Sabbaths, for theirs was not the same parish kirk; seldom coming together on rural festivals or holidays, for in the Highlands now these are not so frequent as of yore; yet all these sweet seldoms, taken together, to loving hearts made a happy many, and thus, though each family passed its life in its own home, there were many invisible threads stretched out through the intermediate air, connecting the two dwellings together, as the gossamer keeps floating from one tree to another, each with its own secret nest. And nest-like both dwellings were.

2. That in Glenco was built beneath a treeless but high heathered rock, lone in all storms, with greensward and garden on a slope down to a rivulet, the clearest of the clear, (oh, once wofully reddened!) and *growing*, so it seems, in the mosses of its own roof, and the huge stones that overshadow it, out of the earth. *That* in Glencreran was more conspicuous, on a knoll among the pastoral meadows, midway between mountain and mountain, so that the grove which shelters it, except when the sun is shining high, is darkened by their meeting shadows, and dark indeed, even in the sunshine, for 'tis a low but wide-armed grove of old oak-like pines.

3. These huts belonged to brothers, and each had an only child, a son and a daughter, born on the same day, and now blooming on the verge of youth. A year ago

and they were but mere children; but what wondrous growth of frame and spirit does nature at that season of life often present before our eyes! So that we almost see the very change going on between morn and morn, and feel that these objects of affection are daily brought closer and closer to ourselves, by partaking daily more and more in all our most sacred thoughts, in our cares and in our duties, and in knowledge of the sorrows as well as the joys of our common lot.

4. Thus had these cousins grown up before their parents' eyes: Flora Macdonald, a name hallowed of yore, the fairest, and Ronald Cameron, the boldest of all the living flowers in Glenco and Glencreran. It was now their seventeenth birthday, and never had a winter sun smiled more serenely over a knoll of snow. Flora, it had been agreed, was to pass that day in Glencreran, and Ronald to meet her among the mountains, that he might bring her down the many precipitous passes to his parents' hut. It was the middle of February, and the snow had lain for weeks with all its drifts unchanged, so calm had been the weather, and so continued the frost. At the same hour, known by horologe on the cliff, touched by the finger of dawn, the happy creatures left each their own glen, and mile after mile of the smooth surface glided away past their feet, almost as the quiet water glides by the little boat, that in favoring breezes walks merrily along the sea. And soon they met at the trysting place, a bank of birch-trees, beneath a cliff that takes its name from the eagles.

5. On their meeting, seemed not to them the whole of nature suddenly inspired with joy and beauty? Insects, unheard by them before, hummed and glittered in the air; from tree roots, where the snow was thin, little flowers, or herbs, flower-like, now for the first time were seen looking out, as if alive; the trees themselves seemed budding, as if it were already spring; and rare as in that rocky region are the birds of song, a faint trill for a moment touched their ears, and a flutter of a wing, telling them that somewhere near, there was preparation for a nest. Deep down beneath the snow they listened to the tinkle of rills un-

reached by the frost, and merry, thought they, was the music of these contented prisoners.

6. Flora sang to Ronald many of her old songs, to those wild Gaelic airs that sound like the sighing winds among fractured cliffs, or the branches of storm-tossed trees, when the subsiding of tempests is about to let them rest. Monotonous music! but irresistible over the heart it has once awakened and enthralled, so sincere seems to be the mournfulness it breathes, a mournfulness brooding and feeding on the same note, that is at once its natural expression and sweetest aliment, of which the singer never wearieth in her dream, while her heart all the time is haunted by all that is most piteous, by the faces of the dead in their paleness returning to the shades of life, only that once more they may pour from their fixed eyes those strange showers of unaccountable tears!

7. How merry were they between those mournful airs! How Flora trembled to see her lover's burning brow and flashing eyes, as he told her tales of great battles fought in foreign lands, far across the sea, tales which he had drunk in with greedy ears from the old heroes scattered all over Lochabar and Badenach, on the brink of the grave, still garrulous of blood!

8. The boy starts to his feet and his keen eye looks along the ready rifle, for his sires had all been famous deer-stalkers, and the passion of the chase was hereditary in his blood. Lo! a deer from Dalness, hound-driven, or sullenly astray, slowly bearing his antlers up the glen, then stopping a moment to snuff the air, then away, away! The rifle-shot rings dully from the scarce echoing snow-cliffs, and the animal leaps aloft, struck by a certain, but not sudden death wound. Oh! for Fingal now to pull him down like a wolf! But laboring and lumbering heavily along, the snow spotted as he bounds with blood, the huge animal disappears round some rocks at the head of the glen.

9. "Follow me, Flora!" the boy-hunter cries; and flinging down their plaids, they turn their bright faces to the mountain, and away up the long glen after the stricken deer. Fleet was the mountain girl, and Ronald, as he

ever and anon looked back to wave her on, with pride admired her lightsome motion as she bounded along the snow. Redder and redder grew that snow, and more heavily trampled, as they winded round the rocks. Yonder is the deer, staggering up the mountain, not half a mile off, now standing at bay, as if before his swimming eyes came Fingal, the terror of the forest, whose howl was known to all the echoes, and quailed the herd while their antlers were yet afar off. "Rest, Flora, rest! while I fly to him with my rifle, and shoot him through the heart!"

10. Up, up, up the interminable glen, that kept winding and winding round many a jutting promontory and many a castellated cliff, the red deer kept dragging his gore-oozing bulk, sometimes almost within, and then for some hundreds of yards just beyond rifle-shot; while the boy, maddened by the chase, pressed forward, now all alone, nor any more looking behind for Flora, who had entirely disappeared: and thus he was hurried on for miles by the whirlwind of passion, till at last he struck the noble quarry, and down sank the antlers in the snow, while the air was spurned by the convulsive beatings of feet. Then leaped Donald upon the red deer, like a beast of prey, and lifted up a look of triumph to the mountain tops.

11. Where is Flora? Her lover has forgotten her, and he is alone, nor knows it; he and the red deer, an enormous animal, fast stiffening in the frost of death.

12. Some large flakes of snow are in the air, and they seemed to wave and whirl, though an hour ago there was not a breath. Faster they fall, and faster: the flakes are almost as large as leaves; and overhead, whence has so suddenly come that huge yellow cloud? "Flora, where are you? Where are you, Flora?" and from the huge hide the boy leaps up, and sees that no Flora is at hand. But yonder is a moving speck, far off upon the snow. 'Tis she, 'tis she; and again Ronald turns his eyes upon the quarry, and the heart of the hunter burns like a new-stirred fire.

13. Shrill as the eagle's cry, disturbed in his eyry, he sends a shout down the glen, and Flora, with cheeks pale and bright by fits, is at last by his side. Panting and

speechless she stands, and then dizzily sinks on his breast. Her hair is ruffled by the wind that revives her, and her face all moistened by the snow-flakes, now not falling, but driven, for the day has undergone a dismal change, and all over the sky are now lowering savage symptoms of a fast-coming night-storm.

14. Bare is poor Flora's head, and sorely drenched her hair, that an hour or two ago glittered in the sunshine. Her shivering frame misses now the warmth of the plaid which almost no cold can penetrate, and which had kept the vital current flowing in many a bitter blast. What would the miserable boy give now for the covering lying far away, which, in his foolish passion, he flung down to chase that fatal deer!

15. "Oh, Flora! if you would not fear to stay here by yourself, under the protection of God, who surely will not forsake you, soon will I go and come from the place where our plaids are lying; and under the shelter of the deer we may be able to outlive the hurricane; you wrapped in them, and folded, oh my dearest sister, in my arms!" "I will go with you down the glen, Ronald!" and she left his breast, but weak as a day-old lamb tottered and sank down on the snow. The cold, intense as if the air were ice, had chilled her very heart, after the heat of that long race: and it was manifest that here she must be for the night, to live or die. And the night seemed already come, so full was the lift of snow; while the glimmer every moment became gloomier, as if the day were expiring long before its time. Howling at a distance down the glen, was heard a sea-born tempest from the Linnhe Loch, where now they both knew the tide was tumbling in, bringing with it sleet and snow-blasts from afar; and from the opposite quarter of the sky an inland tempest was raging to meet it, while every lesser glen had its own uproar, so that on all hands they were environed with death.

16. "I will go, and till I return, leave you with God." "Go, Ronald!" and he went and came as if he had been endowed with the raven's wings.

17. Miles away and miles back had he flown, and an

hour had not been with his going and his coming; but what a dreary wretchedness meanwhile had been hers! She feared that she was dying, that the cold snow-storm was killing her, and that she would never more see Ronald, to say to him farewell. Soon as he was gone, all her courage had died. Alone, she feared death, and wept to think how hard it was for one so young thus miserably to die. He came, and her whole being was changed. Folded up in both the plaids, she felt resigned. "Oh kiss me, kiss me Ronald; for your love, great as it is, is not as my love. You must never forget me, Ronald, when your poor Flora is dead."

XXII. — HIGHLAND SNOW STORM. —Continued.

1. RELIGION with these two young creatures was as clear as the light of the Sabbath-day, and their belief in heaven just the same as in earth. The will of God they thought of, just as they thought of their parents' will, and the same was their living obedience to its decrees. If she was to die, supported now by the presence of her brother, Flora was utterly resigned; if she was to live, her heart imaged to itself the very forms of her grateful worship. But all at once she closed her eyes, ceased breathing, and as the tempest howled and rumbled in the gloom that fell around them like blindness, Ronald almost sunk down, thinking she was dead.

2. "Wretched sinner that I am! My wicked madness brought her here to die of cold!" And he smote his breast and tore his hair, and feared to look up, lest the angry eye of God were looking on him through the storm.

3. All at once, without speaking a word, Ronald lifted Flora in his arms, and walked away up the glen, here almost narrowed into a pass. Distraction gave him super-natural strength, and her weight seemed that of a child. Some walls of what had once been a house, he had suddenly remembered, were but a short way off; whether or not they had any roof he had forgotten, but the thought

even of such a shelter seemed a thought of salvation. There it was, a snowdrift at the opening that had once been a door, snow up to the holes once windows; the wood of the roof had been carried off for fuel, and the snow-flakes were falling in, as if they would soon fill up the inside of the ruin. The snow in front was all trampled, as if by sheep; and carrying in his burden under the low lintel, he saw the place was filled with a flock that had foreknown the hurricane, and that, all huddled together, looked on him as the shepherd, come to see how they were faring in the storm.

4. And a young shepherd he was, with a lamb apparently dying in his arms. All color, all motion, all breath seemed to be gone, and yet something convinced his heart that she was yet alive. The ruined hut was roofless, but across an angle of the walls some pine branches had been flung, as a sort of a shelter for the sheep or cattle that repair thither in cruel weather, some pine branches left by the wood-cutters, who had felled the few trees that once stood at the very head of the glen. Into that corner the snowdrift had not yet forced its way, and he sat down there with Flora in the cherishing of his embrace, hoping that the warmth of his distracted heart might be felt by her, who was as cold as a corpse.

5. The chill air was somewhat softened by the breath of the huddled flock, and the edge of the cutting wind blunted by the stones. It was a place in which it seemed possible that she might revive, miserable as it was, with the mire-mixed snow, and almost as cold as one supposes the grave. And she did revive, and under the half-open lids the dim blue appeared to be not yet life-deserted. It was yet but the afternoon, night-like though it was, and he thought, as he breathed upon her lips, that a faint red returned, and that they felt the kisses he dropt on them to drive death away.

6. "Oh, father, go seek for Ronald, for I dreamed tonight that he was perishing in the snow." "Flora, fear not, God is with us." "Wild swans, they say, are come to Loch Phoil. Let us go, Ronald, and see them; but no

rifle. for why kill creatures said to be so beautiful?" Over them, where they lay, bended down the pine-branch roof, as if it would give way beneath the increasing weight; but there it still hung, though the drift came over their feet, and up to their knees, and seemed stealing upwards to be their shrouds. "Oh! I am overcome with drowsiness, and fain would be allowed to sleep. Who is disturbing me, and what noise is this in our house?" "Fear not. fear not, Flora, God is with us." "Mother, am I lying in your arms? My father surely is not in the storm. Oh, I have had a most dreadful dream!" and with such mutterings as these Flora relapsed again into that perilous sleep. which soon becomes that of death.

7. Night itself came, but Flora and Ronald knew it not; and both lay motionless in one snow-shroud. Many passions, though earth-born, heavenly all, pity, and grief. and love, and hope, and at last despair, had prostrated the strength they had so long supported; and the brave boy, who had been for some time feeble as a very child after a fever, with a mind confused and wandering, and in its perplexities sore afraid of some nameless ill, had submitted to lay down his head beside his Flora's. and had soon become. like her, insensible to the night and all its storms.

8. Bright was the peat fire in the hut of Flora's parents in Glenco, and they were among the happiest of the humble happy, blessing this the birth-day of their blameless child. They thought of her, singing her sweet songs by the fireside of the hut in Glencreran, and tender thoughts of her cousin Ronald, were with them in their prayers. No warning came to their ears in the sough or the howl; for fear it is that creates its own ghosts, and all its own ghostlike visitings; and they had seen their own Flora, in the meekness of the morning, setting forth on her way over the quiet mountains, like a fawn to play.

9. Sometimes, too. love, who starts at shadows as if they were of the grave, is strangely insensible to realities that might well inspire dismay. So it was now with the dwellers in the hut at the head of Glencreran. Their Ronald had left them in the morning, night had come, and he and

Flora were not there, but the day had been almost like a summer day, and in their infatuation they never doubted that the happy creatures had changed their minds, and that Flora had returned with him to Glenco. Ronald had laughingly said, that haply he might surprise the people in that glen by bringing back to them Flora on her birthday, and, strange though it seemed to her afterward to be, that belief prevented one single fear from touching his mother's heart, and she and her husband lay down that night in untroubled slumber.

10. And what could have been done for them, had they been told by some good or evil spirit that their children were in the clutches of such a night? As well seek for a single bark in the middle of the misty main! But the inland storm had been seen brewing among the mountains round Kings-House, and hut had communicated with hut, though far apart in regions where the traveler sees no symptoms of human life. Down through the long cliff-pass of Mealanumy, between Buchael-Etive and the Black Mount, towards the lone House of Dalness, that lies in everlasting shadows, went a band of shepherds, trampling their way across a hundred frozen streams.

11. Following their dogs, who know their duties in their instinct, the band, without seeing it, are now close to that ruined hut. Why bark the sheep-dogs so, and why howls Fingal, as if some spirit passed athwart the night? He scents the dead body of the boy, who had so often shouted him on in the forest, when the antlers went by! Not dead, nor dead she who is on his bosom. Yet life in both is frozen, and will the red blood in their veins ever again be thawed? Almost pitch dark is the roofless ruin; and the frightened sheep know not what is that terrible shape that is howling there. But a man enters and lifts up one of the bodies, giving it into the arms of those at the door-way, and then lifts up the other, and, by the flash of a rifle, they see that it is Ronald Cameron and Flora Macdonald, seemingly both frozen to death. Some of those reeds that the shepherds burn in their huts are kindled, and in that small light they are assured that such are the

corpses. But that noble dog knows that death is not there, and licks the face of Ronald, as if he would restore life to his eyes. Two of the shepherds knew well how to fold the dying in their plaids, how gentlest to carry them along; for they had learnt it on the field of victorious battle, when, without stumbling over the dead and wounded, they bore away the shattered body, yet living, of the youthful warrior who had shown that of such a clan he was worthy to be the chief.

12. The storm was with them all the way down the glen; nor could they have heard each other's voices had they spoken; but, mutely they shifted the burden from strong hand to hand, thinking of the hut in Glenco, and of what would be felt there on their arrival with the dying or the dead.

13. The dip of the hills, in spite of the drifts familiar to their feet, did not deceive them now; and then the dogs, in their instinct, were guides that erred not; and as well as the shepherds knew it themselves, did Fingal know that they were anxious to reach Glenco. He led the way as if he were in the moonlight; and often stood still, when they were shifting their burden, and whined as if in grief. He knew where the bridges were, stones or logs, and he rounded the marshes, where at springs the wild fowl feed. And thus instinct, and reason, and faith, conducted the saving band along, and now they are at Glenco, and at the door of the hut.

14. To life were brought the dead; and there, at midnight, sat they up like ghosts. Strange seemed they for awhile to each other's eyes, and at each other they looked as if they had forgotten how dearly once they loved. Then, as if in holy fear, they gazed in each other's faces, thinking that they had awoke together in heaven. "Flora," said Ronald, and that sweet word, the first he had been able to speak, reminded him of all that had passed, and he knew that the God in whom they had put their trust had sent them deliverance. Flora, too, knew her parents, who were on their knees; and she strove to rise up and kneel down beside them, but she was powerless as a broken

reed; and when she thought to join with them in thanksgiving, her voice was gone. Still as death sat all the people in the hut, and one or two who were fathers were not ashamed to weep.

XXIII. — WINTER AND SUMMER.

FROM THOMSON.

JAMES THOMSON, who lived from 1700 to 1748, is the author of "The Seasons," from which these extracts are taken. He stands high on the list of English poets.

WINTER.

1. Thro' the hush'd air the whitening shower descends,
At first thin-wavering, till at last the flakes
Fall broad, and wide, and fast, dimming the day
With a continual flow.   The cherish'd fields
Put on their winter robe of purest white :
'Tis brightness all, save where the new snow melts
Along the mazy current.   Low the woods
Bow their hoar head ; and ere the languid sun,
Faint from the west, emits his evening ray,
Earth's universal face, deep hid, and chill,
Is one wide dazzling waste, that buries wide
The works of man.

2.   Drooping, the laborer ox
Stands cover'd o'er with snow, and then demands
The fruit of all his toil.   The fowls of heaven,
Tamed by the cruel season, crowd around
The winnowing store, and claim the little boon
Which Providence assigns them.' One alone,
The redbreast, sacred to the household gods,
Wisely regardful of the embroiling sky,
In joyless fields and thorny thickets, leaves
His shivering mates, and pays to trusted man
His annual visit.   Half afraid, he first
Against the window beats ; then, brisk, alights

On the warm hearth; then, hopping o'er the floor,
Eyes all the smiling family askance,
And pecks, and starts, and wonders where he is:
Till more familiar grown, the table crums
Attract his slender feet.

3.   The foodless wilds
Pour forth their brown inhabitants. The hare,
Though timorous of heart, and hard beset
By death in various forms, dark snares and dogs,
And more unpitying men, the garden seeks,
Urged on by fearless want. The bleating kine
Eye the bleak heaven, and next, the glistening earth,
With looks of dumb despair; then, sad dispersed,
Dig for the wither'd herb through heaps of snow.

4. As thus the snows arise, and foul and fierce
All winter drives along the darken'd air,
In his own loose, revolving fields the swain
Disaster'd stands; sees other hills ascend,
Of unknown joyless brow, and other scenes
Of horrid prospect, shag the trackless plain;
Nor finds the river nor the forest, hid
Beneath the formless wild; but wanders on
From hill to dale, still more and more astray,
Impatient flouncing through the drifted heaps,
Stung with the thoughts of home; the thoughts of home
Rush on his nerves, and call their vigor forth
In many a vain attempt.

5.   How sinks his soul!
What black despair, what horror, fills his heart!
When for the dusky spot which fancy feign'd
His tufted cottage rising through the snow,
He meets the roughness of the middle waste,
Far from the track and blest abode of man;
While round him night resistless closes fast,
And every tempest, howling o'er his head,
Renders the savage wilderness more wild.
          H. S. R.—7

Then throng the busy shapes into his mind,
Of cover'd pits, unfathomably deep,
A dire descent! beyond the power of frost;
Of faithless bogs; of precipices huge
Smooth'd up with snow; and what is land unknown,
What water of the still unfrozen spring,
In the loose marsh or solitary lake,
Where the fresh fountain from the bottom boils.

6. These check his fearful steps, and down he sinks
Beneath the shelter of the shapeless drift,
Thinking o'er all the bitterness of death,
Mix'd with the tender anguish nature shoots
Through the rung bosom of the dying man,
His wife, his children, and his friends, unseen.
In vain for him the officious wife prepares
The fire, fair blazing, and the vestment warm:
In vain his little children, peeping out
Into the mingling storm, demand their sire
With tears of artless innocence.

7.   Alas!
Nor wife nor children more shall he behold,
Nor friends nor sacred home. On every nerve
The deadly winter seizes, shuts up sense,
And o'er his inmost vitals creeping cold,
Lays him along the snows a stiffen'd corse,
Stretch'd out, and bleaching in the northern blast.

SUMMER.

1. Low walks the sun, and broadens by degrees,
Just o'er the verge of day. The shifting clouds,
Assembled gay, a richly gorgeous train,
In all their pomp attend his setting throne.
Air, earth, and ocean smile immense.

2. Confess'd from yonder slow-extinguish'd clouds,
All ether softening, sober evening takes

Her wonted station in the middle air;
A thousand shadows at her beck. First this
She sends on earth; then that of deeper dye
Steals soft behind; and then a deeper still,
In circle following circle, gathers round,
To close the face of things. A fresher gale
Begins to wave the wood, and stir the stream,
Sweeping with shadowy gust the fields of corn:
While the quail clamors for his running mate.

3. Wide o'er the thistly lawn, as swells the breeze,
A whitening shower of vegetable down ·
Amusive floats. The kind impartial care
Of nature naught disdains: thoughtful to feed
Her lowest sons, and clothe the coming year,
From field to field the feather'd seeds she wings.

· 4. His folded flock secure, the shepherd home
Hies merry-hearted; and by turns relieves
The ruddy milkmaid of her brimming pail;
The beauty whom perhaps his witless heart,
Unknowing what the joy-mix'd anguish means,
Sincerely loves, by that best language shown
Of cordial glances, and obliging deeds.

5. Onward they pass o'er many a panting hight,
And valley sunk, and unfrequented; where,
At fall of eve, the fairy people throng,
In various game and revelry, to pass
The summer night, as village stories tell.
But far about they wander from the grave
Of him, whom his ungentle fortune urged
Against his own sad breast to lift the hand
Of impious violence. The lonely tower
Is also shunn'd, whose mournful chambers hold,
So night-struck fancy dreams, the yelling ghost.

6. Among the crooked lanes, on every hedge,
The glow-worm lights his gem; and through the dark

A moving radiance twinkles. Evening yields
The world to night; not in her winter robe
Of massy Stygian woof, but loose array'd
In mantle dun. A faint erroneous ray,
Glanced from the imperfect surfaces of things,
Flings half an image on the straining eye;
While wavering woods, and villages, and streams,
And rocks, and mountain-tops, that long retain'd
The ascending gleam, are all one swimming scene,
Uncertain if beheld.

7.   Sudden to heaven
Thence weary vision turns; where, leading soft
The silent hours of love, with purest ray
Sweet Venus shines; and from her genial rise,
When daylight sickens till it springs afresh,
Unrival'd reigns, the fairest lamp of night.

XXIV. — THE MORAL LAW.

1. THERE was once a lawyer, who was a very profane man, and a skeptic. On a certain occasion he asked another lawyer what books he should read on the evidences of Christianity. He was advised to read, in the first instance, the Bible itself; inasmuch as most infidels are very ignorant of it; and furthermore, in order to reason correctly on any subject, it is necessary to understand what it is that we reason about.

2. It was stated to him also, that the internal evidences of the Bible are even stronger than the external. He was advised to begin his perusal of the Bible with the book of Genesis. This advice was complied with: the aid of commentaries, and of his legal friend, was employed in solving difficulties.

3. One evening, some time after this course of study was commenced, the Christian lawyer called on his skeptical friend, and found him walking his room; and so profoundly engaged in thought that his own entrance into the room

was not noticed, until he asked his friend what it was that occupied his attention. The skeptic replied, "I have been reading the moral law." "Well, what do you think of it?" asked the other. "I will tell you what I *used* to think of it," said the skeptic. "I supposed that Moses was the leader of a horde of banditti; that having a strong mind, he acquired great influence over a superstitious people; and that on Mount Sinai he played off some sort of fireworks, to the amazement of his ignorant followers, who imagined, in their mingled fear and superstition, that the exhibition was supernatural."

4. "But what do you think now?" followed his friend. "I have been looking," replied the skeptic, "into the *nature of that law.* I have been trying to see whether I can add any thing to it, or take any thing from it, so as to make it better. Sir, I can not: *it is perfect.*

5. "The First Commandment," continued he, "directs us to make the Creator the object of supreme love and reverence. That is right: if he be our creator, preserver, and supreme benefactor, we ought to treat him, and *no other*, as such. The Second Commandment forbids idolatry: that precept certainly is right. The Third, with equal justness, forbids profanity.

6. "The Fourth fixes a time for religious worship. If there be a God, he ought certainly to be worshiped: it is suitable that there should be an outward homage, significant of our inward regard. If God is to be worshiped, it is proper that some *time* should be set apart for that purpose, when all may worship him harmoniously, and without interruption. One day in seven is certainly not too much; and I do not know that it is too little. The Fifth defines the peculiar duties arising from family relations.

7. "Injuries to our *neighbor* are then classified by the moral law. They are divided into offenses against life, chastity, property, and character; and," said he, "I notice that the greatest offense in each class is expressly forbidden. Thus, the greatest injury to life is murder: to chastity, adultery: to property, theft: to character, perjury. Now the greater offense must include the lesser of the

same kind. Murder must include every injury to life; adultery, every injury to purity; and so of the rest; and the moral code is closed and perfected by a prohibition, forbidding *every improper desire* in regard to our neighbor.

8. "I have been thinking," he proceeded, "WHERE MOSES GOT THAT LAW. I have read history. The Egyptians and the adjacent nations were idolaters; so were the Greeks and Romans; and the wisest and best of Greeks or Romans never gave a code of morals like this. Where did Moses get this law, which surpasses the wisdom and philosophy of the most enlightened ages? He lived at a period comparatively barbarous.

9. "Yet he has given a law, in which the learning and sagacity of all subsequent times can detect no flaw. Where did he get it? He could not have soared so far above his age as to have devised it himself; I am satisfied where he obtained it: IT MUST HAVE COME FROM HEAVEN. I am convinced of the truth of the religion of the Bible."

XXV. — AND WHAT THEN?

1. A STORY is told of a good man who was living at a university, when a young man, whom he had known as a boy, ran up to him with a face full of delight, and told him that what he had long been wishing above all things in the world was at length fulfilled; his parents having just given him leave to study law; and thereupon he had come to the law school at his university on account of his great fame, and meant to spare no labor or pains in getting through his studies as quickly and as well as possible. In this way he ran on a long time; and when at last he came to a stop, the holy man, who had been listening to him with great patience and kindness, said: "Well, and when you have got through your course of studies, what do you mean to do then?"

2. "Then I shall take my doctor's degree," answered the young man. "And what then?" asked he. "And then," continued the youth, "I shall have a number of difficult

and knotty causes to manage, shall catch people's notice by my eloquence, my zeal, my acuteness, and gain a great reputation." "And what then?" repeated the holy man. "And then," replied the youth, "there can't be a question, I shall be promoted to some high office or other; besides I shall make money and grow rich." "And what then," repeated the good man. "And then," pursued the young lawyer, "then I shall live comfortably and honorably in wealth and dignity, and shall be able to look forward quietly to a happy old age." "And what then?" "And then," said the youth, "then I shall die."

3. Here the holy man again asked, "And what then?" Whereupon the young man made no answer, but cast down his head and went away. The last, *And what then?* had pierced like a flash of lightning into his soul, and he could not get clear of it. Soon after he forsook the study of law, and gave himself up to the ministry of Christ, and spent the remainder of his days in godly words and works.

4. The question which was put to the young lawyer, is one which we should put frequently to ourselves. When we have done all that we are doing, all that we aim at doing, all that we dream of doing, even supposing that all our dreams are accomplished, that every wish of our heart is fulfilled, still we may ask, what will we do, what will be then? Whenever we cast our thoughts forward, never let them stop short on this side of the grave; let them not stop short at the grave itself; but when we have followed ourselves thither, and have seen ourselves laid therein, still ask ourselves the searching question, *And what then?*

XXVI.—THE PRODIGAL SON.

FROM THE BIBLE.

1. THEN drew near unto Jesus all the publicans and sinners, to hear him. And the Pharisees and scribes murmured, saying, This man receiveth sinners, and eateth with them.

2. And he spake this parable unto them, saying, What man of you, having an hundred sheep, if he lose one of them, doth not leave the ninety and nine in the wilderness, and go after that which is lost, until he find it? And when he hath found it, he layeth it on his shoulders, rejoicing. And when he cometh home, he calleth together his friends and neighbors, saying unto them, Rejoice with me; for I have found my sheep which was lost. I say unto you, that likewise joy shall be in heaven over one sinner that repenteth, more than over ninety and nine just persons which need no repentance.

3. Either what woman having ten pieces of silver, if she lose one piece, doth not light a candle, and sweep the house, and seek diligently till she find it? And when she hath found it, she calleth her friends and her neighbors together, saying, Rejoice with me; for I have found the piece which I had lost. Likewise I say unto you, there is joy in the presence of the angels of God over one sinner that repenteth.

4. And he said, A certain man had two sons; and the younger of them said to his father, Father, give me the portion of goods that falleth to me. And he divided unto them his living. And not many days after, the younger son gathered all together, and took his journey into a far country, and there wasted his substance in riotous living.

5. And when he had spent all, there arose a mighty famine in that land; and he began to be in want. And he went and joined himself to a citizen of that country; and he sent him into his fields to feed swine. And he would fain have filled his belly with the husks that the swine did eat; and no man gave unto him.

6. And when he came to himself, he said, How many hired servants of my father's have bread enough and to spare, and I perish with hunger! I will arise, and go to my father, and will say unto him, Father, I have sinned against heaven, and before thee, and am no more worthy to be called thy son; make me as one of thy hired servants. And he arose, and came to his father. But when he was yet a great way off, his father saw him, and had compas-

sion, and ran, and fell on his neck, and kissed him. And the son said unto him, Father, I have sinned against heaven, and in thy sight, and am no more worthy to be called thy son.

7. But the father said to his servants, Bring forth the best robe, and put it on him; and put a ring on his hand, and shoes on his feet; and bring hither the fatted calf, and kill it; and let us eat and be merry; for this my son was dead, and is alive again; he was lost, and is found.

XXVII. — THE RAVEN.

FROM POE.

In this poem, one of the most beautiful, in style and poetic fancy, that Poe has written, the *Raven* is supposed to represent *despair*. Poe was a dissipated man and morbidly sensitive. This poem is contained in the "New Sixth Reader" of this series, but is introduced here, for the sake of connecting it with its most admirable and triumphant reply in the succeeding exercise.

I.

Once upon a midnight dreary, while I ponder'd weak and weary,
Over many a quaint and curious volume of forgotten lore,
While I nodded, nearly napping, suddenly there came a tapping,
As of some one gently rapping, rapping at my chamber door;
"'T is some visitor," I mutter'd, "tapping at my chamber door;
    Only this and nothing more."

II.

Ah! distinctly I remember, it was in the bleak December,
And each separate dying ember wrought its ghost upon the floor;
Eagerly I wish'd the morrow: vainly I had tried to borrow,
From my books, surcease of sorrow, sorrow for the lost Lenore,
For the rare and radiant maiden whom the angels name Lenore,
    Nameless here for evermore.

III.

And the silken, sad, uncertain rustling of each purple curtain
Thrill'd me, fill'd me with fantastic terrors, never felt before;

So that now, to still the beating of my heart, I stood repeating,
"'T is some visitor entreating entrance at my chamber door,
Some late visitor entreating entrance at my chamber door;.
        This it is and nothing more."

IV.

Presently my soul grew stronger, hesitating then no longer,
" Sir," said I, "or Madam, truly your forgiveness I implore;
But the fact is, I was napping, and so gently you came rapping,
And so faintly you came tapping, tapping at my chamber door,
That I scarce was sure I heard you." Here I open'd wide the
        door.
        Darkness there, and nothing more.

V.

Deep into that darkness peering, long I stood there, wondering,
        fearing,
Doubting, dreaming dreams no mortal ever dared to dream before;
But the silence was unbroken, and the darkness gave no token,
And the only word there spoken, was the whisper'd word,
        " Lenore!"
        Merely this, and nothing more.

VI.

Then into the chamber turning, all my soul within me burning,
Soon I heard again a tapping, somewhat louder than before;
" Surely," said I, "surely, that is something at my window
        lattice;
Let me see then, what thereat is, and this mystery explore,
Let my heart be still a moment, and this mystery explore,
        'T is the wind, and nothing more!"

VII.

Open here I flung the shutter, when, with many a flirt and flutter,
In there stepp'd a stately raven of the saintly days of yore:
Not the least obeisance made he; not an instant stopp'd or
        stay'd he;
But with mien of lord or lady, perch'd above my chamber door,
Perch'd upon a bust of Pallas, just above my chamber door,
        Perch'd, and sat, and nothing more.

VIII.

Then this ebony bird beguiling my sad fancy into smiling,
By the grave and stern decorum of the countenance it wore ;
"Though thy crest be shorn and shaven, thou," I said, "art sure
    no craven,
Ghastly, grim, and ancient raven, wandering from the nightly
    shore.
Tell me what thy lordly name is on the night's Plutonian shore!"
      Quoth the raven, "Nevermore."

IX.

Much I marvel'd this ungainly fowl to hear discourse so plainly,
Though its answer little meaning, little relevancy bore ;
For we can not help agreeing that no living human being
Ever yet was bless'd with seeing bird above his chamber door,
Bird or beast upon the sculptur'd bust above his chamber door,
      With such name as "Nevermore."

X.

But the raven, sitting lonely on the placid bust, spake only
That one word, as if his soul in that one word he did outpour,
Nothing further then he utter'd, not a feather then he flutter'd,
Till I scarcely more than mutter'd, "Other friends have flown
    before,
On the morrow *he* will leave me, as my hopes have flown before."
      Then the bird said, "Nevermore."

XI.

Startled at the stillness broken by reply so aptly spoken,
"Doubtless," said I, "what it utters is its only stock and store,
Caught from some unhappy master, whom unmerciful disaster
Follow'd fast and follow'd faster, till his song one burden bore,
Till the dirges of his Hope the melancholy burden bore
      Of 'Nevermore,' of 'Nevermore.'"

XII.

But the raven still beguiling all my sad soul into smiling,
Straight I wheel'd a cushion'd seat in front of bird, and bust,
    and door ;

Then .upon the velvet sinking, I betook myself to linking
Fancy unto fancy, thinking what this ominous bird of yore,
What this grim, ungainly, ghastly, gaunt, and ominous bird of yore
    Meant, in croaking "Nevermore."

XIII.

This I sat engaged in guessing, but no syllable expressing
To the fowl whose fiery eyes now burn'd into my bosom's core.
This and more I sat divining, with my head at ease reclining,
On the cushion's velvet lining that the lamplight gloated o'er,
But whose velvet, violet lining, with the lamplight gloating o'er,
    She shall press, ah, Nevermore!

XIV.

Then, methought, the air grew denser, perfumed from an unseen
    censer,
Swung by angels, whose faint foot-falls tinkled on the tufted
    floor.
"Wretch," I cried, "thy God hath lent thee, by these angels he
    hath sent thee,
Respite—respite and nepenthe from thy memories of Lenore!
Quaff, O, quaff this kind nepenthe, and forget this lost Lenore!
    Quoth the raven, "Nevermore."

XV.

"Prophet," cried I, "thing of evil, prophet still, if bird or devil,
Whether tempter sent, or whether tempest toss'd thee here ashore,
Desolate, yet all undaunted, on this desert land enchanted,
On this home by horror haunted, tell me truly, I implore,
Is there, *is* there balm in Gilead, tell me, tell me, I implore,"
    Quoth the raven, "Nevermore."

XVI.

"Prophet," said I, "thing of evil, prophet still, if bird or devil,
By that heaven that bends above us, by that God we both adore,
Tell this soul with sorrow laden, if within the distant Aiden,
It shall clasp a sainted maiden, whom the angels name Lenore,
Clasp a rare and radiant maiden, whom the angels name Lenore,"
    Quoth the raven, "Nevermore."

XVII.

"Be that word our sign of parting, bird or fiend!" I shriek'd
  upstarting;
"Get thee back into the tempest, and the night's Plutonian shore;
Leave no black plume as a token of that lie thy soul hath
  spoken!
Leave my loneliness unbroken! quit the bust above my door!
Take thy beak from out my heart, and take thy form from off
  my door,"
    Quoth the raven, "Nevermore."

XVIII.

And the raven, never flitting, still is sitting, still is sitting,
On the pallid bust of Pallas, just above my chamber door;
And his eyes have all the seeming of a demon that is dreaming,
And the lamp-light, o'er him streaming, throws his shadow on
  the floor;
And my soul from out that shadow, that lies floating on the floor,
    Shall be lifted, Nevermore.

XXVIII. — THE DOVE.

FROM MISS TOWNSEND.

The author of these lines, blind and enfeebled by disease, upon
hearing Poe's Raven read, answered it as follows:

1. 'Twas midnight! solemn, dark, and deep!
   And vainly I had courted sleep,
   When worn with pain, with anguish toss'd,
   Hope, faith, and patience nearly lost,
   I heard a sound, a gentle sound,
   Breaking the solemn stillness round;
   A gentle, soft, and murmuring sound,
   Making the stillness more profound.

2. I hush'd my breath! again it came!
   My heart beat faster, still the same

Low, gentle murmur met my ear,
Approaching nearer and more near;
A single sound, yet soft and clear,
And strangely fraught with memories dear.

3. A flood of clear and silver light
Then burst upon my raptured sight,
Filling my little chamber quite,
And in that light a bird was seen;
Not "grim and black with stately mien,"
But purely white and beautiful,
With look so mild and dutiful;
A lovely bird with plumage white,
In that calm, still, and clear moonlight.

4. Floating a moment round my head,
It rested opposite my bed,
Beside a picture, lovelier
Than heathen god, and holier;
Two beauteous babes, whose sinless eyes
Bespeak them still in Paradise;
Whose loving, soft, and gentle eyes
Tell where that land of beauty lies.

5. There sat the radiant white-wing'd bird;
I listen'd, but no sound I heard;
And then I spoke, "Sweet bird," I said,
"From what far country hast thou fled?
Whence com'st thou; and why com'st thou here?
Canst thou bring aught my soul to cheer?
Hast thou strange news?　Speak, gentle dove!"
And the bird answer'd, "God is love."

6. "They tell me so," I faintly said,
"But joy has flown and hope is dead,
And I am sick, and sad, and weary,
And life is long, and dark, and dreary;
Think not thy words my spirit move!"
Still the bird answer'd, "God is love."

7. "Some dearly lov'd are far away,
   And some, who fondly near me stay,
   Are sick, and sad, and suffering,
   While I am weak and murmuring.
   Each for the other grieves, and tries
   To stay the tears that fill his eyes;
   Why comes not comfort from above?"
   Firmly, but mournfully, the dove
   Distinctly answer'd, "God is love."

8. I started up; "The world," I said,
   "Though beautiful it once was made,
   Is full of crime and misery now;
   Want sits on many a haggard brow;
   The warrior wields his bloody sword,
   Slaves tremble at the tyrant's word;
   Vice honor'd, virtue scorn'd, we see;
   Why are these ills allow'd to be?"
   He rais'd his head, the soft-ey'd dove,
   As though my boldness he'd reprove,
   Then bow'd and answer'd, "God is love."

9. "Forgive," I said, in accents mild,
   "I would I were again a child;
   I've wander'd from the heavenly track,
   And it is late to journey back;
   My wings are clipp'd, I can not soar,
   I strive to mount, but o'er and o'er
   My feeble wings I raise in vain;
   I flutter, sink, and fall again!"
   In low, but earnest tones, the dove
   Still softly murmur'd, "God is love."

10. "Thou mov'st me strangely, wondrous bird!
    My soul is strongly, deeply stirr'd;
    My heart grows lighter. may I still
    My mission upon earth fulfill,
    Proving my love to God sincere,
    By doing all my duty here?

Shall past omissions be forgiven,
And shall the weary rest in Heaven?"
He spread his wings, that radiant dove,
And cheerly answer'd, "God is love."

11. "Thanks, heavenly messenger," I cried,
"Remain that picture still beside;
Surrounded by the light of truth,
Companion meet for sinless youth;
Thou bles-sed type of Love and Peace,
My hope and faith thou'lt still increase;
Be ever near me, gentle dove,
I know, I feel, that 'God is love!'"

XXIX. — THE SCHWEIN-GENERAL.

FROM SIR F. B. HEAD.

SCHWEIN; *pronounced* swine, is the German for *swine.*
SCHWEIN-GENERAL means *swine leader.*

1. EVERY morning, at half-past five o'clock, I hear, as I am dressing, the sudden blast of an immense wooden horn, from which always proceed the same four notes. I have got quite accustomed to this wild sound, and the vibration has scarcely subsided; it is still ringing among the distant hills, when, leisurely proceeding from almost every door in the street, behold a pig! Some, from their jaded, care-worn, dragged appearance, are evidently leaving behind them a numerous litter; others are great, tall, mo-nastic-looking creatures, which seem to have no other object left in this wretched world than to become bacon; while others are thin, tiny, light-hearted, brisk, petulant piglings, with the world and all its loves and sorrows before them. Of their own accord these creatures proceed down the street to join the herdsman, who occasionally continues to repeat the sorrowful blast from his horn.

2. Gregarious, or naturally fond of society, with one curl in their tails, and with their noses almost touching the ground, the pigs trot on, grunting to themselves and to

their comrades, halting only whenever they come to any thing they can manage to swallow. I have observed that the old ones pass all the carcasses, which, trailing to the ground, are hanging before the butchers' shops, as if they were on a sort of bond of honor not to touch them; the middle-aged ones wistfully eye this meat, yet jog on also; while the piglings, that (so like mankind) have more appetite than judgment, can rarely resist taking a nibble; yet, no sooner does the dead calf begin again to move, than from the window immediately above out pops the head of a butcher, who, drinking his coffee, whip in hand, inflicts a prompt punishment, sounding quite equal to the offense.

3. As I have stated, the pigs, generally speaking, proceed of their own accord; but shortly after they have passed, there comes down our street a little bareheaded, barefooted, stunted dab of a child, about eleven years old; a Flibbertigibbet sort of creature, which, in a drawing, one would express by a couple of blots; the small one for her head, the other for her body; while streaming from the latter there would be a long line ending in a flourish, to express the immense whip which the child carries in her hand. This little goblin page, the whipper-in attendant or aid-de-camp of the old pig-driver, facetiously called "Schwein-general," is a being no one looks at, and who looks at nobody.

4. Whether the inns of Schwalbach are full of strangers or empty; whether the promenades are occupied by princes or peasants; whether the weather be good or bad, hot or rainy, she apparently never stóps to consider; upon such vague subjects, it is evident, she never for a moment has reflected. But such a pair of eyes for a pig, have perhaps seldom beamed from human sockets. The little intelligent urchin knows every house from which a pig ought to have proceeded; she can tell by the door being open or shut, and even by foot-marks, whether the creature has joined the herd, or whether, having overslept itself, it is still snoring in its sty: a single glance determines whether she shall pass a yard or enter it; and if a pig, from indolence

II. S. R.—8

or greediness, be loitering on the road, the sting of the wasp can not be sharper or more spiteful than the cut she gives it. As soon as, finishing with one street, she joins her general in the main road, the herd slowly proceed down the town.

5. Besides the little girl who brought up the rear, the herd was preceded by a boy about fourteen, whose duty it was not to let the foremost, the most enterprising, or, in other words, the most empty pig, advance too fast. In the middle of the drove, surrounded like a shepherd by his flock, slowly stalked the "Schwein-general," a wan, spectral-looking old man, worn out, or nearly so, by the arduous and every-day duty of conducting, against their wills, a gang of exactly the most obstinate animals in creation. A single glance at his jaundiced, ill-natured countenance, was sufficient to satisfy one that his temper had been soured by the vexatious contrarieties and "untoward events" it had met with.

6. In his left hand he held a staff to help himself on-ward, while round his right shoulder hung one of the most terrific whips that could possibly be constructed. At the end of a short handle turning upon a swivel there was a lash about nine feet long, formed like the vertebræ of a snake, each joint being an iron ring, which, decreasing in size, was closely connected with its neighbor by a band of hard, greasy leather. The pliability, the weight, and the force of this iron whip, rendered it an argument which the obstinacy even of the pig was unable to resist; yet, as the old man proceeded down the town, he endeavored to speak kindly to the herd, and as the bulk of them preceded him, jostling each other, grumbling and grunting on their way, he occasionally exclaimed in a low, hollow, worn-out tone of encouragement, "Nina! Anina!" (drawling of course very long on the last syllable.)

7. If any little savory morsel caused a contention or stoppage on the march, the old fellow slowly unwound his dreadful whip, and by merely whirling it round his head, like reading the riot act, he generally succeeded in dis-persing the crowd; but if they neglected this solemn

warning, if their stomachs proved stronger than their judgments, and if the group of greedy pigs still continued to stagnate, "Arriff!" the old fellow exclaimed, and rushing forward, the lash whirling round his head, he inflicted, with strength which no one could have fancied he possessed, a smack that seemed absolutely to electrify the leader. As lightning shoots across the heavens, I observed the culprit fly forward; and for many yards, continuing to sidle towards the left, it was quite evident that the thorn was still smarting in his side; and no wonder, poor fellow! for the blow he received would almost have cut a piece out of a door.

8. As soon as the herd got out of the town they began gradually to ascend the rocky, barren mountain which appeared towering above them; and then the labors of the Schwein-general and his staff became greater than ever; for as the animals from their solid column began to extend or deploy themselves into line, it was necessary constantly to ascend or descend the slippery hill, in order to outflank them. "Arriff!" vociferated the old man, striding after one of his rebellious subjects. "Arriff!" in a shrill tone of voice, was reëchoed by the lad, as he ran after another. However, in due time the drove reached the ground which was devoted to their day's exercise, the whole mountain being thus taken in regular succession.

9. The Schwein-general now halted, and the pigs being no longer called upon to advance, but being left entirely to their own notions, I became exceedingly anxious attentively to observe them.

10. No wonder, poor reflecting creatures! that they had come unwillingly to such a spot, for there appeared literally to be nothing for them to eat but hot stones and dust; however, making the best of the bargain, they all very vigorously set themselves to work. Looking up the hill, they dexterously began to lift up with their snouts the largest of the loose stones, and then grubbing their noses into the cool ground, I watched their proceedings for a very long time. Their tough, wet snouts seemed to be sensible of the quality of every thing they touched;

and thus out of the apparently barren ground they managed to get fibres of roots, to say nothing of worms, beetles, or any other traveling insects they met with. As they slowly advanced working up the hill, their ears most philosophically shading their eyes from the hot sun, I could not help feeling how little we appreciate the delicacy of several of their senses, and the extreme acuteness of their instinct.

11. In this situation do the pigs remain every morning for four hours, enjoying little else than air and exercise. At about nine or ten o'clock they begin their march homeward; and nothing can form a greater contrast than their entry into their native town does to their exit from it. Their eager anxiety to get to the dinner trough that awaits them is almost ungovernable; and they no sooner reach the first houses of the town, than a general rush takes place; away each then starts toward his home; and it is really curious to stand still and watch how very quickly they canter by, greedily grunting and snuffing, as if they could smell with their stomachs, as well as their noses, the savory food which was awaiting them.

12. At half-past four the same four notes are heard again; the pigs once more assemble; once more tumble over the hot stones on the mountain; once more remain there for four hours; and in the evening once again return to their sties.

XXX. — LITTLE GRETCHEN.

I.

Little Gretchen, little Gretchen wanders up and down the street;
The snow is on her yellow hair, the frost is at her feet.
The rows of long, dark houses without look cold and damp,
By the struggling of the moonbeam, by the flicker of the lamp.
The clouds ride fast as horses, the wind is from the north,
But no one cares for Gretchen, and no one looketh forth.
Within those dark, damp houses are merry faces bright,
And happy hearts are watching out the old year's latest night.

II.

With the little box of matches she could not sell all day,
And the thin, thin tatter'd mantle the wind blows every way,
She clingeth to the railing, she shivers in the gloom;
There are parents sitting snugly by firelight in the room,
And children with grave faces are whispering one another
Of presents for the new year, for father or for mother.
But no one talks to Gretchen, and no one hears her speak,
No breath of little whisperers comes warmly to her cheek.

III.

No little arms are round her: ah me! that there should be
With so much happiness on earth, so much of misery!
Sure they of many blessings should scatter blessings round,
As laden boughs in autumn fling their ripe fruits to the ground.
And the best love man can offer to the God of love, be sure,
Is kindness to his little ones, and bounty to his poor.
Little Gretchen, little Gretchen goes coldly on her way;
There's no one looketh out at her, there's no one bids her stay.

IV.

Her home is cold and desolate; no smile, no food, no fire,
But children clamorous for bread, and an impatient sire.
So she sits down in an angle where two great houses meet,
And she curleth up beneath her, for warmth, her little feet.
And she looketh on the cold wall, and on the colder sky,
And wonders if the little stars are bright fires up on high.
She hears a clock strike slowly, up in a far church tower,
With such a sad and solemn tone, telling the midnight hour.

V.

And she remember'd her of tales her mother used to tell,
And of the cradle-songs she sang, when summer's twilight fell,
Of good men and of angels, and of the Holy Child,
Who was cradled in a manger, when winter was most wild;
Who was poor, and cold, and hungry, and desolate, and lone;
And she thought the song had told he was ever with his own;
And all the poor and hungry and forsaken ones are his,
"How good of Him to look on me in such a place as this!"

VI.

Colder it grows and colder, but she does not feel it now,
For the pressure at her heart, and the weight upon her brow;
But she struck one little match on the wall so cold and bare
That she might look around her, and see if He were there.
The single match has kindled, and by the light it threw,
It seem'd to little Gretchen the wall was rent in two;
And she could see folks seated at a table richly spread,
With heaps of goodly viands, red wine and pleasant bread.

VII.

She could smell the fragrant savor, she could hear what they did
　　say,
Then all was darkness once again, the match had buru'd away.
She struck another hastily, and now she seem'd to see
Within the same warm chamber a glorious Christmas tree.
The branches were all laden with things that children prize,
Bright gifts for boy and maiden, she saw them with her eyes;
And she almost seem'd to touch them, and to join the welcome
　　shout,
When darkness fell around her, for the little match was out.

VIII.

Another, yet another, she has tried, they will not light;
Till all her little store she took, and struck with all her might:
And the whole miserable place was lighted with the glare,
And she dream'd there stood a little child before her in the air.
There were blood-drops on his forehead, a spear-wound in his side,
And cruel nail-prints in his feet, and in his hands spread wide.
And he look'd upon her gently, and she felt that he had known
Pain, hunger, cold, and sorrow, ay, equal to her own.

IX.

And he pointed to the laden board and to the Christmas tree,
Then up to the cold sky, and said, "Will Gretchen come with
　　me?"
The poor child felt her pulses fail, she felt her eyeballs swim,
And a ringing sound was in her ears, like her dead mother's
　　hymn:

And she folded both her thin white hands, and turn'd from that
    bright board,
And from the golden gifts, and said, "With thee, with thee,
    O Lord!"
The chilly winter morning breaks up in the dull skies
On the city wrapt in vapor, on the spot where Gretchen lies.

x.

In her scant and tatter'd garment, with her back against the wall,
She sitteth cold and rigid, she answers to no call.
They have lifted her up fearfully, they shudder'd as they said,
"It was a bitter, bitter night! the child is frozen dead."
The angels sang their greeting for one more redeem'd from sin;
Men said, "It was a bitter night; would no one let her in?"
And they shiver'd as they spoke of her, and sigh'd. They could
    not see
How much of happiness there was after that misery.

XXXI. — SIEGE OF CALAIS.

FROM BROOKE.

1. EDWARD III., after the battle of Crecy, laid siege
to Calais. He had fortified his camp in so impregnable
a manner, that all the efforts of France proved ineffectual
to raise the siege, or throw succors into the city. The
citizens, under Count Vienne, their gallant governor, made
an admirable defense. France had now put the sickle
into her second harvest, since Edward, with his victorious
army, sat down before the town. The eyes of all Europe
were intent on the issue.

2. At length, famine did more for Edward than arms.
After suffering unheard-of calamities, the French resolved
to attempt the enemy's camp. They boldly sallied forth;
the English joined battle; and after a long and desperate
engagement, Count Vienne was taken prisoner, and the
citizens who survived the slaughter retired within their
gates. The command devolving upon Eustace St. Pierre,

a man of mean birth, but of exalted virtue, he offered to capitulate with Edward, provided he permitted them to depart with life and liberty.

3. Edward, to avoid the imputation of cruelty, consented to spare the bulk of the plebeians, provided they delivered up to him six of their principal citizens with halters about their necks, as victims of due atonement for that spirit of rebellion with which they had inflamed the vulgar. When his messenger, Sir Walter Mauny, delivered the terms, consternation and pale dismay were impressed on every countenance.

4. To a long and dead silence deep sighs and groans succeeded, till Eustace St. Pierre, getting up on a little eminence, thus addressed the assembly: "My friends, we are brought to great straits this day. We must either yield to the terms of our cruel and ensnaring conqueror, or give up our tender infants, our wives and daughters, to the bloody hands of the enraged soldiers.

5. "Is there any expedient left, whereby we may avoid the guilt and infamy of delivering up those who have suffered every misery with you, on the one hand, or the desolation and horror of a sacked city on the other? There is, my friends; there is one expedient left! a gracious, an excellent, a godlike expedient left! Is there any here to whom virtue is dearer than life? Let him offer himself an oblation for the safety of his people! He shall not fail of a blessed approbation from that Power who offered up his only Son for the salvation of mankind."

6. He spoke; but a universal silence ensued. Each man looked around for the example of that virtue and magnanimity which all wished to approve in themselves though they wanted the resolution. At length St. Pierre resumed: "I doubt not but there are many here as ready, nay, more zealous of this martyrdom, than I can be; though the station to which I am raised by the captivity of Lord Vienne imparts a right to be the first in giving my life for your sakes. I give it freely; I give it cheerfully. Who comes next?"

7. "Your son!" exclaimed a youth not yet come to

maturity. "Ah! my child!" cried St. Pierre; "I am, then, twice sacrificed. But no; I have rather begotten thee a second time. Thy years are few, but full, my son. The victim of virtue has reached the utmost purpose and goal of mortality! Who next, my friends? This is the hour of heroes." "Your kinsman," cried John de Aire. "Your kinsman," cried James Wissant. "Your kinsman," cried Peter Wissant. "Ah!" exclaimed Sir Walter Mauny, bursting into tears, "why was not I a citizen of Calais?"

8. The sixth victim was still wanting, but was quickly supplied by lot from numbers who were now emulous of so ennobling an example. The keys of the city were then delivered to Sir Walter. He took the six prisoners into his custody; then ordered the gates to be opened, and gave charge to his attendants to conduct the remaining citizens, with their families, through the camp of the English. Before they departed, however, they desired permission to take a last adieu of their deliverers.

9. What a parting! What a scene! They crowded with their wives and children about St. Pierre and his fellow-prisoners. They embraced; they clung around; they fell prostrate before them; they groaned; they wept aloud; and the joint clamor of their mourning passed the gates of the city, and was heard throughout the English camp.

10. The English, by this time, were apprised of what passed within Calais. They heard the voice of lamentation, and their souls were touched with compassion. Each of the soldiers prepared a portion of his own victuals, to welcome and entertain the half-famished inhabitants; and they loaded them with as much as their present weakness was able to bear, in order to supply them with sustenance by the way.

11. At length, St. Pierre and his fellow-victims appeared, under conduct of Sir Walter and a guard. All the tents of the English were instantly emptied. The soldiers poured from all parts, and arranged themselves on each side, to behold, to contemplate, to admire, this little band of patriots, as they passed. They bowed to them on all sides; they murmured their applause of that virtue which

they could not but revere, even in enemies; and they re-garded those ropes, which they had voluntarily assumed about their necks, as ensigns of greater dignity than that of the British garter.

12. As soon as they had reached the presence, "Mauny," says the monarch, "are these the principal inhabitants of Calais?" "They are," says Mauny; "they are not only the principal men of Calais, they are the principal men of France, my lord, if virtue has any share in the act of ennobling." "Were they delivered peaceably?" says Ed-ward; "was there no resistance, no commotion among the people?" "Not in the least, my lord; the people would all have perished rather than have delivered the least of these to your Majesty. They are self-delivered and self-devoted; and come to offer up their inestimable heads as an ample equivalent for the ransom of thousands."

13. Edward was secretly piqued at this reply of Sir Walter; but he knew the privilege of a British subject, and suppressed his resentment. "Experience," says he, "has ever shown that lenity only serves to invite people to new crimes. Severity, at times is indispensably neces-sary, to compel subjects to submission by punishment and example. Go," he cried to an officer, "lead these men to execution."

14. At this instant, a sound of triumph was heard throughout the camp. The queen had just arrived with a powerful reinforcement of gallant troops. Sir Walter Mauny flew to receive her Majesty, and briefly informed her of the particulars respecting the six victims. As soon as she had been welcomed by Edward and his court, she desired a private audience. "My lord," said she, "the question I am to enter upon is not touching the lives of a few mechanics; it respects the honor of the English nation; it respects the glory of my Edward, my husband, my king. You think you have sentenced six of your enemies to death. No, my lord, they have sentenced themselves; and their execution would be the execution of their own orders, not the orders of Edward.

15. "The stage on which they would suffer would be to

them a stage of honor; but a stage of shame to Edward, a reproach to his conquests, an indelible disgrace to his name. Let us rather disappoint these haughty burghers, who wish to invest themselves with glory at our expense. We cannot wholly deprive them of the merit of a sacrifice so nobly intended; but we may cut them short of their desires. In the place of that death by which their glory would be consummated, let us bury them under gifts; let us put them to confusion with applauses. We shall thereby defeat them of that popular opinion, which never fails to attend those who suffer in the cause of virtue."

16. "I am convinced; you have prevailed. Be it so," replied Edward; "prevent the execution; have them instantly before us." They came; when the Queen, with an aspect and accents diffusing sweetness, thus addressed them: "Natives of France, and inhabitants of Calais, you have put us to a vast expense of blood and treasure, in the recovery of our just and natural inheritance; but you have acted up to the best of an erroneous judgment, and we admire and honor in you that valor and virtue, by which we are so long kept out of our rightful possessions. You noble burghers! you excellent citizens! though you were tenfold the enemies of our person and our throne, we can feel nothing on our part save respect and affection for you. You have been sufficiently tested.

17. "We loose your chains; we snatch you from the scaffold, and we thank you for that lesson of humiliation which you teach us, when you show us, that excellence is not of blood, title, or station; that virtue gives a dignity superior to that of kings; and that those whom the Almighty forms with sentiments like yours, are justly and eminently raised above all human distinctions. You are now free to depart to your kinsfolk, your countrymen; to all those whose lives and liberties you have so nobly defended; provided you refuse not the tokens of our esteem. Yet we would rather bind you to ourselves by every endearing obligation; and, for this purpose, we offer to you your choice of the gifts and honors that Edward has to bestow. Rivals for fame, but always friends to virtue. we

wish that England were entitled to call you her sons."
"Ah, my country," exclaimed Pierre; "it is now that I
tremble for you. King Edward only wins our cities; but
Philippa, the queen, conquers our hearts."

XXXII. — EXILE OF ERIN.

FROM CAMPBELL.

THOMAS CAMPBELL, an English poet, who lived from 1777 to 1844,
is the author of "The Pleasures of Hope," "Gertrude of Wyoming,"
and many exquisite ballads, and occasional poems. His writings are
characterized by fine taste, gorgeous imagery, and perfect polish.

1. THERE came to the beach a poor exile of Erin,
    The dew on his thin robe was heavy and chill;
  For his country he sigh'd, when at twilight repairing,
    To wander alone by the wind-beaten hill.
  But the day-star attracted his eyes' sad devotion,
  For it rose o'er his own native isle of the ocean,
  Where once, in the fire of his youthful emotion,
    He sang the bold anthem of Erin go bragh!

2. Sad is my fate! said the heart-broken stranger,
    The wild deer and wolf to a covert can flee;
  But I have no refuge from famine and danger,
    A home and a country remain not to me.
  Never again in the green sunny bowers,
  Where my forefathers liv'd, shall I spend the sweet hours,
  Or cover my harp with the wild-woven flowers,
    And strike to the numbers of Erin go bragh!

3. Erin, my country! though sad and forsaken,
    In dreams I revisit thy sea-beaten shore;
  But, alas! in a far foreign land I awaken,
    And sigh for the friends who can meet me no more!
  Oh, cruel fate! wilt thou never replace me
  In a mansion of peace, where no perils can chase me?
  Never again shall my brothers embrace me!
    They died to defend me, or live to deplore!

4. Where is my cabin door, fast by the wild wood?
   Sisters and sire! did ye weep for its fall?
Where is the mother that look'd on my childhood?
   And where is the bosom-friend dearer than all?
Oh, my sad heart! long abandon'd by pleasure,
Why did it doat on a fast-fading treasure?
Tears, like the rain-drop, may fall without measure,
   But rapture and beauty they can not recall.

5. Yet all its sad recollections suppressing,
   One dying wish my lone bosom can draw:
Erin! an exile bequeaths thee his blessing!
   Land of my forefathers! Erin go bragh!
Buried and cold, when my heart stills her motion,
Green be thy fields, sweetest isle of the ocean!
And thy harp-striking bards sing aloud with devotion,
   Erin mavournin, Erin go bragh!

XXXIII.—PETER THE GREAT.—Scene 1.

PETER THE GREAT, Emperor of Russia, went in disguise to Holland, to learn the art of ship-building, in order to be able to construct a navy for himself. He introduced that art into his country, and by his energy and good sense laid the foundation of its present prosperity. The following scene is supposed to have occurred while he was in Holland.

Peter. (*Disguised as a carpenter.*) Well, before I quit this place, I may let you into my secret.

Stanmitz. And do you think of leaving us?

Pet. I have now been absent from my native country a twelvemonth. I have acquired some knowledge of ship-building, the object for which I came here, and it is time I should return home.

Sta. Our master, Von Block, will be sorry to lose you, because you are the most industrious fellow in the yard; and I shall be sorry, because — because, Peter, I like you.

Pet. And I don't dislike you.

Sta. Peter, I think I may venture to tell you a secret.

Pet. Why, surely you have done nothing to be ashamed of ?

Sta. No, not ashamed; but I'm considerably *afraid.* Know, then, that I was born at Moscow.

Pet. Well there is no crime in being born at Moscow; besides, that was no fault of yours.

Sta. That's not it.   Listen!   It happened, one day, that a party of soldiers halted near my mother's hut; the commanding officer presently cast an eye at me, and was so amazingly taken with my appearance, that he requested I'd make one of his company.   I was about to decline; but he assured me that the Czar Peter (our namesake, you know), having particular occasion for my services, would take it as an offense if I refused the invitation; so he forthwith clapped a musket on my shoulder, and marched me off.

Pet. Ay, you were enlisted.

Sta. Enlisted! why, I can't say but I was.   Now, I was always an independent sort of fellow, fond of my own way, and could n't stomach being ordered about against my inclination.

Pet. (*Aside.*) So, so! This fellow is a deserter!

Sta. I put up with it a long while, though; till, one bitter cold morning in December, just at three o'clock, I was roused from my comfortable, warm sleep, to turn out and mount guard on the bleak, blustering corner of a rampart, in the snow.   It was too bad, was n't it?

Pet. I don't doubt you would rather have been warm in bed.

Sta. Well, as I could n't keep myself warm, I laid down my musket and began to walk; then I began to run, and — will you believe it? I did n't stop running till I found myself five leagues away from the outposts!

Pet. So, then, you are a deserter!

Sta. A deserter! You call that being a deserter, do you? Well, putting this and that together, I should n't wonder if I were a deserter.

Pet. Do you know, my dear fellow, that if you are dis-covered you will be shot?

Sta. I've some such idea. Indeed, it occurred to me at the time; so, thinking it hardly worth while to be shot for being so short a distance as only five leagues away from my post, I made the best of my way to Saardam; and here I am.

Pet. This is an awkward affair, indeed, and if the burgomaster were informed of it ——— however, be assured your secret is safe in my keeping.

Sta. I don't doubt you, for I suspect you're in a similar scrape yourself.

Pet. I? Ridiculous!

Sta. There's something very mysterious about you at any rate. But, I say, you will keep my secret?

Pet. O! trust me for that.

Sta. Because, if it should get to the ears of any of the agents of the Czar, I should be in rather a bad fix, you know.

Pet. The Czar shall know no more about it than he does now, if I can help it; so don't be afraid. He himself, they say, is rather fond of walking away from his post.

Sta. Ha, ·ha! Is he? Then he has no business to complain of me for running away, — eh?

Pet. You must look out for him, though. They say he has a way of finding out every thing. Don't be too sure of your secret.

Sta. . Come, now; he's in Russia, and I'm in Holland; and I don't see where's the danger unless you mean to blab.

Pet. Fellow-workman, do you take me for a traitor?

Sta. Not so, Peter; but, if I am ever taken up here as a deserter, you will have been the only one to whom I have told my secret.

Pet. A fig for the Czar!

Sta. Don't say that, he's a good fellow, is Peter the Czar; and you'll have to fight me if you say a word in his dispraise.

Pet. O! if that's the case, I'll say no more.

XXXIV. — PETER THE GREAT. — Scene 2.

Stanmitz. Well, mother, I must n't be skulking about here in Moscow any longer. I must leave you, and go back to Holland to my trade. At the risk of my life I came here, and at the risk of my life I must go back.

Mrs. Stanmitz. Ah! Michael, Michael, if it had n't been for your turning deserter, you might have been a corporal by this time!

Sta. Look you, mother, — I was made a soldier against my will, and the more I saw of a soldier's life the more I hated it. As a poor journeyman carpenter, I am at least free and independent; and if you will come with me to Holland, you shall take care of my wages and keep house for me.

Mrs. S. I should be a drag upon you, Michael. You will be wanting to get married by and by; moreover, it will be hard for me to leave the old home at my time of life.

Sta. Some one is knocking at the door. Wait, mother, till I have concealed myself. [*Enter Peter the Great disguised.*]

Peter. What, ho! comrade! No skulking! Come out from behind that screen! Did n't I see you through the window, as I passed?

Sta. Is it possible? Peter! My old fellow-workman! Give us your hand, my hearty! How came you to be here in Moscow? There is no ship-building going on so far inland.

Pet. No; but there is at St. Petersburg, the new city that the Czar is building up.

Sta. They say the Czar is in Moscow just now.

Pet. Yes, he passed through your street this morning.

Sta. So I heard. But I did n't see him. I say, Peter, how did you find me out?

Pet. Why, happening to see your mother's sign over the door, it occurred to me, after I returned to the palace —

Sta. The palace?

Pet. Yes; I always call the place where I put up a palace. It is a way I have.

Sta. You always were a funny fellow, Peter!

Pet. As I was saying, it occurred to me that Mrs. Stanmitz might be the mother or aunt of my old messmate; and so I put on this disguise—

Sta. Ha, ha! Sure enough, it is a disguise, the disguise of a gentleman. Peter, where did you get such fine clothes?

Pet. Don't interrupt me, sir!

Sta. Don't joke in that way again, Peter! Do you know you half frightened me by the stern tone in which you said "Don't interrupt me, sir!" But I see how it is, Peter, and I thank you. You thought you could learn something of your old friend, and so stopped to inquire, and saw me through the window.

Pet. Ah! Stanmitz, many's the big log we have chopped at together through the long summer day in Von Block's ship-yard.

Sta. That we have, Peter! Why not go back with me to Saardam? .

Pet. I can get better wages at St. Petersburg.

Sta. If it were not that I'm afraid of being overhauled for taking that long walk away from my post, I would go to St. Petersburg with you.

Pet. How happened you to venture back here?

Sta. Why, you must know that this old mother of mine wanted to see me badly; and then I had left behind here a sweetheart. Don't laugh, Peter! She has waited all this while for me; and the misery of it is that I am too poor to take her along with me yet. But next year, if my luck continues, I mean to return and marry her.

Pet. What if I should inform against you? I could make a pretty little sum by exposing a deserter.

Sta. Don't joke on that subject! You'll frighten the old woman. Peter, old boy, I'm so glad to see you —— Halloo! Soldiers at the door! What does this mean? An officer? Peter, excuse me, but I must leave you.

Pet. Stay! I give you my word it is not you they want. They are friends of mine.

Sta. O! if that's the case, I'll stay. But do you know one of those fellows looks wonderfully like my old commanding officer?

[*Enter Officer.*]

Officer. A dispatch from St. Petersburg, your majesty, claiming your instant attention.

Mrs. S. Majesty!

Sta. Majesty! I say, Peter, what does he mean by majesty?

Officer. Knave! Know you not that this is the Czar?

Sta. What! — Eh? — This? — Nonsense! This is my old friend Peter.

Officer. Down on your knees, rascal, to Peter the Great, Czar of Russia?

Mrs. S. O! your majesty, your majesty, don't hang the poor boy! He knew no better! He is my only son! Let him be whipped, but don't hang him!

Sta. Nonsense, mother! This is only one of Peter's jokes. Ha, ha, ha! You keep it up well, though. And those are dispatches you are reading, Peter!

Officer. Rascal! Dare you interrupt his majesty?

Sta. Twice you've called me rascal. Don't you think that's being rather familiar? Peter, have you any objection to my pitching your friend out of the window?

Officer. Ha! Now I look closer, I remember you! Soldiers, arrest this fellow! He's a deserter.

Sta. It's all up with me, and there stands Peter, as calm as if nothing had happened.

Mrs. S. I'm all in a maze! Good Mr. Officer, spare the poor boy!

Officer. He must go before a court-martial. He must be shot.

Mrs. S. O! woe is me! woe is me! That ever my poor boy should be shot!

Pet. Officer, I have occasion for the services of your prisoner. Release him.

Officer. Your majesty's will is absolute.

Sta. (*Aside.*) Majesty again? What does it all mean? A light breaks in upon me. There were rumors in Hol-

land, when I left, that the Czar had been working in one of the ship-yards. Can my Peter be the emperor?

Pet. Stanmitz, you have my secret now.

Sta. And you are —

Pet. The emperor! Rise, old woman; — your son, Baron Stanmitz, is safe!

Mrs. S. Baron Stanmitz!

Pet. I want him to superintend my ship-yard at St. Petersburg. No words. Prepare, both of you, to leave for the new city to-morrow. Baron Stanmitz, make that sweetheart of yours a Baroness this very evening, and bring her with you. No words. I have business claiming my care, or I would stop and see the wedding. Here is a purse of ducats. One of my secretaries will call with orders in the morning. Farewell.

Sta. O, Peter! Peter! I mean your majesty! your majesty! I'm in such a bewilderment!

Mrs. S. Down on your knees, Michael! I mean Baron Stanmitz! Down on your knees!

Sta. What! to my old friend, Peter, him that I used to wrestle with? Excuse me, your majesty — I mean friend Peter — Czar Peter — I can't begin to realize it! 'Tis all so like things we dream of.

Pet. Ha, ha! Good-by, messmate! We shall meet again in the morning. Commend me to your sweetheart.

[*Exit.*

Sta. Mr. Officer, that court-martial you spoke of is n't likely to come off.

Officer. Baron, I am your very humble servant. I hope, Baron, you will speak a good word for me to his majesty when opportunity offers. I humbly take my leave of your excellency.

XXXV. — CHASE ON THE ICE.

1. DURING the winter of 1844, being in the northern part of Maine, I had much leisure for the sports of a new country. To none was I more passionately addicted than

to skating. The sequestered lakes, frozen by intense cold, offer a wide plain to the lovers of this pastime. Often would I bind on my skates, and glide away up the glittering river, threading every mazy streamlet that flowed on toward the parent ocean, and feeling every pulse bound with the joyous exercise. It was during one of these excursions that an adventure befell me, that I can rarely think upon, even now, without a certain thrill of astonishment.

2. I had left a friend's house one evening, just before dusk, with the intention of skating a short distance up the noble Kennebec, which, under its icy crust, flowed directly before the door. The air was clear, calm, and bracing. The new moon silvered the lofty pines, and the stars twinkled with rare brilliancy from their dark-blue depths. In the stillness, the solitude, and magnificence of the scene, there was an effect almost preternatural upon the mind. I had gone up the river nearly two miles, when, coming to a little stream which emptied into a larger, I turned in to explore its course. Fir and hemlock trees of a century's growth met overhead, and formed an evergreen archway, radiant with frost-work.

3. All was dark within; but I was young and fearless, and, as I peered into the unbroken forests, I laughed in very joyousness. My wild hurra rang through the woods, and I stood listening to the echo that reverberated again and again, until all was hushed. Occasionally from some tall oak a night-bird would flap its wings. I watched the owls as they fluttered by, and I held my breath to listen to their distant hooting.

4. All of a sudden, a sound arose, which seemed to proceed from the very ice beneath my feet. It was loud and tremendous at first, and ended in a long yell. I was appalled. Coming on the ear amid such an unbroken solitude, it sounded like a blast from an infernal trumpet. Presently I heard the twigs on the shore snap as if from the tread of some animal. The blood rushed to my forehead with a bound that made my skin burn; but I felt a strange relief that I had to contend with things of earthly and not spiritual mold. My energies returned. The

moon shone through the opening by which I had entered the forest, and, considering this the best direction for escape, I shot toward it like an arrow.

5. The opening was hardly a hundred yards distant, and the swallow could not have skimmed them more swiftly; yet, as I turned my eyes to the shore, I could see two dark objects dashing through the underbrush at a pace nearly double that of my own. By their great speed, and the short yells which they gave, I knew at once that they were of the much-dreaded species known as the gray wolf. The untamable fierceness and untiring strength of this animal,

"With its long gallop, that can tire
The hound s deep hate, the hunter's fire,"

render it an object of dread to benighted travelers. The bushes that skirted the shore now seemed to rush by me with the velocity of light, as I dashed on in my flight.

6. The outlet was nearly gained; one second more, and I would be comparatively safe; but my pursuers suddenly appeared on the bank directly above me, which rose to the hight of some ten feet. There was no time for thought; I bent my head and darted wildly forward. The wolves sprang, but, miscalculating my speed, sprang behind, while their intended prey glided out upon the river. Instinct turned me toward home. How my skates made the light, icy mist spin from the glassy surface! The fierce howl of my pursuers again rang in my ears. I did not look back; I thought of the dear ones awaiting my return, and I put in play every faculty of mind and body for my escape. I was perfectly at home on the ice; and many were the days I had spent on my skates.

7. Every half-minute an alternate yelp from my pursuers told me they were close at my heels. Nearer and nearer they came; I could hear them pant. I strained every muscle in my frame to quicken my speed. Still I could hear close behind me the pattering of feet, when an involuntary motion on my part turned me out of my course. The wolves, unable to stop and as unable to turn, slipped and fell, sliding on far ahead, their tongues lolling

out, their white tushes gleaming from their red mouths, their dark, shaggy breasts freckled with foam; and, as they slid on, they howled with redoubled rage.

8. The thought occurred to me, that by thus turning aside whenever they came too near, I could avoid them; for, from the peculiar formation of their feet, they can not run on ice except in a right line. I immediately acted on this plan. The wolves, having regained their feet, sprang directly towards me. The race was renewed for twenty yards up the stream; they were already close on my back, when I glided round and dashed past them. A fierce howl greeted my evolution, and the wolves slipped upon their haunches, and again slid onward, presenting a perfect picture of baffled, bloodthirsty rage.

9. Thus I gained, at each turning, nearly a hundred yards. This was repeated two or three times, the wolves getting more excited every moment, until, coming opposite the house, a couple of stag-hounds, aroused by the noise, bayed furiously from their kennels. Quickly taking the hint, the wolves stopped in their mad career, turned skulkingly, and fled. I watched them till their dusky forms disappeared over a neighboring hill. Then, taking off my skates, I wended my way to the house, grateful to Providence for my escape, and determined never to trust myself again, if I could help it, within the reach of a gray wolf.

XXXVI. — THE CHASE.

From Scott.

Sir Walter Scott, born in Edinburgh, in 1771, was the author of the "Waverly Novels," of the "Life of Napoleon," and of many poems of the highest order, from one of which "The Lady of the Lake," the following extract is taken. The proper names are those of Scottish hills, or lakes, or other localities.

1. The stag at eve had drunk his fill,
    Where danced the moon on Monan's rill,
    And deep his midnight lair had made
    In lone Glenartney's hazel shade;

But, when the sun his beacon red
Had kindled on Benvoirlich's head,
The deep-mouth'd bloodhound's heavy bay
Resounded up the rocky way,
And faint, from farther distance borne,
Were heard the clanging hoof and horn.

2. As chief, who hears his warder call,
  "To arms! the foemen storm the wall,"
  The antler'd monarch of the waste
  Sprung from his heathery couch in haste.
  But, ere his fleet career he took,
  The dew-drops from his flanks he shook;
  Like crested leader proud and high,
  Toss'd his beam'd frontlet to the sky;
  A moment gazed adown the dale,
  A moment snuff'd the tainted gale,
  A moment listen'd to the cry,
  That thicken'd as the chase drew nigh;
  Then, as the headmost foes appear'd,
  With one brave bound the copse he clear'd,
  And, stretching forward free and far,
  Sought the wild heaths of Uam-Var.

3. Yell'd on the view the opening pack;
  Rock, glen, and cavern, paid them back;
  To many a mingled sound at once
  The awaken'd mountain gave response.
  A hundred dogs bay'd deep and strong,
  Clatter'd a hundred steeds along,
  Their peal the merry horns rung out,
  A hundred voices join'd the shout;
  With hark, and whoop, and wild halloo,
  No rest Benvoirlich's echoes knew.

4. Far from the tumult fled the roe,
  Close in her covert cower'd the doe,
  The falcon, from her cairn on high,
  Cast on the rout a wondering eye,

Till far beyond her piercing ken
The hurricane had swept the glen.
Faint, and more faint, its failing din
Return'd from cavern, cliff, and linn,
And silence settled, wide and still,
On the lone wood and mighty hill.

5. Less loud the sounds of silvan war
Disturb'd the hights of Uam-Var,
And rous'd the cavern, where, 'tis told,
A giant made his den of old;
For ere that steep ascent was won,
High in his pathway hung the sun,
And many a gallant, stay'd perforce,
Was fain to breathe his faltering horse,
And of the trackers of the deer,
Scarce half the lessening pack was near;
So shrewdly on the mountain side,
Had the bold burst their mettle tried.

6. The noble stag was pausing now,
Upon the mountain's southern brow,
Where broad extended, far beneath,
The varied realms of fair Menteith.
With anxious eye he wander'd o'er
Mountain and meadow, moss and moor,
And ponder'd refuge from his toil,
By far Lochard or Aberfoyle.
But nearer was the copsewood gray,
That waved and wept on Loch-Achray,
And mingled with the pine-trees blue
On the bold cliffs of Benvenue.
Fresh vigor with the hope return'd,
With flying foot the heath he spurn'd,
Held westward with unwearied race,
And left behind the panting chase.

XXXVII.—THE FIRST AND LAST DINNER.

1. TWELVE friends, much about the same age, and fixed by their pursuits, their family connections, and other local interests, as permanent inhabitants of the metropolis, agreed, one day, when they were drinking wine at the Star and Garter at Richmond, to institute an annual dinner among themselves, under the following regulations: That they should dine alternately at each others' houses on the first and last day of the year; and the first bottle of wine uncorked at the first dinner should be re-corked and put away, to be drank by him who should be the last of their number: that they should never admit a new member; that, when one died, eleven should meet, and when another died, ten should meet, and so on; and when only one remained, he should, on these two days, dine by himself, and sit the usual hours at his solitary table; but the first time he had so dined, lest it should be the only one, he should then uncork the first bottle, and in the first glass drink to the memory of all who were gone.

2. Some thirty years had now glided away, and only ten remained; but the stealing hand of time had written sundry changes in most legible characters. Raven locks had become grizzled; two or three heads had not as many locks as may be reckoned in a walk of half a mile along the Regent's Canal; one was actually covered with a brown wig; the crows' feet were visible in the corner of the eye: good old port and warm Madeira carried it against hock, claret, red Burgundy, and champagne; stews, hashes, and ragouts, grew into favor; crusts were rarely called for to relish the cheese after dinner; conversation was less boisterous, and it turned chiefly upon politics and the state of the funds, or the value of landed property; apologies were made for coming in thick shoes and warm stockings; the doors and windows were more carefully provided with list and sand-bags; the fire was in more request; and a quiet game of whist filled up the hours that were wont to be devoted to drinking, singing, and riotous merriment.

H S. R —10

3. Two rubbers, a cup of coffee, and at home by eleven o'clock, was the usual cry, when the fifth or sixth glass had gone round after the removal of the cloth. At parting, too, there was now a long ceremony in the hall; buttoning up great coats, tying on woollen comforters, fixing silk handkerchiefs over the mouth and up to the ears, and grasping sturdy walking-canes to support unsteady feet.

4. Their fiftieth anniversary came, and death had indeed been busy. Four little old men, of withered appearance and decrepit walk, with cracked voices, and dim, rayless eyes, sat down, by the mercy of Heaven, (as they tremulously declared,) to celebrate for the fiftieth time, the first day of the year, to observe the frolic compact, which, half a century before, they had entered into at the Star and Garter at Richmond. Eight were in their graves! The four that remained stood upon its confines.

5. Yet they chirped cheerily over their glass, though they could scarcely carry it to their lips, if more than half full; and cracked their jokes, though they articulated their words with difficulty, and heard each other with still greater difficulty. They mumbled, they chattered, they laughed, (if a sort of strangled wheezing might be called a laugh,) and as the wine sent their icy blood in warmer pulses through their veins, they talked of their past as if it were but a yesterday that had slipped by them; and of their future as if it were a busy century that lay before them.

6. At length came the last dinner; and the survivor of the twelve, upon whose head fourscore and ten winters had showered their snow, ate his solitary meal. It so chanced that it was in his house, and at his table, they celebrated the first. In his cellar, too, had remained, for more than fifty years, the bottle they had then uncorked, re-corked, and which he was that day to uncork again.

7. It stood beside him. With a feeble and reluctant grasp, he took the " frail memorial " of a youthful vow, and for a moment memory was faithful to her office. She threw open the long vista of buried years; and his heart traveled through them all. Their lusty and blithesome

spring, their bright and fervid summer, their ripe and temperate autumn, their chill, but not too frozen winter. He saw, as in a mirror, one by one, the laughing companions of that hour at Richmond who had dropped into eternity. He felt the loneliness of his condition, (for he had eschewed marriage, and in the veins of no living creature ran a drop of blood whose source was in his own,) and as he drained the glass which he had filled, "to the memory of those who were gone," the tears slowly trickled down the deep furrows of his aged face.

8. He had thus fulfilled one part of his vow; and he prepared himself to discharge the other, by sitting the usual number of hours at his desolate table. With a heavy heart he resigned himself to the gloom of his own thoughts; a lethargic sleep stole over him, his head fell upon his bosom, confused images crowded into his mind, he babbled to himself, was silent, and when his servant entered the room, alarmed by a noise which he heard, he found his master stretched upon the carpet at the foot of the easy-chair, out of which he had slipped in an apoplectic fit. He never spoke again, nor once opened his eyes, though the vital spark was not extinct till the following day. And this was the last dinner.

XXXVIII.—THE LAST MAN.

From Campbell.

1. ALL worldly shapes shall melt in gloom,
    The sun himself must die,
Before the mortal shall assume
    Its immortality.
I saw a vision in my sleep,
That gave my spirit strength to sweep
    Adown the gulf of time:
I saw the last of human mold,
That shall creation's death behold,
    As Adam saw her prime.

2. The sun's eye had a sickly glare,
      The earth with age was wan;
   The skeletons of nations were
      Around that lonely man.
   Some had expired in fight; the brands
   Still rusted in their bony hands;
      In plague and famine, some.
   Earth's cities had no sound nor tread;
   And ships were drifting with the dead
      To shores where all was dumb.

3. Yet, prophet-like, the lone one stood,
      With dauntless words and high,
   That shook the sear leaves from the wood
      As if a storm pass'd by;
   Saying, "We are twins in death, proud Sun,
   Thy face is cold, thy race is run,
      'T is mercy bids thee go;
   For thou, ten thousand thousand years,
   Hast seen the tide of human tears,
      That shall no longer flow.

4. "What though beneath thee, man put forth
      His pomp, his pride, his skill,
   And arts that made fire, flood, and earth,
      The vassals of his will:
   Yet mourn I not thy parted sway,
   Thou dim, discrown-èd king of day;
      For all these trophied arts
   And triumphs, that beneath thee sprang,
   Heal'd not a passion or a pang,
      Entail'd on human hearts.

5. "Go, let oblivion's curtain fall
      Upon the stage of men;
   Nor with thy rising beams, recall
      Life's tragedy again.
   Its piteous pageants bring not back,
   Nor waken flesh, upon the rack

Of pain anew to writhe,
Stretch'd in disease's shapes abhorr'd,
Or mown in battle by the sword,
Like grass beneath the scythe.

6. "Even I am weary, in yon skies
To watch thy fading fire;
Test of all sunless agonies,
Behold not me expire.
My lips, that speak thy dirge of death,
Their rounded gasp and gurgling breath
To see, thou shalt not boast.
The eclipse of nature spreads my pall,
The majesty of darkness shall
Receive my parting ghost.

7. "This spirit shall return to Him
That gave its heavenly spark;
Yet think not, Sun, it shall be dim
When thou thyself art dark.
No! it shall live again, and shine
In bliss unknown to beams of thine,
By Him recall'd to breath,
Who captive led captivity,
Who robb'd the grave of Victory,
And took the sting from Death.

8. "Go, Sun, while mercy holds me up
On nature's awful waste,
To drink this last and bitter cup
Of grief that man shall taste,
Go, tell the night, that hides thy face,
Thou saw'st the last of Adam's race
On earth's sepulchral clod,
The dark'ning universe defy
To quench his immortality,
Or shake his trust in God!"

XXXIX. — THE YOUTH OF WASHINGTON.

FROM EVERETT.

1. JUST as Washington was passing from boyhood to youth, the enterprise and capital of Virginia were seeking a new field for exercise and investment, in the unoccupied public domain beyond the mountains. The business of a surveyor immediately became one of great importance and trust, for no surveys were executed by the government. To this occupation the youthful Washington, not yet sixteen years of age, and well furnished with the requisite mathematical knowledge, zealously devoted himself. Some of his family connections possessed titles to large portions of public land, which he was employed with them in surveying.

2. Thus, at a period of life when, in a more advanced stage of society, the intelligent youth is occupied in the elementary studies of the schools and colleges, Washington was carrying the surveyor's chain through the fertile valleys of the Blue Ridge and the Alleghany Mountains; passing days and weeks in the wilderness, beneath the shadow of eternal forests; listening to the voice of the waterfalls, which man's art had not yet set to the healthful music of the saw-mill or the trip-hammer; reposing from the labors of the day on a bear-skin, with his feet to the blazing logs of a camp-fire; and sometimes startled from the deep slumbers of careless, hard-working youth, by the alarm of the Indian war-whoop.

3. This was the gymnastic school in which Washington was brought up; in which his quick glance was formed, destined to range hereafter across the battle-field, through clouds of smoke and bristling rows of bayonets; the school in which his senses, weaned from the taste for those detestable indulgences, miscalled pleasures, in which the flower of adolescence so often languishes and pines away, were early braced up to the sinewy manhood which becomes the

"Lord of the lion heart and eagle eye."

4. There is preserved among the papers of Washington a letter, written to a friend while he was engaged on his first surveying tour, and when he was, consequently, but sixteen years of age. I quote a sentence from it, in spite of the homeliness of the details, for which I like it the better, and because I wish to set before you, not an ideal hero, wrapped in cloudy generalities and a mist of vague panegyric, but the real, identical man, with all the peculiarities of his life and occupation.

5. "Your letter," says he, "gave me the more pleasure, as I received it among barbarians and an uncouth set of people. Since you received my letter of October last, I have not slept above three or four nights in a bed; but, after walking a good deal all the day, I have lain down before the fire, upon a little hay, straw, fodder, or a bear-skin, whichever was to be had, with man, wife, and children, like dogs and cats; and happy is he who gets the berth nearest the fire. Nothing would make it pass off tolerably but a good reward. A doubloon is my constant gain, every day that the weather will permit my going out, and sometimes six pistoles."

6. If there is an individual in the morning of life who has not yet made his choice between the flowery path of indulgence and the rough ascent of honest industry, if there is one who is ashamed to get his living by any branch of honest labor, let him reflect that the youth who was carrying the theodolite and surveyor's chain through the mountain passes of the Alleghanies, in the month of March, sleeping on a bundle of hay before the fire, in a settler's log-cabin, and not ashamed to boast that he did it for his doubloon a day, is George Washington; that the life he led trained him up to command the armies of United America; that the money he earned was the basis of that fortune which enabled him afterward to bestow his services, without reward, on a bleeding and impoverished country.

7. For three years was the young Washington employed, the greater part of the time, and whenever the season would permit, in this laborious and healthful occupation;

and I know not if it would be deemed unbecoming, were a thoughtful student of our history to say that he could almost hear the voice of Providence, in the language of Milton, announce its high purpose,

> "To exercise him in the wilderness;
>   There shall he first lay down the rudiments
>   Of his great warfare, ere I send him forth
>   To conquer!"

XL.—APPOINTMENT OF WASHINGTON.

JOHN ADAMS was a distinguished patriot of the Revolution, a member of Congress at the time of the appointment of Washington as commander-in-chief of the American Army, and was subsequently President of the United States.

1. THE army was assembled at Cambridge, Mass., under Gen. Ward, and Congress was sitting at Philadelphia. Every day, new applications in behalf of the army arrived. The country was urgent that Congress should legalize the raising of the army, as they were what must be considered, and what was in law considered, only a mob, a band of rebels. The country was placed in circumstances of peculiar difficulty and danger. The struggle had begun, and yet every thing was without order. The great trial now seemed to be this question: Who shall be the commander-in-chief? It was exceedingly important, and was felt to be the hinge on which the contest might turn for or against us. The Southern and the Middle States, warm and rapid in their zeal, for the most part, were jealous of New England, because they felt the real physical force was there; what then was to be done?

2. All New England adored Gen. Ward; he had been in the French war, and went out laden with laurels. He was a scholar and a statesman. Every qualification seemed to cluster in him; and it was confidently believed that the army would not receive any appointment over him. What was then to be done? Difficulties thickened at every

step. The struggle was to be long and bloody. Without union all was lost. The country, and the whole country, must come in. One pulsation must beat through all hearts. The cause was one, and the army must be one. The members had talked, debated, considered, and guessed, and yet the decisive step had not been taken. At length, Mr. Adams came to his conclusion. The means of resolving it were somewhat singular, and nearly as follows. He was walking one morning before Congress Hall, apparently in deep thought, when his cousin Samuel Adams came up to him and said:

3. "What is the topic with you this morning?" O, the army, the army," he replied. "I 'm determined to go into the hall this morning and enter on a full detail of the state of the colonies, in order to show the absolute need of taking some decisive steps. My whole aim will be to induce Congress to appoint the day for adopting the army as the legal army of these united colonies of North America, and then to hint at an election of commander-in-chief." "Well," said Samuel Adams, "I like that, cousin John; but on whom have you fixed as that commander?" "I will tell you; George Washington of Virginia, a member of this house." "O," replied Samuel Adams, quickly, "that will never do, never."

4. "It must do; it shall do;" said John, "and for these reasons: the Southern and Middle States are both to enter heartily in the cause; and their arguments are potent; they say that New England holds the physical power in her hands, and they fear the result. A New England army, a New England commander, with New England perseverance, all united, appall them. For this cause they hang back. Now, the only course is to allay their fears, and give them nothing to complain of; and this can be done in no other way than by appointing a Southern chief over this force, and then all will rush to the standard. This policy will blend us in one mass, and that mass will be resistless."

5. At this, Samuel Adams seemed greatly moved. They talked over the preliminary circumstances, and John asked

H. S. R.—11

his cousin to second the motion. Mr. Adams went in, took the floor, and put all his strength in the delineations he had prepared, all aiming at the adoption of the army. He was ready to own the army, appoint a commander, vote supplies, and proceed to business. After his speech had been finished, some doubted, some feared. His warmth increased with the occasion, and to all those doubts and hesitations he replied: "Gentlemen, if this Congress will not adopt this army, before ten moons have set, New England will adopt it, and she will undertake the struggle alone; yes, with a strong arm, and a clear conscience, she will front the foe single-handed."

6. This had the desired effect. They saw New England was neither playing nor to be played with. They agreed to appoint a day. A day was fixed. It came. Mr. Adams went in, took the floor, urged the measure, and after some debate it passed. The next thing was to get a commander for this army, with supplies, &c. All looked to Mr. Adams on the occasion, and he was ready. He took the floor, and went into a minute delineation of the character of Gen. Ward, bestowing on him the encomiums which then belonged to no one else. At the end of the eulogy, he said, "But this is not the man I have chosen." He then went into the delineation of the character of a commander-in-chief, such as was required by the peculiar situation of the colonists at this juncture. And after he had presented the qualifications in his strongest language, and given the reasons for the nomination he was about to make, he said:

7. "Gentlemen, I know these qualifications are high, but we all know they are needful in this chief. Does any one say they are not to be obtained in this country? In reply, I have to say they are; they reside in one of our own body, and he is the person whom I now nominate; GEORGE WASHINGTON, of Virginia." Washington, who sat on Mr. Adams's right hand, was looking him intently in the face, to watch the name he was about to announce, and not expecting it would be his, sprang from his seat the minute he heard it, and rushed into an adjoining room. Mr. Adams had asked his cousin Samuel to call.

for an adjournment as soon as the nomination was made, in order to give the members time to deliberate, and the result is before the world. I asked Mr. Adams, among other questions, the following: Did you ever doubt the success of the conflict?' 'No, no, not for a moment. I expected to be hung and quartered if I was caught, but no matter for that, my country would be free. I knew George III. could not forge chains long enough and strong enough to reach around these United States."

XLI. — WASHINGTON IN THE CAMP.

From Weems.

Weems is known chiefly as the author of the Life of Washington.

1. In the winter of 1777, while Washington, with the American army, lay encamped at Valley Forge, a certain good old Friend, of the respectable family and name of Potts, if I mistake not, had occasion to pass through the woods near head-quarters. Treading his way along the venerable grove, suddenly he heard the sound of a human voice, which, as he advanced, increased on his ear, and at length became like the voice of one speaking much in earnest.

2. As he approached the spot with a cautious step, whom should he behold, in a dark, natural bower of ancient oaks, but the commander-in-chief of the American armies on his knees at prayer! Motionless with surprise, friend Potts continued on the place till the General, having ended his devotions, arose, and, with a countenance of angelic serenity, retired to head-quarters. Friend Potts then went home; and on entering his parlor, he called out to his wife, "Sarah, my dear! Sarah! all is well! all is well! George Washington will yet prevail." "What is the matter, Isaac?" replied she. "Thee seems moved."

3. "Well, if I *seem* moved, it is no more than I *am*. I have this day seen what I never expected. Thee knows

that I always thought the sword and the gospel inconsistent; and that no man could be a soldier and a Christian at the same time; but George Washington has this day convinced me of my mistake."

4. He then related what he had seen, and concluded with this prophetical remark: "If George Washington be not a man of God, I am greatly deceived; and still more shall I be deceived if God do not, through him, work out a great salvation for America."

XLII. — MARION'S MEN.

FROM BRYANT.

1. OUR band is few, but true and tried,
　　Our leader frank and bold;
　The British soldier trembles
　　When Marion's name is told.
　Our fortress is the good greenwood,
　　Our tent the cypress tree;
　We know the forest round us,
　　As seamen know the sea.
　We know its walls of thorny vines,
　　Its glades of reedy grass,
　Its safe and silent islands
　　Within the dark morass.

2. Woe to the English soldiery
　　That little dread us near!
　On them shall light, at midnight,
　　A strange and sudden fear:
　When, waking to their tents on fire,
　　They grasp their arms in vain,
　And they who stand to face us
　　Are beat to earth again;
　And they who fly in terror deem
　　A mighty host behind,
　And hear the tramp of thousands
　　Upon the hollow wind.

3. Well knows the fair and friendly moon
    The band that Marion leads,
The glitter of their rifles,
    The scampering of their steeds.
'Tis life to guide the fiery barb
    Across the moonlight plain ;
'Tis life to feel the night-wind
    That lifts his tossing mane,
A moment in the British camp,
    A moment and away,
Back to the pathless forest,
    Before the peep of day.

4. Grave men there are by broad Santee,
    Grave men with hoary hairs ;
Their hearts are all with Marion,
    For Marion are their prayers.
And lovely ladies greet our band,
    With kindest welcoming,
With smiles like those of summer,
    And tears like those of spring.
For them we wear these trusty arms,
    And lay them down no more,
Till we have driven the Briton
    Forever from our shore.

XLIII. — MARSEILLES HYMN.

This hymn was popular in France during the French Revolution, and is still one of their patriotic songs.

1. YE sons of France, awake to glory !
    Hark ! hark ! what myriads bid you rise !
Your children, wives, and grandsires hoary ;
    Behold their tears and hear their cries !
Shall hateful tyrants, mischief breeding,
    With hireling hosts, a ruffian band,
    Affright and desolate the land,
While liberty and peace lie bleeding ?

> To arms! to arms! ye brave!
> The avenging sword unsheathe!
> March on! march on! all hearts resolv'd
> On victory or death!

2. Now, now, the dangerous storm is rolling,
> Which treacherous kings confederate raise;
> The dogs of war, let loose, are howling,
> And, lo! our fields and cities blaze.
> And shall we basely view the ruin,
> While lawless force, with guilty stride,
> Spreads desolation far and wide,
> With crimes and blood his hands imbruing?
> To arms! to arms! ye brave!
> The avenging sword unsheathe!
> March on! march on! all hearts resolv'd
> On victory or death!

3. With luxury and pride surrounded,
> The bold, insatiate despots dare,
> Their thirst of gold and power unbounded,
> To mete and vend the light and air.
> Like beasts of burden would they load us,
> Like gods would bid their slaves adore;
> But man is man, and who is more?
> Then shall they longer lash and goad us?
> To arms! to arms! ye brave!
> The avenging sword unsheathe!
> March on! march on! all hearts resolv'd
> On victory or death!

4. O Liberty, can man resign thee,
> Once having felt thy generous flame?
> Can dungeons, bolts, or bars confine thee,
> Or whips thy noble spirit tame?
> Too long the world has wept, bewailing,
> That Falsehood's dagger tyrants wield;
> But Freedom is our sword and shield,
> And all their arts are unavailing.

To arms ! to arms ! ye brave !
The avenging sword unsheathe !
March on ! march on ! all hearts resolv'd
On victory or death !

XLIV.—SHAKSPEARE.

From Hazlitt.

Hazlitt is a popular modern English author, chiefly known as a reviewer, a writer of occasional pieces, and the author of "Table Talk."

1. It has been said, by some critic, that Shakspeare was distinguished from the other dramatic writers of his day, only by his wit; that they had all his other qualities but that; that one writer had as much sense; another, as much fancy; another, as much knowledge of character; another, the same depth of passion; and another, as great power of language. This statement is not true; nor is the inference from it well founded, even if it were. This person does not seem to be aware, that, upon his own showing, the great distinction of Shakspeare's genius was its virtually including the genius of all the great men of his age, and not its differing from them in one accidental particular.

2. The striking peculiarity of Shakspeare's mind was its generic quality; its power of communication with all other minds; so that it contained a universe of thought and feeling within itself, and no one peculiar bias or exclusive excellence, more than another. He was just like any other man, but that he was like all other men. He was the least of an egotist that it was possible to be. He was nothing in himself, but he was all that others were, or that they could become. He not only had in himself the germs of every faculty and feeling, but he could follow them, by anticipation, intuitively, into all their conceivable ramifications, through every change of fortune, or conflict of passion, or turn of thought. He had " a mind,

reflecting ages past," and present; all the people that ever lived are there. There was no respect of persons with him. His genius shone equally on the evil and on the good, on the wise and the foolish, the monarch and the beggar. "All corners of the earth, kings, queens, and states; maids, matrons, nay, the secrets of the grave," are hardly hid from his searching glance. He was like the genius of humanity, changing places with all of us at pleasure, and playing with our purposes as with his own.

3. He turned the globe round for his amusement, and surveyed the generations of men and the individuals as they passed, with their different concerns, passions, follies, vices, virtues, actions, and motives; as well those they knew, as those they did not know or acknowledge to themselves. The dreams of childhood, the ravings of despair, were the toys of his fancy. Airy beings waited at his call and came at his bidding. Harmless fairies "nodded to him and did him their courtesies;" and the night-hag bestrode the blast at the command of "his so potent art."

4. He had only to speak of any thing, in order to become that thing, with all the circumstances belonging to it. When he conceived of a character, whether real or imaginary, he not only entered into all its thoughts and feelings; but seemed instantly, and as if by touching a secret spring, to be surrounded with all the same objects, "subject to the same skyey influences," the same local, outward, and unforeseen accidents which would occur in reality. Thus, the character of Caliban not only stands before us with a language and manners of his own, but the scenery and situation of the enchanted island he inhabits, the traditions of the place, its strange noises, its hidden recesses, "his frequent haunts, and ancient neighborhood," are given with a miraculous truth of nature, and with all the familiarity of an old recollection. "The whole coheres semblably together, in time," place, and circumstance.

5. In reading this author, you do not merely learn what his characters say; you see their persons. By something expressed or understood, you are at no loss to deci-

pher their peculiar physiognomy, the meaning of a look, the grouping, the by-play, as we might see it on the stage. A word, an epithet, paints a whole scene, or throws us back whole years in the history of the person represented. So, (as it has been ingeniously remarked,) when Prospero describes himself as being left alone in the boat with his daughter, the epithet which he applies to her, "Me and thy *crying* self," flings the imagination instantly back from the grown woman, to the helpless condition of infancy, and places the first and most trying scene of his misfortune before us, with all that he must have suffered in the interval.

6. How well the silent anguish of Macduff is conveyed to the reader, by the friendly expostulation of Malcolm, "What! man, ne'er pull your hat upon your brows!" Again, Hamlet, in the scene with Rosencrantz and Guildenstern, somewhat abruptly concludes his fine soliloquy on life, by saying "Man delights me not, nor woman neither, though by your smiling you seem to say so;" which is explained by their answer; "My lord, we had no such stuff in our thoughts; but we smiled to think, if you delight not in man, what scanty entertainment the players shall receive from you, whom we met on the way:" as if, while Hamlet was making his speech, his two old school-fellows from Wittenberg, had been really standing by, and he had seen them smiling by stealth, at the idea of the players crossing their minds. It is not "a combination and a form" of words, a set-speech or two, a preconcerted theory of a character, that will do this; but all the persons concerned must have been present in the poet's imagination, as at a kind of rehearsal; and whatever would have passed through their minds on the occasion, and have been observed by others, passed through his, and is made known to the reader.

XLV. — SHAKSPEARE'S HOME AND TOMB.

FROM IRVING.

Thou soft-flowing Avon, by thy silver stream
Of things more than mortal, sweet Shakspeare would dream;
The fairies by moonlight dance round his green bed,
For hallow'd the turf is which pillows his head.—GARRICK.

1. To a homeless man, who has no spot on this wide world which he can truly call his own, there is a momentary feeling of something like independence and territorial consequence, when after a weary day's travel, he kicks off his boots, thrusts his feet into slippers, and stretches himself before an inn fire. Let the world without go as it may; let kingdoms rise or fall, so long as he has wherewithal to pay his bill, he is, for the time being, the very monarch of all he surveys. The arm-chair is his throne, the poker his scepter, and the little parlor, some twelve feet square, his undisputed empire. It is a morsel of certainty, snatched from the midst of the uncertainties of life; it is a sunny moment, gleaming out kindly on a cloudy day, and he who has advanced some way on the pilgrimage of existence, knows the importance of husbanding even morsels and moments of enjoyment. "Shall I not take mine ease in mine inn?" thought I, as I gave the fire a stir, lolled back in my elbow-chair, and cast a complacent look about the little parlor of the Red Horse at Stratford-on-Avon.

2. The words of sweet Shakspeare were just passing through my mind, as the clock struck midnight, from the tower of the church in which he lies buried. There was a gentle tap at the door, and a pretty chamber-maid, putting in her smiling face, inquired, with a hesitating air, whether I had rung. I understood it as a modest hint that it was time to retire. My dream of absolute dominion was at an end; so, abdicating my throne, like a prudent potentate, to avoid being deposed, and putting the Stratford Guide-Book under my arm, as a pillow companion, I went to bed, and dreamed all night of Shakspeare, the jubilee, and David Garrick.

3. The next morning was one of those quickening mornings which we have in early spring; for it was about the middle of March. The chills of a long winter had suddenly given way; the north wind had spent its last gasp; and a mild air came stealing from the west, breathing the breath of life into nature, and moving every bud and flower to burst forth into fragrance and beauty.

4. I had come to Stratford on a poetical pilgrimage. My first visit was to the house where Shakspeare was born, and where, according to tradition, he was brought up to his father's craft of wool-combing. It is a small, mean-looking edifice of wood and plaster, a true nestling-place of genius, which seems to delight in hatching its offspring in by-corners. The walls of its squalid chambers are covered with names and inscriptions, in every language, by pilgrims of all nations, ranks, and conditions, from the prince to the peasant, and present a simple, but striking instance of the spontaneous and universal homage of mankind to the great poet of nature.

5. The house is shown by a garrulous old lady, in a frosty red face, lighted up by a cold blue anxious eye, and garnished with artificial locks of flaxen hair, curling from under an exceedingly dirty cap. She was peculiarly assiduous in exhibiting the relics with which this, like all other celebrated shrines, abounds. There was the shattered stock of the very matchlock with which Shakspeare shot the deer, on his poaching exploits. There, too, was his tobacco-box, which proves that he was a rival smoker of Sir Walter Raleigh; the sword, also, with which he played Hamlet; and the identical lantern with which Friar Lawrence discovered Romeo and Juliet at the tomb! There was an ample supply also of Shakspeare's mulberry tree.

6. From the birth-place of Shakspeare a few paces brought me to his grave. He lies buried in the chancel of the parish church, a large and venerable pile, moldering with age, but richly ornamented. It stands on the banks of the Avon, on an embowered point, and separated by adjoining gardens from the suburbs of the town. Its situation is quiet and retired; the river runs murmuring at

the foot of the churchyard, and the elms which grow upon its banks droop their branches into its clear bosom. An avenue of limes, the boughs of which are curiously interlaced, so as to form in summer an arched way of foliage, leads up from the gate of the yard to the church porch. The graves are overgrown with grass; the gray tombstones, some of them nearly sunk into the earth, are half covered with moss, which has likewise tinted the reverend old building.

7. The tomb of Shakspeare is in the chancel. The place is solemn and sepulchral. Tall elms wave before the pointed windows, and the Avon, which runs at a short distance from the walls, keeps up a low perpetual murmur. A flat stone marks the spot where the bard is buried. There are four lines inscribed on it, said to have been written by himself, and which have in them something extremely awful. If they are indeed his own, they show that solicitude about the quiet of the grave, which seems natural to fine sensibilities and thoughtful minds.

8. Just over the grave, in a niche of the wall, is a bust of Shakspeare, put up shortly after his death, and considered as a resemblance. The aspect is pleasant and serene, with a finely arched forehead, and I thought I could read in it clear indications of the cheerful, social disposition by which he was as much characterized among his contemporaries as by the vastness of his genius. The inscription mentions his age at the time of his decease, fifty-three years; an untimely death for the world: for what fruit might not have been expected from the golden autumn of such a mind, sheltered as it was from the stormy vicissitudes of life, and flourishing in the sunshine of popular and royal favor.

9. The inscription on the tombstone has not been without its effect. It has prevented the removal of his remains. from the bosom of his native place to Westminster Abbey, which was at one time contemplated. A few years since, also, as some laborers were digging to make an adjoining vault, the earth caved in, so as to leave a vacant space almost like an arch, through which one might have reached

into his grave. No one, however, presumed to meddle with his remains, and lest any of the idle or curious, or any collector of relics should be tempted to commit depredations, the old sexton kept watch over the place for two days, until the vault was finished and the aperture closed again. He told me that he had made bold to look into the hole, but could see neither coffin nor bones; nothing but dust. It was something, I thought, to have seen the dust of Shakspeare.

XLVI. — HAMLET. — Scene 1.

From Shakspeare.

Shakspeare, the great English dramatist, lived from 1564 to 1616. In his life, he was almost unknown, but his posthumous fame will be co-extensive with the existence of English literature. This scene is from Hamlet, one of his best tragedies.

HORATIO, MARCELLUS, BERNARDO.

Hor. Hail to your lordship!

Ham. I am glad to see you well:
Horatio, or I do forget myself.

Hor. The same, my lord, and your poor servant ever.

Ham. Sir, my good *friend;* I'll change *that name* with you.
And what make you from Wittenberg, Horatio?
Marcellus?

Mar. My good lord!

Ham. I am very glad to see you. Good even, sir;
But what, in faith, make you from Wittenberg?

Hor. A truant disposition, good my lord.

Ham. I would not hear your enemy say so;
Nor shall you do mine ear that violence,
To make it truster of your own report
Against yourself. I know you are no truant.
But, what is your affair in Elsinore?
We'll teach you to drink deep, ere you depart.

Hor. My lord, I came to see your father's funeral.

Ham. I pray thee, do not mock me, fellow-student.
I think, it was to see my mother's wedding.

Hor. Indeed, my lord, it follow'd hard upon.

Ham. Thrift, thrift, Horatio! the funeral baked meats
Did coldly furnish forth the marriage tables.
Would I had met my dearest foe in heaven,
Or ever I had seen that day, Horatio!
My father! Methinks I see my father.

Hor. Where,
My lord?

Ham. In my mind's eye, Horatio!

Hor. I saw him once: he was a goodly king.

Ham. He was a man, take him for all in all,
I shall not look upon his like again.

Hor. My lord, I think I saw him yesternight.

Ham. Saw? Who?

Hor. My lord, the king, your father.

Ham. The king, my father?

Hor. Season your imagination for awhile
With an attent ear, till I may deliver,
Upon the witness of these gentlemen,
This marvel to you.

Ham. For heaven's love, let me hear.

Hor. Two nights together had these gentlemen,
Marcellus and Bernardo, on their watch,
In the dead waist and middle of the night,
Been thus encounter'd. A figure like your father,
Arm'd at point, exactly cap-a-pie,
Appears before them, and, with solemn march,
Goes slow and stately by them: thrice he walk'd,
By their oppress'd and fear-surpris-ed eyes,
Within his truncheon's length; while they, distill'd
Almost to jelly with the act of fear,
Stand dumb, and speak not to him. This to me
In dreadful secrecy they did impart;
And I with them, the third night, kept the watch;
Where, as they had deliver'd, both in time,
Form of the thing, each word made true and good.
The apparition comes.

Ham. But where was this?

Mar. My lord, upon the platform where we watch'd.

Ham. Did you not speak to it?

Hor. My lord, I did;
But answer made it none; yet once, methought,
It lifted up its head, and did address
Itself to motion, like as it would speak;
But, even then, the morning cock crew loud;
And, at the sound, it shrunk in haste away,
And vanish'd from our sight.

Ham. 'Tis very strange.

Hor. As I do live, my honor'd lord, 't is true;
And we did think it writ down in our duty
To let you know of it.

Ham. Indeed, indeed, sirs: but this troubles me.
Hold you the watch to-night?

Mar. We do, my lord.

Ham. Arm'd, say you?

Mar. Arm'd, my lord.

Ham. From top to toe?

Mar. My lord, from head to foot.

Ham. Then saw you not his face?

Hor. Oh, yes, my lord, he wore his beaver up.

Ham. What, look'd he frowningly?

Hor. A countenance more in sorrow than in anger.

Ham. Pale or red?

Hor. Nay, very pale.

Ham. And fix'd his eyes upon you?

Hor. Most constantly.

Ham. I would I had been there.

Hor. It would have much amazed you.

Ham. Very like,
Very like. Stay'd it long?

Hor. While one, with moderate haste, might tell a hundred.

Mar. Ber. Longer, longer.

Hor. Not when I saw it.

Ham. His beard was grizzled? No?

Hor. It was as I have seen it in his life,
A sable silver'd.

Ham. I will watch to-night;
Perchance 'twill walk again.
  Hor. I warrant you it will.
  Ham. If it assume my noble father's person,
I 'll speak to it, though hell itself should gape,
And bid me hold my peace. I pray you all,
If you have hitherto conceal'd this sight,
Let it be tenable in your silence still;
And whatsoever else shall hap to-night,
Give it an understanding, but no tongue;
I will requite your loves. So, fare you well.
Upon the platform, 'twixt eleven and twelve,
I 'll visit you.
  Hor. Our duty to your honor.
  Ham. Your loves, as mine to you: Farewell.
                          [*Exeunt all but* Hamlet.
My father's spirit, in arms! All is not well;
I doubt some foul play: would the night were come!
Till then, sit still, my soul. Foul deeds will rise,
Though all the earth o'erwhelm them, to men's eyes.

XLVII. — HAMLET. — Scene 2.

From Shakspeare.

HAMLET, GUILDENSTERN, ROSENCRANTZ.

Hamlet. What have you, my good friends, deserved at
the hands of fortune, that she sends you to prison hither?
  Guildenstern. Prison, my lord?
  Ham. Denmark's a prison.
  Rosencrantz. Then is the world one.
  Ham. A goodly one; in which there are many confines,
wards, and dungeons; Denmark being one of the worst.
  Ros. We think not so, my lord.
  Ham. Why, then, 'tis none to you; for there is nothing
either good or bad, but thinking makes it so : to me it is
a prison.
  Ros. Why, then your ambition makes it one; 'tis too
narrow for your mind.

Ham. O! I could be bounded in a nutshell, and count myself a king of infinite space, were it not that I have bad dreams. But, in the beaten way of friendship, what make you at Elsinore?

Ros. To visit you, my lord; no other occasion.

Ham. Beggar that I am, I am even poor in thanks; but I thank you; and sure, dear friends, my thanks are too dear, a halfpenny. Were you not sent for? Is it your own inclining? Is it a free invitation? Come, come; deal justly with me; come, come; nay, speak.

Guil. What should we say, my lord?

Ham. Any thing; but to the purpose. You were sent for; and there is a kind of confession in your looks, which your modesties have not craft enough to color. I know the good king and queen have sent for you.

Ros. To what end, my lord?

Ham. That you must teach me. But let me conjure you, by the rights of our fellowship, by the consonancy of our youth, by the obligation of our ever-preserved love, and by what more dear a better proposer could charge you withal, be even and direct with me, whether ye were sent for, or no?

Ros. What say you? [*To* GUILDENSTERN.]

Ham. Nay, then I have an eye of you. [*Aside.*] If you love me, hold not off.

Guil. My lord, we were sent for.

Ham. I will tell you why; so shall my anticipation prevent your discovery, and your secrecy to the king and queen moult no feather. I have of late (but wherefore I know not) lost all my mirth, foregone all custom of exercises: and, indeed, it goes so heavily with my disposition, that this goodly frame, the earth, seems to me a sterile promontory; this most excellent canopy, the air, look you, this brave o'erhanging firmament, this majestical roof fretted with golden fire, why, it appears no other thing to me than a foul and pestilent congregation of vapors.

What a piece of work is man! How noble in reason! how infinite in faculties! in form and moving, how express and admirable! in action how like an angel! in

H. S. R.—12

apprehensio'n, how like a god! the beauty of the world! the paragon of animals! And yet, to me, what is this quintessence of dust?

Gentlemen, you are welcome to Elsinore. Your hands. You are welcome; but my uncle-father and aunt-mother are deceived.

Guil. In what, my lord?

Ham. I am but mad north-north-west; when the wind is southerly, I know a hawk from a hand-saw.

Guil. Good, my lord, vouchsafe me a word with you.

Ham. Sir, a whole history.

Guil. The king, sir, —

Ham. Ay, sir, what of him?

Guil. Is, in his retirement, marvelous distempered.

Ham. With drink, sir?

Guil. No, my lord, with choler.

Ham. Your wisdom should show itself richer, to signify this to the doctor; for, for me to put him to his purgation would, perhaps, plunge him into more choler.

Guil. Good, my lord, put your discourse into some frame, and start not so wildly from my affair.

Ham. I am tame, sir; pronounce.

Guil. The queen your mother, in most great affliction of spirit, hath sent me to you.

Ham. You are welcome.

Guil. Nay, good my lord, this courtesy is not of the right breed. If it shall please you to make me a wholesome answer, I will do your mother's commandment; if not, your pardon and my return shall be the end of my business.

Ham. Sir, I can not.

Guil. What, my lord?

Ham. Make you a wholesome answer; my wit's diseased; but, sir, such answer as I can make, you shall command; or, rather, as you say, my mother; therefore no more, but to the matter. My mother, you say, —

Ros. Then thus she says. Your behavior hath struck her into amazement and admiration.

Ham. O wonderful son, that can so astonish a mother! But is there no sequel at the heels of this mother's admiration? Impart.

Ros. She desires to speak with you in her closet, ere you go to bed.

Ham. We shall obey, were she ten times our mother. Have you any further trade with us?

Ros. My lord, you once did love me.

Ham. And do still, by these pickers and stealers! [*Showing his fingers.*]

Ros. Good, my lord; what is your cause of distemper? You do surely but bar the door upon your own liberty, if you deny your griefs to your friend.

Ham. Sir, I lack advancement.

Ros. How can that be, when you have the voice of the king himself for your succession in Denmark?

Ham. Ay, sir, but, "While the grass grows,"—the proverb is something musty. [*Enter the Players with recorders.*] O, the recorders:—let me see one. To withdraw with you:—[*To* GUILDENSTERN.] Why do you go about to recover the wind of me, as if you would drive me into a toil.

Guil. O, my lord, if my duty be too bold, my love is too unmannerly.

Ham. I do not well understand that. Will you play upon this pipe?

Guil. My lord, I can not.

Ham. I pray you.

Guil. Believe me, I can not.

Ham. I do beseech you.

Guil. I know no touch of it, my lord.

Ham. 'Tis as easy as lying; govern these ventages with your fingers and thumb, give it breath with your mouth, and it will discourse most eloquent music. Look you, these are the stops.

Guil. But these can not I command to any utterance of harmony; I have not the skill.

Ham. Why, look you, now, how unworthy a thing you make of me! You would play upon me; you would seem

to know my stops; you would pluck out the heart of my mystery; you would sound me from my lowest note to the top of my compass; and there is much music, excellent voice, in this little organ; yet can not you make it speak. Why, do you think I am easier to be played on than a pipe? Call me what instrument you will, though you can fret me, you can not play upon me.

XLVIII. — BOOK-MAKING.

FROM IRVING.

1. I HAVE often wondered at the extreme fecundity of the press, and how it comes to pass that so many heads on which nature seemed to have inflicted the curse of barrenness, should teem with voluminous productions. As a man travels on, however, in the journey of life, his objects of wonder daily diminish, and he is continually finding out some very simple cause for some great matter of marvel. Thus have I chanced, in my peregrinations about this great metropolis, to blunder upon a scene which unfolded to me some of the mysteries of the book-making craft, and at once put an end to my astonishment.

2. I was one summer's day loitering through the great saloons of the British Museum, with that listlessness with which one is apt to saunter about a museum in warm weather; sometimes lolling over the glass cases of minerals, sometimes studying the hieroglyphics on an Egyptian mummy, and sometimes trying, with nearly equal success, to comprehend the allegorical paintings on the lofty ceilings. While I was gazing about in this idle way, my attention was attracted to a distant door, at the end of a suit of apartments. It was closed, but every now and then it would open, and some strange-favored being, generally clothed in black, would steal forth, and glide through the rooms, without noticing any of the surrounding objects.

3. There was an air of mystery about this that piqued my languid curiosity, and I determined to attempt the

passage of that strait, and to explore the unknown regions beyond. The door yielded to my hand with that facility, with which the portals of enchanted castles yield to the adventurous knight-errant. I found myself in a spacious chamber, surrounded with great cases of venerable books. Above the cases, and just under the cornice, were arranged a great number of black-looking portraits of ancient authors. About the room were placed long tables, with stands for reading and writing, at which sat many pale, studious personages, poring intently over dusty volumes, rummaging among moldy manuscripts, and taking copious notes of their contents.

4. I was, in fact, in the reading-room of the great British Library, an immense collection of volumes of all ages and languages, many of which are now forgotten, and most of which arc seldom read; one of those sequestered pools of obsolete literature, to which modern authors repair, and draw buckets full of classic lore, or "pure English, undefiled," wherewith to swell their own scanty rills of thought. Being now in possession of the secret, I sat down in a corner, and watched the process of this book manufactory.

5. While I was looking on, and indulging in rambling fancies, I had leaned my head against a pile of reverend folios. Whether it was owing to the soporific emanations from these works; or to the profound quiet of the room; or to the lassitude arising from much wandering; or to an unlucky habit of napping at improper times and places, with which I am grievously afflicted, so it was, that I fell into a doze. Still, however, my imagination continued busy, and, indeed, the same scene remained before my mind's eye, only a little changed in some of the details.

6. I dreamed that the chamber was still decorated with the portraits of ancient authors, but that the number was increased. The long tables had disappeared, and, in place of the sage magi, I beheld a ragged, threadbare throng, such as may be seen plying about the great repository of cast-off clothes, Monmouth-street. Whenever they seized upon a book, by one of those incongruities common to

dreams, me-thought it turned into a garment of foreign or antique fashion, with which they proceeded to equip themselves. I noticed, however, that no one pretended to clothe himself from any particular suit, but took a sleeve from one, a cape from another, a skirt from a third, thus decking himself out piecemeal, while some of his original rags would peep out from among his borrowed finery.

7. There was a portly, rosy, well-fed parson, whom I observed ogling several moldy polemical writers through an eye-glass. He soon contrived to slip on the voluminous mantle of one of the old fathers, and, having purloined the gray beard of another, endeavored to look exceedingly wise; but the smirking common-place of his countenance set at naught all the trappings of wisdom. One sickly-looking gentleman was busied embroidering a very flimsy garment with gold thread, drawn out of several old court-dresses of the reign of Queen Elizabeth.

8. Another had trimmed himself magnificently from an illuminated manuscript, had stuck a nosegay in his bosom, culled from "The Paradise of Dautie Devices," and having put Sir Philip Sidney's hat on one side of his head, strutted off with an exquisite air of vulgar elegance. A third, who was but of puny dimensions, had bolstered himself out bravely with the spoils from several obscure tracts of philosophy, so that he had a very imposing front; but he was lamentably tattered in rear, and I perceived that he had patched his small-clothes with scraps of parchment from a Latin author.

9. There were some well-dressed gentlemen, it is true, who only helped themselves to a gem or so, which sparkled among their own ornaments, without eclipsing them. Some, too, seemed to contemplate the costumes of the old writers merely to imbibe their principles of taste, and to catch their air and spirit; but I grieve to say, that too many were apt to array themselves from top to toe, in the patch-work manner I have mentioned. I shall not omit to speak of one genius, in drab breeches and gaiters, and an Areadian hat, who had a violent propensity to the pastoral, but whose rural wanderings had been confined to the classic

haunts of Primrose Hill, and the solitudes of the Regent's Park. He had decked himself in wreaths and ribands from all the old pastoral poets, and, hanging his head on one side, went about with a fantastical lack-a-daisical air, "babbling about green fields."

10. But the personage that most struck my attention, was a pragmatical old gentleman, in clerical robes, with a remarkably large and square, but bald head. He entered the room wheezing and puffing, elbowed his way through the throng, with a look of sturdy self-confidence, and having laid hands upon a thick Greek quarto, clapped it upon his head, and swept majestically away in a formidable frizzled wig.

11. In the hight of this literary masquerade, a cry suddenly resounded from every side, of "Thieves! thieves!" I looked, and lo! the portraits about the wall became animated! The old authors thrust out, first a head, then a shoulder, from the canvas, looked down curiously, for an instant, upon the motley throng, and then descended, with fury in their eyes, to claim their rifled property. The scene of scampering and hubbub that ensued, baffles all description. The unhappy culprits endeavored in vain to escape with their plunder. On one side, might be seen half a dozen old monks stripping a modern professor; on another, there was sad devastation carried into the ranks of modern dramatic writers. Beaumont and Fletcher, side by side, raged round the field like Castor and Pollux, and sturdy Ben Jonson enacted more wonders, than when a volunteer with the army in Flanders.

12. I was grieved to see many men, to whom I had been accustomed to look up with awe and reverence, fain to steal off with scarce a rag to cover their nakedness. Just then my eye was caught by the pragmatical old gentleman in the Greek frizzled wig, who was scrambling away in sore affright, with half a score of authors in full cry after him! They were close upon his haunches: in a twinkling off went his wig; at every turn some strip of raiment was peeled away; until, in a few moments, from his domineering pomp he shrunk into a little, pursy,

wheezy fellow, and made his exit with only a few tags and rags fluttering at his back.

13. There was something so ludicrous in the catastrophe of this learned Theban, that I burst into an immoderate fit of laughter, which broke the whole illusion. The tumult and the scuffle were at an end. The chamber resumed its usual appearance. The old authors shrunk back into their picture-frames, and hung in shadowy solemnity along the walls. In short, I found myself wide awake in my corner, with the whole assemblage of book-worms gazing at me with astonishment. Nothing of the dream had been real but my burst of laughter, a sound never before heard in that grave sanctuary, and so abhorrent to the ears of wisdom, as to electrify the fraternity.

14. The librarian now stepped up to me, and demanded whether I had a card of admission. At first, I did not comprehend him, but I soon found that the library was a kind of literary "preserve," subject to game-laws, and that no one must presume to hunt there without special license and permission. In a word, I stood convicted of being an arrant poacher, and was glad to make a precipitate retreat, lest I should have a whole pack of authors let loose upon me.

XLIX. — SELECTIONS, PROSE AND POETIC.

1. A FUTURE.

I CAN not believe that earth is man's abiding place. It can not be that our life is cast up by the ocean of eternity, to float for a moment on its waves, and sink to nothingness! Else, why is it that the glorious aspirations which leap, like angels, from the temple of our hearts, are forever wandering about unsatisfied? Why is it, that the rainbow and the cloud come over us with a beauty that is not of earth, then pass off and leave us to muse upon their faded loveliness? Why is it, that the stars, who hold their festivals around the midnight throne, are set above our limited faculties, forever mocking us with their

unapproachable glory? And, finally, why is it that the bright forms of human beauty are presented to our view, and then taken from us, leaving the thousand streams of affection to flow back in Alpine torrents upon the heart?

We are born for a higher world than that of earth; there is a realm where rainbows never fade, where the stars will be out before us, like islets that slumber on the ocean, and where the beings that pass before us like shadows, will stay in our presence forever.

2. KINDNESS.

A little spring had lost its way
    Amid the grass and fern;
A passing stranger scoop'd a well,
    Where weary men might turn;
He wall'd it in, and hung, with care,
    A ladle at the brink;
He thought not of the deed he did,
    But judg'd that toil might drink.
He pass'd again, and lo! the well,
    By summers never dried,
Had cool'd ten thousand parch-ed tongues,
    And saved a life beside.

3. HOWARD.

Howard visited all Europe; not to survey the sumptuousness of palaces, or the stateliness of temples; not to make accurate measurements of the remains of ancient grandeur; but to dive into the depths of dungeons; to plunge into the infection of hospitals; to survey the mansions of sorrow and pain; to remember the forgotten, and to visit the forsaken. His plan was original, and it was as full of genius as it was of humanity. It was a voyage of discovery, a circumnavigation of charity. The benefit of his labor is felt more or less in every country; and, at his final reward, he will receive, not by retail, but in gross, the reward of those who visit the prisoner.

H. S. R.—13

4. TIME.

One by one the sands are flowing;
　One by one the moments fall;
Some are coming, some are going,
　Do not strive to grasp them all.

One by one thy duties wait thee,
　Let thy whole strength go to each;
Let no future dreams elate thee,
　Learn thou first what these can teach.

One by one thy griefs shall meet thee,
　Do not fear an arm-ed band;
One will fade as others greet thee,
　Shadows passing through the land.

5. LUCY.

She dwelt among the untrodden ways, beside the springs
　　of Dove,
A maid whom there were none to praise, and very few to
　　love:
A violet by a mossy stone, half hidden from the eye!
Fair as a star, when only one is shining in the sky.
She liv'd unknown, and few could know when Lucy ceas'd
　　to be;
But she is in her grave, and, O, the difference to me!

6. BEAUTY.

There 's beauty in the deep:
The wave is bluer than the sky;
And though the light shine bright on high,
More softly do the sea-gems glow
That sparkle in the depths below;
The rainbow's tints are only made
When on the waters they are laid,
And sun and moon most sweetly shine
Upon the ocean's level brine.
There 's beauty in the deep.

7. MUSIC.

.There 's *music* in the deep:
It is not in the surf's rough roar,
Nor in the whispering, shelly shore,
They are but earthly sounds, that tell
How little of the sea-nymph's shell,
That sends its loud, clear note abroad,
Or winds its softness through the flood,
Echoes through groves with coral gay,
And dies, on spongy banks away.
There 's *music* in the deep.

8. THE BUTTERFLY.

A humming-bird met a butterfly, and, being pleased with the beauty of its person and the glory of its wings, made an offer of perpetual friendship. "I can not think of it," was the reply, "as you once spurned me, and called me a crawling dolt." "Impossible!" exclaimed the humming-bird, "I always entertained the highest respect for such beautiful creatures as you." "Perhaps you do now," said the other; "but when you insulted me, I was a caterpillar. So let me give you a piece of advice: never insult the humble, as they may some day become your superiors."

9. GOD'S LOVE.

There 's not a flower that decks the vale,
    There 's not a beam that lights the mountain,
There 's not a shrub that scents the gale,
    There 's not a wind that stirs the fountain,
There 's not a hue that paints the rose,
    There 's not a leaf around us lying,
But in its use or beauty shows
    God's love to us, and love undying!

L. — THE FALLEN LEAVES.

FROM MRS. NORTON.

MRS. NORTON, a modern author, has written little, but is one of the sweetest of English poets.

1. WE stand among the fallen leaves,
     Young children at our play,
   And laugh to see the yellow things
     Go rustling on their way:
   Right merrily we hunt them down,
     The autumn winds and we,
   Nor pause to gaze where snow-drifts lie,
     Or sunbeams gild the tree.
   With dancing feet we leap along
     Where wither'd boughs are strown.;
   Nor past nor future checks our song,
     The present is our own.

2. We stand among the fallen leaves
     In youth's enchanted spring,
   When Hope (who wearies at the last)
     First spreads her eagle wing:
   We tread with steps of conscious strength
     Beneath the leafless trees,
   And the color kindles on our cheek,
     As blows the winter breeze;
   While, gazing toward the cold gray sky,
     Clouded with snow and rain,
   We wish the old year all past by,
     And the young spring come again.

3. We stand among the fallen leaves
     In manhood's haughty prime,
   When first our pausing hearts begin
     To love " the olden time;"
   And as we gaze, we sigh to think
     How many a year hath pass'd,

Since, 'neath those cold and faded trees
　　Our footsteps wander'd last;
And old companions, now, perchance,
　　Estranged, forgot, or dead,
Come round us, as those autumn leaves
　　Are crush'd beneath our tread.

4. We stand among the fallen leaves
　　In our *own* autumn day,
And, tottering on with feeble steps,
　　Pursue our cheerless way.
We look not back, too long ago
　　Hath all we lov'd been lost;
Nor forward, for we may not live
　　To see our new hope cross'd;
But on we go; the sun's faint beam
　　A feeble warmth imparts:
Childhood, without its joy returns;
　　The present fills our hearts.

LI. — DWIGHT AND DENNIE.

Dr. Dwight was a distinguished theologian of New England, and for many years President of Yale College. Dennie was a literary man of eminence, and editor of the Port Folio and other works. They both died in the early part of the present century.

1. Some time since, as Dr. Dwight was traveling through New Jersey, he chanced to stop at the stage hotel, in one of its populous towns, for the night. At a late hour of the same, arrived also at the inn Mr. Dennie, who had the misfortune to learn from the landlord, that his beds were all paired with lodgers, except one occupied by the celebrated Dr. Dwight. Show me to his apartment, exclaimed Dennie; although I am a stranger to the Reverend Doctor, perhaps I may bargain with him for my lodgings. The landlord accordingly waited on Mr. Dennie to the Doctor's room, and there left him to introduce himself.

2. The Doctor, although in his night-gown, cap, and slippers, and just ready to resign himself to the refreshing

arms of Somnus, politely requested the strange intruder to be seated. Struck with the physiognomy of his companion, he then unbent his austere brow, and commenced a literary conversation.

3. The names of Washington, Franklin, Rittenhouse, and a host of distinguished and literary characters, for some time gave a zest and interest to their conversation, until Dr. Dwight chanced to mention Dennie. "Dennie, the editor of the Port Folio," says the Doctor in a rhapsody, "is the Addison of the United States, the Father of American belles lettres. But, Sir," continued he, "is it not astonishing, that a man of such genius, fancy, and feeling, should abandon himself to the inebriating bowl?"

4. "Sir," said Dennie, "you are mistaken. I have been intimately acquainted with Dennie for several years; and I never knew or saw him intoxicated." "Sir," says the Doctor, "you err. I have my information from a particular friend; I am confident that I am right and you are wrong." Dennie now ingeniously changed the conversation to the clergy, remarking, that Abercrombie and Mason were among the most distinguished divines; "nevertheless, he considered Dr. Dwight, President of Yale College, the most learned theologian, the first logician, and the greatest poet that America has produced. But, Sir," continued Dennie, "there are traits in his character, unworthy of so wise and great a man, and of the most detestable description; he is the greatest *bigot* and *dogmatist* of the age!"

5. "Sir," says the Doctor, "you are grossly mistaken; I am intimately acquainted with Dr. Dwight, and I know to the contrary." "Sir," says Dennie, "you are mistaken; I have it from an intimate acquaintance of his, who I am confident would not tell me an untruth." "No more slander!" says the Doctor; "I am Dr. Dwight, of whom you speak!" "And I, too," exclaimed Dennie, "am Mr. Dennie, of whom *you spoke!*" The astonishment of Dr. Dwight may be better conceived than told. Suffice it to say, they mutually shook hands, and were extremely happy in each other's acquaintance.

LII. — MONEY MAKES THE MARE GO.

FROM BERQUIN.

DERBY AND SCRAPEWELL.

Derby. Good morning, neighbor Scrapewell. I have half a dozen miles to ride to-day, and should be extremely obliged to you if you would lend me your gray mare.

Scrapewell. I should be happy, friend Derby, to oblige you, but I'm under the necessity of going immediately to the mill with three bags of corn. My wife wants the meal this very morning.

Der. Then she must want it still, for I can assure you the mill does not go to-day. I heard the miller tell Will Davis that the water was too low.

Scrape. You don't say so? That is bad indeed; for in that case I shall be obliged to gallop off to town for the meal. My wife would comb my head for me, if I should neglect it.

Der. I can save you this journey, for I have plenty of meal at home, and will lend your wife as much as she wants.

Scrape. Ah! neighbor Derby, I am sure your meal will never suit my wife. You can't conceive how whimsical she is.

Der. If she were ten times more whimsical than she is, I am certain she would like it; for you sold it to me yourself, and you assured me that it was the best you ever had.

Scrape. Yes, yes, that's true, indeed; I always have the best of every thing. You know, neighbor Derby, that no one is more ready to oblige a friend than I am; but I must tell you, the mare this morning refused to eat hay; and truly, I am afraid she will not carry you.

Der. Oh, never fear, I will feed her well with oats on the road.

Scrape. Oats! neighbor; oats are very dear.

Der. Never mind that. When I have a good job in view, I never stand for trifles.

Scrape. But it is very slippery; and I am really afraid she will fall and break your neck.

Der. Give yourself no uneasiness about that. The mare is certainly sure-footed; and, besides, you were just now talking of galloping her to town.

Scrape. Well, then, to tell you the plain truth, though I wish to oblige you with all my heart, my saddle is torn quite in pieces, and I have just sent my bridle to be mended.

Der. Luckily, I have both a bridle and a saddle hanging up at home.

Scrape. Ah! that may be; but I am sure your saddle will never fit my mare.

Der. Why, then I'll borrow neighbor Clodpole's.

Scrape. Clodpole's! his will no more fit than yours will.

Der. At the worst, then, I will go to my friend 'Squire Jones. He has half a score of them; and I am sure he will lend me one that will fit her.

Scrape. You know, friend Derby, that no one is more willing to oblige his neighbors than I am. I do assure you, the beast should be at your service, with all my heart; but she has not been curried, I believe for three weeks past. Her foretop and mane want combing and cutting very much. If any one should see her in her present plight, it would ruin the sale of her.

Der. O! a horse is soon curried, and my son Sam shall dispatch her at once.

Scrape. Yes, very likely; but I this moment recollect the creature has no shoes on.

Der. Well, is there not a blacksmith hard by?

Scrape. What! that tinker of a Dobson? I would not trust such a bungler to shoe a goat. No, no; none but uncle Tom Thumper is capable of shoeing my mare.

Der. As good luck would have it, then, I shall pass right by his door.

Scrape. (*Calling to his son.*) Timothy, Timothy. Here's neighbor Derby, who wants the loan of the gray mare, to ride to town to-day. You know the skin was rubbed off her back last week a hand's breadth or more. (*He gives*

Tim a wink.) However, I believe she is well enough by this time. You know, Tim, how ready I am to oblige my neighbors. And, indeed, we ought to do all the good we can in this world. We must certainly let neighbor Derby have her, if she will possibly answer his purpose. Yes, yes; I see plainly, by Tim's countenance, neighbor Derby, that he's disposed to oblige you. I would not have refused you the mare for the worth of her. If I had, I should have expected you would have refused me in your turn. None of my neighbors can accuse me of being backward in doing them a kindness. Come, Timothy, what do you say?

Tim. What do I say, father? Why, I say, sir, that I am no less ready than you are to do a neighborly kindness. But the mare is by no means capable of performing the journey. About a band's-breadth did you say, sir? Why, the skin is torn from the poor creature's back, of the bigness of your broad-brimmed hat. And, besides, I have promised her, as soon as she is able to travel, to Ned Saunders, to carry a load of apples to the market.

Scrape. Do you hear that, neighbor? I am very sorry matters turn out thus. I would not have disobliged you for the price of two such mares. Believe me, neighbor Derby, I am really sorry, for your sake, that matters turn out thus.

Der. And I as much for yours, neighbor Scrapewell; for, to tell you the truth, I received a letter this morning from Mr. Griffin, who tells me, if I will be in town this day, he will give me the refusal of all that lot of timber which he is about cutting down upon the back of Cobble-hill; and I intended you should have shared half of it, which would have been not less than fifty dollars in your pocket. But, as your—

Scrape. Fifty dollars, did you say?

Der. Ay, truly did I; but as your mare is out of order, I'll go and see if I can get old Roan, the blacksmith's horse.

Scrape. Old Roan! My mare is at your service, neighbor. Here, Tim, tell Ned Saunders he can't have the mare.

Neighbor Derby wants her; and I won't refuse so good a friend any thing he asks for.

Der. But what are you to do for meal?

Scrape. My wife can do without it this fortnight, if you want the mare so long.

Der. But then your saddle is all in pieces.

Scrape. I meant the old one. I have bought a new one since, and you shall have the first use of it.

Der. And you would have me call at Thumper's, and get her shod?

Scrape. No, no; I had forgotten to tell you, that I let neighbor Dobson shoe her last week, by way of trial; and, to do him justice, I must own, he shoes extremely well.

Der. But if the poor creature has lost so much skin from off her back.

Scrape. Poh, poh! That is just one of our Tim's large stories. I do assure you, it was not at first bigger than my thumb-nail; and I am certain it has not grown any since.

Der. At least, however, let her have something she will eat, since she refuses hay.

Scrape. She did indeed refuse hay this morning; but the only reason was, that she was crammed full of oats. You have nothing to fear, neighbor; the mare is in perfect trim; and she will skim you over the ground like a bird. I wish you a good journey and a profitable job.

LIII.—MISCELLANEOUS EXTRACTS.

1. RESIGNATION.

God sendeth sun, he sendeth shower,
Alike they're needful to the flower;
And joys and tears alike are sent
To give the soul fit nourishment.
As comes to me or cloud or sun,
Father! thy will, not mine, be done.

Can loving children e'er reprove
With murmurs whom they trust and love?
Creator, I would ever be
A trusting, loving child to thee;
As comes to me or cloud or sun,
Father! thy will, not mine, be done.

2. FUTURITY.

Too curious man, why dost thou seek to know
Events, which, good or ill, foreknown are woe?
The all-seeing Power, that made thee mortal, gave
Thee every thing a mortal state should have;
Foreknowledge only is enjoy'd by Heaven,
And, for his peace of mind, to man forbidden;
Wretched were life, if he foreknew his doom;
Even joys foreseen give pleasing hope no room,
And griefs assured are felt before they come.

3. DISTRUST.

A dew-drop, falling on the ocean wave,
Exclaim'd, in fear, " I perish in this grave;"
But, in a shell receiv'd, that drop of dew
Unto a pearl of marvelous beauty grew;
And happy now, the grace did magnify
Which thrust it forth, as it had fear'd, to die;
Until again, " I perish quite," it said,
Torn by rude diver from its ocean bed;
O, unbelieving! So it came to gleam
Chief jewel in a monarch's diadem.

4. KNOWLEDGE AND WISDOM.

Knowledge and Wisdom, far from being one,
Have oftimes no connection. Knowledge dwells
In heads replete with thoughts of other men;
Wisdom, in minds attentive to their own.
Knowledge, a rude, unprofitable mass,
The mere materials with which Wisdom builds,
Till smooth'd and squared, and fitted to its place,
Does but encumber whom it seems to enrich.

Knowledge is proud that he has learn'd so much ;
Wisdom is humble, that he knows no more.

5. NIGHT.

How beautiful is night !
A dewy freshness fills the silent air :
No mist obscures, nor cloud, nor speck, nor stain,
Breaks the serene of heaven ;
In full orb'd glory yonder moon divine
Rolls through the dark-blue depths.
Beneath her steady ray
The desert-circle spreads
Like the round ocean, girdled with the sky.
How beautiful is night !

6. ADVANCE.

God bade the Sun with golden step sublime,
Advance !
He whisper'd in the listening ear of Time,
Advance !
He bade the guiding Spirit of the stars,
With lightning speed, in silver-shining cars,
Along the bright floor of his azure hall,
Advance !
Sun, Stars, and Time obey the voice, and all
Advance !

7. COURAGE.

Onward ! throw all terrors off !
Slight the scorner, scorn the scoff.
In the *race*, and not the *prize*,
Glory's *true* distinction lies.
Triumph herds with meanest things,
Common robbers, vilest kings,
Mid the reckless multitude !
But the generous, but the good,
Stand in modesty alone,
Still serenely struggling on,

Planting peacefully the seeds
Of bright hopes and better deeds.

8. HAPPINESS.

To be good, is to be happy; angels
Are happier than men, because they 're better.
Guilt is the source of sorrow : 'tis the fiend,
The avenging fiend, that follows us behind
With whips and stings : the blest know none of this,
But rest in everlasting peace of mind,
And find the hight of all their heaven is goodness.

9. NATURE.

The love of Nature and the scenes she draws,
Is Nature's dictate. Strange ! there should be found
Who, self-imprison'd in their proud saloons,
Renounce the odors of the open field
For the unscented fictions of the loom;
Who, satisfied with only pencil'd scenes,
Prefer to the performance of a God
The inferior wonders of an artist's hand !
Lovely, indeed, the mimic works of art,
But Nature's works far lovelier.

10. BE JUST.

Dare nobly then ; but, conscious of your trust,
As ever warm and bold, be ever just ;
Nor court applause in these degenerate days :
The villain's censure is extorted praise.
But chief, be steady in a noble end,
And show mankind that truth has yet a friend.

'Tis mean for empty praise of wit to write,
As foplings grin to show their teeth are white ;
To brand a doubtful folly with a smile,
Or madly blaze unknown defects, is vile :
'Tis doubly vile, when, but to prove your art,
You fix an arrow in a blameless heart.

11. SCRIPTURAL PRECEPTS.

Trust in the Lord, and do good,
So shalt thou dwell in the land,
And, verily, thou shalt be fed.

Cast thy burden on the Lord,
And he will sustain thee.
He will never suffer the righteous to be moved.

Those that wait upon the Lord,
They shall inherit the land.
The steps of a good man are ordered by the Lord,
And he delighteth in his way:
Though he fall, he shall not be utterly cast down.

I have seen the wicked in great power,
And spreading himself like a green bay tree.
Yet he passed away, and, lo! he was not.
Yea, I sought him, but he could not be found.

Mark the perfect man, and behold the upright;
For the end of that man is peace.

12. SUMMER.

It is a sultry day; the sun has drunk
The dew that lay upon the morning grass;
There is no rustling in the lofty elm
That canopies my dwelling, and its shade
Scarce cools me.

    All is silent, save the faint
And interrupted murmur of the bee,
Settling on the sick flowers, and then again
Instantly on the wing. The plants around
Feel the too potent fervors; the tall maize
Rolls up its long green leaves; the clover droops
Its tender foliage, and declines its blooms.
But far in the fierce sunshine tower the hills,
With all their growth of woods, silent and stern,
As if the scorching heat and dazzling light
Were but an element they lov'd.

For me, I lie
Languidly in the shade, where the thick turf
Retains some freshness, and I woo the wind
That still delays its coming.

13. FRIENDSHIP.

Green be the turf above thee, friend of my better days!
None knew thee but to love thee, nor named thee but to praise.
Tears fell when thou wert dying from eyes unused to weep,
And long where thou art lying will tears the cold turf steep.

When hearts whose truth is proven, like thine, are laid in earth,
There should a wreath be woven to tell the world their worth;
And I, who woke each morrow, to clasp thy hand in mine,
Who shared thy joy and sorrow, whose weal and woe were thine,
It should be mine to braid it around thy faded brow,
But I've in vain essay'd it, and feel I can not now.
While memory bids me weep thee, nor thoughts nor words are free,
The grief is fix'd too deeply that mourns a man like thee.

14. SUSPICION.

Let me have men about me that are *fat*,
Sleek-headed men, and such as sleep o' nights;
Yond Cassius has a lean and hungry look;
He *thinks* too much: such men are dangerous.
'Would he were fatter.

If my name were liable to fear,
I do not know the man I should avoid,
So soon as that spare Cassius.   He reads much;
He is a great observer, and he looks
Quite through the deeds of men.   He hears no music;
Seldom he smiles; and smiles in such a sort,
As if he mock'd himself, and scorn'd his spirit,
That could be moved to smile at any thing.
Such men as he are never at heart's ease
While they behold a greater than themselves;
And therefore are they very dangerous.

LIV.—FULTON'S FIRST STEAMBOAT.

FROM STORY.

JUDGE STORY was one of the most distinguished lawyers in the United States. He was born in 1779, and died in 1845. At the age of thirty-two, he was made Judge of the Supreme Court of the United States, and continued in that office until his death. He has written much both upon legal topics and other subjects.

ROBERT FULTON, as is well known, was the inventor of steamboats.

1. IT was in reference to the astonishing impulse given to mechanical pursuits, that Dr. Darwin, more than forty years ago, broke out in strains equally remarkable for their poetical enthusiasm and prophetic truth, and predicted the future triumph of the steam-engine:

> "Soon shall thy arm, unconquer'd steam, afar
> Drag the slow barge, or drive the rapid car;
> Or on wide waving wing expanded bear
> The flying chariot through the fields of air,
> Fair crews triumphant, leaning from above,
> Shall wave their fluttering kerchiefs as they move,
> Or warrior bands alarm the gaping crowd,
> And armies shrink beneath the shadowy cloud."

2. What would he have said, if he had but lived to witness the immortal invention of Fulton, which seems almost to move in the air, and to fly on the wings of the wind? And yet how slowly did this enterprise obtain the public favor? I myself have heard the illustrious inventor relate, in an animated and affecting manner, the history of his labors and discouragements. "When," said he, "I was building my first steamboat at New York, the project was viewed by the public either with indifference or with contempt, as a visionary scheme. My friends, indeed, were civil, but they were shy. They listened with patience to my explanations, but with a settled cast of incredulity on their countenances. I felt the full force of the lamentation of the poet,

> "Truths would you teach, to save a sinking land,
> All shun, none aid you, and few understand."

3. "As I had occasion to pass daily to and from the building-yard, while my boat was in progress, I have often loitered unknown near the idle groups of strangers, gathering in little circles, and heard various inquiries as to the object of this new vehicle. The language was uniformly that of scorn, or sneer, or ridicule. The loud laugh often rose at my expense; the dry jest; the wise calculation of losses and expenditures; the dull but endless repetition of 'The Fulton Folly.' Never did a single encouraging remark, a bright hope, or a warm wish, cross my path. Silence itself was but politeness vailing its doubts, or hiding its reproaches.

4. "At length the day arrived when the experiment was to be put into operation. To me it was a most trying and interesting occasion. I invited many friends to go on board to witness the first successful trip. Many of them did me the favor to attend, as a matter of personal respect; but it was manifest that they did it with reluctance, fearing to be the partners of my mortification, and not of my triumph. I was well aware that, in my case, there were many reasons to doubt of my own success. The machinery was new and ill made; many parts of it were constructed by mechanics unaccustomed to such work; and unexpected difficulties might reasonably be presumed to present themselves from other causes. The moment arrived in which the word was to be given for the vessel to move. My friends were in groups on the deck. There was anxiety mixed with fear among them. They were silent, and sad, and weary. I read in their looks nothing but disaster, and almost repented of my efforts.

5. "The signal was given, and the boat moved on a short distance, and then stopped, and became immovable. To the silence of the preceding moment now came murmurs of discontent, and agitation, and whispers, and shrugs. I could hear distinctly repeated, 'I told you it would be so. It is a foolish scheme. I wish we were well out of it.' I elevated myself upon a platform, and addressed the assembly. I stated that I knew not what was the matter; but, if they would be quiet and indulge me for a half-hour, I

H. S. R.—14

would either go on or abandon the voyage for that time. This short respite was conceded without objection. I went below, examined the machinery, and discovered that the cause was a slight mal-adjustment of some of the work. In a short period it was obviated.

6. "The boat was again put in motion. She continued to move on. All were still incredulous. None seemed willing to trust the evidence of their own senses. We left the fair city of New York; we passed through the romantic and ever-varying scenery of the highlands; we descried the clustering houses of Albany; we reached its shores; and then, even then, when all seemed achieved, I was the victim of disappointment. Imagination superseded the influence of fact. It was then doubted if it could be done again; or, if done, it was doubted if it could be made of any great value."

7. Such was the history of the first experiment, as it fell, not in the very language which I have used, but in its substance, from the lips of the inventor. He did not live, indeed, to enjoy the full glory of his invention. It is mournful to say that attempts were made to rob him, in the first place, of the merits of the invention, and next of its fruits. He fell a victim to his efforts to sustain his title to both.

LV. — THE STEAMBOAT.

FROM HOLMES.

OLIVER WENDELL HOLMES, born in 1809, is an American poet, distinguished for purity, finish, and grace. He was for some years a Professor in the Medical College at Dartmouth, and more recently in Harvard University.

1. SEE how yon flaming herald treads
    The ridg'd and rolling waves,
   As, crashing o'er their crested heads,
    She bows her surly slaves!
  With foam before and fire behind,
    She rends the clinging sea,

That flies before the roaring wind,
   Beneath her hissing lee.

2. The morning spray, like sea-born flowers,
   With heap'd and glistening bells
Falls round her fast in ringing showers,
   With every wave that swells;
And, flaming o'er the midnight deep,
   In lurid fringes thrown,
The living gems of ocean sweep
   Along her flashing zone.

3. With clashing wheel, and lifting keel,
   And smoking torch on high,
Where winds are loud, and billows reel,
   She thunders foaming by!
Where seas are silent and serene,
   With even beam she glides,
The sunshine gleaming through the green
   That skirts her gleaming sides.

4. Now, like a wild nymph, far apart
   She vails her shadowy form,
The beating of her restless heart
   Still sounding through the storm;
Now answers, like a courtly dame,
   The reddening surges o'er,
With flying scarf of spangled flame,
   The Pharos of the shore.

5. To-night yon pilot shall not sleep,
   Who trims his narrow'd sail;
To-night yon frigate scarce shall keep
   Her broad breast to the gale;
And many a fore-sail, scoop'd and strain'd,
   Shall break from yard and stay,
Before this smoky wreath has stain'd
   The rising mist of day.

6. Hark! hark! I hear yon whistling shroud,
    I see yon quivering mast;
The black throat of the hunted cloud
    Is panting forth the blast!
An hour, and, whirl'd like winnowing chaff
    The giant surge shall fling
His tresses o'er yon pennon-staff
    White as the sea-bird's wing.

7. Yet rest, ye wanderers of the deep;
    No wind nor wave shall tire
Those fleshless arms, whose pulses beat
    With floods of living fire;
Sleep on, and when the morning light
    Streams o'er the shining bay,
Oh, think of those for whom the night
    Shall never wake in day!

LVI. — GRACE DARLING.

1. "Honor and shame from no condition rise;
    Act well your part—there all the honor lies."
The truth of this saying is strikingly illustrated in the history of Grace Darling. Her situation in life was humble, yet she possessed a truly heroic soul, and nobly and well did she act her part, manifesting on one occasion some of the highest qualities that belong to human nature. Her daring and magnanimous conduct secured to her the respect and admiration of persons of every rank and condition, and a celebrity which may be said to have spread over the greater part of the civilized world.

2. Her father, William Darling, was keeper of the lighthouse on Longstone, one of the Farne group, a cluster of twenty-five small islands, on the coast of Northumberland, England. Though situated at no great distance from the main land, these islands are desolate in an uncommon degree. Composed of rugged rock, with a slight covering of herbage, and in some instances surrounded by black and

splintered precipices, they are the residence of little beside wild sea-fowl. Through the broken channels between the smaller islands, the restless sea rushes with great force; and many an unrecorded shipwreck must have happened here in former times, when no beacon light blazed amid the storm to guide the daring mariner in his perilous pathway along the tempestuous deep.

3. Mr. Darling was a man of superior character, worthy and intelligent, of modest manners, and possessing within himself those resources demanded in so solitary a situation, where weeks often passed without any communication with the main land. Although in humble circumstances and the father of a large family, he managed to educate all his children in a respectable manner. Grace, his seventh child, was born Nov. 24, 1815. She was remarkable for a retiring and somewhat reserved disposition. In person, she was about the middle size, of fair complexion and a comely countenance, gentle in manners, and with an expression of the greatest mildness and benevolence. She had reached her twenty-second year, when the incident occurred which has rendered her name so famous.

4. The Forfarshire steamer, commanded by Captain John Humble, sailed from Hull, on her voyage to Dundee, Scotland, Wednesday, Sept. 5, 1838. She was laden with a valuable cargo, and had on board, in addition to her officers and crew, twenty-two cabin, and nineteen steerage passengers—sixty-three persons in all. During Wednesday night a leak was discovered. This was partially repaired and the vessel proceeded on her course. On Thursday evening she neared Farne Islands, the sea running high and the wind blowing strong from the north. Owing to the motion of the vessel, the leak increased to such a degree as to extinguish the fires. The engines were now entirely useless; the vessel soon became unmanageable; and, the tide setting strongly to the south, she drifted in the direction of the island.

5. Meantime it rained heavily, and the fog was so dense that it became impossible to tell their situation. About four o'clock on Friday morning, she struck upon the

rocks, and lay at the mercy of the waves. Soon after the first shock a powerful sea struck the vessel, raising her off the rock, but immediately allowing her to fall violently back upon the sharp reef, fairly breaking her in two. The afterpart, with many of the passengers upon it, was borne away through a tremendous current, and every soul perished; while the forepart of the vessel remained fast upon the rock. The survivors, nine in number, continued in their dreadful situation till daybreak, clinging to the wreck, exposed to the buffeting of the waves, and fearful that every rising surge would sweep the fragment to which they clung, away into the yawning deep.

6. Such was the situation when, as day broke, they were descried from the Longstone, by the Darlings, at nearly a mile's distance. There were at the lighthouse only Mr. Darling, his wife, and Grace. A mist hovered over the desolate island; and though the wind had somewhat abated its violence, the wild and heaving sea, which, in the calmest weather, is never at rest among the winding gorges between these iron pinnacles, still raged and roared fearfully. To have braved the perils of that terrible passage, would have done the highest honor to the well-tried nerves of the stoutest man. But what shall be said of the errand of mercy being undertaken and accomplished, mainly through the strength of a female heart and arm?

7. Through the dim mist of the stormy morning, by the aid of a glass, the figures of the sufferers were seen clinging to the shattered wreck. But who could dare tempt the raging abyss that boiled and surged and maddened around them; and bear across the crested billows relief to the poor victims of the tempest? Mr. Darling at first shrank from the attempt: not so his intrepid daughter. At her solicitation the boat was launched, the mother assisting, and father and daughter entered it, each taking an oar.

8. It could have been only by the exertion of great muscular power, as well as of determined courage, that the boat was rowed to the rock. When there, a greater danger even than that which they had encountered in approaching, arose from the difficulty of steadying the boat, and

preventing its being dashed in pieces upon the sharp reef, by the ever-restless and heaving billows, still wild and turbulent from the dreadful lashing of the storm. However, the sufferers were safely rescued.

9. The delight experienced when the boat was observed approaching the rock, was converted into amazement, when it was discovered that one of its inmates was a female. The sufferers were at once conveyed to the lighthouse where, owing to the violent seas that continued to prevail among the islands, they were obliged to remain from Friday morning till Sunday. The Darlings rendered every attention in their power, to alleviate the sufferings of the rescued; and Grace gave up her own bed to a poor woman, whose children had perished on the wreck.

10. The subsequent events of Grace Darling's life are soon told. Her heroic conduct wafted her name over all Europe. Immediately on the circumstances being made known, the lonely lighthouse of Longstone became the center of attraction to curious and sympathizing thousands. Her name was echoed with applause among all ranks; and the noble and the good testified their sincere admiration of the young heroine, by many valuable contributions and substantial tokens of regard. The Humane Society sent her a flattering vote of thanks, and a public subscription was raised as a reward for her bravery and humanity.

11. It is gratifying to know that, amid all this attention and applause, Grace never for a moment forgot the modest dignity of conduct becoming her sex and character. The flattering testimonials showered upon her failed to produce in her mind any feeling but a sense of wonder and grateful pleasure. She continued to reside at the lighthouse with her parents, attending to the duties of her own limited sphere, thus affording, by her conduct, the best proof that the liberality of the public had not been unworthily bestowed.

12. It is a melancholy reflection that one so noble and deserving, should have been stricken down, almost ere the plaudits excited by her heroic deed had died away. Toward the latter end of 1841, she showed symptoms of declining

health. Consumption soon developed itself; and, notwith-
standing the best medical advice and skill, and all the
attentions which kindness and affection- could bestow, she
gradually declined, but lingered on through the ensuing
spring and summer, in calm Christian resignation awaiting
her approaching death.

13. Not less lovely than they, she drooped and faded
with the flowers of autumn, and ere the storms of winter
again swept over her island home, she passed calmly away
to her eternal rest. Her funeral was attended by an im-
mense concourse of persons of all ages and rank, and a
neat monument has been erected above her early grave,
inscribed with the immortal name of Grace Darling.

LVII. — THE HEROINE.

FROM WORDSWORTH.

WILLIAM WORDSWORTH, who lived from 1770 to 1850, a Poet Lau-
reate of England, a wealthy man, and a poet at thirteen, is emi-
nently a painter of nature in its affections and natural beauty. He
is one of the three, whom Byron designated as the *Lake Poets*,
Coleridge and Southey being the other two. In these lines he
celebrates the heroism of Grace Darling, described in the preceding
exercise.

1. All night the storm had raged, nor ceas'd, nor paus'd,
When, as day broke, the maid, through misty air,
Espies far off a wreck, amid the surf,
Beating on one of those disastrous isles,
Half of a vessel, half, no more; the rest
Had vanish'd, swallow'd up with all that there
Had for the common safety striven in vain,
Or thither throng'd for refuge.

2. With quick glance,
Daughter and sire through optic-glass discern,
Clinging about the remnant of this ship,
Creatures; how precious in the maiden's sight!
For whom, belike, the old man grieves still more
Than for their fellow-sufferers engulf'd,

Where every parting agony is hush'd,
And hope and fear mix not in further strife.
"But courage, father! let us out to sea,
A few may yet be saved."

3. The daughter's words,
Her earnest tone, and looks beaming with faith,
Dispel the father's doubts; nor do they lack
The noble-minded mother's helping hand
To launch the boat; and, with her blessing cheer'd,
And inwardly sustain'd by silent prayer,
Together they put forth, father and child!

4. Each grasps an oar, and struggling on they go,
Rivals in effort; and, alike intent,
Here to elude and there surmount, they watch
The billows lengthening, mutually cross'd
And shatter'd, and re-gathering their might;
As if the tumult by the Almighty's will
Were, in the conscious sea, rous'd and prolong'd,
That woman's fortitude, so tried, so proved,
May brighten more and more!

5. True to the mark,
They stem the current of that perilous gorge,
Their arms still strengthening with the strengthening
        heart,
Though danger, as the wreck is near'd, becomes
More imminent. Not unseen do they approach;
And rapture, with varieties of fear
Incessantly conflicting, thrills the frames
Of those who in that dauntless energy
Foretaste deliverance.

6. But the least perturb'd
Can scarcely trust his eyes, when he perceives
That of the pair, toss'd on the waves to bring
Hope to the hopeless, to the dying life,
One is a woman, a poor earthly sister!
H. S. R —15

Or, be the visitant other than she seems,
A guardian spirit sent from pitying Heaven,
In woman's shape?

7. But why prolong the tale,
Casting weak words amid a host of thoughts
Arm'd to repel them? Every hazard faced
And difficulty master'd, with resolve
That no one breathing should be left to perish,
This last remainder of the crew are all
Placed in the little boat, then o'er the deep
Are safely borne, landed upon the beach,
And, in fulfillment of God's mercy, lodg'd
Within the sheltering light-house.

8. Shout, ye waves!
Send forth a sound of triumph. Waves and winds,
Exult in this deliverance wrought through faith
In Him whose providence your rage has serv'd!
Ye screaming sea-mews, in the concert join!

9. And would that some immortal voice, a voice
Fitly attuned to all that gratitude   . .
Breathes out from floor or couch, through pallid lips
Of the survivors, to the clouds might bear,
Blended with praise of that parental love,
Beneath whose watchful eye the maiden grew
Pious and pure, modest, and yet so brave,
Though young, so wise, though meek, so resolute,
Might carry to the clouds and to the stars,
Yea, to celestial choirs, Grace Darling's name!

LVIII. — THE ROYAL GEORGE.

FROM COWPER.

COWPER, an English poet, who lived from 1731 to 1800, is remarkable for the playful humor and fascinating ease of much of his poetry, for the deep pathos of his more somber pieces, and for the unexceptionable moral and religious character of all his writings.

The Royal George, a ship of the English navy, commanded by Admiral Kempenfelt, was sunk by a flaw of wind, in 1782, near the shore, with one thousand men and three hundred visitors on board. Only three hundred were saved.

1. TOLL for the brave,
     The brave that are no more;
   All sunk beneath the wave,
     Fast by their native shore.

2. Eight hundred of the brave,
     Whose courage well was tried,
   Had made the vessel heel,
     And laid her on her side.

3. A land breeze shook the shrouds,
     And she was overset;
   Down went the Royal George,
     With all her crew complete.

4. Toll for the brave;
     Brave Kempenfelt is gone;
   His last sea fight is fought;
     His work of glory done.

5. It was not in the battle;
     No tempest gave the shock;
   She sprang no fatal leak;
     She ran upon no rock.

6. His sword was in its sheath,
     His fingers held the pen,
   When Kempenfelt went down,
     With twice four hundred men.

7. Weigh the vessel up,
   Once dreaded by our foes,
   And mingle with her cup
   The tear that England owes.

8. Her timbers yet are sound,
   And she may float again,
   Full charged with England's thunder,
   And plow the distant main.

9. But Kempenfelt is gone;
   His victories are o'er;
   And he and his eight hundred
   Shall plow the waves no more.

LIX. — SELF-KILLING.

1. As the world is at present situated, it is possible to acquire learning upon almost every subject, and an infinite amount of knowledge, useful and otherwise, without even by chance lighting upon a knowledge of the most indispensable observances necessary for the preservation of a sound mind in a sound body. Half of the multiform languages of Asia may be mastered, while the prodigy who boasts of much learning knows not that to sit a whole day within doors at close study is detrimental to health; or, if he knows so much, deliberately prefers the course which leads to ruin. Leyden, an enthusiast of this order, was ill with a fever and liver complaint at Mysore, and yet continued to study ten hours a day.

2. His physician warned him of the dangerous consequences that were likely to ensue, when he answered, "Very well, doctor, you have done your duty, but I *can not be idle:* whether I am to die or live, the wheel must go round to the last." "I may perish in the attempt," he said, on another occasion; "but, if I die without surpassing Sir William Jones a hundred-fold in Oriental learning, let never tear for me profane the eye of a Borderer."

And he eventually sank, in his thirty-sixth year, under the consequences of spending some time in an ill-ventilated library, which a slight acquaintance with one of the most familiar of the sciences, would have warned him against entering. Alexander Nicoll, a recent professor of Hebrew at Oxford, who was said to be able to walk to the wall of China without the aid of an interpreter, died at the same age, partly through the effects of that intense study which so effectually but so uselessly had gained him distinction.

3. Dr. Alexander Murray, a similar prodigy, died in his thirty-eighth year of over-severe study; making the third of a set of men remarkable for the same wonderful attainments, and natives of the same country, who, within a space of twenty years, fell victims to their deficiency in a piece of knowledge which any well-cultivated mind may acquire in a day. Excessive application unquestionably cut short the days of Sir Walter Scott, and also of the celebrated Weber, whose mournful exclamation in the midst of his numerous engagements can never be forgotten; "Would that I were a tailor, for then I should have a Sunday's holiday!" The premature extinction of early prodigies of genius is generally traceable to the same cause. We read that while all other children played, they remained at home to study, and then we learn that they perished in the bud, and balked the hopes of all their admiring friends.

4. The ignorant wonder is, of course, always the greater, when life is broken short in the midst of honorable undertakings. We wonder at the inscrutable decrees which permit the idle and the dissolute to live, and remove the ardent benefactor of his kind, the hope of parents, the virtuous and the self-devoted; never reflecting that the highest moral and intellectual qualities avail nothing in repairing or warding off a decided injury to the physical system, which is regulated by an entirely distinct code of laws. The conduct of the Portuguese sailors in a storm, when, instead of working the vessel properly, they employ themselves in paying vows to their saints, is just as

rational as most of the notions which prevail on this subject.

5. When Sir Philip Sidney was at Frankfort, he was advised by the celebrated printer Languet in the midst of his studies not to neglect his health, "lest he should resemble a traveler who, during a long journey, attends to himself, but not to his horse." The body may indeed be well likened to a horse, and the mind to its rider; for the one is the vehicle of the other, and whatever be the object of the journey, whether to perform the most generous actions, or engage in the most patriotic enterprises, the animal will sink under excessive labor or inadequate nutrition; there being only this important difference, that with the horse the rider sinks also, as their existence can not be separated without death.

6. It ought to be universally made known, by means of education, and for this purpose the best informed amongst us would be required to go back to school, that the uses of our intellectual nature are not to be properly realized, without a just regard to the laws of that perishable frame with which it is connected; that, in cultivating the mind, we must neither over-task nor under-task the body, neither push it to too great a speed, nor leave it neglected; and that, notwithstanding this intimate connection and mutual dependence, the highest merits on the part of the mind will not compensate for muscles mistreated, or soothe a nervous system which severe study has tortured into insanity.

7. To come to detail, it ought to be impressed on all, that to spend more than a moderate number of hours in mental exercise diminishes insensibly the powers of future application, and tends to abbreviate life; that no mental exercise should be attempted immediately after meals, as the processes of thought and of digestion can not be safely prosecuted together; that pure air and thoroughly ventilated apartments are essential to health; and that, without a due share of exercise to the whole of the mental faculties, there can be no soundness in any, while the whole corporeal system will give way beneath a severe pressure

upon any one in particular. These are truths completely established with physiologists, and upon which it is undeniable that a great portion of human happiness depends.

LX.—THE STOMACH.

1. BEING allowed for once to speak, I would fain take the opportunity to set forth how ill, in all respects, we stomachs are used. From the beginning to the end of life, we are either afflicted with too little or too much, or not the right thing, or things which are horribly disagreeable to us; or are otherwise thrown into a state of discomfort. I do not think it proper to take up a moment in bewailing the Too Little, for that is an evil which is never the fault of our masters, but rather the result of their misfortunes; and indeed we would sometimes feel as if it were a relief from other kinds of distress, if we were put upon short allowance for a few days. But we conceive ourselves to have matter for a true bill against mankind in respect to the Too Much, which is always a voluntarily-incurred evil.

2. What a pity that in the progress of discovery we can not establish some means of a good understanding between mankind and their stomachs; for really the effects of their non-acquaintance are most vexatious Human beings seem to be, to this day, completely in the dark as to what they ought to take at any time, and err almost as often from ignorance as from depraved appetite. Sometimes, for instance, when we of the inner house are rather weakly, they will send us down an article that we only could deal with when in a state of robust health. Sometimes, when we would require mild semi-farinaceous or vegetable diet, they will persist in all the most stimulating and irritating of viands.

3. What sputtering we poor stomachs have when mistakes of that kind occur! What remarks we indulge in, regarding our masters! "What's this, now?" will a stomach-genius say; "ah, detestable stuff! What an ever-

lasting fool that man is! Will he never learn? Just the very thing I did not want. If he would, only send down a bowl of fresh leek soup, or barley broth, there would be some sense in it:" and so on. If we had only been allowed to give the slightest hint now and then, like faithful servants as we are, from how many miseries might we have saved both our masters and ourselves!

4. I have been a stomach for about forty years, during all of which time I have endeavored to do my duty faithfully and punctually. My master, however, is so reckless, that I would defy any stomach of ordinary ability and capacity to get along pleasantly with him. The fact is, like almost all other men, he, in his eating and drinking, considers his own pleasure only, and never once reflects on the poor wretch who has to be responsible for the disposal of every thing down stairs. Scarcely on any day does he fail to exceed the strict rule of temperance; nay, there is scarcely a single meal which is altogether what it ought to be, either in its constituents or its general amount. My life is therefore one of continual worry and fret; I am never off the drudge from morning till night, and have not a moment in the four-and-twenty hours that I can safely call my own.

5. My greatest trial takes place in the evening, when my master has dined. If you only saw what a mess this said dinner is; soup, fish, flesh, fowl, ham, curry, rice, potatoes, table-beer, sherry, tart, pudding, cheese, bread, all mixed up together. I am accustomed to the thing, so don't feel much shocked; but my master himself would faint at the sight. The slave of duty in all circumstances, I call in my friend Gastric Juice, and to it we set, with as much good-will as if we had the most agreeable task in the world before us. But, unluckily, my master has an impression very firmly fixed upon him that our business is apt to be vastly promoted by an hour or two's drinking; so he continues at table among his friends, and pours me down some bottle and a half of wine, perhaps of various sorts, that bothers Gastric Juice and me to a degree of which no one can have any conception.

6. In fact, this said wine undoes our work almost as fast as we do it, besides blinding and poisoning us poor genii into the bargain. On many occasions I am obliged to give up my task for the time altogether; for while this vinous shower is going on I would defy the most vigorous stomach in the world to make any advance in its business worth speaking of. Sometimes things go to a much greater length than at others; and my master will paralyze us in this manner for hours, not always, indeed, with wine, but occasionally with punch, one ingredient of which, the lemon, is particularly odious to us ministers of the interior. All this time I can hear him jollifying away at a great rate, drinking healths to his neighbors, and ruining his own.

7. I am a lover of early hours, as are my brethren generally. To this we are very much disposed by the extremely hard work which we usually undergo during the day. About ten o'clock, having, perhaps, at that time, got all our labors past, and feeling fatigued and exhausted, we like to sink into repose, not to be again disturbed till next morning at breakfast-time. Well, how it may be with others I can't tell; but so it is, that my master never scruples to rouse me up from my first sleep, and give me charge of an entirely new meal, after I thought I was to be my own master for the night. This is a hardship of the most grievous kind.

8. Only imagine an innocent stomach genius, who has gathered his coal, drawn on his night-cap, and gone to bed, rung up and made to stand attention to receive a succession of things, all of them superfluous and in excess, which he knows he will not be able to get off his hands all night. Such, O mankind, are the woes which befall our tribe in consequence of your occasionally yielding to the temptation of a "little supper." I see turkey and tongue in grief and terror. Macaroni fills me with frantic alarm. I behold jelly and trifle follow in mute despair. O that I had the power of standing beside my master, and holding his unreflecting hand, as he thus prepares for my torment and his own!

9. Here, too, the old mistaken notion about the need of something stimulating besets him, and down comes a deluge of hot spirits and water, that causes every villicle in my coat to writhe in agony, and almost sends Gastric Juice off in the sulks to bed. Nor does the infatuated man rest here. If the company be agreeable, rummer will follow upon rummer, while I am kept standing, as it were, with my sleeves tucked up, ready to begin, but unable to perform a single stroke of work.

10. I feel that the strength which I ought to have had at my present time of life has passed from me. I am getting weak, and peevish, and evil-disposed. A comparatively small trouble sits long and sore upon me. Bile, from being my servant, is becoming my master; and a bad one he makes, as all good servants ever do. I see nothing before me but a premature old age of pains and groans, and gripes and grumblings, which will, of course, not last over long; and thus I shall be cut short in my career when I should have been enjoying life's tranquil evening, without a single vexation of any kind to trouble me.

11. Were I of a rancorous temper, it might be a consolation to think that my master, the cause of all my woes, must suffer and sink with me; but I don't see how this can mend my own case; and, from old acquaintance, I am rather disposed to feel sorry for him, as one who has been more ignorant and imprudent than ill-meaning. In the same spirit let me hope that this true and unaffected account of my case may prove a warning to other persons how they use their stomachs; for they may depend upon it, that whatever injustice they do to *us* in their days of health and pride will be repaid to *themselves* in the long-run, our friend Madam Nature being an inveterately accurate accountant, who makes no allowance for revokes or mistakes.

LXI. — SELECTIONS IN POETRY.

1. TIME.

TIME moveth not; our being 'tis that moves;
And we, swift gliding down life's rapid stream,
Dream of swift ages and revolving years,
Ordain'd to chronicle our passing days.
So, the young sailor, in the gallant bark,
Scudding before the wind, beholds the coast
Receding from his eye, and thinks the while,
Struck with amaze, that *he* is motionless,
And that the *land* is sailing.

2. HUMILITY.

Humility! the sweetest, loveliest flower
That bloom'd in Paradise, the first that died,
Has rarely blossom'd since upon our soil.
It is so frail, so delicate a thing,
'Tis gone if it but look upon itself;
And she who ventures to esteem it hers,
Proves by that single thought she has it not.

3. DEATH TO THE OLD.

Of no distemper, of no blast, he died,
But fell, like autumn fruit, that mellow'd long;
E'en wonder'd at, because he dropp'd no sooner.
Fate seem'd to wind him up for threescore years,
Yet freshly ran he on ten winters more;
Till like a clock worn out with eating time,
The wheels of weary life at last stood still.

4. FAME.

Of all the phantoms, fleeting in the mist
Of time, though meager all, and ghostly thin,
Most unsubstantial, unessential shade,
Was earthly FAME. She was a voice alone,
And dwelt upon the noisy tongues of men.
She never *thought*, but gabbled ever on,

Applauding most what least deserv'd applause.
As changed the wind, her organ, so *she* changed
Perpetually; and whom she prais'd to-day,
Vexing his ears with acclamations loud,
To-morrow blamed, and hiss'd him out of sight.

5. PLEASURE.

But pleasures are like poppies spread,
You seize the flower, its bloom is fled;
Or as the snow flake in the river,
A moment white, then lost forever;
Or like the borealis race,
That flit, ere you can point the place;
Or like the rainbow's lovely form,
Evanishing amid the storm.

6. CHEERFULNESS.

It gives to beauty half its power,
    The nameless charm, worth all the rest,
The light that dances o'er the face,
    And speaks of sunshine in the breast.
If beauty ne'er have set her seal,
    It will supply her absence too,
And many a face looks passing fair,
    Because a merry heart shines through.

LXII.—SELECTIONS IN PROSE.

THE MAN AND THE VINE.

1. IN one of the early years after the creation of the
world, man began to plant a vine, and Satan saw it and
drew near.

"What plantest thou, son of the earth?" said the prince
of demons.

"A vine!" replied the man.

"What are the properties of this tree?"

"Oh, its fruit is pleasant to look at, and delicious to the

taste; from it is produced a liquid which fills the heart with joy."

"Well, since wine makes glad the heart of man, I will help thee plant this tree."

2. So saying, the demon brought a lamb and slew it, then a lion, then an ape, and, last of all, a pig, killing each in succession, and moistened the roots of the vine with the blood.

Thence it has happened ever since, that, when a man drinks a small portion of wine, he becomes gentle and caressing as a lamb; after a little more, strong and bold as a lion; when he takes still more, he resembles an ape in his folly and absurd and mischievous actions; but when he has swallowed the liquid to excess, he is like a pig wallowing in the mire.

A HEBREW LEGEND.

1. "You teach," said the Emperor Trajan, to a famous Rabbi, "that your God is every-where, and boast that he resides among your nation. I should like to see him."

"God's presence is, indeed, every-where," the Rabbi replied, "but he can not be seen, for no mortal eye can look upon his splendor."

The emperor had the obstinacy of power, and persisted in his demand.

"Well," answered the Rabbi, "suppose we begin by endeavoring to gaze at one of his embassadors."

2. Trajan assented; and the Rabbi, leading him into the open air, for it was the noon of the day, bade him raise his eyes to the sun, then shining down upon the world in his meridian glory. The emperor made the attempt, but relinquished it.

"I can not," he said, "the light dazzles me."

"If, then," rejoined the triumphant Rabbi, "thou art unable to endure the light of one of his creatures, how canst thou expect to behold the unclouded glory of the Creator?"

TIME.

1. I saw the temple reared by the hands of men, standing with its high pinnacles in the distant plain. The stream beat upon it, the God of nature hurled his thunderbolts against it, and yet it stood as firm as adamant. Revelry was in its hall; the gay, the happy, the young, and the beautiful, were there. I returned, and the temple was no more; its high walls lay in scattered ruins; moss and wild grass grew wildly there, and, at the midnight hour, the owl's cry was heard where the young and gay once reveled, but now had passed away.

2. I saw a child rejoicing in his youth, the idol of his father. I returned, and the child had become old. Trembling with weight of years, he stood the last of his generation, a stranger amid the desolation around him.

3. I saw the old oak stand in all its pride on the mountain; the birds were caroling on its boughs. I returned, the oak was leafless and sapless; the winds were playing through the branches.

"Who is the destroyer?" said I, to my guardian angel.

4. "It is Time," said he. "When the morning stars sang together with joy over the new-made world, he commenced his course; and when he shall have destroyed all that is beautiful on earth, plucked the sun from its sphere, vailed the moon in blood, yea, when he shall have rolled the heavens and earth away as a scroll, then shall an angel from the throne of God come forth, and, with one foot on the sea and one on the land, lift up his head toward heaven and Heaven's Eternal, and say, 'Time is, time was, but time shall be no longer.'"

THE ROSES OF EARTH.

1. Eve, the mother of mortals, walked one day alone and mournful on the desecrated soil of this sinful earth. Suddenly she espied a rose-tree laden with expanded blossoms, which, like the blush of dawn, shed a rosy light upon the green leaves around them.

2. "Ah," cried she, with rapture, "is it a deception, or do I indeed behold even here the lovely roses of Eden?

Already do I breathe from afar their paradisiacal sweetness. Hail, the gentle type of innocence and joy! Art thou not a silent pledge that, even among the thorns of earth, Eden's happiness may bloom? Surely it is bliss even to inhale the pure fragrance of thy flowers!"

3. Even while she was speaking, with her joyous gaze bent upon a profusion of roses, there sprang up a light breeze, which stirred the boughs of the tree; and lo! the petals of the full-blown flowers silently detached themselves and sank upon the ground. Eve exclaimed, with a sigh:

"Alas! ye also are children of death! I read your meaning, types of earthly joys."

4. And, in mournful silence, she looked upon the fallen leaves. Soon, however, did a gleam of joy lighten up her countenance while she spoke, saying:

"Still shall your blossoms, as they are unfolded in the bud, be unto me the types of holy innocence."

5. So saying, she stooped down to gaze upon the half-closed buds, when suddenly she became aware of the thorns that grew beneath them, and her soul was sorely troubled.

"Oh!" cried she, "do ye also need some defense? Do you indeed bear within the consciousness of sin, and are these thorns the symptoms of your shame? Nevertheless, I bid you welcome, beauteous children of the spring, as an image of heaven's bright and rosy dawn upon this thorny earth!"

JUPITER AND THE HORSE.

1. "Father of beasts and men," said the horse, approaching the throne of Jupiter, "I am said to be one of the most beautiful of animals with which thou hast adorned the world; and my self-love leads me to believe it. Nevertheless, I believe there are some things capable of improvement even in me; may there not be?"

"And what in thee thinkest thou admits of improvement? Speak! I am open to instruction," said indulgent Jupiter, with a smile.

2. "Perhaps," returned the horse, "I should be fleeter. if my legs were taller and thinner. A long. swan-like

neck would not disfigure me.   A broader breast would add to my strength.   And since thou hast destined me to bear thy favorite, man, the saddle which my well-meaning rider puts upon me might be created a part of me."

"Good!" replied Jupiter, "wait a moment." Jupiter, with earnest countenance, pronounced the creative word. Then flowed life into dust; then matter organized and combined; and suddenly stood before the throne the ugly camel.

The horse saw, shuddered, and trembled with fear and abhorrence.

3. "Here," said Jupiter, "are taller and thinner legs; here is a long, swan neck; here is a broad breast; here is a created saddle! Wilt thou, oh horse! that I should transform thee after this fashion?" The horse trembled.

"Go!" said Jupiter; "be instructed for this once without being punished. But, to remind thee occasionally of thy presumption, the new creation shall continue." Jupiter cast a preserving glance on the camel. And never shall the horse behold thee without shuddering.

LXIII. — I MUST DIE.

FROM LANGHORNE.

RICHARD LANGHORNE, during the reign of Charles II, of England, was unjustly condemned and executed. Just before his death, he wrote the following lines, most exquisite in all the essentials of true poetry, except meter and rhyme.

1. It is told me I must die:
O, happiness!
Be glad, O my soul!
And rejoice in Jesus, thy Savior!
If he intended thy perdition,
Would he have laid down his life for thee?
Would he have called thee with so much love,
And illuminated thee with the light of the Spirit?
Would he have given thee his cross,
And given thee shoulders to bear it with patience.

2. It is told me I must die:
O, happy news!
Come on, my dearest soul;
Behold, thy Jesus calls thee!
He prayed for thee upon his cross;
There he extended his arms to receive thee;
There he bowed down his head to kiss thee;
There he opened his heart to give thee entrance,
There he gave up his life to purchase life for thee.

3. It is told me I must die:
O, what happiness!
I am going
To the place of my rest;
To the land of the living;
To the heaven of security;
To the kingdom of peace;
To the palace of my God;
To the nuptials of the Lamb;
To sit at the table of my King;
To feed on the bread of angels;
To see what no eye hath seen;
To hear what no ear hath heard;
To enjoy what the heart of man can not comprehend.

4. O, my Father!
O, thou best of all Fathers,
Have pity on the most wretched of all thy children!
I was lost, but by thy mercy found;
I was dead, but by thy grace am now raised again;
I was gone astray after vanity,
But I am now ready to appear before thee.
O, my Father!
Come, now, in mercy, receive thy child!
Give him thy kiss of peace;
Remit unto him all his sins;
Clothe him with thy nuptial robe;
Permit him to have a place at thy feast;
And forgive all those who are guilty of his death.
H. S. R.—16

LXIV. — THE RESURRECTION.

FROM THE BIBLE.

1. MOREOVER, brethren, I declare unto you the gospel which I preached unto you, which also ye have received, and wherein ye stand; by which also ye are saved, if ye keep in memory what I preached unto you, unless ye have believed in vain.

2. For I delivered unto you first of all that which I also received, how that Christ died for our sins according to the scriptures; and that he was buried, and that he rose again the third day, according to the scriptures; and that he was seen of Cephas, then of the twelve. After that, he was seen of above five hundred brethren at once; of whom the greater part remain unto this present, but some are fallen asleep.

3. After that, he was seen of James; then of all the apostles; and last of all he was seen of me also, as of one born out of due time. For I am the least of the apostles, that am not meet to be called an apostle, because I persecuted the church of God. But by the grace of God I am what I am; and his grace which was bestowed upon me was not in vain; but I labored more abundantly than they all: yet not I, but the grace of God which was with me. Therefore, whether it were I or they, so we preach, and so ye believed.

4. Now if Christ be preached that he rose from the dead, how say some among you that there is no resurrection of the dead? But if there be no resurrection of the dead, then is Christ not risen. And if Christ be not risen, then is our preaching vain, and your faith is also vain. Yea, and we are found false witnesses of God; because we have testified of God that he raised up Christ: whom he raised not up, if so be that the dead rise not. For if the dead rise not, then is not Christ raised: and if Christ be not raised, your faith is vain; ye are yet in your sins. Then they also which are fallen asleep in Christ are perished.

If in this life only we have hope in Christ, we are of all men most miserable.

5. But now is Christ risen from the dead, and become the first fruits of them that slept. For since by man came death, by man came also the resurrection of the dead. For as in Adam all die, even so in Christ shall all be made alive.

6. But every man in his own order: Christ the first fruits; afterward they that are Christ's at his coming. Then cometh the end, when he shall have delivered up the kingdom to God, even the Father; when he shall have put down all rule, and all authority, and power. For he must reign till he hath put all enemies under his feet. The last enemy that shall be destroyed is death. For he hath put all things under his feet.

7. But when he saith, all things are put under him, it is manifest that he is excepted which did put all things under him. And when all things shall be subdued unto him, then shall the Son also himself be subject unto him that put all things under him, that God may be all in all.

8. Else what shall they do which are baptized for the dead, if the dead rise not at all? why are they then baptized for the dead? and why stand we in jeopardy every hour? I protest by your rejoicing, which I have, in Christ Jesus our Lord, I die daily. If after the manner of men I have fought with beasts, at Ephesus, what advantageth me it if the dead rise not? Let us eat and drink; for to-morrow we die.

9. Be not deceived; evil communications corrupt good manners. Awake to righteousness, and sin not; for some have not the knowledge of God. I speak this to your shame.

10. But some man will say, How are the dead raised up? and with what body do they come? Thou fool, that which thou sowest is not quickened, except it die. And that which thou sowest, thou sowest not that body that shall be, but bare grain; it may chance of wheat, or of some other grain: but God giveth it a body as it hath pleased him, and to every seed his own body.

11. All flesh is not the same flesh: but there is one kind

of flesh of men, another flesh of beasts, another of fishes, and another of birds. There are also celestial bodies, and bodies terrestrial: but the glory of the celestial is one, and the glory of the terrestrial is another.

12. There is one glory of the sun, and another glory of the moon, and another glory of the stars: for one star differeth from another star in glory. So also is the resurrection of the dead: it is sown in corruption, it is raised in incorruption: it is sown in dishonor, it is raised in glory: it is sown in weakness, it is raised in power: it is sown a natural body, it is raised a spiritual body.

13. There is a natural body, and there is a spiritual body. And so it is written, The first man Adam was made a living soul, the last Adam was made a quickening spirit. Howbeit, that was not first which is spiritual, but that which is natural; and afterward that which is spiritual. The first man is of the earth, earthy; the second man is the Lord from heaven. As is the earthy, such are they also that are earthy; and as is the heavenly, such are they also that are heavenly. And as we have borne the image of the earthy, we shall also bear the image of the heavenly.

14. Now this I say, brethren, that flesh and blood can not inherit the kingdom of God; neither doth corruption inherit incorruption. Behold, I show you a mystery. We shall not all sleep, but we shall all be changed in a moment, in the twinkling of an eye, at the last trump; for the trumpet shall sound; and the dead shall be raised incorruptible, and we shall be changed. For this corruptible must put on incorruption, and this mortal must put on immortality.

15. So when this corruptible shall have put on incorruption, and this mortal shall have put on immortality, then shall be brought to pass the saying that is written, Death is swallowed up in victory. O death, where is thy sting? O grave, where is thy victory? The sting of death is sin, and the strength of sin is the law. But thanks be to God which giveth us the victory through our Lord Jesus Christ.

16. Therefore, my beloved brethren, be ye steadfast, unmovable, always abounding in the work of the Lord, forasmuch as ye know that your labor is not in vain in the Lord.

LXV.— THE LEPER.

FROM WILLIS.

N. P. WILLIS, an American poet and prose writer of distinction, born in 1807, for some years past editor of the "Home Journal," will probably live and be best known through his exquisitely poetical description of Scripture scenes, as "Absalom," "Jephthah's Daughter," "Hagar," and the following piece.

4. ELD; old age.   5. JEREED; a javelin.

1. " ROOM for the leper! room!" and as he came,
The cry pass'd on, "Room for the leper! room!"
Sunrise was slanting on the city,
Rosy and beautiful, and from the hills
The early-risen poor were coming in,
Duly and cheerfully, to their toil, and up
Rose the sharp hammer's click, and the far hum
Of moving wheels and multitudes astir,
And all that in a city murmur swells,
Unheard but by the watcher's weary ear,
Aching with night's dull silence, or the sick,
Hailing the welcome light, and sounds that chase
The death-like images of the dark away.

2. "Room for the leper!" And aside they stood,
Matron, and child, and pitiless manhood, all
Who met him on his way, and let him pass.
And onward through the open gate he came,
A leper, with the ashes on his brow,
Sackcloth about his loins, and on his lip
A covering; stepping painfully and slow,
And with a difficult utterance, like one
Whose heart is with an iron nerve put down,
Crying, "Unclean! Unclean!"

3. 'Twas now the depth
Of the Judæan summer, and the leaves,
Whose shadows lay so still upon the path,
Had budded on the clear and flashing eye
Of Judah's loftiest noble. He was young,
And eminently beautiful, and life
Mantled with eloquent fullness on his lip,
And sparkled in his glance; and in his mien
There was a gracious pride that every eye
Follow'd with benisons; and this was he!

4. With the soft air of summer there had come
A torpor on his frame, which not the speed
Of his best barb, nor music, nor the blast
Of the bold huntsman's horn, nor aught that stirs
The spirit to its bent, might drive away.
The blood beat not as wont within his veins;
Dimness crept o'er his eye; a drowsy sloth
Fetter'd his limbs like palsy, and his port
With all his loftiness, seem'd struck with eld.

5. Even his voice was changed, a languid moan
Taking the place of the clear, silver key;
And brain and sense grew faint, as if the light,
And very air, were steep'd in sluggishness.
He strove with it awhile, as manhood will,
Ever too proud for weakness, till the rein
Slacken'd within his grasp, and in its poise
The arrowy jereed like an aspen shook.
Day after day, he lay as if in sleep;
His skin grew dry and bloodless, and white scales,
Circled with livid purple, cover'd him.
And then his nails grew black, and fell
From the dull flesh about them, and the hues
Deepen'd beneath the hard, unmoisten'd scales,
And from their edges grew the rank white hair,
   And Helon was a *leper!*

6. Day was breaking,
When at the altar of the temple stood

The holy priest of God.   The incense lamp
Buru'd with a struggling light, and a low chant
Swell'd through the hollow arches of the roof,
Like an articulate wail, and there alone,
Wasted to ghastly thinness, Helon knelt.
The echoes of the melancholy strain
Died in the distant aisles, and he rose up
Struggling with weakness and how'd down his head
Unto the sprinkled ashes, and put off
His costly raiment for the leper's garb,
And with the sackcloth round him, and his lip
Hid in a loathful covering, stood still,
  Waiting to hear his doom.

7. Depart! Depart, O child
Of Israel, from the temple of thy God;
For He has smote thee with his chastening rod,
  And to the desert wild
From all thou lovest, away thy feet must flee,
That from thy plague His people may be free.

8. Depart; and come not near
The busy mart, the crowded city, more;
Nor set thy foot a human threshold o'er.
  And stay thou not to hear
Voices that call thee in the way; and fly
From all who in the wilderness pass by.

9. Wet not thy burning lip
In streams that to a human dwelling glide;
Nor rest thee where the covert fountains bide;
  Nor kneel thee down to dip
The water where the pilgrim bends to drink,
By desert well, or river's grassy brink.

10. And pass thee not between
The weary traveler and the cooling breeze;
And lie not down to sleep beneath the trees
  Where human tracks are seen;

Nor milk the goat that browseth on the plain,
Nor pluck the standing corn, or yellow grain.

11. And now depart! and when
Thy heart is heavy, and thine eyes are dim,
Lift up thy prayer beseechingly to Him
    Who, from the tribes of men,
Selected thee to feel his chastening rod.
Depart, O leper! and forget not God!

12. And he went forth, alone; not one, of all
The many whom he lov'd, nor she whose name
Was woven in the fibers of the heart
Breaking within him now, to come and speak
Comfort unto him. Yea, he went his way,
Sick, and heart-broken, and alone, to die;
For God had curs'd the leper!

13. It was noon,
And Helon knelt beside a stagnant pool
In the lone wilderness, and bathed his brow,
Hot with the burning leprosy, and touch'd
The loathsome water to his parch-ed lips,
Praying that he might be so bless'd, to die!
Footsteps approach'd, and with no strength to flee,
He drew the covering closer on his lip,
Crying "Unclean! Unclean!" and in the folds
Of the coarse sackcloth, shrouding up his face,
He fell upon the earth till they should pass.

14. Nearer the stranger came, and bending o'er
The leper's prostrate form, pronounced his name,
"Helon!" the voice was like the master-tone
Of a rich instrument, most strangely sweet;
And the dull pulses of disease awoke,
And for a moment beat beneath the hot
And leprous scales with a restoring thrill.
"Helon, arise!" and he forgot his curse,
And rose and stood before him.

15. Love and awe
Mingled in the regard of Helon's eye
As he beheld the stranger. He was not
In costly raiment clad, nor on his brow
The symbol of a princely lineage wore;
No followers at his back, nor in his hand
Buckler, or sword, or spear; yet in his mien
Command sat throned serene, and, if he smiled,
A kindly condescension graced his lips,
The lion would have crouch'd to in his lair.
His garb was simple, and his sandals worn,
His statue model'd with a perfect grace;
His countenance, the impress of a God,
Touch'd with the open innocence of a child;
His eye was blue and calm, as is the sky,
In the serenest noon; his hair, unshorn,
Fell on his shoulders; and his curling beard
The fullness of perfected manhood bore.

16. He look'd on Helon earnestly awhile,
As if his heart was moved, and stooping down,
He took a little water in his hand
And laid it on his brow, and said "Be clean!"
And lo! the scales fell from him, and his blood
Cours'd with delicious coolness through his veins,
And his dry palms grew moist, and on his brow
The dewy softness of an infant stole.

17. His leprosy was cleans'd, and he fell down
Prostrate at Jesus' feet, and worship'd him.

LXVI.—THE GYPSIES.

From Scott.

5. COLOTTE; a noted painter.	10. STIRK; cattle.
10. GLOWR; stare.	10. SUNKETS; delicacies.
10. BIELDS; hovels.	11. REISE; rod.

1. IT was in a hollow way, near the top of a steep ascent upon the verge of the Ellangowan estate, that Mr. Bertram

II. S. R —17

met the gypsy procession. Four or five men formed the advanced guard, wrapped in long, loose great coats, that hid their tall, slender figures, as the large slouched hats, drawn over their brows, concealed their wild features, dark eyes, and swarthy faces. Two of them carried long fowling pieces, one wore a broad-sword without a sheath, and all had the Highland dirk, though they did not wear that weapon openly or ostentatiously.

2. Behind them followed the train of laden asses, and small carts, or tumblers, as they were called in that country, on which were laid the decrepit and the helpless, the aged and infant part of the exiled community. The women, in their red cloaks and straw hats, the elder children, with bare heads and bare feet, and almost naked bodies, had the immediate care of the little caravan. The road was narrow, running between two broken banks of sand, and Mr. Bertram's servant rode forward, smacking his whip with an air of authority, and motioning to their drivers to allow free passage to their betters.

3. His signal was unattended to. He then called to the men who lounged idly on before, "Stand to your beasts' heads, and make room for the laird to pass." "He shall have his share of the road," answered a male gypsy from under his slouched and large-brimmed hat, and without raising his face, "and he shall have no more; the highway is as free to our cuddies as to his geldings."

4. The tone of the man being sulky, and even menacing, Mr. Bertram thought it best to put his dignity into his pocket, and pass by the procession quietly, upon such space as they chose to leave for his accommodation, which was narrow enough. To cover with an appearance of indifference his feeling of the want of respect with which he was treated, he addressed one of the men, as he passed him, without any show of greeting, salute, or recognition, "Giles Baillie," he said, "have you heard that your son Gabriel is well?" (the question referred to a young man who had been pressed.)

5. "If I had heard otherwise," said the old man, looking up with a stern and menacing countenance, "you should

have heard it too." And he plodded his way, tarrying no further question. When the laird had pressed onward with difficulty among a crowd of familiar faces, in which he now only read hatred and contempt, but which had on all former occasions marked his approach with the reverence due to that of a superior being, and had got clear of the throng, he could not help turning his horse and looking back to mark the progress of the march. The group would have been an excellent subject for the pencil of Colotte. The van had already reached a small and stunted thicket, which was at the bottom of the hill, and which gradually hid the line of march until the last stragglers disappeared.

6. His sensations were bitter enough. The race, it is true, which he had thus summarily dismissed from their ancient place of refuge, was idle and vicious; but had he endeavored to render them otherwise? They were not more irregular characters now, than they had been while they were admitted to consider themselves as a sort of subordinate dependents of his family; and ought the circumstance of his becoming a magistrate to have made at once such a change in his conduct toward them? Some means of reformation ought at least to have been tried, before sending seven families at once upon the wide world, and depriving them of a degree of countenance which withheld them at least from atrocious guilt.

7. There was also a natural yearning of heart upon parting with so many known and familiar faces; and to this feeling Godfrey Bertram was peculiarly accessible, from the limited qualities of his mind, which sought its principal amusements among the petty objects around him.

8. As he was about to turn his horse's head to pursue his journey, Meg Merrilies, who had lagged behind the troops, unexpectedly presented herself. She was standing upon one of those high banks, which, as we before noticed, overhung the road; so that she was placed considerably higher than Ellangowan, even though he was on horseback; and her tall figure, relieved against the clear blue sky, seemed almost of supernatural hight. We have noticed that there was in her general attire, or rather in her mode

of adjusting it, somewhat of a foreign costume, artfully adopted, perhaps, for the purpose of adding to the effect of her spells and predictions, or perhaps from some traditional notions respecting the dress of her ancestors. On this occasion, she had a large piece of red cotton cloth rolled about her head in the form of a turban, from beneath which her dark eyes flashed with uncommon luster.

9. Her long and tangled black hair fell in elf locks from the folds of this singular head-gear. Her attitude was that of a sibyl in frenzy, as she stretched out, in her right hand, a sapling bough which seemed just pulled. "I'll be sworn, said the groom, "she has been cutting the young ashes in the Dukit Park." The laird made no answer, but continued to look at the figure which was thus perched above his path.

10. "Ride your ways," said the gypsy, "ride your ways, Laird of Ellangowan; ride your ways, Godfrey Bertram! This day have ye quenched seven smoking hearths; see if the fire in your ain parlor burn the blyther for that! Ye have riven the thack off seven cottar houses; look if your ain roof-tree stand the faster! Ye may stable your stirks in the shealings at Derncleugh; see that the hare does not couch on the hearthstane at Ellangowan! Ride your ways, Godfrey Bertram! what do ye glowr after our folk for? There's thirty hearts there, that wad hae wanted bread ere ye had wanted sunkets, and spent their life-blood ere ye had scratched your finger; yes, there's thirty yonder, from the auld wife of an hundred to the babe that was born last week, that ye hae turned out o' their bits o' bields, to sleep with the toad and the black-cock in the muirs!

11. "Ride your ways, Ellangowan! Our bairns are hanging at our weary backs; look that your braw cradle at hame be the fairer spread up! Not that I am wishing ill to little Harry, or to the babe that's yet to be born; God forbid, and make them kind to the poor, and better folk than their father! And now, ride e'en your ways, for these are the last words ye'll ever hear Meg Merrilies speak, and this is the last reise that I'll ever cut in the bonny woods of Ellangowan."

12. So saying, she broke the sapling she held in her hand, and flung it into the road. Margaret of Anjou, bestowing on her triumphant foes her keen-edged malediction, could not have turned from them with a gesture more proudly contemptuous. The laird was clearing his voice to speak, and thrusting his hand in his pocket to find half a crown; the gypsy waited neither for his reply nor his donation, but strode down the hill to overtake the caravan.

13. Ellangowan rode pensively home; and it was remarkable that he did not mention this interview to any of his family. The groom was not so reserved: he told the story at great length to a full audience in the kitchen, and concluded by swearing, that "if ever the devil spoke by the mouth of a woman, he had spoken by that of Meg Merrilies that blessed day."

LXVII. — THE LAST OF THE MAMELUKES.

FROM DUMAS.

1. THE Mamelukes were a powerful body of soldiers, that had long been in the service of the Pacha of Egypt. A few years since, the Pacha, or chief of that country, finding them troublesome and dangerous to his power, determined to destroy them. Accordingly, they were invited to a feast in a citadel, the place being surrounded by the Pacha's garrison, except on one side, where there was a deep precipice.

2. They came, according to custom, superbly mounted on the finest horses, and in their richest costume. At a signal given by the Pacha, death burst forth on all sides. Crossing and enfilading batteries poured forth their flame and iron, and men and horses were at once weltering in their blood.

3. Many precipitated themselves from the summit of the citadel, and were destroyed in the abyss below. Two, however, recovered themselves. At the first shock of the concussion both horses and riders were stunned; they trembled for an instant, like equestrian riders shaken by an

earthquake, and then darted off with the rapidity of light-ning; they passed the nearest gate, which fortunately was not closed, and found themselves out of Cairo. One of the fugitives took the road to Ell Azish, the other darted up the mountains. The pursuers divided, one-half follow-ing each.

4. It was a fearful thing, that race for life and death! The steeds of the desert, let loose on the mountains, bounded from rock to rock, forded torrents, or sped along the edges of precipices. Three times the horse of one Mameluke fell breathless; three times, hearing the tramp of the pursuers, he arose and renewed his flight. He fell at length not to rise again.

5. His master exhibited a touching instance of reciprocal fidelity. Instead of gliding down the rocks into some defile, or gaining a peak inaccessible to cavalry, he seated himself by the side of his courser, threw the bridle over his arm, and awaited the arrival of his executioners. They came up, and he fell beneath a score of sabers, without a motion of resistance, a word of complaint, or a prayer for mercy.

6. The other Mameluke, more fortunate than his com-panion, traversed Ell Azish, gained the desert, escaped unhurt, and, in time, became the Governor of Jerusalem, where, at a later date, I had the pleasure to see him, the last and only remnant of that redoubtable corps, which, thirty years ago, rivaled in courage, though not in fortune, the chosen men of Napoleon's army.

LXVIII. — FATHER IS COMING.

FROM HOWITT.

1. THE clock is on the stroke of six,
    The father's work is done;
 Sweep up the hearth and mend the fire,
    And put the kettle on.
 The wild night-wind is blowing cold,
 'Tis dreary crossing o'er the wold.

2. He's crossing o'er the wold apace,
    He's stronger than the storm;
He does not feel the cold, not he;
    His heart it is so warm.

3. He makes all toil, all hardship light:
    Would all men were the same!
So ready to be pleas'd, so kind,
    So very slow to blame!
Folks need not be unkind, austere,
For love hath readier will than fear.

4. Nay, do not close the shutters, child;
    For far along the lane,
The little window looks, and he
    Can see it shining plain.
I've heard him say he loves to mark
The cheerful fire-light through the dark.

5. And we'll do all that father asks,
    His wishes are so few;
Would they were more! that every hour
    Some wish of his I knew!
I'm sure it makes a happy day,
When I can please him every way.

6. I know he's coming by the sign
    That baby's almost wild,
See how he laughs, and crows, and stares;
    Heaven bless the merry child!
He's father's self in face and limb,
And father's heart is strong in him.

7. Hark! hark! I hear his footsteps now,
    He's at the garden gate;
Run, little Bess, and ope the door,
    And do not let him wait.
Shout, baby, shout, and clap thy hands,
For father on the threshold stands.

LXIX. — I SEE THEE STILL.

1. I SEE thee still!
Remembrance, faithful to her trust,
Calls thee in beauty from the dust;
Thou comest in the morning light,
Thou 'rt with me through the gloomy night;
In dreams I meet thee as of old;
Then thy soft arms my neck enfold,
And thy sweet voice is in my ear;
In every scene to memory dear
      I see thee still!

2. I see thee still
In every hallow'd token round;
This little ring thy finger bound,
This lock of hair thy forehead shaded,
This silken chain by thee was braided;
These flowers, all wither'd now, like thee,
Sweet sister, thou didst cull for me;
This book was thine; here thou didst read;
This picture, ah, yes! here, indeed,
      I see thee still!

3. I see thee still!
Here was thy summer noon's retreat,
Here was thy favorite fireside seat;
This was thy chamber; here, each day,
I sat and watch'd thy sad decay;
Here, on this bed, thou last didst lie;
Here, on this pillow, thou didst die!
Dark hour! Once more its woes unfold;
As then I saw thee pale and cold,
      I see thee still!

4. I see thee still!
Thou art not in the grave confined,
Death can not claim the immortal mind;

Let earth close o'er its sacred trust,
But goodness dies not in the dust!
Thee, O my sister! 'tis not thee
Beneath the coffin's lid I see!
Thou to a fairer land art gone;
There, let me hope, my journey done,
            To see thee still!

LXX.—TO AN ABSENT WIFE.

FROM GEORGE D. PRENTICE.

GEORGE D. PRENTICE, one of the sweetest and most talented of American poets, has been, for many years, editor of a leading paper in Louisville, Kentucky. He has written little, but all that he has written, is of the highest order of poetry.

1. 'TIS morn; the sea breeze seems to bring
Joy, health, and freshness on its wing;
Bright flowers, to me all strange and new,
Are glittering in the early dew;
And perfumes rise from many a grove
As incense to the clouds that move
Like spirits o'er yon welkin clear;
But I am sad, thou art not here.

2. 'Tis noon; a calm, unbroken sleep
Is on the blue waves of the deep;
A soft haze, like a fairy dream,
Is floating over hill and stream;
And many a broad magnolia flower
Within its shadowy woodland bower
Is gleaming like a lovely star;
But I am sad, thou art afar.

3. 'Tis eve; on earth the sunset skies
Are painting their own Eden dyes;
The stars come down, and trembling glow
Like blossoms in the waves below;

And, like some unseen sprite, the breeze
Seems lingering 'mid the orange trees,
Breathing in music round the spot;
But I am sad, I see thee not.

4. 'Tis midnight; with a soothing spell
The far tones of the ocean swell,
Soft as a mother's cadence mild,
Low bending o'er her sleeping child;
And on each wandering breeze are heard
The rich notes of the mocking-bird
In many a wild and wondrous lay;
But I am sad, thou art away.

5. I sink in dreams, low, sweet, and clear;
Thy own dear voice is in my ear;
Around my cheek thy tresses twine,
Thy own lov'd hand is clasp'd in mine,
Thy own soft lip to mine is press'd,
Thy head is pillow'd on my breast,
O! I have all my heart holds dear;
And I am happy, thou art here.

LXXI. — RURAL LIFE IN ENGLAND.

FROM IRVING.

1. THE stranger who would form a correct opinion of
the English character, must not confine his observations to
the metropolis. He must go forth into the country; he
must sojourn in villages and hamlets; he must visit castles,
villas, farm-houses, cottages; he must wander through
parks and gardens; along hedges and green lanes; he must
loiter about country churches; attend wakes and fairs, and
other rural festivals; and cope with the people in all their
conditions, and all their habits and humors.

2. In some countries the *large cities* absorb the wealth
and fashion of the nation; they are the only fixed abodes

of elegant and intelligent society, and the *country* is inhabited almost entirely by boorish peasantry. In England, on the contrary, the metropolis is a mere gathering-place, or general rendezvous, of the polite classes, where they devote a small portion of the year to a hurry of gayety and dissipation, and having indulged this carnival, return again to the apparently more congenial habits of rural life. The various orders of society are therefore diffused over the whole surface of the kingdom, and the most retired neighborhoods afford specimens of the different ranks.

3. The English, in fact, are strongly gifted with the rural feeling. They possess a quick sensibility to the beauties of nature, and a keen relish for the pleasures and employments of the country. Even the inhabitants of cities, born and brought up among brick walls and bustling streets, enter with facility into rural habits, and evince a turn for rural occupation. The merchant has his snug retreat in the vicinity of the metropolis, where he often displays as much pride and zeal in the cultivation of his flower-garden and the watering of his fruits, as he does in the conduct of his business and the success of his commercial enterprises. Even those less fortunate individuals who are doomed to pass their lives in the midst of din and traffic, contrive to have something which shall remind them of the green aspect of nature. In the most dark and dingy quarters of the city, the drawing-room window resembles frequently a bank of flowers. Every spot capable of vegetation has its grass-plot and flower-bed; and every square its mimic park, laid out with picturesque taste, and gleaming with refreshing verdure.

4. Those who see the Englishman only in town, are apt to form an unfavorable opinion of his social character. He is either absorbed in business, or distracted by the thousand engagements that dissipate time, thought, and feeling, in this huge metropolis; he has, therefore, too commonly, a look of hurry and abstraction. Wherever he happens to be, he is on the point of going somewhere else; at the moment he is talking on one subject, his mind is wandering to another; and while paying a friendly visit, he is

calculating how he shall economize time, so as to pay the other visits allotted to the morning.

5. It is in the country that the Englishman gives scope to his natural feelings. He breaks loose gladly from the cold formalities and negative civilities of town; throws off his habits of shy reserve, and becomes joyous and free-hearted. He manages to collect around him all the conveniences and elegancies of polite life, and to banish its restraint. His country-seat abounds with every requisite, either for studious retirement, tasteful gratification, or rural exercise. Books, music, paintings, horses, dogs, and sporting implements of all kinds, are at hand. He puts no constraint either upon his guests or himself, but in the true spirit of hospitality provides the means of enjoyment, and leaves every one to partake according to his inclination.

6. The taste of the English in the cultivation of land, and in what is called landscape gardening, is unrivaled. They have studied nature intently, and discover an exquisite sense of her beautiful forms and harmonious combinations. Those charms, which in other countries she lavishes in wild solitudes, are here assembled round the haunts of domestic life. They seem to have caught her coy and furtive glances, and spread them, like witchery, about their rural abodes.

7. The fondness for rural life among the higher classes of the English, has had a great and salutary effect upon the national character. I do not know a finer race of men than the English gentlemen. Instead of the softness and effeminacy which characterize the men of rank in most countries, they exhibit a union of elegance and strength, a robustness of frame and freshness of complexion, which I am inclined to attribute to their living so much in the open air, and pursuing so eagerly the invigorating recreations of the country. These hardy exercises produce also a healthful tone of mind and spirits, and a manliness and simplicity of manners, which even the follies and dissipations of the town can not pervert, and can never entirely destroy.

8. In rural occupations there is nothing mean and debasing. It leads a man forth among scenes of natural grandeur and beauty; it leaves him to the workings of his own mind, operated upon by the purest and most elevating of external influences. Such a man may be simple and rough, but he can not be vulgar. The man of refinement, therefore, finds nothing revolting in an intercourse with the lower orders of rural life. He lays aside his distance and reserve, and is glad to waive the distinctions of rank, and to enter into the honest, heartfelt enjoyments of common life. Indeed, the very amusements of the country bring men more and more together, and the sound of hound and horn blend all feelings into harmony.

9. The great charm, however, of English scenery is the moral feeling that seems to pervade it. It is associated in the mind with the idea of order, of quiet, of sober, well-established principles, of hoary usage and revered custom. Every thing seems to be the growth of ages, of regular and peaceful existence. The old church of remote architecture, with its low, massive portal; its Gothic tower; its windows, rich with tracery and painted glass; its stately monuments of warriors and worthies of the olden time, ancestors of the present lords of the soil; its tombstones, recording successive generations of sturdy yeomanry, whose progeny still plow the same fields and kneel at the same altar; the parsonage, a quaint, irregular pile, partly antiquated, but repaired and altered in the taste of various ages and occupants; the stile and foot-path leading from the church-yard, across pleasant fields, and along shady hedge rows, according to an immemorial right of way; the neighboring village, with its venerable cottages, its public green sheltered by trees, under which the forefathers of the present race have sported; the antique family mansion, standing apart in some little rural domain, but looking down with a protecting air on the surrounding scene: *all these* common features of English landscape evince a calm and settled security, and hereditary transmission of home-bred virtues and local attachments, that speak deeply and touchingly for the moral character of the nation.

10. It is a pleasant sight on a Sunday morning, when the bell is sending its sober melody across the quiet fields, to behold the peasantry, in their best finery, with ruddy faces, and modest cheerfulness, thronging tranquilly along the green lanes to church; but it is still more pleasant to see them in the evenings, gathering about their cottage doors, and appearing to exult in the humble comforts and embellishments which their own hands have spread around them.

11. It is this sweet home-feeling, this settled repose of affection in the domestic scene, that is, after all, the parent of the steadiest virtues and purest enjoyments; and I can not close these desultory remarks better, than by quoting the words of a modern English poet, who has depicted it with remarkable felicity.

12. Through each gradation, from the castled hall,
The city dome, the villa crown'd with shade,
But chief from modest mansions numberless,
In town or hamlet, shelt'ring middle life,
Down to the cottaged vale, and straw-roof'd shed,
The western isle hath long been famed for scenes
Where bliss domestic finds a dwelling-place:
Domestic bliss, that, like a harmless dove,
(Honor and sweet endearment keeping guard,)
Can center in a quiet little nest
All that desire would fly for through the earth;
That can, the world eluding, be itself
A world enjoy'd; that wants no witnesses
But its own sharers, and approving Heaven;
That, like a flower deep hid in rocky cleft,
Smiles, though 'tis looking only at the sky.

LXXII.— THE MAY QUEEN.

FROM TENNYSON.

ALFRED TENNYSON is an English poet still living, and is the present Poet Laureate of England. He is among the first of modern poets. The following refers to one of the most beautiful customs of English rural life.

MAY DAY.

I.

You must wake and call me early, call me early, mother dear;
To-morrow 'll be the happiest time of all the glad new year;

Of all the glad new year, mother, the maddest, merriest day;
For I'm to be Queen o' the May, mother, I'm to be Queen o'
    the May.

II.

I sleep so sound, all night, mother, that I shall never wake,
If you do not call me loud, when the day begins to break;
But I must gather knots of flowers, and buds and garlands gay,
For I'm to be Queen o' the May, mother, I'm to be Queen o'
    the May.

III.

Little Effie shall go with me to-morrow to the green,
And you'll be there, too, mother, to see me made the Queen;
For the shepherd lads on every side 'll come from far away,
And I'm to be Queen o' the May, mother, I'm to be Queen o'
    the May.

IV.

The honeysuckle round the porch has woven its rosy bowers;
And by the meadow trenches blow the faint, sweet cuckoo-
    flowers;
And the wild marsh-marigold shines like fire in swamps and
    hollows gray,
And I'm to be Queen o' the May, mother, I'm to be Queen o'
    the May.

V.

The night-winds come and go, mother, upon the meadow grass,
And the happy stars above them seem to brighten as they pass;
There will not be a drop of rain the whole of the livelong day,
And I'm to be Queen o' the May, mother, I'm to be Queen o'
    the May.

VI.

All the valley, mother, 'll be fresh, and green, and still,
And the cowslip and the crow-foot are over all the hill,
And the rivulet in the flowery dale 'll merrily glance and play,
For I'm to be Queen o' the May, mother, I'm to be Queen o'
    the May.

VII.

So you must wake and call me early, call me early, mother dear,
To-morrow 'll be the happiest time of all the glad new year;

To-morrow 'll be of all the year the maddest, merriest day,
For I 'm to be Queen o' the May, mother, I 'm to be Queen o'
the May.

NEW YEAR'S EVE.

VIII.

If you 're waking, call me early, call me early, mother dear,
For I would see the sun rise upon the glad New-Year,
It is the last new-year that I shall ever see,
Then you may lay me low i' the mold, and think no more of me.

IX.

To-night I saw the sun set: he set, and left behind
The good old year, the dear old time, and all my peace of mind,
And the new-year's coming up, mother, but I shall never see
The blossoms on the black-thorn, the leaf upon the tree.

X.

There 's not a flower on all the hills: the frost is on the pane;
I only wish to live till the snow-drops come again:
I wish the snow would melt, and the sun come out on high;
I long to see a flower so, before the day I die.

XI.

When the flowers come again, mother, beneath the waning light,
You 'll never see me more in the long gray fields at night;
When from the dry, dark wold the summer airs blow cool
On the oat-grass and the sword-grass, and the bulrush in the pool.

XII.

You 'll bury me, my mother, just beneath the hawthorn shade,
And you 'll come sometimes and see me where I am lowly laid;
I shall not forget you, mother, I shall hear you when you pass,
With your feet above my head in the long and pleasant grass.

XIII.

I have been wild and wayward, but you 'll forgive me now;
You 'll kiss me, my own mother, upon my cheek and brow;
Nay, nay, you must not weep, nor let your grief be wild,
You should not fret for me, mother, you have another child.

XIV.

If I can, I 'll come again, mother, from out my resting-place;
Though you 'll not see me, mother, I shall look upon your face,
Though I can not speak a word, I shall hearken what you say,
And be often, often with you when you think I 'm far away.

XV.

Good night, good night, when I have said good night for evermore,
And you see me carried out from the threshhold of the door,
Don't let Effie come to see me till my grave be growing green;
She 'll be a better child to you than I have ever been.

XVI.

She 'll find my garden tools upon the granary floor;
Let her take them: they are hers: I shall never garden more.
But tell her when I 'm gone, to train the rose-bush that I set
About the parlor window, and the box of mignonnette.

XVII.

Good night, sweet mother; call me before the day is born,
All night I lie awake, but I fall asleep at morn;
But I would see the sun rise upon the glad new-year,
So, if you 're waking, call me, call me early, mother dear.

LXXIII.— GOD'S MERCY.

JEREMY TAYLOR, who lived from 1613 to 1667, is one of the most celebrated divines of the Church of England. His sermons are among the richest treasures of theological literature. He is sometimes styled the *Shakspeare of Divinity*. The following is a good specimen of his richness of imagery, beauty of style, and force of thought and expression.

1. MAN, having destroyed that which God delighted in, that is, the beauty of the soul, fell into an evil portion, and being seized on by the divine justice, grew miserable, and condemned to an incurable sorrow. Poor Adam, being famished and undone, went and lived a sad life in the mountains of India, and turned his face and his prayers toward Paradise; thither he sent his sighs, to that place

H. S. R.—18

he directed his devotions; there was his heart now, where his felicity sometimes had been: but he knew not how to return thither, for God was his enemy, and, by many of his attributes, opposed himself against him; and poor man, whom a fly or a fish could kill, was assaulted and beaten with a sword of fire in the hand of a cherubim. God's eye watched him, his omniscience was man's accuser, his serenity was his judge, his justice the executioner.

2. It was a mighty calamity that man was to undergo, when he that made him armed himself against his creature, which would have died or turned to nothing, if he had but withdrawn the miracles or the almightiness of his power. If God had taken his arm from under him, man had perished. But it was, therefore, a greater evil when God laid his arm on him and against him, and seemed to support him, that he might be longer killing him. In the midst of these sadnesses, God remembered his own creature, and pitied it; and by his mercy, rescued him from the hands of his power, and the sword of his justice, and the guilt of his punishment, and the disorder of his sin; and placed him in that order of good things where he ought to have stood.

3. It was mercy that preserved the noblest of God's creatures here below; he who stood condemned and undone under all other attributes of God, was saved and rescued by his mercy; that it may be evident that God's mercy is above all his works, and above all ours, greater than the creation, and greater than our sins. As is his majesty, so is his mercy, that is, without measures and without rules, sitting in heaven and filling all the world, calling for a duty that he may give a blessing, making man that he may save him, punishing him that he may preserve him.

4. And God's justice bowed down to his mercy, and all his power passed into mercy, and his omniscience changed into care and watchfulness, into providence and observation for man's avail, and heaven gave its influence for man, and rained showers for our food and drink; and the attributes and acts of God sat at the foot of mercy, and all *that* mercy descended upon the head of man.

5. For so the light of the world in the turning of crea-
tion was spread abroad like a curtain, and dwelt nowhere,
but filled the *expansum* with a dissemination great as the
unfoldings of the air's looser garment, or the wilder fringes
of the fire, without knots, or order, or combination; but
God gathered the beams in his hand, and united them into
a globe of fire, and all the light of the world became the
body of the sun; and he lent some to his weaker sister
that walks in the night, and guides a traveler, and teaches
him to distinguish a house from a river, or a rock from a
plain field. So is the mercy of God a vast *expansum* and a
huge ocean. From eternal ages it dwelt around the throne
of God, and it filled all that infinite distance and space,
that hath no measure but the will of God; until God, de-
siring to communicate that excellency and make it relative,
created angels, that he might have persons capable of huge
gifts; and man, who he knew would need forgiveness.

6. For so the angels, our elder brothers, dwelt forever
in the house of their Father, and never broke his com-
mandments; but we, the younger, like prodigals, forsook
our Father's house, and went into a strange country, and
followed stranger courses, and spent the portion of our
nature, and forfeited all our title to the family, and came to
need another portion. For, ever since the fall of Adam,
who, like an unfortunate man, spent all that a wretched
man could need, or a happy man could have, our life is
repentance, and forgiveness is all our portion; and though
angels were objects of God's bounty, yet man only is, in
proper speaking, the object of his mercy; and the mercy
which dwells in an infinite circle, became confined to a little
ring, and dwelt here below, till it hath carried all God's
portion up to heaven, where it shall reign and glory upon
our crowned heads forever and ever!

7. But for him that considers God's mercies, and dwells
awhile in that depth, it is hard not to talk widely, and
without art and order of discoursings. St. Peter talked he
knew not what, when he entered into a cloud with Jesus
on Mount Tabor, though it passed over him like the little
curtains that ride upon the north wind, and pass between

the sun and us. And when we converse with a light greater than the sun, and taste a sweetness more delicious than the dew of heaven, and in our thoughts entertain the ravishments and harmony of that atonement, which reconciles God to man, and man to felicity, it will be more easily pardoned, if we should be like persons that admire much, and say but little; and, indeed, we can but confess the glories of the Lord by dazzled eyes, and a stammering tongue, and a heart overcharged with the miracles of this infinity.

8. For so those little drops that run over, though they be not much in themselves, yet they tell that the vessel was full, and could express the greatness of the shower no otherwise but by spilling, and in artificial expressions and runnings over. But because I have undertaken to tell the drops of the ocean, and to span the measures of eternity, I must do it by the great lines of revelation and experience, and tell concerning God's mercy as we do concerning God himself, that he is that great Fountain of which we all drink, and the great Rock of which we all eat, and on which we all dwell, and under whose shadow we all are refreshed.

9. God's mercy is all this; and we can only draw the great lines of it, and reckon the constellations of our hemisphere, instead of telling the number of the stars; we can only reckon what we feel and what we live by; and though there be in every one of these lines of life, enough to engage us forever to do God's service, and to give him praises, yet it is certain there are very many mercies of God on us, and toward us, and concerning us, which we neither feel, nor see, nor understand as yet, but yet we are blessed by them, and are preserved and secure, and we shall then know them, when we come to give God thanks in the festivities of an eternal Sabbath.

LXXIV. — MERCY.

FROM SHAKSPEARE.

1. THE quality of mercy is not strain'd;
It droppeth as the gentle rain from heaven,
Upon the place beneath: it is twice bless'd;
It blesseth him that gives, and him that takes:
'Tis mightiest in the mightiest: it becomes
The thro-ned monarch better than his crown:
His scepter shows the force of temporal power,
The attribute to awe and majesty,
Wherein doth sit the fear and dread of kings.

2. But mercy is above the scepter'd sway;
It is enthro-ned in the hearts of kings,
It is an attribute of God himself;
And earthly power doth then show likest God's,
When mercy seasons justice: therefore, man,
Though justice be thy plea, consider this
That, in the course of justice, none of us
Should see salvation. We do pray for mercy;
And that same prayer doth teach us all to render
The deeds of mercy.

LXXV. — THE SISTER'S PLEA.

FROM SHAKSPEARE.

Isabella. I am a woeful suitor to your honor,
Please but your honor hear me.
Angelo. Well; what's your suit?
Isab. There is a vice, that most I do abhor,
And most desire should meet the blow of justice;
For which I would not plead, but that I must;
For which I must not plead, but that I am
At war 'twixt will and will not.
Ang. Well; the matter?

Isab. I have a brother is condemn'd to die:
I do beseech you, let it be his fault,
And not my brother.

Ang. Condemn the fault, and not the actor of it?
Why, every fault's condemn'd, ere it be done:
Mine were the very cipher of a function,
To fine the faults, whose fine stands in record,
And let go by the actor.

Isab. O just, but severe law!
Must he needs die?

Ang. Maiden, no remedy.

Isab. Yes; I do think that you might pardon him,
And neither Heaven nor man grieve at the mercy.

Ang. I will not do 't.

Isab. But can you, if you would?

Ang. Look! what I will not, that I can not do.

Isab. But might you do 't, and do the world no wrong,
If so your heart were touch'd with that remorse
As mine is to him?

Ang. He 's sentenced; 'tis too late.

Isab. Too late? why, no; I, that do speak a word,
May call it back again. Well, believe this:
No ceremony that to great ones 'longs,
Not the king's crown, nor the deputed sword,
The marshal's truncheon, nor the judge's robe,
Become them with one-half so good a grace
As mercy does. If he had been as you,
And you as he, you would have slipt like him;
But he, like you, would not have been so stern.

Ang. Pray you, begone.

Isab. I would to Heaven I had your potency,
And you were Isabel! should it then be thus?
No! I would tell what 't were to be a judge,
And what a prisoner.

Ang. Your brother is a forfeit of the law,
And you but waste your words.

Isab. Alas! alas!
Why, all the souls that are were forfeit once;
And he that might the 'vantage best have took

Found out the remedy! How would you be,
If He, which is the top of judgment, should
But judge you as you are? O, think on that,
And mercy then will breathe within your lips,
Like man new made.

    Ang. Be you content, fair maid;
It is the law, not I, condemns your brother;
Were he my kinsman, brother, or my son,
It should be thus with him; he must die to-morrow.

    Isab. To-morrow? O, that's sudden! Spare him, spare
      him!
He's not prepared for death! Even for our kitchens
We kill the fowl of season : shall we serve Heaven
With less respect than we do minister
To our gross selves? Good, good, my lord, bethink you
Who it is that hath died for this offense :
There's many have committed it.

    Ang. The law hath not been dead, though it hath slept:
Those many had not dared to do that evil,
If the first man that did the edict infringe
Had answer'd for his deed: now, 'tis awake;
Takes note of what is done; and, like a prophet,
Looks in a glass, that shows what future evils
(Either now, or by remissness new-conceiv'd,
And so in progress to be hatch'd and born),
Are now to have no successive degrees,
But, where they live, to end.

    Isab. Yet show some pity!

    Ang. I show it most of all when I show justice;
For then I pity those I do not know,
Which a dismiss'd offense would after gall;
And do him right, that, answering one foul wrong,
Lives not to act another. Be satisfied :
Your brother dies to-morrow; be content.

    Isab. So you must be the first that gives this sentence,
And he, that suffers! O, it is excellent
To have a giant's strength; but it is tyrannous
To use it like a giant. Could great men thunder
As Jove himself does, Jove would ne'er be quiet,

For every pelting, petty officer
Would use his heaven for thunder; nothing but thunder.
Merciful Heaven!
Thou rather, with thy sharp and sulphurous bolt,
Split'st the unwedgeable and gnarl-ed oak,
Than the soft myrtle.   But man, proud man!
Drest in a little brief authority,
Most ignorant of what he's most assured,
His glassy essence, like an angry ape,
Plays such fantastic tricks before high Heaven
As make the angels weep.
We can not weigh our brother with ourself.
Great men may jest with saints: 'tis wit in them!
But, in the less, foul profanation.
That in the captain's but a choleric word,
Which in the soldier is flat blasphemy.

Ang. Why do you put these sayings upon me?

Isab. Because authority, though it err like others,
Hath yet a kind of medicine in itself.
Go to your bosom:
Knock there, and ask your heart what it doth know
That's like my brother's fault; if it confess
A natural guiltiness, such as is his,
Let it not sound a thought upon your tongue
Against my brother's life.

Ang. [*Aside.*] She speaks, and 'tis
Such sense, my sense breeds with it. [*To her.*] Fare you
    well.

Isab. Gentle, my lord, turn back.

Ang. I will bethink me. Come again to-morrow.

Isab. Hark, how I'll bribe you! Good, my lord, turn
    back.

Ang. How? bribe me?

Isab. Ay, with such gifts that heaven shall share with
    you.
Not with fond shekels of the tested gold,
Or stones, whose rates are either rich or poor,
As fancy values them: but with true prayers,
That shall be up at heaven, and enter there,

Ere sunrise; prayers from preserv-ed souls,
From fasting maids, whose minds are dedicate
To nothing temporal.

    Ang. Well; come to me
To-morrow.

    Isab. Heaven keep your honor safe!

    Ang. Amen.

LXXVI. — GOD IN NATURE.

FROM COWPER.

1. THERE lives and works
A soul in all things, and that soul is God;
The beauties of the wilderness are his,
That make so gay the solitary place
Where no eye sees them. And the fairer forms
That cultivation glories in are his.

    2. He sets the *bright procession* on its way,
And marshals all the order of the year;
He marks the bounds that winter may not pass,
And blunts his pointed fury; in its case,
Russet and rude, folds up the tender germ,
Uninjur'd, with inimitable art:
And ere one flowery season fades and dies,
Designs the blooming wonders of the next.
The Lord of all, himself through all diffused,
Sustains, and is the life of all that lives.

    3. Nature is but a name for an effect,
Whose cause is God. Not a flower
But shows some touch, in freckle, streak, or stain,
Of His unrival'd pencil. He inspires
Their balmy odors, and imparts their hues,
And bathes their eyes in nectar, and includes
In grains as countless as the sea-side sands,
The forms with which they sprinkle all the earth.

    4. Happy who walks with Him! whom, what he finds
Of flavor, or of scent, in fruit, or flower,
Of what he views of beautiful or grand

    11. S. R.—19

In Nature, from the broad, majestic oak,
To the green blade that twinkles in the sun,
Prompts with the remembrance of a present God.

LXXVII. — ALEXANDER AND THE ROBBER.

FROM AIKEN.

Alexander. What! art thou the Thracian robber, of whose exploits I have heard so much?

Robber. I am a Thracian, and a soldier.

Alexander. A soldier? a thief, a plunderer, an assassin! the pest of the country! I could honor thy courage; but I must detest and punish thy crimes.

Robber. What have I done of which you can complain?

Alexander. Hast thou not set at defiance my authority; violated the public peace, and passed thy life in injuring the persons and properties of thy fellow-subjects?

Robber. Alexander, I am your captive; I must hear what you please to say, and endure what you please to inflict. But my soul is unconquered; and if I reply at all to your reproaches, I will reply like a free man.

Alexander. Speak freely. Far be it from me to take the advantage of my power, to silence those with whom I deign to converse!

Robber. I must, then, answer your question by another. How have you passed your life?

Alexander. Like a hero. Ask Fame, and she will tell you. Among the brave, I have been the bravest; among sovereigns, the noblest; among conquerors, the mightiest.

Robber. And does not Fame speak of me, too? Was there ever a bolder captain of a more valiant band? Was there ever — but I scorn to boast. You yourself know that I have not been easily subdued.

Alexander. Still, what are you but a robber, a base, dishonest robber?

Robber. And what is a conqueror? Have not you, too, gone about the earth like an evil genius, blasting the fair

fruits of peace and industry; plundering, ravaging, killing without law, without justice, merely to gratify an insatiable lust for dominion? All that I have done to a single district, with a hundred followers, you have done to whole nations, with a hundred thousand. If I have stripped individuals, you have ruined kings and princes. If I have burned a few hamlets, you have desolated the most flourishing kingdoms and cities of the earth. What is then the difference, but that as you were born a king, and I a private man, you have been able to become a mightier robber than I?

Alexander. But if I have taken like a king, I have given like a king. If I have subverted empires, I have founded greater. I have cherished arts, commerce, and philosophy.

Robber. I, too, have freely given to the poor, what I took from the rich. I have established order and discipline among the most ferocious of mankind; and have stretched out my protecting arm over the oppressed. I know, indeed, little of the philosophy you talk of; but I believe neither you nor I shall ever atone to the world for the mischief we have done it.

Alexander. Leave me. Take off his chains and use him well. Are we, then, so much alike? Alexander like a robber? Let me reflect! ✕

LXXVIII. — SELECTIONS.

THE LIFE OF MAN.

1. WHEN the world was created, and all creatures assembled to have their life-time appointed, the ass first advanced, and asked how long he would have to live. "Thirty years," replied Nature; "will that be agreeable to thee?" "Alas!" answered the ass, "it is a long while! Remember what a wearisome existence mine will be; from morning until night I shall have to bear heavy burdens, dragging corn sacks to the mill, that others may eat bread

while I have no encouragement but blows and kicks. Give but a portion of that time, I pray." Nature was moved with compassion, and granted to him but eighteen years. The ass went away comforted, and the dog came forward.

2. "How long dost thou require to live?" asked Nature. "Thirty years was too long for the ass; but wilt thou be contented with them?" "Is it thy will that I should?" replied the dog. "Think how much I shall have to run about; my feet will not last for so long a time; and when I have lost my voice for barking, and my teeth for biting, what else shall I be fit for, but to lie in a corner, and growl?" Nature thought he was right, and gave him twelve years.

3. The ape then approached. "Thou wilt, doubtless, willingly live the thirty years," said Nature; "thou wilt not have to labor as the ass and the dog. Life will be pleasant to thee." "Ah, no!" cried he; "so it may seem to others, but it does not to me! Should puddings ever rain down, I should have no spoon! I shall play many tricks, and excite laughter by my grimaces, and then be rewarded with a sour apple! How often sorrow lies concealed behind a jest! I shall not be able to endure for thirty years!" Nature was gracious, and he received but ten.

4. At last came man, healthy and strong, and asked the measure of his days. "Will thirty years content thee?" asked Nature. "How short a time!" exclaimed man. "When I shall have built my house, and kindled a fire in my own hearth; when the trees I shall have planted are about to bloom and bear fruit; when life will seem most desirable, I shall die! Oh, Nature, grant me a longer period!" "Thou shalt have the eighteen years of the ass besides." "That is not yet sufficient," replied the man. "Take likewise the twelve years of the dog." "It is not yet sufficient," reiterated the man; "give me more!" "I give thee, then, the ten years of the ape; in vain wilt thou crave more!" Man departed dissatisfied.

5. Thus man lives seventy years. The first thirty of

his life are his human years, and pass swiftly by. He is then healthy and happy; he labors cheerfully, and rejoices in his existence. The eighteen years of the ass come next, and burden upon burden is heaped upon him; he carries the corn that is to feed others, and blows and kicks are the wages of his faithful service. The twelve years of the dog follow, and he loses his teeth, and lies in a corner, and growls. When these are gone, the ape's ten years form the conclusion. The man, weak and silly, becomes the sport of children.

REMEMBRANCE.

1. Ah! there it stands, the same old house!
   And there that ancient tree,
   Where I first trod in boyish pride
   And laugh'd in happy glee.
   But it is changed; the fence is gone
   Which girded it around;
   And here and there the fragments lie
   Scatter'd upon the ground.

2. I lov'd that house with boyish love,
   For it did shelter me,
   When I was but an infant, toss'd
   Upon my mother's knee;
   And oft I 've look'd, in youthful pride,
   Upon that hallow'd spot,
   And though I 've wander'd far from it,
   It never was forgot.

3. And now 'tis changed; the door unhinged,
   The shutters, too, are gone;
   The pretty green that coated them
   Is faded by the sun;
   The roof is old, and crumbling in,
   Fast yielding to decay;
   And those whom God had welcom'd there,
   Were call'd by him away.

while I have no encouragement but blows and kicks. Give but a portion of that time, I pray." Nature was moved with compassion, and granted to him but eighteen years. The ass went away comforted, and the dog came forward.

2. "How long dost thou require to live?" asked Nature. "Thirty years was too long for the ass; but wilt thou be contented with them?" "Is it thy will that I should?" replied the dog. "Think how much I shall have to run about; my feet will not last for so long a time; and when I have lost my voice for barking, and my teeth for biting, what else shall I be fit for, but to lie in a corner, and growl?" Nature thought he was right, and gave him twelve years.

3. The ape then approached. "Thou wilt, doubtless, willingly live the thirty years," said Nature; "thou wilt not have to labor as the ass and the dog. Life will be pleasant to thee." "Ah, no!" cried he; "so it may seem to others, but it does not to me! Should puddings ever rain down, I should have no spoon! I shall play many tricks, and excite laughter by my grimaces, and then be rewarded with a sour apple! How often sorrow lies concealed behind a jest! I shall not be able to endure for thirty years!" Nature was gracious, and he received but ten.

4. At last came man, healthy and strong, and asked the measure of his days. "Will thirty years content thee?" asked Nature. "How short a time!" exclaimed man. "When I shall have built my house, and kindled a fire in my own hearth; when the trees I shall have planted are about to bloom and bear fruit; when life will seem most desirable, I shall die! Oh, Nature, grant me a longer period!" "Thou shalt have the eighteen years of the ass besides." "That is not yet sufficient," replied the man. "Take likewise the twelve years of the dog." "It is not yet sufficient," reiterated the man; "give me more!" "I give thee, then, the ten years of the ape; in vain wilt thou crave more!" Man departed dissatisfied.

5. Thus man lives seventy years. The first thirty of

his life are his human years, and pass swiftly by. He is then healthy and happy; he labors cheerfully, and rejoices in his existence. The eighteen years of the ass come next, and burden upon burden is heaped upon him; he carries the corn that is to feed others, and blows and kicks are the wages of his faithful service. The twelve years of the dog follow, and he loses his teeth, and lies in a corner, and growls. When these are gone, the ape's ten years form the conclusion. The man, weak and silly, becomes the sport of children.

REMEMBRANCE.

1. Ah! there it stands, the same old house!
  And there that ancient tree,
 Where I first trod in boyish pride
  And laugh'd in happy glee.
 But it is changed; the fence is gone
  Which girded it around;
 And here and there the fragments lie
  Scatter'd upon the ground.

2. I lov'd that house with boyish love,
  For it did shelter me,
 When I was but an infant, toss'd
  Upon my mother's knee;
 And oft I 've look'd, in youthful pride,
  Upon that hallow'd spot,
 And though I 've wander'd far from it,
  It never was forgot.

3. And now 'tis changed; the door unhinged,
  The shutters, too, are gone;
 The pretty green that coated them
  Is faded by the sun;
 The roof is old, and crumbling in,
  Fast yielding to decay;
 And those whom God had welcom'd there,
  Were call'd by him away.

LXXIX. — THE PRISONER OF CHILLON.

FROM BYRON.

LORD BYRON, (GEORGE GORDON BYRON,) one of the most celebrated of modern English poets, lived from 1788 to 1824. With intellectual power and poetic talent of the highest order, his entire want of moral and religious principle will consign him to an oblivion, redeemed only by a few brilliant and untainted gems, like the following.

CHILLON is a castle on Lake Geneva. The speaker in this poem is one of three brothers who were imprisoned on account of their religious opinions.

1. THERE are seven pillars of Gothic mold
In Chillon's dungeons deep and old,
And in each pillar there is a ring,
    And in each ring there is a chain.
That iron is a cankering thing,
    For in these limbs its teeth remain,
With marks that will not wear away,
Till I have done with this new day,
Which now is painful to these eyes,
Which have not seen the sun so rise
For years—I can not count them o'er.
I lost their long and heavy score
When my last brother droop'd and died,
And I lay living by his side.

2. They chain'd us each to a column stone,
And we were three, yet each alone:
We could not move a single pace,
We could not see each other's face, ,
But with that pale and livid light
That made us strangers in our sight.
And thus together, yet apart,
Fetter'd in hand, but pined in heart,
'Twas still some solace, in the dearth
Of the pure elements of earth,
To hearken to each other's speech,
And each turn comforter to each,

With some new hope, or legend old,
Or song heroically bold;
But even these at length grew cold.

3. Our voices took a dreary tone,
An echo of the dungeon stone,
A grating sound, not full and free,
As they of yore were wont to be;
It might be fancy, but to me
They never sounded like our own.

4. I was the eldest of the three,
And to uphold and cheer the rest,
I ought to do, and did, my best;
And each did well in his degree.
The youngest, whom my father lov'd,
Because our mother's brow was given
To him, with eyes as blue as heaven,
For him my soul was sorely moved:
And truly might it be distress'd
To see such bird in such a nest;
For he was beautiful as day,
And in his natural spirit gay,
With tears for naught but others' ills;
And then they flowed like mountain rills,
Unless he could assuage the woe
Which he abhorr'd to view below.

5. The other was as pure of mind,
But form'd to combat with his kind;
Strong in his frame, and of a mood
Which 'gainst the world in war had stood,
And perish'd in the foremost rank
With joy; but not in chains to pine;
His spirit wither'd with their clank;
I saw it silently decline,
And so perchance in sooth did mine;
But yet I forced it on to cheer
Those relics of a home so dear.

He was a hunter of the hills,
  Had follow'd there the deer and wolf;
  To him this dungeon was a gulf,
And fetter'd feet the worst of ills.

     *   *   *   *

  6. I said my nearer brother pined,
I said his mighty heart declined,
He loath'd and put away his food;
It was not that 'twas coarse and rude,
For we were used to hunters' fare,
And for the like had little care;
The milk drawn from the mountain goat
Was changed for water from the moat;
Our bread was such as captives' tears
Have moisten'd many a thousand years,
Since man first pent his fellow-men
Like brutes within an iron den.

  7. But what were these to us or him?
These wasted not his heart or limb;
My brother's soul was of that mold
Which in a palace had grown cold,
Had his free breathing been denied
The range of the steep mountain's side:
But why delay the truth? He died.
I saw, and could not hold his head,
Nor reach his dying hand, nor dead;
Though hard I strove, but strove in vain,
To rend and gnash my bonds in twain.
He died, and they unlock'd his chain,
And scoop'd for him a shallow grave
Even from the cold earth of our cave.

  8. I begg'd them, as a boon, to lay
His corse in dust whereon the day
Might shine: it was a foolish thought;
But then within my brain it wrought,
That even in death his freeborn breast
In such a dungeon could not rest.

I might have spared my idle prayer;
They coldly laugh'd, and laid him there,
The flat and turfless earth above
The being we so much did love;
His empty chain above it leant,
Such murder's fitting monument!

9. But he, the favorite and the flower,
Most cherish'd since his natal hour,
His mother's image in fair face,
The infant love of all his race,
His martyr'd father's dearest thought,
My latest care, for whom I sought
To hoard my life, that his might be
Less wretched now, and one day free;
He, too, who yet had held untired,
A spirit natural or inspired,
He too, was struck, and day by day
Was wither'd on the stalk away.

10. O God! it is a fearful thing
To see the human soul take wing
In any shape, in any mood:
I 've seen it rushing forth in blood,
I 've seen it on the breaking ocean
Strive with a swoln, convulsive motion,
I 've seen the sick and ghastly bed
Of sin delirious with its dread;
But these were horrors; this was woe
Unmix'd with such, but sure and slow.

11. He faded, and so calm and meek,
So softly worn, so sweetly weak,
So tearless, yet so tender, kind,
And griev'd for those he left behind;
With, all the while, a cheek whose bloom
Was as a mockery of the tomb,
Whose tints as gently sunk away
As a departing rainbow's ray;

toward the abode of the bittern, and to those especially who dwell where all around is art, and where the tremulous motion of the ever-trundling wheel of society dizzies the understanding, till one fancies that the stable laws of nature turn round in concert with the minor revolutions of our pursuits, it is far from being unprofitable. Man, so circumstanced, is apt to descend as low, or even lower, than those unclad men of the woods whom he despises; and there is no better way of enabling him to win back his birthright as a rational and reflecting being, than the taste of the cup of wild nature, even though its acerbity should make him writhe at the time. That is the genuine medicine of the mind, far better than all the opiates of the library; and the bounding pulse of glowing and glorious thought returns all the sooner for its being a little drastic.

6. In the tuft of tall herbage, not very far from the firm ground, but yet placed so near, or rather *in* the water, that you can not very easily reach it, the bittern may be close all the time, wakeful, noting you well, and holding herself prepared to "keep her castle;" but you can not rouse her by shouting, or even by throwing stones, the last of which is treason against nature, in a place solely under nature's dominion. Wait till the sun is down, and the last glimmer of the twilight has got westward of the zenith, and then return to the place where you expect the bird.

7. The reeds begin to rustle with the little winds, in which the day settles accounts with the night; but there is a shorter and sharper rustle, accompanied by the brush of rather a powerful wing. You look around the dim horizon, but there is no bird; another rustle of the wing, and another, still weaker and weaker, but not a moving thing between you and the sky around. You feel rather disappointed; foolish, if you are daring; fearful, if you are timid. Anon, a burst of savage and uncouth laughter breaks over you, piercingly, or rather gratingly loud, and so unwonted and odd, that it sounds as if the voices of a bull and a horse were combined, the former breaking down his bellow to suit the neigh of the latter, in mocking you from the sky.

8. That is the love-song of the bittern, with which he serenades his mate; and uncouth and hard as it sounds to you, that mate hears it with far more pleasure than she would the sweetest chorus of the grove; and when the surprise with which you are first taken is over, you begin to discover that there is a sort of modulation in the singular sound. As the bird utters it, he wheels in a spiral, expanding his voice as the loops widen, and sinking it as they close; and though you can just dimly discover him between you and the zenith, it is worth while to lie down on your back, and watch the style of his flight, which is as fine as it is peculiar. The sound comes better out, too, when you are in that position; and there is an echo, and, as you would readily imagine, a shaking of the ground; not that, according to the tale of the poets, the bird thrusts his bill into the marsh, and shakes it with his booming, though (familiar as I once was with the sound, and all the observable habits of the bitterns) some kindly critic labored to convert me from that heresy.

9. The length of the bird is about twenty-eight inches, and the extent of the wings about forty-four. It is heavier, in proportion to the extent of the wings, than the heron; and, though it flies more steadily than that bird, it is not very powerful in forward flight, or in gaining hight without wheeling; but when once it is up, it can keep the sky with considerable ease; and while it does so, it is safe from the buzzards and harriers, which are the chief birds of prey in its locality.

10. Though the bittern is an unoffending and retiring bird, easily hawked when on a low flight, and not very difficult to shoot when out of its cover, as it flies short and soon alights, it is both a vigilant and powerful bird on the ground. It stands high, so that, without being seen, it sees all around it, and is not easily surprised. Its bill, too, is so strong, yet so sharp, and the thrust of it is given with so much rapidity and effect, that other animals are not very fond of going in upon it; and even when wounded, it makes a very determined resistance, throwing itself upon its back, using both its bill and its claws.

LXXXI. — TROUT FISHING.

FROM THOMSON.

1. Now when the first foul torrent of the brooks,
Swell'd with the vernal rains, is ebb'd away,
And, whitening, down their mossy-tinctur'd stream
Descends the billowy foam : now is the time,
While yet the dark-brown water aids the guile,
To tempt the trout.   The well-dissembled fly,
The rod fine-tapering with elastic spring,
Snatch'd from the hoary steed the floating line,
And all thy slender watery stores prepare.

2. But let not on thy hook the tortur'd worm
Convulsive twist in agonizing folds;
Which, by rapacious hunger swallow'd deep,
Gives, as you tear it from the bleeding breast
Of the weak, helpless, uncomplaining wretch,
Harsh pain, and horror to the tender hand.

3. When with his lively ray the potent sun
Has pierced the streams, and rous'd the finny race,
Then, issuing cheerful, to thy sport repair;
Chief should the western breezes curling play,
And light o'er ether bear the shadowy clouds.
High to their fount, this day, amid the hills,
And woodlands warbling round, trace up the brooks;
The next, pursue their rocky-channel'd maze
Down to the river, in whose ample wave
Their little naiads love to sport at large.

4. Just in the dubious point, where with the pool
Is mix'd the trembling stream, or where it boils
Around the stone, or from the hollow'd bank
Reverted plays in undulating flow,
There throw, nice judging, the delusive fly;
And, as you lead it round in artful curve,
With eye attentive mark the springing game.

Straight as above the surface of the flood
They wanton rise, or, urged by hunger, leap,
Then fix, with gentle twitch, the barb-ed hook;
Some lightly tossing to the grassy bank,
And to the shelving shore slow dragging some,
With various hand proportion'd to their force.

5. If yet too young, and easily deceiv'd,
A worthless prey scarce bends your pliant rod,
Him, piteous of his youth and the short space
He has enjoy'd the vital light of heaven,
Soft disengage, and back into the stream
The speckled captive throw. But should you lure
From his dark haunt, beneath the tangled roots
Of pendent trees, the monarch of the brook,
Behooves you then to ply your finest art.
Long time he, following cautious, scans the fly;
And oft attempts to seize it, but as oft
The dimpled water speaks his jealous fear.

6. At last, while haply o'er the shaded sun
Passes a cloud, he desperate takes the death,
With sullen plunge. At once he darts along,
Deep struck, and runs out all the lengthen'd line:
Then seeks the furthest ooze, the sheltering weed,
The cavern'd bank, his old secure abode;
And flies aloft, and flounces round the pool,
Indignant of the guile.

7. With yielding hand
That feels him still, yet to his furious course ·
Gives way, you, now retiring, following now
Across the stream, exhaust his idle rage:
Till, floating broad upon his breathless side,
And to his fate abandon'd, to the shore
You gayly drag your unresisting prize.

LXXXII. — THE SPIDER.

FROM GOLDSMITH.

OLIVER GOLDSMITH, who lived from 1731 to 1774, was a celebrated poet. Though born and educated in Ireland, he spent most of his life in London, writing for his daily bread. "The Traveler," "The Deserted Village," "The Vicar of Wakefield," and his "Animated Nature," are among his principal works.

1. ANIMALS in general are sagacious in proportion as they cultivate society. The elephant and the beaver show the greatest signs of this, when united; but when man intrudes into their communities, they lose all their spirit of industry, and testify but a very small share of that sagacity for which in a social state they are so remarkable.

2. Among insects, the labors of the bee and the ant have employed the attention and admiration of the naturalist; but their whole sagacity is lost upon separation, and a single bee or ant seems destitute of every degree of industry, is the most stupid insect imaginable, languishes for a time in solitude, and soon dies.

3 Of all the solitary insects I have ever remarked, the spider is the most sagacious, and its actions, to me, who have attentively considered them, seem almost to exceed belief. The insect is formed by nature for a state of war not only upon other insects, but upon its own kind. For this state, nature seems perfectly well to have formed it. Its head and breast are covered with a strong natural coat of mail, which is impenetrable to the attempts of every other insect, and its abdomen is enveloped in a soft pliant skin, which eludes the sting even of a wasp. Its legs are terminated by strong claws, not unlike those of a lobster; and their vast length, like spears, serves to keep every assailant at a distance.

4. Not worse furnished for observation than for attack or defense, it has several eyes, large, transparent, and covered with a horny substance, which, however, does not impede its vision. Besides this, it is furnished with a

forceps above the mouth, which serves to kill or secure the prey already caught in its claws or its net.

5. Such are the implements of war with which the body is immediately furnished; but its net to entangle the enemy seems what it chiefly trusts to, and what it takes most pains to render as complete as possible. Nature has furnished the body of this little creature with a glutinous liquid, which it spins into thread coarser or finer, as it chooses to contract or dilate the opening through which it comes. In order to fix its threads when it begins to weave, it emits a small drop of its liquid against the wall, which hardening by degrees, serves to hold the thread very firmly. Then receding from the first point, the thread lengthens; and when the spider has come to the place where the other end of the thread should be fixed, gathering up with its claws the thread, which would otherwise be too slack, it is stretched tightly, and fixed in the same manner to the wall as before.

6. In this manner it spins and fixes several threads parallel to each other, which, so to speak, serve as the warp to the intended web. To form the woof, it spins in the same manner its thread, transversely fixing one end to the first thread that was spun, and which is always the strongest of the whole web, and the other to the wall. All these threads being newly spun, are glutinous, and therefore stick to each other, wherever they happen to touch; and in those parts of the web most exposed to be torn, our natural artist strengthens them, by doubling the threads sometimes six-fold.

7. Thus far, naturalists have gone into the description of this animal: what follows is the result of my own observation upon that species of the insect called the house spider. I perceived, about four years ago, a large spider in one corner of my room, making its web, and though the maid frequently leveled her fatal broom against the labors of the little animal, I had the good fortune then to prevent its destruction, and, I may say, it more than paid me by the entertainment it afforded.

8. In three days, the web was with incredible diligence

completed; nor could I avoid thinking that the insect seemed to exult in its new abode. It frequently traversed it round, and examined the strength of every part of it. The first enemy, however, it had to encounter, was another and a much larger spider, which, having no web of its own, and having probably exhausted all its stock in former labors of this kind, came to invade the property of its neighbor. Soon, then, a terrible encounter ensued, in which the invader seemed to have the victory, and the laborious spider was obliged to take refuge in its hole. Upon this, I perceived the victor using every art to draw the enemy from his stronghold. He seemed to go off, but quickly returned, and when he found all arts vain, began to demolish the new web without mercy. This brought on a new battle, and, contrary to my expectations, the laborious spider became conqueror, and fairly killed his antagonist.

9. Now then, in peaceful possession of what was justly its own, it waited three days with the utmost impatience, repairing the breaches of its web, and taking no sustenance, that I could perceive. At last, however, a large blue fly fell into the snare, and struggled hard to get loose. The spider gave it leave to entangle itself as much as possible, but it seemed to be too strong for the cobweb. I must own I was greatly surprised when I saw the spider immediately sally out, and in less than a minute weave a new net around its captive, by which the motion of its wings was stopped; and when it was fairly hampered in this manner, it was seized and dragged into the hole.

10. In this manner it lived, in a precarious state, and nature seemed to have fitted it for such a life; for upon a single fly it subsisted for more than a week. I once put a wasp into the nest, but when the spider came out in order to seize it, as usual, upon perceiving what kind of an enemy it had to deal with, it instantly broke all the bands that held it fast, and contributed all that lay in its power to disengage so formidable an antagonist. When the wasp was at liberty, I expected the spider would set about repairing the breaches that were made in its net; but those,

it seems, were irreparable, wherefore the cobweb was now entirely forsaken, and a new one begun, which was completed in the usual time.

11. I had now a mind to see how many cobwebs a single spider could furnish; wherefore I destroyed this, and the insect set about another. When I destroyed the other also, its whole stock seemed entirely exhausted, and it could spin no more. The arts it made use of to support itself, now deprived of its principal means of subsistence, were indeed surprising. I have seen it roll up its legs like a ball, and lie motionless for hours together, but cautiously watching all the time; when a fly happened to approach sufficiently near, it would dart out all at once, and often seize its prey.

12. Of this life, however, it soon began to grow weary, and resolved to invade the possession of some other spider, since it could not make a web of its own. It made an attack upon a neighboring fortification with great vigor, and at first was as vigorously repulsed. Not daunted, however, with one defeat, it continued to lay siege to another's webb for three days, and, at length, having killed the defendant, actually took possession. When smaller flies happen to fall into the snare, the spider does not sally out at once, but very patiently waits until it is sure of them; for upon his immediately approaching, the terror of his appearance might give the captive strength sufficient to get loose. Its manner is, to wait patiently, till, by ineffectual and impotent struggles, the captive has wasted all its strength, and then it becomes a certain and easy conquest.

13. The insect I am now describing lived three years. Every year it changed its skin, and got a new set of legs. I have sometimes plucked off a leg, which grew again in two or three days. At first, it dreaded my approach to its web; but, at last, it became so familiar as to take a fly out of my hand; and, upon my touching any part of the web, would immediately leave its hole, prepared either for defense or attack.

LXXXIII. — SELECTIONS FROM THE BIBLE.

1. The Lord is my shepherd;
I shall not want.
He maketh me to lie down in green pastures,
He leadeth me beside the still waters.

2. O give thanks unto the Lord, for he is good;
For his mercy endureth forever.
Sing unto him, sing psalms unto him;
Talk ye of all his wondrous works.

3. Oh that men would praise the Lord for his goodness,
And for his wonderful works to the children of men!
And let them sacrifice the sacrifices of thanksgiving,
And declare his works with rejoicing.

4. The works of the Lord are great,
Sought out of all them that have pleasure therein.
His work is honorable and glorious;
And his righteousness endureth forever.

5. Blessed is the man that feareth the Lord,
That delighteth greatly in his commandments:
His seed shall be mighty upon the earth:
The generation of the upright shall be blessed.

6. Blessed be the name of the Lord
From this time forth and for evermore.
From the rising of the sun unto the going down of the same,
The Lord's name is to be praised.

7. Return unto thy rest, O my soul!
For the Lord hath dealt bountifully with thee,
For thou hast delivered my soul from death,
Mine eyes from tears and my feet from falling.

8. I will pay my vows unto the Lord,
Now in the presence of all his people,
In the courts of the Lord's house,
In the midst of thee, O Jerusalem!   [of the ungodly,

9. Blessed is the man that walketh not in the counsel

Nor standeth in the way of sinners,
Nor sitteth in the seat of the scornful.

10. The Lord shall preserve thee from all evil:
He shall preserve thy soul.
The Lord shall preserve thy going out and thy coming in.
From this time forth and for evermore.

LXXXIV. — THE HERO OF HAARLEM.

1. At an early period in the history of Holland, a boy was born in Haarlem, a town remarkable for its variety of fortune in war, but, happily, still more so for its manufactures and inventions in peace. His father was a *sluicer*, that is, one whose employment it was to open and shut the sluices, or large oak gates, which, placed at certain regular distances, close the entrance of the canals, and secure Holland from the danger to which it seems exposed, of finding itself *under* water, rather than *above* it.

2. When water is wanted, the sluicer raises the sluices more or less, as required, as a cook turns the cock of a fountain, and closes it again carefully at night; otherwise, the water would flow into the canals, then overflow them, and inundate the whole country; so that even the little children in Holland are fully aware of the importance of a punctual discharge of· the sluicer's duties.

3. The boy was about eight years old when, one day, he asked permission to take some cakes to a poor blind man, who lived at the other side of the dyke. His father gave him leave, but charged him not to stay too late. The child promised, and set off on his little journey. The blind man thankfully partook of his young friend's cakes, and the boy, mindful of his father's orders, did not wait, as usual, to hear one of the old man's stories, but as soon as he had seen him eat one muffin, took leave of him to return home.

4. As he went along by the canals, then quite full, for it was in October, and the autumn rains had swelled the

waters, the boy now stopped to pull the little blue flowers which his mother loved so well, now, in childish gayety, hummed some merry song. The road gradually became more solitary, and soon neither the joyous shout of the villager, returning to his cottage-home, nor the rough voice of the carter, grumbling at his lazy horses, was any longer to be heard. The little fellow now perceived that the blue of the flowers in his hand was scarcely distinguishable from the green of the surrounding herbage, and he looked up in sore dismay.

5. The night was falling; not, however, a dark winter-night, but one of those beautiful, clear, moonlight nights, in which every object is perceptible, though not as distinctly as by day. The child thought of his father, of his injunction, and was preparing to quit the ravine in which he was almost buried, and to regain the beach, when suddenly a slight noise, like the trickling of water upon pebbles, attracted his attention. He was near one of the large sluices, and he now carefully examines it, and soon discovers a hole in the wood, through which the water was flowing.

6. With the instant perception which every child in Holland would have, the boy saw that the water must soon enlarge the hole through which it was now only dropping, and that utter and general ruin would be the consequence of the inundation of the country that must follow. To see, to throw away the flowers, to climb from stone to stone till he reached the hole, and to put his finger into it, was the work of a moment, and, to his delight, he finds that he has succeeded in stopping the flow of the water.

7. This was all very well for a little while, and the child thought only of the success of his device. But the night was closing in, and with the night came the cold. The little boy looked around in vain. No one came. He shouted, he called loudly; no one answered. He resolved to stay there all night; but, alas! the cold was becoming every moment more biting, and the poor finger fixed in the hole began to feel benumbed, and the numbness soon extended to the hand, and thence throughout the whole

arm. The pain became still greater, still harder to bear, but yet the boy moved not.

8. Tears rolled down his cheeks as he thought of his father, of his mother, of his little bed, where he might now be sleeping so soundly; but still the little fellow stirred not, for he knew that did he remove the small, slender finger which he had opposed to the escape of the water, not only would he himself be drowned, but his father, his brothers, his neighbors, nay, the whole village.

9. We know not what faltering of purpose, what momentary failures of courage there might have been during that long and terrible night; but certain it is, that, at daybreak, he was found in the same painful position by a clergyman returning from attendance on a death-bed, who, as he advanced, thought he heard groans, and bending over the dyke, discovered a child seated on a stone, writhing from pain, and with pale face and tearful eyes.

10. "In the name of wonder, boy," he exclaimed, "what are you doing there?" "I am hindering the water from running out," was the answer, in perfect simplicity, of the child, who, during that whole night had been evincing such heroic fortitude and undaunted courage.

11. The Muse of History, too often blind to true glory, has handed down to posterity many a warrior, the destroyer of thousands of his fellow-men; she has left us in ignorance of the name of this real, little hero of Haarlem.

LXXXV.—THE CUP OF WATER.

THE following beautiful ballad illustrates the proverbial inviolability of promise in the estimation of many eastern nations.

1. MOSLEM; Mohammedan.

I.

Now the third and fatal conflict for the Persian throne was done,
And the Moslem's fiery valor had the crowning victory won.

II.

Harmosan, the last and boldest, the invader to defy,
Captive, overborne by numbers, they were bringing forth to die.

Then exclaim'd that noble captive, "Lo, I perish in my thirst;
Give me but one drink of water, and then let arrive the worst!"

III.

In his hand he took the goblet, but awhile the draught forbore,
Seeming doubtfully the purpose of the foeman to explore.
Well might then have paus'd the bravest, for around him angry
foes
With a hedge of naked weapons did that lonely man enclose.

IV.

" But what fear'st thou?" cried the monarch; "is it, friend, a
secret blow?
Fear it not! our gallant Moslems no such treacherous dealing
know;
Thou may'st quench thy thirst securely, for thou shalt not die,
before
Thou hast drank that cup of water; this reprieve is thine, no
more!"

V.

Harmosan quick dash'd the goblet down to earth with ready hand,
And the liquid sank forever, lost amid the burning sand.
" Thou hast said that mine my life is, till the water of that cup
I have drain'd: then bid thy servants that spill'd water gather
up!"

VI.

For a moment stood the monarch, as by doubtful passions stirr'd;
Then exclaim'd, "Forever sacred must remain a monarch's word.
Bring another cup, and straightway to the noble Persian give:
Drink, I said before, and perish: now I bid thee, drink and live!"

LXXXVI. — THE BATTLE OF IVRY.

FROM MACAULAY.

IVRY; *pronounced,* E-vree.   2. COLIGNI; *pronounced,* Co-leen-yee.
3. ORIFLAMME; *pronounced,* or-ree-flam, the French standard.
5. D'AUMALE; *pronounced,* Do-mal.
5. ST. BARTHOLOMEW; on the eve of St. Bartholomew's day, in
1572, an indiscriminate massacre of Huguenots took place, by order
of Charles IX., King of France.

Henry the Fourth, on his accession to the French throne, was op-
posed by a large part of his subjects, under the Duke of Mayenne,
with the assistance of Spain and Savoy, and, from the union of these
several nations, their army was called the "army of the league." In
March, 1590, he gained a decisive victory over that party, at Ivry, a
small town in France. Before the battle, he said to his troops, "My
children, if you lose sight of your colors, rally to my white plume;
you will always find it in the path to honor and glory." His con-
duct was answerable to his promise. Nothing could resist his im-
petuous valor, and the leaguers underwent a total and bloody defeat.
In the midst of the rout, Henry followed, crying, "Save the French!"
and his clemency added a number of the enemy to his own army.

I.

Now glory to the Lord of Hosts, from whom all glories are!
And glory to our sovereign liege, King Henry of Navarre.
Now let there be the merry sound of music and the dance,
Through thy corn-fields green, and sunny vines, O pleasant land
    of France!
And thou, Rochelle, our own Rochelle, proud city of the waters,
Again let rapture light the eye of all thy mourning daughters.
As thou wert constant in our ills, be joyous in our joy,
For cold, and stiff, and still are they who would thy walls annoy;
Hurrah! hurrah! a single field hath turu'd the chance of war,
Hurrah! hurrah! for Ivry, and King Henry of Navarre!

II.

O! how our hearts were beating, when, at the dawn of day,
We saw the army of the league drawn out in long array;
With all its priest-led citizens, and all its rebel peers,
And Appenzel's stout infantry, and Egmont's Flemish spears
There, rode the brood of false Lorraine, the curses of our land!
And dark Mayenne was in the midst, a truncheon in his hand!

And, as we look'd on them, we thought of Seine's empurpled
    flood,
And good Coligni's hoary hair, all dabbled with his blood;
And we cried unto the living God who rules the fate of war;
To fight for his own holy name, and Henry of Navarre.

III.

The king is come to marshal us, in all his armor drest,
And he has bound a snow-white plume upon his gallant crest.
He look'd upon his people, and a tear was in his eye;
He look'd upon the traitors, and his glance was stern and high.
Right graciously he smiled on us, as rolled from wing to wing,
Down all our line, a deafening shout, "God save our lord, the
    king!"
"And if my standard-bearer fall, and fall full well he may,
For never saw I promise yet of such a bloody fray,
Press where you see my white plume shine, amid the ranks of
    war,
And be your oriflamme to-day, the helmet of Navarre."

IV.

Hurrah! the foes are moving! Hark to the mingled din
Of fife, and steed, and trump, and drum, and roaring culverin!
The fiery duke is pricking fast across St. Andre's plain,
With all the hireling chivalry of Guelders and Almayne.
Now, by the lips of those ye love, fair gentlemen of France,
Charge for the golden lilies, now upon them with the lance!
A thousand spurs are striking deep, a thousand spears in rest,
A thousand knights are pressing close behind the snow-white
    crest;
And in they burst, and on they rush'd, while, like a guiding star,
Amid the thickest carnage, blazed the helmet of Navarre.

V.

Now, God be prais'd! the day is ours! Mayenne hath turn'd his
    rein;
D'Aumale hath cried for quarter; the Flemish count is slain;
Their ranks are breaking like thin clouds before a Biscay gale;
The field is heap'd with bleeding steeds, and flags, and cloven
    mail.

And then we thought on vengeance, and all along our van,
"Remember Saint Bartholomew," was pass'd from man to man;
But out spake gentle Henry then, "No Frenchman is my foe;
Down, down with every foreigner; but let your brethren go."
Oh! was there ever such a knight, in friendship or in war,
As our sovereign lord, King Henry, the soldier of Navarre!

VI.

Ho! maidens of Vienna! Ho! matrons of Lucerne!
Weep, weep, and rend your hair for those who never shall return.
Ho! Philip, send, for charity, thy Mexican pistoles,
That Antwerp monks may sing a mass for thy poor spearmen's
    souls!
Ho! gallant nobles of the league, look that your arms be bright!
Ho! burghers of Saint Genevieve, keep watch and ward to-night!
For our God hath crush'd the tyrant, our God hath rais'd the slave,
And mock'd the counsel of the wise and the valor of the brave.
Then glory to His holy name, from whom all glories are;
And honor to our sovereign lord, King Henry of Navarre.

LXXXVII.—POMPEII.

2. IMPLUVIUM; a room with an opening above, through which
water fell into the cistern.
3. PERISTYLE; a room encompassed with columns.
4. ARABESQUE; an Arabian painting.

1. ONCE there stood a town in Italy, at the foot of Mount
Vesuvius, which was to Rome what Brighton or Hastings
is to London, a very fashionable watering-place, at which
Roman gentlemen and members of the senate built villas,
to which they were in the habit of retiring from the fa-
tigues of business or the broils of politics. The outsides
of all the houses were adorned with frescoes, and every shop
glittered with all the colors of the rainbow. At the end
of each street there was a charming fountain, and any one
who sat down beside it to cool himself, had a delightful
view of the Mediterranean, then as beautiful, as blue, and
sunny, as it is now. On a fine day, crowds might be seen

lounging here, some sauntering up and down, in gala dresses of purple, while slaves passed to and fro, bearing on their heads splendid vases; others sat on marble benches, shaded from the sun by awnings, and having before them tables covered with wine, and fruit, and flowers. Every house in that town was a little palace, and every palace was like a temple, or one of our great public buildings.

2. Any one who thinks a mansion in London the acme of splendor, would have been astonished, had he lived in those days, to find how completely the abodes of those Roman lords outshone "the stately homes of England." On entering the former, the visitor passed through a vestibule decorated with rows of pillars, and then found himself in the *impluvium*, in which the household gods kept guard over the owner's treasure, which was placed in a safe, or strong box, secured with brass or iron bands. In this apartment guests were received with imposing ceremony, and the patron heard the complaints, supplications, and adulations of his great band of clients or dependants, who lived on his smiles and bounty, but chiefly on the latter.

3. Issuing thence, the visitor found himself in the *tablinum*, an apartment paved with mosaic and decorated with paintings, in which were kept the family papers and archives. It contained a dining room and a supper room, and a number of sleeping rooms hung with the softest of Syrian cloths, a cabinet filled with rare jewels and antiquities, and sometimes a fine collection of paintings; and last of all, a pillared peristyle, opening out upon the garden, in which the finest fruit hung temptingly in the rich light of a golden sky; and fountains, which flung their waters aloft in every imaginable form and device, cooled the air and discoursed sweet music to the ear; while from behind every shrub there peeped out a statue, or the bust of some great man, carved from the purest white marble, and placed in charming contrast with bouquets of rare flowers springing from stone vases. On the gate there was always the image of a dog, and underneath it the inscription, "Beware the dog."

4. The frescoes on the walls represented scenes in the

Greek legends, such as "The Seizure of Europa," "The Battle of the Amazons," etc., many of which are still to be seen in the museum at Naples. The pillars in this peristyle of which we have just spoken, were encircled with garlands of flowers, which were renewed every morning. The tables of citron wood were inlaid with silver arabesques; the couches were of bronze, gilt and jeweled, and were furnished with thick cushions and tapestry, embroidered with marvelous skill. When the master gave a dinner party, the guests reclined upon these cushions, washed their hands in silver basins, and dried them with napkins fringed with purple; and having made a libation on the altar of Bacchus, ate oysters brought from the shores of Britain, kids which were carved to the sound of music, and fruits served up on ice in the hottest days of summer; and while the cup-bearers filled their golden cups with the rarest and most delicate wine in all the world, other attendants crowned them with flowers wet with the dew, and dancers executed the most graceful movements, and singers accompanied by the lyre, poured forth an ode of Horace or of Anacreon.

5. After the banquet, a shower of scented water, scattered from invisible pipes, spread perfume over the apartment, and every thing around, even the oil, and the lamps, and the jets of the fountain, shed forth the most grateful odor; and suddenly, from the mosaic of the floor, tables of rich dainties, of which we have at the present day no idea, rose, as if by magic, to stimulate the palled appetites of the revelers into fresh activity. When these had disappeared, other tables succeeded them, upon which senators, and consuls, and proconsuls, gambled away provinces and empires by the throw of dice; and last of all, the tapestry was suddenly raised, and young girls, lightly attired, wreathed with flowers, and bearing lyres in their hands, issued forth, and charmed sight and hearing by the graceful mazes of the dance.

6. One day, when such festivities as these were in full activity, Vesuvius sent up a tall and very black column of smoke, something like a pine-tree; and suddenly, in broad

noonday, darkness black as pitch came over the scene. There was a frightful din of cries, groans, and imprecations, mingled confusedly together. The brother lost his sister, the husband his wife, the mother her child; for the darkness became so dense that nothing could be seen but the flashes which every now and then darted forth from the summit of the neighboring mountain. The earth trembled, the houses shook and began to fall, and the sea rolled back from the land as if terrified; the air became thick with dust; and then, amid tremendous and awful noise, a shower of stones, scoriæ, and pumice, fell upon the town and blotted it out forever.

7. The inhabitants died just as the catastrophe found them; guests in their banqueting halls, brides in their chambers, soldiers at their post, prisoners in their dungeons, thieves in their theft, maidens at the mirror, slaves at the fountain, traders in their shops, students at their books. Some people attempted flight, guided by some blind people, who had walked so long in darkness that no thicker shadows could ever come upon them; but of these many were struck down on the way. When, a few days afterward, people came from the surrounding country to the place, they found naught but a black, level, smoking plain, sloping to the sea, and covered thickly with ashes. Down, down, beneath, thousands and thousands were sleeping the sleep that knows no waking, with all their little pomps, and vanities, and frivolities, and pleasures, and luxuries, buried with them.

8. This took place on the 23d of August, A. D. 79, and the name of the town thus suddenly overwhelmed with ruins was Pompeii. Sixteen hundred and seventeen years afterward, curious persons began to dig and excavate on the spot, and lo, they found the city pretty much as it was when overwhelmed. The houses were standing, the paintings were fresh, and the skeletons stood in the very positions and the very places in which death had overtaken their owners so long ago.

9. The marks left by the cups of the tipplers still remained on the counters; the prisoners still wore their

fetters, the belles their chains and bracelets; the miser held his hand on his hoarded coin, and the priests were lurking in the hollow images of their gods, from which they uttered responses and deceived the worshipers. There were the altars, with the blood dry and crusted upon them, the stables in which the victims of the sacrifice were kept, and the hall of mysteries, in which were symbolical paintings. The researches are still going on, new wonders are every day coming to light, and we soon shall have almost as perfect an idea of a Roman town in the first century of the Christian era, as if we had walked the streets and gossiped with the idle loungers at the fountains.

LXXXVIII. — THE DESERTED VILLAGE.

FROM GOLDSMITH.

1. SWEET was the sound, when oft, at evening's close,
Up yonder hill the village murmur rose;
There, as I pass'd with careless steps and slow,
The mingling notes came soften'd from below:
The swain responsive as the milkmaid sung;
The sober herd that lowed to meet their young;
The noisy geese that gabbled o'er the pool;
The playful children just let loose from school;
The watch-dog's voice, that bay'd the whispering wind;
And the loud laugh that spoke the vacant mind;
These all in sweet confusion sought the shade,
And fill'd each pause the nightingale had made.

2. But now the sounds of population fail;
No cheerful murmurs fluctuate in the gale,
No busy steps the grass-grown footway tread,
But all the bloomy flush of life is fled,
All but yon widow'd, solitary thing,
That feebly bends beside the plashy spring;
She, wretched matron, forced in age for bread
To strip the brook with mantling cresses spread,

To pick her wintry fagot from the thorn,
To seek her nightly shed, and weep till morn;
She only left of all the harmless train,
The sad historian of the pensive plain.

3. Near yonder copse, where once the garden smiled,
And still where many a garden flower grows wild,
There, where a few torn shrubs the place disclose,
The village preacher's modest mansion rose.
A man he was to all the country dear,
And passing rich with forty pounds a year.
Remote from towns he ran his godly race,
Nor e'er had changed, nor wish'd to change, his place;
Unskillful he to fawn, or seek for power,
By doctrines fashion'd to the varying hour;
Far other aims his heart had learn'd to prize,
More bent to raise the wretched than to rise.

4. His house was known to all the vagrant train;
He chid their wanderings, but reliev'd their pain;
The long-remember'd beggar was his guest,
Whose beard descending swept his aged breast;
The ruin'd spendthrift, now no longer proud,
Claim'd kindred there, and had his claims allow'd;
The broken soldier, kindly bade to stay,
Sat by his fire, and talk'd the night away,
Wept o'er his wounds, or, tales of sorrow done,
Shoulder'd his crutch, and showed how fields were won.
Pleas'd with his guests, the good man learn'd to glow,
And quite forgot their vices in their woe.
Careless their merits or their faults to scan,
His pity gave, ere charity began.

5. Thus to relieve the wretched was his pride,
And e'en his failings leau'd to virtue's side;
But in his duty prompt at every call,
He watch'd and wept, he pray'd and felt for all;
And, as a bird each fond endearment tries
To tempt its new-fledg'd offspring to the skies,

He tried each art, reproved each dull delay,
Allured to brighter worlds, and led the way.

6. Beside the bed where parting life was laid,
And sorrow, guilt, and pain, by turns dismay'd,
The reverend champion stood. At his control
Despair and anguish fled the struggling soul;
Comfort came down the trembling wretch to raise.
And his last faltering accents whisper'd praise.

7. At church, with meek and unaffected grace.
His looks adorn'd the venerable place;
Truth from his lips prevail'd with double sway,
And fools, who came to scoff, remain'd to pray.
The service past, around the pious man,
With steady zeal, each honest rustic ran;
E'en children follow'd with endearing wile,
And pluck'd his gown, to share the good man's smile.

8. His ready smile a parent's warmth express'd;
Their welfare pleas'd him, and their cares distress'd;
To them his heart, his love, his griefs were given,
But all his serious thoughts had rest in heaven.
As some tall cliff that lifts its awful form,
Swells from the vale, and midway leaves the storm,
Though round its breast the rolling clouds are spread,
Eternal sunshine settles on its head.

LXXXIX. — THE BELLS.

FROM POE.

1. RUNIC; Gothic. TINTINABULATION; sound of a bell.
5. PÆAN; joyous singing.

1. HEAR the sledges with the bells,
        Silver bells!
What a world of merriment their melody foretells!
    How they tinkle, tinkle, tinkle,
        In the icy air of night!

While the stars that oversprinkle
All the heavens, seem to twinkle
   With a crystalline delight;
Keeping time, time, time,
In a sort of Runic rhyme,
To the tintinabulation that so musically wells
   From the bells, bells, bells, bells,
      Bells, bells, bells;
From the jingling and the tinkling of the bells.

   2. Hear the mellow *wedding* bells,
      Golden bells!
What a world of happiness their harmony fortells!
   Through the balmy air of night
   How they ring out their delight!
    From the molten golden notes,
      And all in tune,
   What a liquid ditty floats
To the turtle-dove that listens, while she gloats
      On the moon!
   O, from out the sounding cells,
What a gush of euphony voluminously wells!
      How it swells!
      How it dwells
   On the Future! how it tells
   Of the rapture that impels,
   To the swinging and the ringing
   Of the bells, bells, bells,
   Of the bells, bells, bells, bells,
      Bells, bells, bells;
To the rhyming and the chiming of the bells!

   3. Hear the loud *alarum* bells;
      Brazen bells!
What a tale of terror, now, their turbulency tells!
   In the startled ear of night
   How they scream out their affright!
   Too much horrified to speak,
   They can only shriek, shriek,

Out of tune,
In a clamorous appealing to the mercy of the fire,
In a mad expostulation with the deaf and frantic fire,
Leaping higher, higher, higher,
With a desperate desire,
And a resolute endeavor
Now, now to sit, or never,
By the side of the pale-faced moon !
O, the bells, bells, bells!
What a tale their terror tells
Of despair!
How they clang, and clash, and roar!
What a horror they outpour
On the bosom of the palpitating air!

4. Yet the ear, it fully knows,
By the twanging
And the clanging,
How the danger ebbs and flows;
Yet the ear distinctly tells,
In the jangling
And the wrangling,
How the danger sinks and swells,
By the sinking or the swelling in the anger of the bells;
Of the bells;
Of the bells, bells, bells, bells,
Bells, bells, bells;
In the clamor and the clangor of the bells!

5. Hear the *tolling* of the bells;
Iron bells!
What a world of solemn thought their monody compels!
In the silence of the night,
How we shiver with affright,
At the melancholy menace of their tone!
For every sound that floats
From the rust within their throats
Is a groan.

And the people, ah, the people!
They that dwell up in the steeple,
        All alone,
And who, tolling, tolling, tolling,
    In that muffled monotone,
Feel a glory in so rolling
    On the human heart a stone;
They are neither man nor woman;
They are neither brute nor human;
        They are Ghouls:
And their king it is who tolls;
And he rolls, rolls, rolls,
        Rolls
    A pæan from the bells!

6. And his merry bosom swells
    With the pæan of the bells!
And he dances, and he yells;
Keeping time, time, time,
In a sort of Runic rhyme,
    To the pæan of the bells;
        Of the bells:
Keeping time, time, time,
In a sort of Runic rhyme,
    To the throbbing of the bells;
Of the bells, bells, bells;
    To the sobbing of the bells;
Keeping time, time, time,
    As he knells, knells, knells,
In a happy Runic rhyme,
    To the rolling of the bells;
Of the bells, bells, bells;
    To the tolling of the bells;
Of the bells, bells, bells, bells,
        Bells, bells, bells;
To the moaning and the groaning of the bells!

XC. — THE HEAD-STONE.

FROM WILSON.

1. THE coffin was let down to the bottom of the grave, the planks were removed from the heaped-up brink, the first rattling clods had struck their knell, the quick shoveling was over, and the long, broad, skillfully cut pieces of turf were aptly joined together, and trimly laid by the beating spade, so that the newest mound in the church-yard was scarcely distinguishable from those that were grown over by the undisturbed grass and daisies of a luxuriant spring. The burial was soon over; and the party, with one consenting motion, having uncovered their heads, in decent reverence of the place and occasion, were beginning to separate, and about to leave the church-yard.

2. Here, some acquaintances, from distant parts of the parish, who had not had opportunity of addressing each other in the house, that had belonged to the deceased, nor in the course of the few hundred yards, that the little procession had to move over, from his bed to his grave, were shaking hands quietly but cheerfully, and inquiring after the welfare of each other's families. There, a small knot of neighbors were speaking, without exaggeration, of the respectable character which the deceased had borne, and mentioning to one another little incidents of his life, some of them so remote as to be known only to the gray-headed persons of the group; while a few yards further removed from the spot, were standing together parties, who discussed ordinary concerns, altogether unconnected with the funeral, such as the state of the markets, the promise of the season, or change of tenants; but still with a sobriety of manner and voice, that was insensibly produced by the influence of the simple ceremony now closed, by the quiet graves around, and the shadow of the spire and gray walls of the house of God.

3. Two men yet stood together at the head of the grave, with countenances of sincere, but unimpassioned grief. They were brothers, the only sons of him who had been

buried. And there was something in their situation, that naturally kept the eyes of many directed upon them, for a long time, and more intently than would have been the case, had there been nothing more observable about them than the common symptoms of a common sorrow. But these two brothers, who were now standing at the head of their father's grave, had for some years been totally estranged from each other, and the only words that had passed between them, during all that time, had been uttered within a few days past, during the necessary preparations for the old man's funeral.

4. No deep and deadly quarrel was between these brothers, and neither of them could distinctly tell the cause of this unnatural estrangement. Perhaps dim jealousies of their father's favor; selfish thoughts that will sometimes force themselves into poor men's hearts, respecting temporal expectations; unaccommodating manners on both sides; taunting words, that mean little when uttered, but which rankle and fester in remembrance; imagined opposition of interests, that, duly considered, would have been found one and the same; these, and many other causes, slight when single, but strong when rising up together in one baneful band, had gradually but fatally infected their hearts, till at last they, who in youth had been seldom separate, and truly attached, now met at market, and miserable to say, at church, with dark and averted faces, like different clansmen during a feud.

5. Surely if any thing could have softened their hearts toward each other, it must have been to stand silently, side by side, while the earth, stones, and clods, were falling down upon their father's coffin. And doubtless their hearts were so softened. But pride, though it can not prevent the holy affections of nature from being felt, may prevent them from being shown; and these two brothers stood there together, determined not to let each other know the mutual tenderness that, in spite of them, was gushing up in their hearts, and teaching them the unconfessed folly and wickedness of their causeless quarrel.

6. A head-stone had been prepared, and a person came

forward to plant it. The elder brother directed him how to place it, a plain stone with a sand-glass, skull, and cross-bones, chiseled not rudely, and a few words inscribed. The younger brother regarded the operation with a troubled eye, and said, loudly enough to be heard by several of the bystanders, "William, this was not kind in you; you should have told me of this. I loved my father as well as you could love him. You were the elder, and, it may be, the favorite son; but I had a right in nature to have joined you in ordering this head-stone, had I not?"

7. During these words, the stone was sinking into the earth, and many persons, who were on their way from the grave, returned. For awhile the elder brother said nothing, for he had a consciousness in his heart that he ought to have consulted his father's son, in designing this last becoming mark of affection and respect to his memory; so the stone was planted in silence, and now stood erect, decently and simply, among the other unostentatious memorials of the humble dead.

8. The inscription merely gave the name and age of the deceased, and told that the stone had been erected "by his affectionate sons." The sight of these words seemed to soften the displeasure of the angry man, and he said, somewhat more mildly, "Yes, we were his affectionate sons, and since my name is on the stone, I am satisfied, brother. We have not drawn together kindly of late years, and perhaps never may; but I acknowledge and respect your worth; and here, before our own friends, and before the friends of our father, with my foot above his head, I express my willingness to be on other and better terms with you, and if we can not command love in our hearts, let us, at least, brother, bar out all unkindness."

9. The minister, who had attended the funeral, and had something intrusted to him to say publicly before he left the church-yard, now came forward, and asked the elder brother, why he spake not regarding this matter. He saw that there was something of a cold and sullen pride rising up in his heart, for not easily may any man hope to dismiss from the chamber of his heart even the vilest guest,

if once cherished there. With a solemn, and almost severe air, he looked upon the relenting man, and then, changing his countenance into serenity, said gently,

> "Behold how good a thing it is,
> And how becoming well,
> Together such as brethren are,
> In unity to dwell."

The time, the place, and this beautiful expression of a natural sentiment, quite overcame a heart, in which many kind, if not warm affections, dwelt; and the man thus appealed to, bowed down his head and wept. "Give me your hand, brother;" and it was given, while a murmur of satisfaction arose from all present, and all hearts felt kindlier and more humanely toward each other.

10. As the brothers stood fervently, but composedly, grasping each other's hand, in the little hollow that lay between the grave of their mother, long since dead, and of their father, whose shroud was haply not yet still from the fall of dust to dust, the minister stood beside them with a pleasant countenance, and said, "I must fulfill the promise I made to your father on his death-bed. I must read to you a few words which his hands wrote at an hour when his tongue denied its office. I must not say that you did your duty to your old father; for did he not often beseech you, apart from one another, to be reconciled, for your own sakes as Christians, for his sake, and for the sake of the mother who bare you, and, Stephen, who died that you might be born? When the palsy struck him for the last time, you were both absent, nor was it your fault that you were not beside the old man when he died.

11. "As long as sense continued with him here, did he think of you two, and of you two alone. Tears were in his eyes; I saw them there, and on his cheek too, when no breath came from his lips. But of this no more. He died with this paper in his hand; and he made me know that I was to read it to you over his grave. I now obey him. 'My sons, if you will let my bones lie quiet in the grave, near the dust of your mother, depart not from my

burial till, in the name of God and Christ, you promise to love one another as you used to do. Dear boys, receive my blessing."

12. Some turned their heads away to hide the tears that needed not to be hidden, and when the brothers had released each other from a long and sobbing embrace, many went up to them, and, in a single word or two, expressed their joy at this perfect reconcilement. The brothers themselves walked away from the church-yard arm in arm with the minister to the manse. On the following Sabbath, they were seen sitting with their families in the same pew, and it was observed that they read together off the same Bible, when the minister gave out the text, and that they sang together, taking hold of the same psalm-book. The same psalm was sung (given out at their own request,) of which one verse had been repeated at their father's grave; a larger sum than usual was, on that Sabbath, found in the plate for the poor, for Love and Charity are sisters. And ever after, both during the peace and the troubles of this life, the hearts of the brothers were as one, and in nothing were they divided.

XCI.—THE DYING YEAR.

FROM LONGFELLOW.

12. KYRIE ELEYSON; Lord, have mercy.
12. CHRISTE ELEYSON; Christ, have mercy.

1. YES, the year is growing old,
   And his eye is pale and blear'd:
Death, with frosty hand and cold,
   Plucks the old man by the beard,
      Sorely, sorely!

2. The leaves are falling, falling,
   Solemnly and slow;
Caw! caw! the rooks are calling,
   It is a sound of woe,
      A sound of woe!

3. Through woods and mountain-passes
    The winds like anthems roll;
  They are chanting solemn masses,
    Singing; Pray for this poor soul!
        Pray! pray!

4. The hooded clouds, like friars,
    Tell their beads in drops of rain,
  And patter their doleful prayers;
    But their prayers are all in vain,
        All in vain!

5. There he stands, in the foul weather,
    The foolish, fond Old Year,
  Crown'd with wild flowers and with heather,
    Like weak, despi-sed Lear,
        A king! a king!

6. Then comes the summer-like day,
    Bids the old man rejoice!
  His joy! his last! O, the old man gray
    Loveth her ever soft voice,
        Gentle and low.

7. To the crimson woods he saith,
    And the voice gentle and low
  Of the soft air, like a daughter's breath,
    Pray, do not mock me so!
        Do not laugh at me!

8. And now, the sweet day is dead;
    Cold in his arms it lies,
  No stain from its breath is spread
    Over the glassy skies,
        No mist or stain!

9. Then, too, the *Old Year* dieth,
    And the forests utter a moan,

Like the voice of one who crieth
In the wilderness alone,
Vex not his ghost!

10. Then comes with an awful roar,
Gathering and sounding on,
The storm-wind from Labrador,
The wind Euroclydon,
The storm-wind!

11. Howl! howl! and from the forest
Sweep the red leaves away!
Would the sins that thou abhorrest,
O soul, could thus decay,
And be swept away!

12. For there shall come a mightier blast,
There shall be a darker day;
And the stars from heaven downcast,
Like red leaves be swept away!
Kyrie Eleyson!
Christe Eleyson!

XCII.—DIONYSIUS, PYTHIAS, AND DAMON.

FROM FENELON.

Dionysius. Amazing! What do I see? It is Pythias just arrived. It is indeed Pythias. I did not think it possible. He is come to die, and to redeem his friend.

Pythias. Yes, it is Pythias. I left the place of my confinement with no other views than to pay to heaven the vows I had made; to settle my family concerns according to the rules of justice; and to bid adieu to my children, that I might die tranquil and satisfied.

Dionysius. But why dost thou return? Hast thou no fear of death? Is it not the character of a madman, to seek it thus voluntarily?

Pythias. I return to suffer, though I have not deserved

death.   Every principle of honor and goodness forbids me to allow my friend to die for me.

Dionysius. Dost thou then love him better than thyself?

Pythias. No: I love him as myself. But I am persuaded that I ought to suffer death, rather than my friend; since it was Pythias whom thou hadst decreed to die. It were not just that Damon should suffer, to deliver me from death which was designed not for him, but for me only.

Dionysius. But thou supposest that it is as unjust to inflict death upon thee, as upon thy friend.

Pythias. Very true; we are both perfectly innocent; and it is equally unjust to make either of us suffer.

Dionysius. Why dost thou then assert, that it were injustice to put him to death, instead of thee?

Pythias. It is unjust in the same degree to inflict death either on Damon or on myself; but Pythias were highly culpable to let Damon suffer that death which the tyrant had prepared for Pythias only.

Dionysius. Dost thou then return hither, on the day appointed, with no other view than to save the life of a friend by losing thy own?

Pythias. I return in regard to thee, to suffer an act of injustice which it is common for tyrants to inflict; and, with respect to Damon, to perform my duty, by rescuing him from the danger he incurred by his generosity to me.

Dionysius. And now, Damon, let me address myself to thee. Didst thou not really fear that Pythias would never return; and that thou wouldst be put to death on his account?

Damon. I was too well assured that Pythias would punctually return; and that he would be more solicitous to keep his promise than to preserve his life. Would to heaven that his relations and friends had forcibly detained him! He would then have lived for the comfort and benefit of good men; and I should have the satisfaction of dying for him.

Dionysius. What, does life displease thee?

Damon. Yes; it displeases me when I see and feel the power of a tyrant.

Dyonisius. It is well! Thou shalt see him no more. I will order thee to be put to death immediately.

Pythias. Pardon the feelings of a man who sympathizes with his dying friend. But remember it was Pythias who was devoted by thee to destruction. I come to submit to it, that I may redeem my friend. Do not refuse me this consolation in my last hour.

Dionysius. I can not endure men who despise death, and set my power at defiance.

Damon. Thou canst not, then, endure virtue.

Dionysius. No; I can not endure that proud, disdainful virtue which contemns life, which dreads no punishment, and which is insensible to the charms of riches and pleasure.

Damon. Thou seest, however, that it is a virtue which is not insensible to the dictates of honor, justice, and friendship.

Dionysius. Guards, take Pythias to execution. We shall see whether Damon will continue to despise my authority.

Damon. Pythias, by returning to submit himself to thy pleasure, has merited his life, and deserved thy favor; but I have excited thy indignation, by resigning myself to thy power in order to save him; be satisfied, then, with this sacrifice, and put me to death.

Pythias. Hold, Dionysius! Remember it was Pythias alone who offended thee; Damon could not—

Dionysius. Alas! what do I see and hear? Where am I? How miserable; and how worthy to be so! I have hitherto known nothing of true virtue. I have spent my life in darkness and error. All my power and honors are insufficient to produce love. I can not boast of having acquired a single friend in the course of a reign of thirty years. And yet these two persons, in a private condition, love one another tenderly, unreservedly confide in each other, are mutually happy, and ready to die for each other's preservation.

Pythias. How couldst thou, who hast never loved any person, expect to have friends? If thou hadst loved and respected men, thou wouldst have secured their love and

respect.   Thou hast feared mankind, and they fear thee; they detest thee.

Dionysius. Damon, Pythias, condescend to admit me as a third friend, in a connection so perfect.   I give you your lives, and I will load you with riches.

Damon. We have no desire to be enriched by thee; and, in regard to thy friendship, we can not expect or enjoy it, till thou become good and just.   Without these qualities, thou canst be connected with none but trembling slaves and base flatterers.   To be loved and esteemed by men of free and generous minds, thou must be virtuous, affectionate, disinterested, beneficent; and know how to live in a sort of equality with those who share and deserve thy friendship.

XCIII.—HARVEY BIRCH AND CAPTAIN WHARTON.

FROM COOPER.

JAMES FENIMORE COOPER, an American author of distinction, was born in 1789. His works are remarkable for their delineation of Indian character and their description of naval scenes.

The following extract is from the "Spy," in which Harvey Birch is a spy in the confidence of Washington, and Captain Wharton is a prisoner whom Birch is attempting to rescue in the disguise of a negro, Cæsar, who has taken his place in the prison.

1. THE road which it was necessary for Harvey Birch, the pedler, and Captain Wharton to travel, in order to reach the shelter of the hills, lay, for half a mile, in full view from the door of the building that had so recently been the prison of the latter; running for the whole distance over the rich plain, that spreads to the very foot of the mountains, which here rise in a nearly perpendicular ascent from their bases; it then turned short to the right, and was obliged to follow the windings of nature, as it won its way into the bosom of the Highlands.

2. To preserve the supposed difference in their stations, Harvey rode a short distance ahead of his companion, and maintained the sober, dignified pace that was suited to his assumed character.   On their right, the British regiment

of foot lay in tents and the sentinels, who guarded their encampments, were to be seen moving, with measured tread, under the skirts of the hills themselves. The first impulse of Wharton was, certainly, to urge the beast he rode to his greatest speed at once, and, by a coup-de-main, not only to accomplish his escape, but relieve himself from the torturing suspense of his situation. But the forward movement that the youth made for this purpose was instantly checked by the pedler.

3. "Hold up!" he cried, dextrously reining his own horse across the path of the other; "would you ruin us both? Fall into the place of a black following his master. Did you not see their blooded chargers, all saddled and bridled, standing in the sun before the house? How long do you think that miserable Dutch horse you are on would hold his speed, if pursued by the British? Every foot that we can gain without giving the alarm, counts us a day in our lives. Ride steadily after me, and on no account look back. They are as subtle as foxes, ay, and as ravenous for blood as wolves."

4. Henry Wharton reluctantly restrained his impatience, and followed the direction of the pedler. His imagination, however, continually alarmed him with the fancied sounds of pursuit; though Birch, who occasionally looked back under the pretence of addressing his companion, assured him that all continued quiet and peaceful. "But," said Henry, "it will not be possible for Cæsar to remain long undiscovered: had we not better put our horses to the gallop? and, by the time they can reflect on the cause of our flight, we can reach the corner of the woods."

5. "Ah! you little know them, Captain Wharton," returned the pedler; "there is a sergeant at this moment looking after us, as if he thought all was not right; the keen-eyed fellow watches me like a tiger lying in wait for his leap; when I stood on the horse-block, he half suspected something was wrong; nay, check your beast; we must let the animals walk a little, for he is laying his hand on the pommel of his saddle; if he mounts now, we are gone. The foot soldiers could reach us with their

muskets." "What does he do?" asked Henry, reining his horse to a walk, but, at the same time, pressing his heels into the animal's sides, to be in readiness for a spring.

6. "He turns from his charger, and looks the other way. Now trot on gently; not so fast, not so fast; observe the sentinel in the field a little ahead of us; he eyes us keenly." "Never mind the footman," said Henry, impatiently; he can do nothing but shoot us; whereas these dragoons may make me a captive again. Surely, Harvey, there are horsemen moving down the road behind us. Do you see nothing particular?" "Humph!" ejaculated the pedler; "there is something particular, indeed, to be seen behind the thicket on your left; turn your head a little, and you may see and profit by it, too."

7. Henry eagerly seized his permission to look aside, and his blood curdled to the heart as he observed they were passing a gallows, that had unquestionably been erected for his own execution. He turned his face from the sight in undisguised horror. "There is a warning to be prudent in that bit of wood," said the pedler, in that sententious manner that he often adopted. "It is a terrific sight indeed!" cried Henry, for a moment vailing his face with his hands, as if to drive a vision from before him.

8. The pedler moved his body partly around, and spoke with energetic, but gloomy bitterness, "And yet, Captain Wharton, you see it when the setting sun shines full upon you; the air you breathe is clear, and fresh from the hills before you. Every step that you take leaves that hated gallows behind; and every dark hollow, and every shapeless rock in the mountains, offers you a hiding-place from the vengeance of your enemies. But I have seen the gibbet raised when no place of refuge offered. Twice have I been buried in dungeons, where, fettered and in chains, I have passed nights in torture, looking forward to the morning's dawn, that was to light me to a death of infamy. The sweat has started from limbs that seemed already drained of their moisture, and if I ventured to the hole, that admitted air through grates of iron, to look out upon the smiles of nature, which God has bestowed for the

meanest of his creatures, the gibbet has glared before my eyes, like an evil conscience, harrowing the soul of a dying man. Four times have I been in their power, besides this last; but, twice, twice did I think that my hour had come.

9. "It is hard to die at the best, Captain Wharton; but to spend your last moments alone and unpitied, to know that none near you so much as think of the fate that is to you the closing of all that is earthly; to think that in a few hours you are to be led from the gloom, which, as you dwell on what follows, becomes dear to you, to the face of day, and there to meet all eyes upon you, as if you were a wild beast; and to lose sight of every thing amid the jeers and scoffs of your fellow creatures; that, Captain Wharton, that indeed is to die."

10. Henry listened in amazement, as his companion uttered this speech with a vehemence altogether new to him; both seemed to have forgotten their danger and their disguises, as he cried, "What! were you ever so near death as that?" "Have I not been the hunted beast of these hills for three years past?" resumed Harvey; "and once they even led me to the foot of the gallows itself, and I escaped only by an alarm from the royal troops. Had they been a quarter of an hour later, I must have died. There was I placed, in the midst of unfeeling men, and gaping women and children, as a monster to be cursed. When I would pray to God, my ears were insulted with the history of my crimes; and when, in all that multitude, I looked around for a single face that showed me any pity, I could find none, no, not even one; all cursed me as a wretch who would sell his country for gold.

11. "The sun was brighter to my eyes than common, but then it was the last time I should see it. The fields were gay and pleasant, and every thing seemed as if this world was a kind of heaven. Oh! how sweet life was to me at that moment! 'Twas a dreadful hour, Captain Wharton, and such as you have never known. You have friends to feel for you; but I had none but a father to mourn my loss when he might hear of it; there was no pity, no consolation near to soothe my anguish. Every thing seemed

to have deserted me; I even thought that He had forgotten that I lived."

12. "What! did you feel that God had forsaken you, Harvey?" cried the youth, with strong sympathy. "God never forsakes his servants," returned Birch, with reverence, and exhibiting naturally a devotion that hitherto he had only assumed. "And who did you mean by He?" The pedler raised himself in his saddle to the stiff and upright posture that was suited to the outward appearance. The look of fire that, for a short time, glowed upon his countenance, disappeared in the solemn lines of unbending self-abasement, and, speaking as if addressing a negro, he replied, "In heaven there is no distinction of color, my brother; therefore you have a precious charge within you, that you must hereafter render an account of," dropping his voice; "this is the last sentinel near the road; look not back, as you value your life."

13. Henry remembered his situation, and instantly assumed the humble demeanor of his adopted character. The unaccountable energy of the pedler's manner was soon forgotten in the sense of his own immediate danger; and with the recollection of his critical situation returned all the uneasiness that he had momentarily forgotten. "What see you, Harvey?" he cried, observing the pedler to gaze toward the building they had left, with ominous interest; "What see you at the house?" "That which bodes no good to us," returned the pretended priest. "Throw aside the mask and wig; you will need all your senses without much delay; throw them in the road: there are none before us that I dread, but there are those behind us who will give us a fearful race."

14. "Nay, then," cried the captain, casting the implements of his disguise into the highway, "let us improve our time to the utmost; we want a full quarter to the turn; why not push for it at once?" "Be cool, they are in alarm, but they will not mount without an officer, unless they see us fly; now he comes; he moves to the stables; trot briskly; a dozen are in their saddles, but the officer stops to tighten his girths; they hope to steal a march upon

us; he is mounted; now ride, Captain Wharton, for your life, and keep at my heels. If you quit me you will be lost."

15. A second request was unnecessary. The instant that Harvey put his horse to his speed, Captain Wharton was at his heels, urging the miserable animal that he rode to the utmost. Birch had selected the beast on which he rode, and, although vastly inferior to the high-fed and blooded chargers of the dragoons, still it was much superior to the little pony that had been thought good enough to carry Cæsar Thompson on an errand. A very few jumps convinced the captain that his companion was fast leaving him, and a fearful glance that he threw behind informed the fugitive that his enemies were as speedily approaching. With that abandonment that makes misery doubly grievous when it is to be supported alone, Henry called aloud to the pedler not to desert him. Harvey instantly drew up, and suffered his companion to run alongside of his own horse. The cocked hat and wig of the pedler fell from his head the moment that his steed began to move briskly, and this development of their disguise, as it might be termed, was witnessed by the dragoons, who announced their observation by a boisterous shout, that seemed to be uttered in the very ears of the fugitives, so loud was the cry, and so short the distance between them.

16. "Had we not better leave our horses," said Henry, "and make for the hills across the fields on our left? the fence will stop our pursuers." "That way lies the gallows," returned the pedler; "these fellows go three feet to our two, and would mind those fences no more than we do these ruts; but it is a short quarter to the turn, and there are two roads behind the wood. They may stand to choose until they can take the track, and we shall gain a little upon them there." "But this miserable horse is blown already," cried Henry, urging his beast with the end of his bridle, at the same time that Harvey aided his efforts by applying the lash of a heavy riding-whip that he carried; "he will never stand it for half a mile further." "A quarter will do, a quarter will do," said the pedler; "a single quarter will save us, if you follow my directions."

17. Somewhat cheered by the cool and confident manner of his companion, Henry continued silently urging his horse forward. A few moments brought them to the desired turn, and, as they doubled round a point of low under-brush, the fugitives caught a glimpse of their pursuers scattered along the highway. Mason and the sergeant, being better mounted than the rest of the company, were much nearer to their heels than even the pedler thought could be possible.

18. At the foot of the hills, and for some distance up the dark valley that wound among the mountains, a thick underwood of saplings had been suffered to shoot up, when the heavier growth was felled for the sake of fuel. At the sight of this cover, Henry again urged the pedler to dismount, and to plunge into the woods; but his request was promptly refused. The two roads before mentioned met at a very sharp angle, at a short distance from the turn, and both were circuitous, so that but little of either could be seen at a time. The pedler took the one which led to the left, but held it only a moment, for, on reaching a partial opening in the thicket, he darted across the right hand path, and led the way up a steep ascent, which lay directly before them. This maneuver saved them. On reaching the fork, the dragoons followed the track, and passed the spot where the fugitives had crossed to the other road, before they missed the marks of the footsteps. Their loud cries were heard by Henry and the pedler, as their wearied and breathless animals toiled up the hill, ordering their comrades in the rear to ride in the right direction. The captain again proposed to leave their horses, and dash into the thicket.

19. Not yet, not yet," said Birch, in a low voice; "the road falls from the top of this hill as steep as it rises; first let us gain the top." While speaking, they reached the desired summit, and both threw themselves from their horses. Henry plunged into the thick underwood, which covered the side of the mountain for some distance above them. Harvey stopped to give each of their beasts a few severe blows of his whip, that drove them headlong down

the path on the other side of the eminence, and then followed his example.

20. The pedler entered the thicket with a little caution, and avoided, as much as possible, rustling or breaking the branches in his way. There was but time only to shelter his person from view, when a dragoon led up the ascent, and, on reaching the hight, he cried aloud, "I saw one of their horses turning the hill this minute." "Drive on, spur forward, my lads," shouted Mason; "give the Englishman quarter, but cut down the pedler, and make an end of him."

21. Henry felt his companion gripe his arm hard, as he listened in a great tremor to this cry, which was followed by the passage of a dozen horsemen, with a vigor and speed that showed too plainly how little security their over-tired steeds could have afforded them. "Now," said the pedler, rising from his cover to reconnoiter, and standing for a moment in suspense, "all that we gain is clear gain; for as we go up, they go down. Let us be stirring." "But will they not follow us, and surround this mountain?" said Henry, rising, and imitating the labored but rapid progress of his companion; "remember they have foot as well as horse; and, at any rate, we shall starve in the hills."

22. "Fear nothing, Captain Wharton," returned the pedler with confidence; "this is not the mountain that I would be on, but necessity has made me a dexterous pilot among these hills. I will lead you where no man will dare to follow. See, the sun is already setting behind the tops of the western mountains, and it will be two hours to the rising of the moon. Who, think you, will follow us far, on a November night, among these rocks and precipices?" "But listen!" exclaimed Henry; "the dragoons are shouting to each other; they miss us already." "Come to the point of this rock, and you may see them," said Harvey, composedly setting himself down to rest. "Nay, they can see us; notice, they are pointing up with their fingers. There! one has fired his pistol, but the distance is too great for even a musket to carry upward." "They will pursue us," cried the impatient Henry; "let us be moving."

23. "They will not think of such a thing," returned the pedler, picking the chickerberries that grew on the thin soil where he sat, and very deliberately chewing them, leaves and all, to refresh his mouth. "What progress could they make here, in their boots and spurs, with their long swords, or even pistols? No, no; they may go back and turn out the foot; but the horse pass through these defiles, when they can keep the saddle, with fear and trembling. Come, follow me, Captain Wharton; we have a troublesome march before us, but I will bring you where none will think of venturing this night." So saying, they both arose, and were soon hid from view among the rocks and caverns of the mountain.

XCIV. — THE CONVICT SHIP.

1. MORN on the waters! and purple and bright
Bursts on the billows the flashing of light;
O'er the glad waves, like a child of the sun,
See the tall vessel goes gallantly on;
Full to the breeze she unbosoms her sail,
And her pennon streams onward, like hope, in the gale;
The winds come around her, and murmur and song,
And the surges rejoice as they bear her along.
See! see, she looks up to the golden-edge clouds,
And the sailor sings gayly aloft in her shrouds.

2. Onward she glides amid ripple and spray,
Over the waters, away and away!
Bright as the visions of youth ere they part,
Passing away like a dream of the heart!
Who, as the beautiful pageant sweeps by,
Music around her, and sunshine on high,
Pauses to think, amid glitter and glow,
Oh! there be hearts that are breaking below.

3. Night on the waves! and the moon is on high,
Hung like a gem on the brow of the sky,

Treading its depths in the power of her might,
And turning the clouds, as they pass her, to light;
Look to the waters! asleep on their breast
Seems not the ship like an island of rest?
Bright and alone on the shadowy main,
Like a heart-cherish'd home on some desolate plain.

4. Who, as she smiles in the silvery light,
Spreading her wings on the bosom of night,
Alone on the deep, as the moon on the sky,
A phantom of beauty, could deem, with a sigh,
That so lovely a thing is the mansion of sin,
And souls that are smitten lie bursting within?
Who, as he watches her silently gliding,
Remembers that wave after wave is dividing
Bosoms that sorrow and guilt could not sever,
Hearts that are parted and broken forever?
Or dreams that he watches, afloat on the wave
The death-bed of hope, or the young spirit's grave?

5. 'Tis thus with our life: while it passes along,
Like a vessel at sea, amid sunshine and song,
Gayly we glide in the gaze of the world,
With streamers afloat, and with canvas unfurl'd;
All gladness and glory, to wandering eyes,
Yet charter'd by sorrow, and freighted with sighs;
Fading and false is the aspect it wears,
As the smiles we put on, just to cover our tears;
And the withering thoughts that the world can not know,
Like heart-broken exiles, lie burning below;
While the vessel drives on to that desolate shore,
Where the dreams of our childhood are vanish'd and o'er.

XCV. — THE SHIPWRECK.

FROM BYRON.

1. THERE were two fathers in this ghastly crew,
   And with them their two sons, of whom the one

Was more robust and hardy to the view;
　　But he died early: and when he was gone,
His nearest messmate told his sire, who threw
.　　One glance on him, and said, "Heaven's will be done!
I can do nothing;" and he saw him thrown
Into the deep without a tear or groan.

2. The other father had a weaklier child,
　　Of a soft cheek, and aspect delicate;
But the boy bore up long, and with a mild
　　And patient spirit held aloof his fate;
Little he said, and now and then he smiled,
　　As if to win a part from off the weight
He saw increasing on his father's heart,
With the deep deadly thought that they must part.

3. And o'er him bent his sire, and never rais'd
　　His eyes from off his face, but wiped the foam
From his pale lips, and ever on him gazed:
　　And when the wish'd for shower at length was come,
And the boy's eyes, which the dull film half glazed,
　　Brighten'd, and for a moment seem'd to roam,
He squeez'd from out a rag some drops of rain
Into his dying child's mouth; but in vain!

4. The boy expired, the father held the clay,
　　And look'd upon it long; and when, at last,
Death left no doubt, and the dead burden lay
　　Stiff on his heart, and pulse and hope were past,
He watch'd it wistfully, until away
　　'Twas borne by the rude wave wherein 'twas cast,
Then he himself sunk down all dumb and shivering,
And gave no sign of life, save his limbs quivering.

———————

5. As day advanced, the weather seem'd to abate,
　　And then the leak they reckon'd to reduce,
And keep the ship afloat, though three feet yet

The wind blew fresh again: as it grew late
    A squall came on, and while some guns broke loose,
A gust, which all descriptive power transcends,
Laid with one blast the ship on her beam ends.

6. Immediately the masts were cut away,
    Both main and mizen; first the mizen went,
The mainmast follow'd; but the ship still lay
    Like a mere log, and baffled our intent.
Foremast and bowsprit were cut down, and they
    Eas'd her at last (although we never meant
To part with all till every hope was blighted),
And then with violence the old ship righted.

7. 'Twas twilight, and the sunless day went down
    Over the waste of waters; like a vail,
Which, if withdrawn, would but disclose the frown
    Of one whose fate is masked but to assail.
Thus to their hopeless eyes the night was shown,
    And grimly darkled o'er the faces pale,
And the dim desolate deep: twelve days had Fear
Been their familiar, and now Death was here.

8. At half-past eight o'clock, booms, hencoops, spars,
    And all things, for a chance, had been cast loose,
That still could keep afloat the struggling tars;
    For yet they strove, although of no great use.
There was no light in heaven but a few stars;
    The boats put off o'ercrowded with their crews:
She gave a heel, and then a lurch to port,
And, going down head-foremost, sunk, in short.

9. Then rose from sea to sky the wild farewell,
    Then shriek'd the timid, and stood still the brave;
Then some leap'd overboard with dreadful yell,
    As eager to anticipate their grave;
And the sea yawn'd around her like a hell,
    And down she suck'd with her the whirling wave,
Like one who grapples with his enemy,
And strives to strangle him before he die.

10. And first one universal shriek there rush'd,
    Louder than the loud ocean, like a crash
Of echoing thunder; and then all was hush'd,
    Save the wild wind and the remorseless dash
Of billows; but at intervals there gush'd,
    Accompanied with a convulsive splash,
A solitary shriek, the bubbling cry
Of some strong swimmer in his agony.

XCVI. — THE ARIEL AMONG THE SHOALS.

FROM COOPER.

The following description of a ship among the shoals, is one of Cooper's best pictures of nautical scenes.

1. The extraordinary activity of Griffith, which communicated itself with promptitude to the whole crew, was produced by a sudden alteration in the weather. In place of the well-defined streak along the horizon, that has been already described, an immense body of misty light appeared to be moving in with rapidity from the ocean, while a distinct but distant roaring announced the sure approach of the tempest that had so long troubled the waters. Even Griffith, while thundering his orders through the trumpet, and urging the men by his cries to expedition, would pause for an instant to cast anxious glances in the direction of the coming storm, and the faces of the sailors who lay on the yards, were turned instinctively toward the same quarter of the heavens, while they knotted the reef-points, that were to confine the unruly canvas to the prescribed limits.

2. The pilot alone, in that confused and busy throng, where voice rose above voice, and cry echoed cry, in quick succession, appeared as if he held no interest in the important stake. With his eyes steadily fixed on the approaching mist, and his arms folded together in composure, he stood calmly awaiting the result. The ship had fallen off with her broadside to the sea, and had become unmanageable. "The schooner has it!" cried Griffith, " We

are falling off before the wind; shall we try a cast of lead?"

3. The pilot turned from his contemplative posture, and moved slowly across the deck before he returned any reply to this question, like a man who not only felt that every thing depended upon himself, but that he was equal to the emergency. "'Tis unnecessary," he at length said; "'twould be certain destruction to be taken aback, and it is difficult to say, within several points, how the wind may strike us." "'Tis difficult no longer," cried Griffith; "and here it comes, and in right earnest."

4. The rushing sounds of the wind were now indeed heard at hand, and the words had hardly passed the lips of the young lieutenant, before the vessel bowed down heavily to one side, and then, as she began to move through the water, rose again majestically to her upright position, as if saluting, like a courteous champion, the powerful antagonist with which she was about to contend. Not another moment elapsed before the ship was throwing the waters aside with a lively progress. The hurry and bustle gradually subsided, and the men slowly descended to the deck, all straining their eyes to pierce the gloom in which they were enveloped, and some shaking their heads in melancholy doubt, afraid to express the apprehensions they really entertained.

5. All on board anxiously awaited for the fury of the gale; for there were none so ignorant in that gallant frigate as not to know that they as yet only felt the infant efforts of the wind. Each moment, however, it increased in power, though so gradually that the relieved mariners began to believe that all their gloomy forebodings were not to be realized. During this short interval of uncertainty, no other sounds were heard than the whistling of the breeze, as it passed quickly through the mass of rigging, and the dashing of the spray that began to fly from her bows like the foam of a cataract.

6. "It blows fresh," cried Griffith, who was the first to speak in that moment of anxiety; "but it is no more than a cap-full of wind, after all. Give us elbow room, and the

right canvas, Mr. Pilot, and I'll handle the ship like a gentleman's yacht, in this breeze." "Will she stay, think ye, under this sail?" said the low voice of the stranger. "She will do all that man can ask of wood and iron," returned the lieutenant, "but the vessel don't float that will tack under double-reefed topsails alone against a heavy sea. Help her with the canvas, pilot, and you'll see her come round like a dancing-master." "Let us feel the strength of the gale first," returned the man who was called Mr. Gray, moving from Griffith to the weather side of the vessel, where he stood in silence, looking ahead of the ship with an air of singular coolness and abstraction.

7. All the lanterns had been extinguished. The land could be faintly discerned, rising like a heavy bank of black fog above the margin of the waters, and was only distinguishable from the heavens, by its deeper obscurity. For several minutes the stillness of death pervaded the crowded decks. It was evident to every one that their ship was dashing at a prodigious rate through the waves; and she was approaching, with such velocity, the quarter of the bay, where the shoals and dangers were known to be situated, that nothing but the habits of the most exact discipline could suppress the uneasiness of the officers and men. At length, the voice of Captain Munson was heard calling to the pilot, "Shall I send a hand into the chains, Mr. Gray, and try our water?" "Tack your ship, sir, tack your ship; I would see how she works, before we reach the point where she *must* behave well."

8. Griffith gazed after him in wonder, while the pilot slowly paced the quarter-deck, and then, rousing from his trance, gave forth the cheering order that called each man to his station. The confident assurances which the young gentleman had given to the pilot respecting the qualities of his vessel, and his own ability to manage her, were fully realized by the result. The helm was no sooner put down, than the huge ship bore up gallantly against the wind, and, dashing directly through the waves, threw the foam high into the air as she looked boldly into the very eye of the wind, and then, yielding gracefully to its power,

she fell aft on the other tack, with her head pointed from those dangerous shoals that she had so recently approached with such terrifying velocity. The heavy yards sprung round as if they had been vanes to indicate the currents of the air, and, in a few moments, the frigate again moved with stately progress through the water, leaving the rocks and shoals behind her on one side of the bay, but advancing toward those that offered equal danger on the other.

9. During this time, the sea was becoming more agitated, and the violence of the wind was gradually increasing. An endless succession of white surges rose above the heavy billows, and the very air was glittering with the light that was disengaged from the ocean. The ship yielded each moment more and more before the storm, and, in less than half an hour, she was driven along with tremendous fury by the full power of a gale of wind. Still the hardy and experienced mariners who directed her movements, held her to the course that was necessary to their preservation, and still Griffith gave forth, when directed by their unknown pilot, those orders that turned her in the narrow channel where safety was alone to be found.

XCVII. — THE ARIEL. — Continued.

1. So far the performance of his duty seemed easy to the stranger, and he gave the required directions in those still, calm tones that formed so remarkable a contrast to the responsibility of his situation. But when the land was becoming dim, in distance as well as darkness, and the agitated sea was only to be discovered as it swept by them in foam, he broke in upon the monotonous roaring of the tempest with the sound of his voice, seeming to shake off his apathy and rouse himself to the occasion.

2. "Now is the time to watch her closely, Mr. Griffith," he cried; "here we get the true tide and the real danger. Place the best quarter-master of your ship in those chains, and let an officer stand by him and see that he gives

us the right water." "I will take that office on myself," said the captain; "pass a light into the weather main-chains." "Stand by your braces!" exclaimed the pilot, with startling quickness. "Heave away that lead!"

3. These preparations taught the crew to expect the crisis, and every officer and man stood in fearful silence, at his assigned station, awaiting the issue of the trial. Even the quarter-master gave out his orders to the men at the wheel in deeper and hoarser tones than usual, as if anxious not to disturb the quiet and order of the vessel. While this deep expectation pervaded the frigate, the piercing cry of the leadsman, as he called, "By the mark seven!" rose above the tempest, crossed over the decks, and appeared to pass away to leeward, borne on the blast like the warnings of some water spirit.

4. "'Tis well," returned the pilot, calmly; "try again." The short pause was succeeded by another cry, "And a half five!" "She shoals! she shoals!" exclaimed Griffith; "keep her a good full." "Ay, you must hold the vessel in command now," said the pilot, with those cool tones that are most appalling in critical moments, because they seem to denote most preparation and care. The third call, "By the deep four!" was followed by a prompt direction from the stranger to tack.

5. Griffith seemed to emulate the coolness of the pilot, in issuing the necessary order to execute their maneuver. The vessel rose slowly from the inclined position into which she had been forced by the tempest, and the sails were shaking violently, as if to release themselves from their confinement, while the ship stemmed the billows, when the well-known voice of the sailing-master was heard shouting from the forecastle, "Breakers, breakers, dead ahead!" This appalling sound seemed yet to be lingering about the ship, when a second voice cried, "Breakers on our lee-bow!"

6. "We are in a bight of the shoals, Mr. Gray," said the commander. "She loses her way; perhaps an anchor might hold her." "Clear away that best-bower!" shouted Griffith, through his trumpet. "Hold on," cried the pilot,

in a voice that reached the very hearts of all who heard him; "hold on every thing."

7. The young man turned fiercely to the daring stranger who thus defied the discipline of his vessel, and at once demanded, "Who is it that dares to countermand my orders? Is it not enough that you run the ship into danger, but you must interfere to keep her there? If another word——"

8. "Peace, Mr. Griffith," interrupted the captain, bending from the rigging, his gray locks blowing about in the wind, and adding a look of wildness to the haggard care that he exhibited by the light of his lantern; "yield the trumpet to Mr. Gray; he alone can save us." Griffith threw his speaking trumpet on the deck, and as he walked proudly away, muttered in bitterness of feeling, "Then all is lost, indeed, and among the rest, the foolish hopes with which I visited this coast."

9. There was, however, no time for reply; the ship had been rapidly running into the wind, and, as the efforts of the crew were paralyzed by the contradictory orders they had heard, she gradually lost her way, and in a few seconds all her sails were taken aback. Before the crew understood their situation, the pilot had applied the trumpet to his mouth, and, in a voice that rose above the tempest, he thundered forth his orders. Each command was given distinctly, and with a precision that showed him to be master of his profession. The helm was kept fast, the head-yards swung up heavily against the wind, and the vessel was soon whirling round on her keel with a retrograde movement.

10. Griffith was too much of a seaman not to perceive that the pilot had seized with a perception almost intuitive, the only method that promised to extract the vessel from her situation. He was young, impetuous, and proud; but he was also generous. Forgetting his resentment and his mortification, he rushed forward among the men, and, by his presence and example, added certainty to the experiment. The ship fell off slowly before the gale, and bowed her yards nearly to the water, as she felt the blast pouring

its fury on her broadside, while the surly waves beat violently against her stern, as if in reproach at departing from her usual manner of moving.

XCVIII. — THE ARIEL. — Continued.

1. THE voice of the pilot, however, was still heard, steady, and calm, and yet so clear and high as to reach every ear; and the obedient seamen whirled the yards at his bidding in despite of the tempest, as if they handled the toys of their childhood. The beautiful fabric, obedient to her government, threw her bows up gracefully to the wind again, and, as her sails were trimmed, moved out from among the dangerous shoals in which she had been embayed, as steadily and swiftly as she had approached them.

2. A moment of breathless astonishment succeeded the accomplishment of this fine maneuver, but there was no time for the usual expressions of surprise. The stranger still held the trumpet, and continued to lift his voice amid the howlings of the blast, whenever prudence or skill directed any change in the management of the ship. For an hour longer there was a fearful struggle for their preservation, the channel at each step becoming more complicated, and the shoals thickening around the mariners on every side. The lead was cast rapidly, and the quick eye of the pilot seemed to pierce the darkness with a keenness of vision that exceeded human power.

3. It was apparent to all in the vessel, that they were under the guidance of one who understood the navigation thoroughly, and their exertions kept pace with their reviving confidence. Again and again the frigate appeared to be rushing blindly on shoals, where the sea was covered with foam, and where destruction would have been as sudden as it was certain, when the clear voice of the stranger was heard warning them of their danger, and inciting them to their duty. The vessel was implicitly yielded to his government, and during those anxious moments, when she was dashing the waters aside, throwing the spray

over her enormous yards, each ear would listen eagerly for those sounds that had obtained a command over the crew, that can only be acquired, under such circumstances, by great steadiness and consummate skill. The ship was recovering from the inaction of changing her course, in one of those critical tacks she had made so often, when the pilot, for the first time, addressed the commander of the frigate.

4. "Now is the pinch," he said; "and if the ship behaves well, we are safe; but, if otherwise, all we have yet done will be useless." The veteran seaman whom he addressed left the chains at this portentous notice, and, calling to his first lieutenant, required of the stranger an explanation of his warning. "See yon light on the southern headland?" returned the pilot; "you may know it from the star near it by its sinking, at times, in the ocean. Now observe the hummock, a little north of it, looking like a shadow in the horizon; 'tis a hill far inland. If we keep that light open from the hill, we shall do well, but if not, we surely go to pieces. "Let us tack again!" exclaimed the lieutenant.

5. The pilot shook his head, as he replied, "There is no more tacking or box-hauling to be done to-night. We have barely room to pass out of the shoals on this course, and if we can weather the 'Devil's Grip,' we clear their outermost point, but if not, as I said before, there is but one alternative." "If we had beaten out the way we entered," exclaimed Griffith, "we should have done well." "Say, also, if the tide would have let us do so," returned the pilot, calmly. "Gentlemen, we must be prompt; we have but a mile to go, and the ship appears to fly. That topsail is not enough to keep her up to the wind; we want both jib and mainsail." "Tis a perilous thing to loosen canvas in such a tempest!" observed the doubtful captain. "It must be done!" returned the collected stranger; "we perish without. See! the light already touches the edge of the hummock; the sea casts us to leeward." "It shall be done!" cried Griffith, seizing the trumpet from the hand of the pilot.

H. S. R.—24

6. The orders of the lieutenant were executed almost as soon as issued, and, every thing being ready, the enormous folds of the mainsail were trusted loose to the blast. There was an instant when the result was doubtful; the tremendous thrashing of the heavy sails seeming to bid defiance to all restraint, shaking the ship to her center; but art and strength prevailed, and gradually the canvas was distended, and bellying as it filled, was drawn down to its usual place by the power of a hundred men. The vessel yielded to this immense addition of force, and bowed before it like a reed bending to a breeze. The success of the measure was announced by a joyful cry from the stranger, that seemed to burst from his inmost soul.

7. "She feels it! She springs! Observe," he said; "the light opens from the hummock already; if she will only bear her canvas, we shall go clear!" A report like that of a cannon interrupted his exclamation, and something like a white cloud was seen drifting before the wind from the head of the ship, till it was driven into the gloom far to leeward. " 'Tis the jib blown from the bolt-ropes," said the commander of the frigate. "This is no time to spread light duck, but the mainsail may stand it yet." "The sail would laugh at a tornado," returned the lieutenant; "but that mast springs like a piece of steel." "Silence, all!" cried the pilot. "Now, gentlemen, we shall soon know our fate. Let her luff, luff you can."

8. This warning effectually closed all discourse, and the hardy mariners, knowing that they had done all in the power of man to insure their safety, stood in breathless anxiety, awaiting the result. At a short distance ahead of them, the whole ocean was white with foam, and the waves, instead of rolling on in regular succession, appeared to be tossing about in mad gambols. A single streak of dark billows, not half a cable's length in width, could be discerned running into this chaos of water; but it was soon lost to the eye amid the confusion of the disturbed element. Along this narrow path the vessel moved more heavily than before, being brought so near the wind as to keep her sails touching.

9. The pilot silently proceeded to the wheel, and with his own hands he undertook the steerage of the ship. No noise proceeded from the ship to interrupt the horrid tumult of the ocean, and she entered the channel among the breakers with the silence of a desperate calmness. Twenty times, as the foam rolled away to leeward, the crew were on the eve of uttering their joy, as they supposed the vessel past the danger; but breaker after breaker would still rise before them, following each other into the general mass, to check their exultation. Occasionally, the fluttering of the sails would be heard; and when the looks of the startled seamen were turned to the wheel, they beheld the stranger grasping its spokes, with his quick eye glancing from the water to the canvas. At length, the ship reached a place where she appeared to be rushing directly into the jaws of destruction, when suddenly her course was changed, and her head receded rapidly from the wind. At the same instant, the voice of the pilot was heard shouting, "Square away the yards!—*in* mainsail!"

10. A general burst from the crew echoed, "Square away the yards!" and, quick as thought, the frigate was seen gliding along the channel before the wind. The eye had hardly time to dwell on the foam, which seemed like clouds driving in the heavens, when the gallant vessel issued from her perils, and rose and fell on the heavy waves of the open sea.

XCIX.—THE BRAVE MAN.

FROM THE GERMAN.

1. LOUD let the Brave Man's praises swell
   As organ blast, or clang of bell!
   Of lofty soul and spirit strong,
   He asks not gold, he asks but song!
Then glory to God, by whose gift I raise
The tribute of song to the Brave Man's praise!

2. The thaw wind came from the southern sea,
   Dewy and dark o'er Italy;
   The scatter'd clouds fled far aloof,
   As flies the flock before the wolf;
It swept o'er the plain, and it strew'd the wood,
And it burst the ice-bands on river and flood.

3. The snow-drifts melt, till the mountain calls
   With the voice of a thousand waterfalls;
   The waters are over both field and dell;
   Still doth the land-flood wax and swell;
And high roll its billows, as in their track
They hurry the ice-crags, a floating wrack.

4. On pillars stout, and arches wide,
   A bridge of granite stems the tide;
   And midway o'er the foaming flood,
   Upon the bridge the toll-house stood;
There dwelleth the toll-man, with babes and wife;
O, toll-man! O, toll-man! quick! flee for thy life!

5. Near and more near the wild waves urge;
   Loud howls the wind, loud roars the surge;
   The toll-man sprang on the roof in fright,
   And he gazed on the waves in their gathering might.
"All-merciful God! to our sins be good!
We are lost! we are lost! The flood! the flood!"

6. High rolled the waves! In headlong track
   Hither and thither dash'd the wrack!
   On either bank uprose the flood;
   Scarce on their base the arches stood!
The toll-man, trembling for house and life,
Out-screams the storm with his babes and wife.

7. High heaves the flood-wreck, block on block;
   The sturdy pillars feel the shock;
   On either arch the surges break,
   On either side the arches shake.

They totter! they sink 'neath the whelming wave!
All-merciful Heaven, have pity and save!

8. Upon the river's further strand
    A trembling crowd of gazers stand;
    In wild despair their hands they wring,
    Yet none may aid or succor bring;
And the hapless toll-man, with babes and wife,
Is screaming for help through the stormy strife.

9. *When* shall the Brave Man's praises swell
    As organ blast or clang of bell?
    Ah! name him *now*, he tarries long;
    Name him at last, my glorious song!
O! speed, for the terrible death draws near;
O, Brave Man! O, Brave Man! arise, appear!

10. Quick gallops up, with headlong speed,
    A noble Count on noble steed!
    And, lo! on high his fingers hold
    A purse well stored with shining gold.
"Two hundred pistoles for the man who shall save
Yon perishing wretch from the yawning wave!"

11. Who is the Brave Man, say, my song:
    Shall to the Count thy meed belong?
    Though, Heaven be prais'd, right brave he be,
    I know a braver still than he:
O, Brave Man! O, Brave Man! arise, appear!
O, speed, for the terrible death draws near!

12. And ever higher swell the waves,
    And louder still the storm wind raves,
    And lower sink their hearts in fear;
    O, Brave Man! O, Brave Man! haste, appear.
Buttress and pillar, they groan and strain,
And the rocking arches are rent in twain!

13. Again, again before their eyes,
    High holds the Count the glittering prize;

All see, but all the danger shun;
Of all the thousand stirs not one.
And the toll-man in vain, through the tumult wild,
Out-screams the tempest with wife and child.

14. But who amid the crowd is seen,
    In peasant garb, with simple mien,
    Firm, leaning on a trusty stave,
    In form and feature tall and grave?
He hears the Count, and the scream of fear;
He sees that the moment of death draws near!

15. Into a skiff he boldly sprang;
    He braved the storm that round him rang;
    He call'd aloud on God's great name,
    And forward, a deliverer came.
But the fisher's skiff seems all too small
From the raging waters to save them all.

16. The river round him boil'd and surged;
    Thrice through the waves his skiff he urged,
    And back through wind and water's roar,
    He bore them safely to the shore:
So fierce rolled the river, that scarce the last
In the fisher's skiff through the danger pass'd.

17. Who is the Brave Man? Say, my song,
    To whom shall that high name belong?
    Bravely the peasant ventur'd in,
    But 'twas, perchance, the prize to win.
If the generous Count had proffer'd no gold,
The peasant, methinks, had not been so bold.

18. Out spake the Count, "Right boldly done!
    Here, take thy purse; 'twas nobly won."
    A generous act, in truth, was this,
    And truly the Count right noble is;
But loftier still was the soul display'd
By him in the peasant garb array'd.

19. "Poor though I be, thy hand withhold;
  I barter not my life for gold!
  Yon hapless man is ruin'd now:
  Great Count, on him thy gift bestow."
He spake from his heart in his honest pride,
And he turn'd on his heel and strode aside.

20. Then loudly let his praises swell
  As organ blast or clang of bell;
  Of lofty soul and spirit strong,
  He asks not gold, he asks but song!
So glory to God, by whose gift I raise
The tribute of song to the Brave Man's praise!

C.—CLEON AND I.

1. CLEON hath a million acres, ne'er a one have I;
Cleon dwelleth in a palace, in a cottage I;
Cleon hath a dozen fortunes, not a penny I;
But the poorer of the twain is Cleon, and not I.

2. Cleon, true, possesseth acres, but the landscape, I;
Half the charms to *me* it yieldeth money can not buy;
Cleon harbors sloth and dullness, freshening vigor, I;
He in velvet, I in fustian; richer man am I.

3. Cleon is a slave to grandeur, free as thought am I;
Cleon fees a score of doctors, need of none have I.
Wealth-surrounded, care-environ'd, Cleon fears to die;
Death may come, he'll find me ready; happier man am I.

4. Cleon sees no charm in nature, in a daisy, I;
Cleon hears no anthems ringing in the sea and sky.
Nature sings to me forever; earnest listener I;
State for state, with all attendants, who would change?
    Not I.

CI. — THE RETORT.

1. ONE day, a rich man, flush'd with pride and wine,
    Sitting with guests at table, all quite merry,
   Conceiv'd it would be vastly fine
        To crack a joke upon his secretary.

2. "Young man," said he, by what art, craft, or trade,
    Did your good father earn his livelihood?"
   "He was a saddler, sir," the young man said,
    "And in his line was always reckon'd good."

3. "A saddler, eh? and had you stuff'd with Greek,
    Instead of teaching you like him to do!
   And pray, sir, why did not your father make
        A saddler, too, of you?"
   At this each flatterer, as in duty bound,
    The joke applauded, and the laugh went round.

4. At length the secretary, bowing low,
    Said, (craving pardon if too free he made,)
   "Sir, by your leave, I fain would know
        Your father's trade."

5. "My father's trade? Why, sir, but that's too bad!
    My father's trade? Why, blockhead, art thou mad?
   My father, sir, was never brought so low:
        He was a gentleman, I'd have you know."

6. "Indeed! excuse the liberty I take;
        But if your story's true,
   How happen'd it your father did not make
        A gentleman of you?"

CII. — THE BACHELOR'S DREAM.

FROM HOOD.

3. TETE-A-TETES; (pro. tate-a-tates,) private conversations.

1. MY fire is lit, my tea is fix'd,
    My curtains drawn, and all is snug,
   Old Puss is in her elbow chair,

And Tray is sitting on the rug.
Last night I had a curious dream,
Miss Susan Bates was Mistress Mogg;
What d'ye think of that, my cat?
What d'ye think of that, my dog?

2. She look'd so fair, she sang so well,
   I could but woo and she was won;
   Myself in blue, the bride in white,
   The ring was placed, the deed was done!
   Away we went in chaise-and-four,
   As fast as grinning boys could flog;
   What d'ye think of that, my cat?
   What d'ye think of that, my dog?

3. What loving *tete-a-tetes* to come!
   What *tete-a-tetes* must still defer!
   When Susan came to live with me,
   Her mother came to live with her!
   With sister Belle she could n't part,
   But all *my* ties had leave to jog;
   What d'ye think of that, my cat?
   What d'ye think of that, my dog?

4. The mother brought a pretty Poll;
   A monkey, too, what work he made!
   The sister introduced a beau;
   My Susan brought a favorite maid.
   She had a tabby of her own,
   A snappish mongrel christen'd Gog;
   What d'ye think of that, my cat?
   What d'ye think of that, my dog?

5. My clothes, they were the queerest shape!
   Such coats and hats she never met!
   My ways, they were the oddest ways!
   My friends were such a vulgar set!
   Poor Tompkinson was snubb'd and huff'd,
   She could not bear that Mister Blogg;
   What d'ye think of that, my cat?
   What d'ye think of that, my dog?

6. At times we had a spar, and then
   Mamma must mingle in the song;
   The sister took a sister's part;
   The maid declared her master wrong:
   The parrot learn'd to call me "Fool;"
   My life was like a London fog;
   What d'ye think of that, my cat?
   What d'ye think of that, my dog?

7. Now was not that an awful dream
   For one who single is and snug,
   With Pussy in the elbow-chair,
   And Tray reposing on the rug?
   If I must totter down the hill,
   'Tis safest done without a clog;
   What d'ye think of that, my cat?
   What d'ye think of that, my dog?

CIII.—RALEIGH'S LAST LETTER.

Sir Walter Raleigh was one of the most distinguished men who adorned the reigns of Elizabeth and James I. of England. As a patriot, statesman, general, and literary man, he had few equals in his day. When James I. ascended the throne, he was accused of high treason, unjustly condemned, and, after twelve years' imprisonment, was executed. The following is his last letter.

1. You shall receive, my dear wife, my last words, in these my last lines: my love I send you, that you may keep when I am dead; and my counsel, that you may remember it when I am no more. I would not, with my will, present you sorrows, dear Bess; let them go to the grave with me, and be buried in the dust. And seeing that it is not the will of God that I shall see you any more, bear my destruction patiently, and with a heart like yourself.

2. First, I send all the thanks which my heart can conceive, or my words express, for your many cares for me, which, though they have not taken effect as you wished,

yet my debt to you is not the less; but pay it I never shall, in this world.

3. Secondly, I beseech you, for the love you bear me living, that you do not hide yourself many days, but by your patience seek to help my miserable fortunes, and the right of your poor child. Your mourning can not avail me, that am but dust.

4. Dear wife, I beseech you, for my soul's sake, pay all poor men. When I am dead, no doubt you shall be much sought unto; for the world thinks I was very rich: have a care to fair pretenses of men: for no greater misery can befall you, in this life, than to become a prey unto the world, and after to be despised. I speak, God knows, not to dissuade you from marriage; for it will be best for you, both in respect of God and the world. As for me, I am no more yours, nor you mine; death has cut us asunder, and God hath divided me from the world, and you from me.

5. Remember your poor child, for his father's sake, who loved you in his happiest estate. I sued for my life, but God knows, it was for you and yours that I desired it; for know it, my dear wife, your child is the child of a true man, who, in his own respect, despiseth death and his misshapen and ugly forms. I can not write much, (God knows how hardly I steal this time, when all sleep!) and it is also time for me to separate my thoughts from the world. Beg my dead body, which, living, was denied you, and either lay it in Sherburne or Exeter church, by my father and mother. I can say no more; time and death call me away.

6. The everlasting God, powerful, infinite, and inscrutable, God Almighty, who is goodness itself, the true light and life, keep you and yours, and have mercy upon me, and forgive my persecutors and false accusers, and send us to meet in his glorious kingdom! My dear wife, farewell: bless my boy: pray for me, and let my true God hold you both in his arms.

CIV. — "NOT TO MYSELF."

1. "Not to myself alone,"
The little opening flower transported cries,
   "Not to myself alone I bud and bloom;
With fragrant breath the breezes I perfume,
And gladden all things with my rainbow dyes.
   The bee comes sipping, every eventide,
            His dainty fill;
   The butterfly within my cup doth hide
            From threatening ill."

2. "Not to myself alone,"
The circling star with honest pride doth boast,
   "Not to myself alone I rise and set;
I write upon night's coronal of jet
His power and skill who form'd our myriad host;
   A friendly beacon at heaven's open gate
            I gem the sky,
   That man might ne'er forget, in every fate,
            His home on high."

3. "Not to myself alone,"
The heavy laden bee doth murmuring hum;
   "Not to myself alone from flower to flower,
I rove the wood, the garden, and the bower,
And to the hive at evening weary come;
   For man, for man, the luscious food I pile
            With busy care,
   Content if he repay my ceaseless toil
            With scanty share."

4. "Not to myself alone,"
The soaring bird with lusty pinion sings,
   "Not to myself alone I raise my song;
I cheer the drooping with my warbling tongue,
And bear the mourner on my viewless wings;

I bid the hymnless churl my anthem learn,
 And God adore;
I call the worldling from his dross to turn,
 And sing and soar."

5. "Not to myself alone,"
The streamlet whispers on its pebbly way,
 "Not to myself alone I sparkling glide;
I scatter life and health on every side,
And strew the fields with herb and flow'ret gay.
I sing unto the common, bleak and bare, .
 My gladsome tune;
I sweeten and refresh the languid air
 In droughty June."

6. "Not to myself alone."
O man, forget not thou, earth's honor'd priest,
 Its tongue, its soul, its life, its pulse, its heart,
 In earth's great chorus to sustain *thy* part!
Chiefest of guests at Love's ungrudging feast,
 Play not the niggard; spurn thy native clod,
  And *self* disown;
Live to thy neighbor; live unto thy God;
  Not to thyself alone!

CV. — MAJOR ANDRE.

FROM HAMILTON.

MAJOR ANDRE was an officer in the English army during the revolutionary war. He was entrusted with the very delicate duty of communicating with Benedict Arnold, an American officer, who proposed treacherously to deliver the garrison at West Point to the English. Andre was detected, and, though a noble, honorable man, was, according to the rules of war, executed as a spy.

ALEXANDER HAMILTON, from whose letter to a friend this extract is taken, was one of the most distinguished patriots and officers of the Revolution, and was the first Secretary of the Treasury under the Constitution.

1. NEVER, perhaps, did any man suffer death with more justice, or deserve it less. The first step he took, after

his capture, was to write a letter to General Washington, conceived in terms of dignity without insolence, and apology without meanness. The scope of it was to vindicate himself from the imputation of having assumed a mean character, for treacherous or interested purposes: asserting that he had been involuntarily an impostor; that, contrary to his intention, which was to meet a person for intelligence on neutral ground, he had been betrayed within our posts, and forced into the vile condition of an enemy in disguise; soliciting only, that, to whatever rigor policy might devote him, a decency of treatment might be observed, due to a person who, though unfortunate, had been guilty of nothing dishonorable. His request was granted in its full extent; for, in the whole progress of the affair, he was treated with the most scrupulous delicacy. The board of officers were not more impressed with the candor and firmness, mixed with a becoming sensibility, which he displayed, than he was penetrated with their liberality and politeness. He acknowledged the generosity of the behavior toward him in every respect, but particularly in this, in the strongest terms of manly gratitude.

2. In one of the visits I made to him, said he, "There is only one thing that disturbs my tranquillity. Sir Henry Clinton has been too good to me; he has been lavish of his kindness. I am bound to him by too many obligations, and love him too well, to bear the thought that he should reproach himself, or that others should reproach him, on the supposition of my having conceived myself obliged, by his instructions, to run the risk I did. I would not, for the world, leave a sting in his mind that should embitter his future days." He could scarce finish the sentence, bursting into tears, in spite of his efforts to suppress them; and with difficulty collected himself enough afterward to add: "I wish to be permitted to assure him I did not act under this impression, but submitted to a necessity imposed upon me, as contrary to my own inelination as to his orders."

3. When his sentence was announced to him, he remarked that, since it was his lot to die, there was still a

choice in the mode which would make a material difference in his feelings; and he would be happy, if possible, to be indulged with a professional death. He made a second application by letter, in concise but pursuasive terms. It was thought this indulgence, being incompatible with the customs of war, could not be granted; and it was therefore determined, in both cases, to evade an answer, to spare him the sensations which a certain knowledge of the mode would inflict.

4. In going to the place of execution, he bowed familiarly, as he went along, to all those with whom he had been acquainted in his confinement. A smile of complacency expressed the serene fortitude of his mind. Arrived at the fatal spot, he asked, with some emotion, "Must I, then, die in this manner?" He was told it had been unavoidable. "I am reconciled to my fate," said he, "but not to the mode." Soon, however, recollecting himself, he added, "It will be but a momentary pang;" and, springing upon the cart, performed the last offices to himself, with a composure that excited the admiration and melted the hearts of the beholders.

5. Upon being told the final moment was at hand, and asked if he had any thing to say, he answered, "Nothing, but to request you will witness to the world, that I die like a brave man." Among the extraordinary circumstances that attended him, in the midst of his enemies, he died universally esteemed and universally regretted.

CVI. — ARNOLD AND TALLEYRAND.

FROM WOODWORTH.

1. THERE was a day when Talleyrand arrived in Havre direct from Paris. It was the darkest hour of the French Revolution. Pursued by the bloodhounds of the Reign of Terror, stripped of every wreck of property or power, Talleyrand secured a passage to America, in a ship about

to sail. He was a beggar and a wanderer to a strange land, to earn his bread by daily labor.

2. "Is there an American staying at your house?" he asked the landlord of the hotel. "I am bound to cross the water, and would like a letter to a person of influence in the New World." The landlord hesitated a moment, then replied, "There is a gentleman up-stairs, either from America or Britain, but whether an American or an Englishman, I can not tell." He pointed the way, and Talleyrand, who, in his life, was Bishop, Prince, and Prime Minister, ascended the stairs. A miserable suppliant, he stood before the stranger's door, knocked, and entered.

3. In the far corner of the dimly lighted room, sat a man of some fifty years: his arms folded, and his head bowed on his breast. From a window directly opposite, a flood of light poured over his forehead. His eyes looked from beneath the downcast brows, and gazed on Talleyrand's face with a peculiar and searching expression. His face was striking in outline; the mouth and chin indicative of an iron will. His form, vigorous, even with the snows of fifty, was clad in a dark, but rich and distinguished costume.

4. Talleyrand advanced, stated that he was a fugitive, and, under the impression that the gentleman before him was an American, he solicited his kind and feeling offices. He poured forth his history in eloquent French and broken English: "I am a wanderer and an exile. I am forced to fly to the New World, without a friend or home. You are an American! Give me, then, I beseech you, a letter of yours, so that I may be able to earn my bread. I am willing to toil in any manner; the scenes of Paris have seized me with such horror, that a life of labor would be a paradise to a career of luxury in France. Will you give me a letter to one of your friends? A gentleman like yourself has doubtless many friends."

5. The strange gentleman rose. With a look that Talleyrand never forgot, he retreated toward the door of the next chamber; his eyes looking still from beneath his darkened brow. He spoke as he retreated backward: his

voice was full of meaning. "I am the only man born in the New World who can raise his hand to God and say, I have not a friend, not one, in all America!" Talleyrand never forgot the overwhelming sadness of the look which accompanied these words.

6. "Who are you?" he cried, as the strange man retreated to the next room: "your name?" "My name," he replied, with a smile that had more mockery than joy in its convulsive expression, "my name is Benedict Arnold!" He was gone. Talleyrand sank into his chair, gasping the words, "ARNOLD, THE TRAITOR!"

7. Thus Arnold wandered over the earth, another Cain, with the wanderer's mark upon his brow. Even in that secluded room in that inn at Havre, his crimes found him out, and forced him to tell his name: that name the synonym of infamy. The last twenty years of his life are covered with a cloud, from whose darkness but a few gleams of light flash out upon the page of history.

8. The manner of his death is not exactly known; but we can not doubt that he died utterly friendless; that remorse pursued him to the grave, whispering John Andre! in his ear; and that the memory of his course of glory gnawed like a canker at his heart, murmuring forever, "True to your country, what might you have been, Oh! Arnold, the Traitor!"

CVII.—INGRATITUDE—PATRIOTISM—THE BRAVE.

INGRATITUDE.

1. BLOW, blow, thou wintry wind,
Thou art not so unkind
  As man's ingratitude:
Thy tooth is not so keen,
Because thou art not seen,
  Although thy breath be rude.

2. Freeze, freeze, thou bitter sky,
Thou dost not bite so nigh
   As benefits forgot:
Though thou the waters warp,
Thy sting is not so sharp
   As friend remember'd not.

PATRIOTISM.

3. Breathes there the man, with soul so dead,
Who never to himself hath said,
   This is my own, my native land?
Whose heart hath ne'er within him buru'd,
As home his footsteps he hath turu'd,
   From wandering on a foreign strand?

4. If such there breathe, go, mark him well:
For him no minstrel raptures swell.
High though his titles, proud his name,
Boundless his wealth, as wish can claim;
Despite those titles, power, and pelf,
The wretch concenter'd all in self,
Living, shall forfeit fair renown,
And, doubly dying, shall go down
To the vile dust from whence he sprung,
Unwept, unhonor'd, and unsung.

5. O Caledonia! stern and wild,
Meet nurse for a poetic child!
Land of brown heath and shaggy wood,
Land of the mountain and the flood,
Land of my sires! what mortal hand
Can e'er untie the filial band
That knits me to thy rugged strand!

THE BRAVE.

6. How sleep the brave, who sink to rest
By all their country's wishes blest!

When Spring, with dewy fingers cold,
Returns to deck the hallow'd mold,
She there shall dress a sweeter sod
Than Fancy's feet have ever trod.

7. By fairy hands their knell is rung,
By forms unseen their dirge is sung;
There Honor comes, a pilgrim gray,
To bless the turf that wraps their clay;
And Freedom shall awhile repair
To dwell a weeping hermit there!

———————

CVIII.—AMERICA.

1. My country! 'tis of thee,
  Sweet land of liberty,
    Of thee I sing;
  Land where my fathers died,
  Land of the pilgrims' pride;
  From every mountain side,
    Let freedom ring.

2. My native country! thee,
  Land of the noble free,
    Thy name I love:
  I love thy rocks and rills,
  Thy woods and templed hills;
  My heart with rapture thrills,
    Like that above.

3. Let music swell the breeze,
  And ring from all the trees,
    Sweet freedom's song;
  Let mortal tongues awake,
  Let all that breathe partake,
  Let rocks their silence break,
    The sound prolong.

4. Our fathers' God! to thee,
   Author of liberty!
     To thee we sing;
   Long may our land be bright
   With freedom's holy light;
   Protect us by thy might,
     Great God, our King!

CIX. — THE POETRY OF THE BIBLE.

FROM DR. SPRING.

1. ONE of the most eminent critics has said, that "devotional poetry can not please." If it be so, then has the Bible carried the dominion of poetry into regions that are inaccessible to worldly ambition. It has crossed the enchanted circle, and, by the beauty, boldness, and originality of its conceptions, has given to devotional poetry a glow, a richness, a tenderness, in vain sought for in Shakspeare or Cowper, in Scott, or in Byron.

2. Where is there poetry that can be compared with the song of Moses, after the destruction of Pharaoh; with the psalms of David; with the song of Solomon; and with the prophecies of Isaiah? Where is there an elegiac ode to be compared with the song of David, upon the death of Saul and Jonathan, or the lamentations of Jeremiah? Where, in ancient or modern poetry, is there a passage like this? "In thoughts from the visions of the night, when deep sleep falleth on man, fear came upon me, and trembling, which made all my bones to shake. Then a spirit passed before my face: the hair of my flesh stood up. It stood still, but I could not discern the form thereof. An image was before mine eyes. There was silence. And I heard a voice, saying, Shall mortal man be more just than God? shall a man be more pure than his Maker? Behold he putteth no trust in his servants, and his angels he chargeth with folly. How much less in them that dwell in houses of clay, whose foundation is as the dust, and who are crushed before the moth!"

3. Men, who have felt the power of poetry, when they have marked the "deep-working passion of Dante," and observed the elevation of Milton, as he "combined image with image, in lofty gradations," have thought that they discovered the indebtedness of these writers to the poetry of the Old Testament. But how much more sublime is Isaiah than Milton! How much more enkindling than Dante is David! How much more picturesque than Homer is Solomon or Job! Like the rapid and glowing argumentations of Paul, the poetic parts of the Bible may be read a thousand times, and they have all the freshness and glow of the first perusal.

4. Where, in the compass of human language, is there a paragraph, which, for boldness and variety of metaphor, delicacy and majesty of thought, strength and invention, elegance and refinement, equals the passage in which "God answers Job out of the whirlwind?" What merely human imagination, in the natural progress of a single discourse, and, apparently, without effort, ever thus went down to "the foundations of the earth;" stood at "the doors of the ocean;" visited "the place where the day-spring from on high takes hold of the uttermost parts of the earth;" entered into "the treasures of the snow and the hail;" traced "the path of the thunderbolt;" and, penetrating the retired chambers of nature, demanded, "Hath the rain a father? or, who hath begotten the drops of the dew?" And how bold its flights, how inexpressibly striking and beautiful its antithesis, when, from the warm and sweet Pleiades, it wanders to the sterner Orion; and, in its rapid course, hears the "young lions crying unto God, for lack of meat;" sees the war-horse pawing in the valley; descries the eagle on the crag of the rock; and, in all that is vast and minute, dreadful and beautiful, discovers and proclaims the glory of Him, who is "excellent in counsel, and wonderful in working!"

5. The style of Hebrew poetry is every-where forcible and figurative, beyond example. The book of Job stands not alone in this sententious, spirited, and energetic form and manner. It prevails throughout the poetic parts of

the Scriptures; and they stand, confessedly, the most eminent examples to be found of the truly sublime and beautiful. I confess, I have not much of the spirit of poetry. It is a fire that is enkindled at the living lamp of nature, and glows only on a few favored altars. And yet, I can not but love the poetic associations of the Bible. Now, they are sublime and beautiful, like the mountain torrent, swollen and impetuous, by the sudden bursting of the cloud; now, they are grand and awful, like the stormy Galilee, when the tempest beat upon the fearful disciples; again, they are placid as that calm lake, when the Savior's feet have touched its waters, and stilled them into peace.

6. There is, also, a sublimity, an invention, in the *imagery* of the Bible, that is found in no other book. In the Bible, you have allegory, apologue, parable, and enigma, all clearly intelligible, and enforcing truth with a strong and indelible impression. You have significant actions, uttering volumes of instruction; as when "Jesus called a little child, and set him in the midst of his disciples, and said, Except ye be converted, and become as little children, ye shall not enter into the kingdom of heaven;" as when he cursed the barren fig-tree; as when he "washed his disciples' feet." And where is there a *comparison* like this? "And the heavens departed as a scroll, when it is rolled together." Where is there a *description* like this? "And I saw an angel standing in the sun, and he cried with a loud voice, saying to all the fowls that fly in the midst of heaven, Come, and gather yourselves together unto the supper of the great God." Or, where is there a sentence like the following? "And I saw a great white throne, and him that sat on it, from whose face the earth and the heavens fled away, and there was found no place for them."

7. English literature is no common debtor to the Bible. In what department of English literature may not the difference be discovered between the spirit and sentiments of Christian writers, and those who have drawn all their materials of thought and of ornament from pagan writers? We find a proof of the superiority of Christian principles.

even in those works of imagination, which are deemed scarcely susceptible of influence from religion. The common romance and the novel, with all their fooleries and ravings, would be more contemptible than they are, did they not, sometimes, undesignedly, catch a conception, or adorn a character, from the rich treasury of revelation. And the more splendid fictions of the poet derive their highest charm from the evangelical philanthropy, tenderness, and sublimity, that invest them. But for the Bible, Homer and Milton might have stood upon the same shelf, equal in morality, as they are competitors for renown; Young had been ranked with Juvenal; and Cowper had united with Horace and with Ovid, to swell the tide of voluptuousness.

CX. — SONG OF MOSES.

FROM THE BIBLE.

1. I WILL sing unto the Lord, for he hath triumphed
   gloriously;
The horse and his rider hath he whelmed in the sea.
My praise and my song is Jehovah,
And he is become my salvation:
He is my God, and I will praise him;
My father's God, and I will exalt him.

2. Jehovah is a man of war: Jehovah is his name.
The chariots of Pharaoh and his hosts hath he cast into
   the sea,
And his choicest leaders into the Red sea.
The floods have covered them; they went down;
Into the abyss they went down as a stone.
Thy right hand, O Jehovah, hath made itself glorious in
   power:
Thy right hand, O Jehovah, hath dashed in pieces the
   enemy;

And in the strength of thy majesty thou hast destroyed
    thine adversaries.
Thou didst let loose thy wrath: it consumed them like
    stubble.

3. With the blast of thy nostrils, the waters were heaped
    together;
The flowing waters stood upright as a heap:
The floods were congealed in the heart of the sea.
The enemy said, "I will pursue, I will overtake;
I will divide the spoil; my soul shall be satisfied:
I will draw my sword, my hand shall destroy them."
Thou didst blow with thy breath, the sea covered them:
They sank as lead in the mighty waters.

4. Who is like unto thee among the gods, O Jehovah?
Who is like unto thee, making thyself glorious in holiness,
Fearful in praises, executing wonders?
Thou didst stretch out thy right hand, the earth swallowed
    them.
Thou hast led forth, in thy mercy, the people whom thou
    hast redeemed;
Thou hast guided them in thy strength to the habitation
    of thy holiness.

5. The people shall hear, and be disquieted;
Terror shall seize the inhabitants of Philistia.
Then, the nobles of Edom shall be confounded:
The mighty ones of Moab, trembling shall take hold upon
    them:
All the inhabitants of Canaan shall melt away:
Terror and perplexities shall fall upon them:
Because of the greatness of thine arm, they shall be still
    as a stone,
Till thy people pass over, O Jehovah,
Till the people pass over whom thou hast redeemed.
Thou shalt bring them in, and plant them in the mountains
    of thine inheritance,

The place for thy dwelling which thou hast prepared, O Jehovah!

The sanctuary, O Lord, which thy hands have established.

Jehovah shall reign forever and ever!

CXI.—THE KING OF GLORY.

FROM THE BIBLE.

In this piece, one of the class should read what is marked, *"First Voice;"* another should read what is marked, *"Second Voice;"* and the whole class should read in concert what is marked, *"Chorus."*

1st Voice. THE earth is the Lord's, and the fullness thereof,
The world, and they that dwell therein;
For he hath founded it upon the seas,
And established it upon the floods.

2d Voice. Who shall ascend into the hill of the Lord?
Or who shall stand in his holy place?

1st Voice. He that hath clean hands, and a pure heart,
Who hath not lifted up his heart unto vanity;
He shall receive the blessing from the Lord,
And righteousness from the God of his salvation.

Chorus. Lift up your heads, O ye gates!
And be ye lifted up, ye everlasting doors!
And the King of glory shall come in.

1st Voice. Who is this King of glory?

2d Voice. The Lord, strong and mighty;
The Lord, mighty in battle.

Chorus. Lift up your heads, O ye gates!
Even lift them up, ye everlasting doors!
And the King of glory shall come in.

1st Voice. Who is this King of glory? Who?

2d Voice. The Lord of hosts, *He* is the King of glory.

Chorus. Lift up your heads, O ye gates!
Even lift them up, ye everlasting doors!
And the King of glory shall come in.

H S. R.—26

CXII. — THE DUELIST.

FROM DIALOGUES OF THE DEAD.

Duelist. Mercury, Charon's boat is on the other side of the water; allow me, before it returns, to have some conversation with the North American Savage, whom you brought hither at the same time that you conducted me to the shades. I never saw one of that species before, and am curious to know what the animal is. He looks very grim. Pray, sir, what is your name? I understand you speak English.

Savage. Yes, I learned it in my childhood, having been bred up for some years in the town of New York: but before I was a man, I returned to my countrymen, the valiant Mohawks, and having been cheated by one of yours in the sale of some rum, I wished never to have any thing to do with them afterward. Yet, with the rest of my tribe, I took up the hatchet for them, in the war against France, and was killed while I was upon a scalping party. But I died very well satisfied; for my friends were vietorious, and before I was shot, I had scalped seven men and five women and children. In a former war, I had done still greater exploits. My name is the Bloody Bear: it was given me to denote my fierceness and valor.

Duelist. Bloody Bear, I respect you, and am much your humble servant. My name is Tom Pushwell, very well known at Arthur's. I am a gentleman by birth, and by profession a gamester, and a man of honor. I have killed men in fair fighting, in honorable single combat, but I do not understand cutting the throats of women and children.

Savage. Sir, that's our way of making war. Every nation has its own customs. But, by the grimness in your countenance, and that hole in your breast, I presume you were killed, as I was myself, in some scalping party. How happened it that your enemy did not take off your scalp?

Duelist. Sir, I was killed in a duel. A friend of mine had lent me some money; after two or three years, being himself in great want, he asked me to pay him; I thought

his demand an affront to my honor, and sent him a challenge. We met in Hyde Park; the fellow could not fence; I was the most adroit swordsman in England. I gave him three or four wounds; but, at last, he ran upon me with such impetuosity that he put me out of my play, and I could not prevent him from whipping me through the lungs. I died the next day, as a man of honor should, without any sniveling signs of repentance; and he will follow me soon, for his surgeon has declared his wounds to be mortal. It is said that his wife is dead of her fright, and that his family of seven children will be undone by his death. So I am well revenged, and that is a comfort. For my part, I had no wife. I always hated marriage.

Savage. Mercury, I won't go in a boat with that fellow. He has murdered his countryman; he has murdered his friend. I say I won't go in a boat with that fellow, I will swim over the river; I can swim like a duck.

Mercury. Swim over the Styx! it must not be done: it is against the laws of Pluto's empire. You must go in the boat, so be quiet.

Savage. Do not tell me of laws; I am a savage! I value no laws. Talk of laws to the Englishman; there are laws in his country, and yet you see he did not regard them, for they could never allow him to kill his fellow-subject in time of peace, because he asked him to pay a debt. The English can not be so brutal as to make such things lawful.

Mercury. You reason well against him. But how comes it that you are so offended with murder; you who have massacred women in their sleep, and children in their cradles?

Savage. I killed none but my enemies; I never killed my own countryman; I never killed my friend. Here, take my blanket, and let it come over in the boat, but see that the murderer does not sit upon it or touch it; if he does, I will burn it in the fire I see yonder. Farewell. I am resol d to swim over the water.

Mercury. By this touch of my wand, I take all thy strength from thee. Swim now if thou canst.

Savage. This is a very potent enchanter. Restore me my strength, and I will obey thee.

Mercury. I restore it; but be orderly and do as I bid you, otherwise worse will befall you.

Duelist. Mercury, leave him to me; I will tutor him for you. Sirrah Savage, dost thou pretend to be ashamed of my company? Dost thou know that I have kept the best company in England?

Savage. I know thou art a scoundrel! Not pay thy debts! kill thy friend who lent thee money, for asking thee for it! Get out of my sight, or I will drive thee into the Styx.

Mercury. Stop, I command thee. No violence. Talk to him calmly.

Savage. I must obey thee. Well, sir, let me know what merit you had to introduce you into good company. What could you do?

Duelist. Sir, I gamed as I told you. Besides that, I kept a good table. I ate as well as any man in England or France.

Savage. Eat! Did you ever eat the chine of a Frenchman, or his leg, or his shoulder? There is fine eating! I have eaten twenty. My table was always well served. My wife was the best cook for dressing man's flesh in all North America. You will not pretend to compare your eating with mine.

Duelist. I danced very finely.

Savage. I will dance with thee for thy ears. I can dance all day long. I can dance the war-dance with more spirit and vigor than any man of my nation; let us see thee begin it. How thou standest like a post! Has Mercury struck thee with his enfeebling rod; or art thou ashamed to betray thy awkwardness? If he would permit me, I would teach thee to dance in a way that thou hast not yet seen. I would make thee caper and leap like a buck. But what else canst thou do, thou bragging rascal?

Duelist. O, heavens! must I bear this? What can I do with this fellow? I have neither sword nor pistol; and his shade seems to be twice as strong as mine.

Mercury. You must answer his questions. It was your own desire to have a conversation with him. He is not well bred, but he will tell you some truths which you must hear in this place. It would have been well for you if you had heard them above. He asked of you what you could do besides eating and dancing.

Duelist. I sang very agreeably.

Savage. Let me hear you sing your death-song, or the war-whoop. I challenge you to sing; the fellow is mute. Mercury, this is a liar. He tells us nothing but lies. Let me pull out his tongue.

Duelist. The lie given me! and, alas! I dare not resent it. O, what a disgrace to the family of the Pushwells!

Mercury. Here, Charon, take these two savages to your care. How far the barbarism of the Mohawk will excuse his horrid acts, I leave Minos to judge; but what excuse can the Englishman plead? The custom of dueling? An excuse this, that, in these regions, can not avail. The spirit that made him draw his sword in the combat against his friend, is not the spirit of honor; it is the spirit of the furies, of Alecto herself. To her he must go, for she has long dwelt in his merciless bosom.

Savage. If he is to be punished, turn him over to me. I understand the art of tormenting. Sirrah, I begin with this kick, as a tribute to your boasted honor. Get you into the boat, or I will give you another. I am impatient to have you condemned.

Duelist. O my honor, my honor, to what infamy art thou fallen!

CXIII. — THE DUEL.

FROM HOOD.

THOMAS HOOD, an English poet, who lived from 1798 to 1845, is chiefly known as a humorist and comic writer. In this department he has no superior, and is rivaled only by Saxe and Holmes of our own country.

1. IN Brentford town, of old renown,
   There liv'd a Mister Bray,

Who fell in love with Lucy Bell,
And so did Mister Clay.

2. Said Mr. Bray to Mr. Clay,
"You choose to rival me,
And court Miss Bell; but there your *court*
No *thoroughfare* shall be.

3. "Unless you now give up your suit,
You may repent your love;
I, who have shot a *pigeon* match,
Can shoot a *turtle dove.*

4. "So, pray, before you woo her more,
Consider what you do:
If you pop aught to Lucy Bell,
I'll *pop* it into you."

5. Said Mr. Clay to Mr. Bray,
"Your threats I do explode;
One who has been a volunteer
Knows how to prime and load.

6. "And so I say to you, unless
Your passion quiet keeps,
I, who have shot and hit *bulls' eyes,*
May chance to hit a *sheep's!*"

7. Now gold is oft for silver changed,
And that for copper red;
But these two went away to give
Each other change for *lead.*

8. But first they found a friend apiece,
This pleasant thought to give,
That when they both were dead they'd have
Two *second*s yet to live.

9. To measure out the ground, not long
The seconds next forbore;

And having taken *one rash step*,
  They took *a dozen more.*

10. They next prepared each pistol **pan**,
    Against the deadly strife;
By putting in the *prime of death*
    Against the *prime of life.*

11. Now all was ready for the foes;
    But when they took their stands,
Fear made them tremble so, they **found**
    They both were *shaking hands.*

12. Said Mr. C. to Mr. B.,
    "Here one of us may fall,
And like St. Paul's Cathedral **now**,
    Be doom'd to have a *ball.*

13. "I do confess I did attach
    Misconduct to your name!
If I withdraw the charge, will **then**
    Your *ramrod* do the same?"

14. Said Mr. B., "I do agree;
    But think of Honor's courts,
If we go off without a shot,
    There will be strange *reports.*

15. "But look! the morning now is bright,
    Though cloudy it begun;
Why can't we aim above, as if
    We had *call'd out* the sun?"

16. So up into the harmless air
    Their bullets they did send;
And may all other duels have
    That *upshot* in the end.

CXIV. — THE WINDMILLS.

FROM DON QUIXOTE, BY CERVANTES.

CERVANTES was a celebrated Spanish author, who lived from 1547 to 1623. His principal work is "Don Quixote," in which he ridicules the "knight errantry," then so fashionable. Sancho Panza is the squire, and is a man of shrewd mother wit, and rich humor. The book abounds in wit, in beautiful description, in poetry, and eloquence.

1. As they were thus discoursing, they came in sight of thirty or forty windmills, which are in that plain; and, as soon as Don Quixote espied them, he said to his squire, "Fortune disposes our affairs better than we ourselves could have desired; look yonder, friend Sancho Panza, where thou mayest discover somewhat more than thirty monstrous giants, whom I intend to encounter and slay, and with their spoils we will begin to enrich ourselves; for it is lawful war, and doing God good service, to remove so wicked a generation from off the face of the earth." "What giants?" said Sancho Panza. "Those thou seest yonder," answered his master, "with their long arms; for some are wont to have them almost of the length of two leagues." "Look, sir," answered Sancho; "those which appear yonder are not giants, but windmills; and what seem to be arms are the sails, which, whirled about by the wind, make the millstone go."

2. "It is very evident," answered Don Quixote, "that thou art not versed in the business of adventures. They are giants; and, if thou art afraid, get thee aside and pray, while I engage with them in fierce and unequal combat." So saying, he clapped spurs to his steed, notwithstanding the cries his squire sent after him, assuring him that they were certainly windmills, and not giants. But he was so fully possessed that they were giants, that he neither heard the outcries of his squire Sancho, nor yet discerned what they were, though he was very near them; but went on, crying out aloud, "Fly not, ye cowards, and vile caitiffs, for it is a single knight who assaults you!" The

wind now rising a little, the great sails began to move; upon which Don Quixote called out, "Although ye should move more arms than the giant Briareus, ye shall pay for it!"

3. Then recommending himself devoutly to his lady, Dulcinea, beseeching her to succor him in the present danger, being well covered with his buckler, and setting his lance in the rest, he rushed on as fast as Rozinante could gallop, and attacked the first mill before him; when, running his lance into the sail, the wind whirled it about with so much violence, that it broke the lance to shivers, dragging horse and rider after it, and tumbling them over and over on the plain, in very evil plight. Sancho Panza hastened to his assistance, as fast as he could; and when he came up to his master, he found him unable to stir, so violent was the blow which he and Rozinante had received in their fall.

4. "Save me!" quoth Sancho; "did not I warn you to have a care of what you did, for that they were nothing but windmills? And nobody could mistake them, but one that had the like in his head." "Peace, friend Sancho!" answered Don Quixote; "for matters of war are, of all others, most subject to continual change. Now, I verily believe, and it is most certainly the fact, that the sage Freston, who stole away my study and books, has metamorphosed these giants into windmills, on purpose to deprive me of the glory of vanquishing them, so great is the enmity he bears me! But his wicked arts will finally avail but little against the goodness of my sword!" "God grant it!" answered Sancho Panza; then helping him to rise, he mounted him again upon his steed, which was almost disjointed.

H. S. R.—27

CXV.—SANCHO PANZA.

FROM CERVANTES.

In this extract from Don Quixote, Sancho Panza enters upon the government of an island, which had been promised to him for his faithful services.

1. SANCHO, with all his attendants, came to a town that had about a thousand inhabitants, and was one of the best where the Duke had any power. As soon as he came to the gates, (for it was walled,) the chief officers and inhabitants, in their formalities, came out to receive him; the bells rung, and all the people gave general demonstration of their joy. The new governor was then carried in mighty pomp to the great church, to give Heaven thanks; and, after some ridiculous ceremonies, they delivered him the keys of the gates, and received him as perpetual governor of the island of Barataria. In the meantime, the garb, the port, the huge beard, and the short and thick shape of the new governor, made every one, who knew nothing of the jest, wonder; and even those who were privy to the plot, who were many, were not a little surprised.

2. In short, from the church they carried him to the court of justice; where, when they had placed him in his seat, "My Lord Governor," said the Duke's steward to him, "it is an ancient custom here, that he who takes possession of this famous island, must answer to some difficult and intricate question that is propounded to him; and, by the return that he makes, the people feel the pulse of his understanding, and, by an estimate of his abilities, judge whether they ought to rejoice or be sorry for his coming."

3. All the while the steward was speaking, Sancho was staring on an inscription, in large characters, on the wall over against his seat; and, as he could not read, he asked what was the meaning of that which he saw painted there upon the wall. "Sir," said they, "it is an account of the day when your lordship took possession of this island; and the inscription runs thus: 'This day, being such a day of

this month, in such a year, the Lord Don Sancho Panza took possession of this island, which may he long enjoy.'"

4. "And who is he?" asked Sancho. "Your lordship," answered the steward, "for we know of no other Panza in this island but yourself, who now sit in this chair." "Well, friend," said Sancho, "pray take notice that Don does not belong to me, nor was it borne by any of my family before me. Plain Sancho Panza is my name. Now do I already guess that your Dons are as thick as stones in this island. But it is enough that Heaven knows my meaning; if my government happen to last but four days to an end, it shall go hard but I will clear the island of these Dons, that must needs be as troublesome as so many flesh-flies. Come, now for your question, good Mr. Steward, and I will answer it as well as I can, whether the town be sorry or pleased."

5. At the same instant two men came into the court, the one dressed like a country fellow, the other looking like a tailor with a pair of shears in his hand. "If it please you, my lord," cried the tailor, "I and this farmer are come before your worship. This honest man came to my shop yesterday; for, saving your presence, I am a tailor, and, Heaven be praised, free of my company; so, my lord, he showed me a piece of cloth. 'Sir,' quoth he, is there enough of this to make a cap?' Whereupon I measured the stuff, and answered him, 'Yes, if it like your worship.'

6. "Now, as I imagined, do you see, he could not but imagine (and perhaps he imagined right enough) that I had a mind to cabbage some of his cloth, judging hard of us honest tailors. 'Prithee,' quoth he, 'look there be not enough for two caps?' Now I smelt him out, and told him there was. Whereupon the old knave, (if it like your worship,) going on to the same tune, bid me look again, and see whether it would not make *three?* And, at last, if it would not make *five?* I was resolved to humor my customer, and said it might; so we struck a bargain.

7. "Just now the man is come for his caps, which I gave him; but when I asked him for my money, he will

have me give him his cloth again, or pay him for it." "Is this true, honest man?" said Sancho to the farmer. "Yes, if it please you, answered the fellow, "but pray let him show the five caps he has made me." "With all my heart," cried the tailor; and with that, pulling his hand from under his cloak, he held up five little tiny caps, hanging upon his four fingers and thumb, as upon so many pins. "There," quoth he, "you see the fine caps this good gaffer asks for; and may I never whip a stitch more if I have wronged him of the least snip of his cloth, and let any workman be judge."

8. The sight of the caps, and the oddness of the cause, set the whole court a laughing. Only Sancho sat gravely, considering awhile, and then, "Methinks," said he, "this suit needs not be long depending, but may be decided without any more ado, with a great deal of equity; and, therefore, the judgment is, that the tailor shall lose his making, and the countryman his cloth, and that the caps be given to the poor prisoners, and so let there be an end of the business."

9. If this sentence provoked the laughter of the whole court, the next no less raised their admiration. For, after the governor's order was executed, two old men appeared before him, one of them with a large cane in his hand, which he used as a staff. "My lord," said the other, who had none, "some time ago I lent this man ten gold crowns, to do him a kindness, which money he was to pay me on demand. I did not ask him for it again in a good while, lest it should prove a greater inconvenience to him to repay me, than he labored under when he borrowed it. However, perceiving that he took no care to pay me, I have asked him for my due; nay, I have been forced to dun him hard for it.

10. "But still he did not only refuse to pay me again, but denied that he owed me any thing, and said, 'that if I lent him so much money, he certainly returned it.' Now, because I have no witnesses of the loan, nor he of the pretended payment, I beseech your lordship to put him to his oath, and if he will swear that he has paid me, I will

freely forgive him before God and the world." "What say you to this, old gentleman with the staff?" asked Sancho. "Sir," answered the old man, "I own he lent me the gold; and, since he requires my oath, I beg you will be pleased to hold down your rod of justice, that I may swear upon it how I have honestly and truly returned him his money."

11. Thereupon the governor held down his rod, and, in the meantime, the defendant gave the plaintiff his cane to hold, as if it hindered him, while he was to make a cross, and swear over the judge's rod. This done, he declared that it was true the other had lent him ten crowns, but that he really had returned him the sum into his own hands; and that, because he supposed the plaintiff had for-gotten it, he was continually asking him for it."

12. The great governor, hearing this, asked the creditor what he had to reply? He made answer that, since his adversary had sworn it, he was satisfied; for he believed him to be a better Christian than to forswear himself, and perhaps he had forgotten that he had been repaid. Then the defendant took his cane again, and, having made a low obeisance to the judge, was leaving the court; which, when Sancho perceived, reflecting on the passage of the cane, and admiring the creditor's patience, after he had studied awhile, with his head leaning over his stomach, and his forefinger on his nose, on a sudden, he ordered the old man with the staff to be called back.

13. When he returned, "Honest man," said Sancho, "let me see that cane a little. I have a use for it." "With all my heart," answered the other; "sir, here it is," and with that he gave it to him. Sancho took it, and giving it to the other old man, "There," said he, "go your ways, and Heaven be with you, for now you are paid." "How so, my lord?" cried the old man, "do you judge this cane to be worth ten gold crowns? "Certainly," said the gov-ernor, "or else I am the greatest dunce in the world. And now you shall see whether I have not a head-piece fit to govern a whole kingdom upon a shift."

14. This said, he ordered the cane to be broken in open

court, which was no sooner done, than out dropped the
ten crowns.   All the spectators were amazed, and began to
look on their governor as a second Solomon.   They asked
him how he could conjecture that the ten crowns were in
the cane? He told them that, having observed how the
defendant gave it to the plaintiff to hold while he took
his oath, and then swore he had truly returned the money
into his own hands, after which he took his cane again
from the plaintiff, it came into his head that the money
was lodged within the reed; from whence may be learned,
that, though sometimes those that govern may be destitute
of sense, yet it often pleases God to direct them in their
judgment.

CXVI. — OTHELLO'S APOLOGY.

FROM SHAKSPEARE.

1. MOST potent, grave, and reverend seigniors,
My very noble and approved good masters,
That I have ta'en away this old man's daughter,
It is most true; true, I have married her;
The very head and front of my offending
Hath this extent, no more.

2. Rude am I in speech,
And little bless'd with the set phrase of peace,
For since these arms of mine had seven years' pith,
Till now some nine moons wasted, they have used
Their dearest action in the tented field;
And little of this great world can I speak
More than pertains to feats of broil and battle,
And therefore little shall I grace my cause,
In speaking of myself.   Yet, by your gracious patience,
I will a round, unvarnish'd tale deliver
Of my whole course of love; what drugs, what charms,
What conjuration, and what mighty magic,
(For such proceedings I am charged withal,)
I won his daughter with.

3. Her father lov'd me; oft invited me;
Still question'd me the story of my life,
From year to year; the battles, sieges, fortunes,
That I have pass'd.
I ran it through, even from my boyish days,
To the very moment that he bade me tell it.
Wherein I spoke of most disastrous chances,
Of moving accidents, by flood and field;
Of hair-breadth 'scapes in the imminent deadly breach;
Of being taken by the insolent foe,
And sold to slavery; of my redemption thence;
And with it, all my travel's history.

4. These things to hear
Would Desdemona seriously incline:
But still the house affairs would draw her thence:
Which ever as she could with haste dispatch,
She 'd come again, and with a greedy ear
Devour up my discourse: which I observing,
Took once a pliant hour, and found good means
To draw from her a prayer of earnest heart,
That I would all my pilgrimage dilate,
Whereof by parcels she had something heard,
But not attentively.

5. I did consent:
And often did beguile her of her tears,
When I did speak of some distressful stroke,
That my youth suffer'd. My story being done,
She gave me for my pains a world of sighs:
She said, In faith, 'twas strange, 'twas passing strange;
'Twas pitiful, 'twas wondrous pitiful;
She wish'd she had not heard it; yet she wish'd,
That heaven had made her such a man.

6. She thank'd me;
And bade me, if I had a friend that lov'd her,
I should but teach him how to tell my story,
And that would woo her. On this hint, I spake.

She lov'd me for the dangers I had pass'd;
And I lov'd her, that she did pity them.
This only is the witchcraft I have used.

CXVII. — GIL BLAS.

FROM LE SAGE.

Archbishop. What is your business with me, my friend?

Gil Blas. I am the young man who was recommended to you by your nephew, Don Fernando.

Arch. O! you are the person of whom he spoke so handsomely. I retain you in my service; I regard you as an acquisition. Your education, it would seem, has not been neglected; you know enough of Greek and Latin for my purpose, and your handwriting suits me. I am obliged to my nephew for sending me so clever a young fellow. So good a copyist must be also a grammarian. Tell me, did you find nothing in the sermon you transcribed for me which shocked your taste? no little negligence of style, or impropriety of diction?

Gil B. O, sir! I am not qualified to play the critic; and if I were, I am persuaded that your Grace's compositions would defy censure.

Arch. Ahem! well I do flatter myself that not many flaws could be picked in them. But, my young friend, tell me what passages struck you most forcibly.

Gil B. If, where all was excellent, any passages more particularly moved me, they were those personifying hope, and describing the good man's death.

Arch. You show an accurate taste and delicate appreciation. I see your judgment may be relied upon. Give yourself no inquietude, Gil Blas, in regard to your advancement in life. I will take care of that. I have an affection for you, and, to prove it, I will now make you my confidant. Yes, my young friend, I will make you the depository of my most secret thoughts. Listen to what I have to say. I am fond of preaching, and my sermons are

not without effect upon my hearers. The conversions of which I am the humble instrument ought to content me. But, shall I confess my weakness? my reputation as a finished orator is what gratifies me most. My productions are celebrated as at once vigorous and elegant. But I would, of all things, avoid the mistake of those authors who do not know when to stop; I would produce nothing beneath my reputation; I would retire seasonably, ere that is impaired. And so, my dear Gil Blas, one thing I exact of your zeal, which is, that when you shall find that my pen begins to flag and to give signs of old age in the owner, you shall not hesitate to apprise me of the fact. Do not be afraid that I shall take it unkindly. I cannot trust my own judgment on this point; self-love may mislead me. A disinterested understanding is what I require for my guidance. I make choice of yours, and mean to abide by your decision.

Gil B. Thank Heaven, sir, the period is likely to be far distant when any such hint shall be needed. Besides, a genius like yours will wear better than that of an inferior man; or, to speak more justly, your faculties are above the encroachments of age. Instead of being weakened, they promise to be invigorated, by time.

Arch. No flattery, my friend. I am well aware that I am liable to give way at any time, all at once. At my age, certain infirmities of the flesh are unavoidable, and they must needs affect the mental powers. I repeat it, Gil Blas, so soon as you shall perceive the slightest symptom of deterioration in my writings, give me fair warning. Do not shrink from being perfectly candid and sincere; for I shall receive such a monition as a token of your regard for me.

Gil B. In good faith, sir, I shall endeavor to merit your confidence.

Arch. Nay, your interests are bound up with your obedience in this respect; for if, unfortunately for you, I should hear in the city a whisper of a falling off in my discourses, an intimation that I ought to stop preaching, I should hold you responsible, and consider myself ex-

empted from all care for your fortunes. Such will be the result of your false discretion.

Gil B. Indeed sir, I shall be vigilant to observe your wishes, and to detect any blemish in your writings.

Arch. And now tell me, Gil Blas, what does the world say of my last discourse? Think you it gave general satisfaction?

Gil B. Since you exact it of me in so pressing a manner to be frank —

Arch. Frank? O, certainly, by all means, speak out, my young friend.

Gil B. Your Grace's sermons never fail to be admired; but —

Arch. But—Well? Do not be afraid to let me know all.

Gil B. If I may venture the observation, it seemed to me that your last discourse did not have that effect upon your audience which your former efforts have had. Perhaps your grace's recent illness —

Arch. What, what! Has it encountered, then, some Aristarchus?

Gil B. No, sir, no. Such productions as yours are beyond criticism. Everybody was charmed with it; but— since you have demanded it of me to be frank and sincere— I take the liberty to remark that your last discourse did not seem to me altogether equal to your preceding. It lacked the strength—the—Do you not agree with me, sir?

Arch. Mr. Gil Blas, that discourse, then, is not to your taste?

Gil B. I did not say that, sir. I found it excellent, only a little inferior to your others.

Arch. So! Now I understand. I seem to you to be on the wane; eh? Out with it. You think it about time that I should retire?

Gil B. I should not have presumed, sir, to speak so freely, but for your express commands. I have simply ren- dered you obedience; and I humbly trust that you will not be offended at my hardihood.

Arch. Offended! O! not at all, Mr. Gil Blas, I utter no reproaches. I don't take it at all ill that you should

speak your sentiments; it is your sentiment only that I find ill. I have been duped in supposing you to be a person of any intelligence; that is all.

Gil B. But, sir, in my zeal to serve you, I have erred in —

Arch. Say no more, say no more! You are yet too raw to discriminate. Know that I never composed a better sermon than that which has had the misfortune to lack your approbation. My faculties, thank Heaven, have lost nothing of their vigor. Hereafter I will make a better choice of an adviser. Go, tell my treasurer to count you out a hundred ducats, and may Heaven conduct you with that sum. Adieu, Mr. Gil Blas! I wish you all manner of prosperity—with a little more taste.

CXVIII. — LOSS OF THE ARCTIC.

From H. W. Beecher.

1. It was autumn. Hundreds had wended their way from pilgrimages; from Rome and its treasures of dead art, and its glory of living nature; from the sides of the Switzer's mountains, from the capitals of various nations; all of them saying in their hearts, we will wait for the September gales to have done with their equinoctial fury, and then we will embark; we will slide across the appeased ocean, and in the gorgeous month of October, we will greet our longed-for native land, and our heart-loved homes.

2. And so the throng streamed along from Berlin, from Paris, from the Orient, converging upon London, still hastening toward the welcome ship, and narrowing every day the circle of engagements and preparations. They crowded aboard. Never had the Arctic borne such a host of passengers, nor passengers so nearly related to so many of us.

3. The hour was come. The signal ball fell at Greenwich. It was noon also at Liverpool. The anchors were weighed; the great hull swayed to the current; the national colors streamed abroad, as if themselves instinct with life

and national sympathy. The bell strikes; the wheels re-
volve; the signal gun beats its echoes in upon every
structure along the shore, and the Arctic glides joyfully
forth from the Mersey, and turns her prow to the winding
channel, and begins her homeward run. The pilot stood
at the wheel, and men saw him. Death sat upon the prow,
and no eye beheld him. Whoever stood at the wheel in
all the voyage, Death was the pilot that steered the craft,
and none knew it. He neither revealed his presence nor
whispered his errand.

4. And so hope was effulgent, and lithe gayety disported
itself, and joy was with every guest. Amid all the incon-
veniencies of the voyage, there was still that which hushed
every murmur,—"Home is not far away." And every
morning it was still one night nearer home! Eight days
had passed. They beheld that distant bank of mist that
for ever haunts the vast shallows of Newfoundland. Boldly
they made for it; and plunging in, its pliant wreaths
wrapped them about. They shall never emerge. The last
sunlight has flashed from that deck. The last voyage is
done to ship and passengers. At noon there came noise-
lessly stealing from the north that fated instrument of
destruction. In that mysterious shroud, that vast atmos-
phere of mist, both steamers were holding their way with
rushing prow and roaring wheels, but invisible.

5. At a league's distance, unconscious, and at nearer
approach unwarned; within hail, and bearing right toward
each other, unseen, unfelt, till in a moment more, emerging
from the gray mists, the ill-omened Vesta dealt her deadly
stroke to the Arctic. The death-blow was scarcely felt
along the mighty hull. She neither reeled nor shivered.
Neither commander nor officers deemed that they had suf-
fered harm. Prompt upon humanity, the brave Luce (let
his name be ever spoken with admiration and respect,)
ordered away his boat with the first officer to inquire if
the stranger had suffered harm. As Gourley went over
the ship's side, O, that some good angel had called to the
brave commander in the words of Paul on a like occasion,
"Except these abide in the ship, ye can not be saved."

6. They departed, and with them the hope of the ship, for now the waters, gaining upon the hold, and rising up upon the fires, revealed the mortal blow. Oh, had now that stern, brave mate, Gourley, been on deck, whom the sailors were wont to mind; had he stood to execute efficiently the commander's will; we may believe that we should not have had to blush for the cowardice and reereancy of the crew, nor weep for the untimely dead. But, apparently, each subordinate officer lost all presence of mind, then courage, and so honor. In a wild scramble, that ignoble mob of firemen, engineers, waiters, and crew, rushed for the boats, and abandoned the helpless women, children, and men, to the mercy of the deep! Four hours there were from the catastrophe of the collision to the catastrophe of SINKING.

7. Oh, what a burial was here! Not as when one is borne from his home, among weeping throngs, and gently carried to the green fields, and laid peacefully beneath the turf and the flowers. No priest stood to pronounce a burial service. It was an ocean grave. The mists alone shrouded the burial-place. No spade prepared the grave, nor sexton filled up the hollowed earth. Down, down, they sank, and the quick returning waters smoothed out every ripple, and left the sea as if it had not been.

CXIX. — THE HESPERUS.

FROM LONGFELLOW.

1. IT was the schooner Hesperus,
   That sail'd the wintry sea;
   And the skipper had taken his little daughter,
   To bear him company.

2. Blue were her eyes as the fairy flax,
   Her cheeks like the dawn of day,
   And her bosom white as the hawthorn buds,
   That ope in the month of May.

3. The skipper, he stood beside the helm,
   His pipe was in his mouth;
And he watch'd how the veering flaw did blow
   The smoke, now west, now south.

4. Then up and spake an old sailor
   Had sail'd the Spanish Main,
"I pray thee, put into yonder port,
   For I fear a hurricane.

5. " Last night the moon had a golden ring,
   And to-night no moon we see."
The skipper he blew a whiff from his pipe,
   And a scornful laugh laugh'd he.

6. Colder and louder blew the wind,
   A gale from the north-east;
The snow fell hissing in the brine,
   And the billows froth'd like yeast.

7. Down came the storm, and smote amain
   The vessel in its strength;
She shudder'd and paus'd like a frighted steed,
   Then leap'd her cable's length.

8. "Come hither, come hither, my little daughter,
   And do not tremble so;
For I can weather the roughest gale
   That ever wind did blow."

9. He wrapp'd her warm in his seaman's coat,
   Against the stinging blast;
He cut a rope from a broken spar,
   And bound her to the mast.

10. "O father, I hear the church bells ring;
   O, say, what may it be?"
" 'Tis a fog-bell, on a rock-bound coast;"
   And he steer'd for the open sea.

11. "O father, I hear the sound of guns;
    O, say, what may it be?"
"Some ship in distress, that can not live
    In such an angry sea."

12. "O father, I see a gleaming light;
    O, say, what may it be?"
But the father answer'd never a word:
    A frozen corpse was he.

13. Lash'd to the helm, all stiff and stark,
    With his face unto the skies,
The lantern gleam'd, through the gleaming snow,
    On his fix'd and glassy eyes.

14. Then the maiden clasp'd her hands and pray'd
    That sa-ved she might be;
And she thought of Christ, who still'd the wave
    On the Lake of Galilee.

15. And fast through the midnight, dark and drear,
    Through the whistling sleet and snow,
Like a sheeted ghost, the vessel swept
    Toward the reef of Norman's Woe.

16. And ever, the fitful gusts between,
    A sound came from the land;
It was the sound of the trampling surf,
    On the rocks and the hard sea sand.

17. The breakers were right beneath her bows;
    She drifted a dreary wreck;
And a whooping billow swept the crew,
    Like icicles, from her deck.

18. She struck where the white and fleecy waves
    Look'd soft as carded wool;
But the cruel rocks, they gored her side
    Like the horns of an angry bull.

19. Her rattling shrouds, all sheath'd in ice,
    With the masts, went by the board;
    Like a vessel of glass she stove and sank:
    Ho! ho! the breakers roar'd.

20. At day-break, on the bleak sea beach,
    A fisherman stood aghast
    To see the form of a maiden fair
    Lash'd close to a drifting mast.

21. The salt sea was frozen on her breast,
    The salt tears in her eyes;
    And he saw her hair, like the brown sea-weed,
    On the billows fall and rise.

22. Such was the wreck of the Hesperus,
    In the midnight and the snow:
    Christ save us all from a death like this,
    On the reef of Norman's Woe.

CXX. — BREAK, BREAK, BREAK.

FROM TENNYSON.

1. BREAK, break, break,
    On thy cold, gray stones, O Sea,
    And I would that my tongue could utter
    The thoughts that arise in me.

2. O, well for the fisherman's boy
    That he shouts with his sister at play!
    O, well for the sailor lad
    That he sings in his boat on the bay!

3. And the stately ships go on
    To the haven under the hill;
    But, O, for the touch of a vanish'd hand,
    And the sound of a voice that is still!

4. Break, break, break,
   At the foot of thy crags, O Sea,
   But the tender grace of a day that is dead
   Will never come back to me.

CXXI. — LAND AND SEA.

1. On! give me to tread the steadfast earth,
   With a firm step, bold and free;
   For surely a rood of land is worth
   More than an acre of sea:
   The pleasure that lies in the deep, deep sea,
   Lieth all too deep for me.

2. The tiller I leave where the fierce winds blow,
   And I'll be a tiller of ground:
   The only bark that I wish to know,
   Is the bark of my faithful hound:
   For the pleasure that lies in the deep, deep sea,
   Lieth all too deep for me.

3. A summer-day's cruise 'neath a squalless sky
   Is doubtless a right merry thing,
   As swiftly past cape and headland we fly,
   On our seagull's snowy wing;
   Yet the pleasure that lies in the deep, deep sea,
   Lieth all too deep for me.

4. Though to woo the sea may be full of bliss,
   While her voice is sweet and low,
   Yet her wavelet lips seem meeting your kiss
   When you reel to the might of a blow.
   Oh! the pleasure that lies in the deep, deep sea,
   Lieth all too deep for me.

5. Then the night-capp'd waves grow wild in their glee,
   And the wooer grows queerish and pale;
   H. S. R.—28

And the *tribute* he offers his mistress, the sea,
It seemeth of little avail:
Ah! the pleasure that lies in the deep, deep sea,
Lieth all too deep for me.

6. The perfumed Earth for a bride I take,
And our nuptial couch of flowers
Shall be placed by the brink of some reedy lake,
Where Nature rules the Hours;
For the pleasure that lies in the deep, deep sea,
Lieth all too deep for me.

7. There the music tones of each brooklet and bird,
And the wind through the old woods sweeping,
In our leafy home shall alone be heard,
While our tryst we are fondly keeping:
Ah! the pleasure that lies in the deep, deep sea,
Lieth all too deep for me.

8. Then give me to tread the steadfast earth,
With a firm step bold and free;
For surely a rood of land is worth
More than an acre of sea;
The pleasure that lies in the deep, deep sea,
Lieth all too deep for me.

CXXII. — VANITY OF RICHES.

FROM JOHNSON.

Dr. SAMUEL JOHNSON, who lived from 1709 to 1784, stands at the head of the English authors of his day. He was the principal writer in many of the magazines and periodicals of the time, and the author of the celebrated *English Dictionary* which bears his name.

1. As Ortogrul, of Basra, was one day wandering along the streets of Bagdat, musing on the varieties of merchandise which the shops opened to his view, and observing the different occupations which busied the multitude on

every side, he was awakened from the tranquillity of medi-
tation by a crowd that obstructed his passage. He raised
his eyes, and saw the chief vizier, who, having returned
from the divan, was entering his palace.

2. Ortogrul mingled with the attendants; and, being sup-
posed to have some petition for the vizier, was permitted
to enter. He surveyed the spaciousness of the apartments,
admired the walls hung with golden tapestry, and the floors
covered with silken carpets; and despised the simple neat-
ness of his own little habitation.

3. "Surely," said he to himself, "this palace is the seat
of happiness; where pleasure succeeds to pleasure, and
discontent and sorrow can have no admission. Whatever
nature has provided for the delight of sense is here spread
forth to be enjoyed. What can mortals hope or imagine
which the master of this palace has not obtained?

4. "The dishes of luxury cover his table; the voice of
harmony lulls him in his bowers; he breathes the fragrance
of the groves of Java, and sleeps upon the down of the
cygnets of the Ganges. He speaks, and his mandate is
obeyed; he wishes, and his wish is gratified; all whom he
sees obey him, and all whom he hears flatter him.

5. "How different, O Ortogrul! is thy condition, who art
doomed to the perpetual torments of unsatisfied desire;
and who hast no amusement in thy power that can with-
hold thee from thy own reflections! They tell thee that
thou art wise; but what does wisdom avail with poverty?
None will flatter the poor; and the wise have very little
power of flattering themselves.

6. "That man is surely the most wretched of the sons
of wretchedness, who lives with his own faults and follies
always before him, and who has none to reconcile him to
himself by praise and veneration. I have long sought
content, and have not found it; I will from this moment
endeavor to be rich."

7. Full of this new resolution, he shut himself in his
chamber for six months, to deliberate how he should grow
rich. He sometimes purposed to offer himself as a coun-
selor to one of the kings in India, and sometimes resolved

to dig for diamonds in the mines of Golconda. One day, after some hours passed in violent fluctuation of opinion, sleep insensibly seized him in his chair. He dreamed that he was ranging a desert country, in search of some one that might teach him how to grow rich; and as he stood on the top of a hill, shaded with cypress, in doubt whither to direct his steps, his father appeared on a sudden standing before him.

8. "Ortogrul," said the old man, "I know thy perplexity; listen to thy father. Turn thine eye on the opposite mountain." Ortogrul looked, and saw a torrent tumbling down the rocks, roaring with the noise of thunder, and scattering its foam on the impending woods. "Now," said his father, "behold the valley that lies between the hills." Ortogrul looked, and espied a little well, out of which issued a small rivulet. "Tell me, now," said his father, "dost thou wish for sudden affluence, that may pour upon thee like the mountain torrent; or for a slow and gradual increase, resembling the rill gliding from the well?"

9. "Let me be quickly rich," said Ortogrul; "let the golden stream be quick and violent." "Look around thee," said his father, "once again." Ortogrul looked, and perceived the channel of the torrent dry and dusty; but following the rivulet from the well, he traced it to a wide lake, which the supply, slow and constant, kept always full. He awoke, and determined to grow rich by silent profit, and persevering industry.

10. Having sold his patrimony, he engaged in merchandise; and in twenty years purchased lands, on which he raised a house equal in sumptuousness to that of the vizier; to this mansion he invited all the ministers of pleasure, expecting to enjoy all the felicity which he had imagined riches able to afford. Leisure soon made him weary of himself, and he longed to be persuaded that he was great and happy. He was courteous and liberal; he gave all that approached him hopes of pleasing him, and all who should please him hopes of being rewarded. Every art of praise was tried, and every source of adulatory fiction was exhausted.

11. Ortogrul heard his flatterers without delight, because he found himself unable to believe them. His own heart told him its frailties; his own understanding reproached him with his faults. "How long," said he, with a deep sigh, "have I been laboring in vain to amass wealth, which at last is useless! Let no man hereafter wish to be rich, who is already too wise to be flattered."

CXXIII. — VANITY.

FROM GOETHE.

GOETHE, a celebrated German author, lived from 1749 to 1832. He wrote in almost every department of literature, and exercised great influence in Germany.

1. I 've set my heart upon nothing, you see;
   Hurrah!
And so the world goes well with me.
   Hurrah!
And who has a mind to be fellow of mine,
Why, let him take hold and help me twine
   A wreath for the rosy Nine.

2. I set my heart at first upon wealth:
   Hurrah!
And barter'd away my peace and health;
   But, ah!
The slippery change went about like air;
And when I had clutch'd a handful here,
   Away it went there.

3. I set my heart upon travels grand;
   Hurrah!
And spurn'd our plain old fatherland;
   But, ah!
Naught seem'd to be just the thing it should,
Most comfortless beds and indifferent food,
   My tastes misunderstood.

4. I set my heart upon sounding fame;
    Hurrah!
And, lo! I 'm eclips'd by some upstart's name;
    And, ah!
When in public life I loom'd quite high,
The folks that pass'd me would look awry;
  Their very worst friend was I.

5. And then I set my heart upon war;
    Hurrah!
We gain'd some battles with eclat.
    Hurrah!
We troubled the foe with sword and flame,
And some of our friends fared quite the same.
  I lost a leg for fame.

6. Now I 've set my heart upon nothing, you see;
    Hurrah!
And the whole wide world belongs to me.
    Hurrah!
The feast begins to run low, no doubt;
But there 's a fountain above that will never run out,
  It will never run out.

CXXIV. — A HERD OF BISONS.

FROM COOPER.

1. "THERE come the buffaloes themselves, and a noble
herd it is." Every eye was now drawn to the striking
spectacle that succeeded. A few enormous bisons were
first discovered scouring along the most distant roll of the
prairie, and then succeeded long files of single beasts,
which, in their turns, were followed by a dark mass of
bodies, until the dun-colored herbage of the plain was en-
tirely lost in the deeper hue of their shaggy coats.

2. The herd, as the column spread and thickened, was
like the endless flocks of the smaller birds, whose extended

flanks are so often seen to heave up out of the abyss of the heavens, until they appear as countless as the leaves in those forests over which they wing their endless flight. Clouds of dust shot up in little columns from the center of the mass, as some animal more furious than the rest plowed the plains with his horns, and, from time to time, a deep, hollow bellowing was borne along on the wind, as though a thousand throats vented their plaints in a discordant murmuring.

3. A long and musing silence reigned in the party, as they gazed on this spectacle of wild and peculiar grandeur. It was at length broken by the trapper, who, having been long accustomed to similar sights, felt less of its influence, or rather felt it in a less thrilling and absorbing manner, than those to whom the scene was more novel. "There," said he, "go ten thousand oxen in one drove, without keeper or master, except Him who made them, and gave them these open plains for their pasture!

4. "But the herd is heading a little this way, and it behooves us to make ready for their visit. If we hide ourselves altogether, the horned brutes will break through the place, and trample us beneath their feet, like so many creeping worms; so we will just put the weak ones apart, and take post, as becomes men and hunters, in the van."

5. As there was but little time to make the necessary arrangements, the whole party set about them in good earnest. By the vacillating movements of some fifty or a hundred males, that led the advance, it remained questionable, for many moments, what course they intended to pursue. But a tremendous and painful roar, which came from behind the cloud of dust that rose in the center of the herd, and which was horridly answered by the screams of carrion birds, that were greedily sailing directly above the flying drove, appeared to give a new impulse to their flight, and at once to remove every symptom of indecision.

6. As if glad to seek the smallest signs of the forest, the whole of the affrighted herd became steady in its direction, rushing in a straight line toward the little cover of bushes, which has already been so often named. The

appearance of danger was now, in reality, of a character to try the stoutest nerves. The flanks of the dark, moving mass, were advanced in such a manner as to make a concave line of the front, and every fierce eye, that was glaring from the shaggy wilderness of hair, in which the entire heads of the males were enveloped, was riveted with mad anxiety on the thicket.

7. It seemed as if each beast strove to outstrip his neighbor in gaining this desired cover, and as thousands in the rear pressed blindly on those in front, there was the appearance of an imminent risk that the leaders of the herd would be precipitated on the concealed party, in which case the destruction of every one of them was certain. Each of our adventurers felt the danger of his situation in a manner peculiar to his individual character and circumstances.

8. The old man, who had stood all this while leaning on his rifle, and regarding the movements of the herd with a steady eye, now deemed it time to strike his blow. Leveling his piece at the foremost bison, with an agility that would have done credit to his youth, he fired. The animal received the bullet on the matted hair between his horns, and fell to his knees; but, shaking his head, he instantly arose, the very shock seeming to increase his exertions. There was now no longer time to hesitate. Throwing down his rifle, the trapper stretched forth his arms, and advanced from the cover with naked hands, directly towards the rushing column of the beasts.

9. The figure of a man, when sustained by the firmness and steadiness that intellect only can impart, rarely fails of commanding respect from all the inferior animals of the creation. The leading bisons recoiled, and, for a single instant, there was a sudden stop to their speed, a dense mass of bodies rolling up in front, until hundreds were seen floundering and tumbling on the plain. Then came another of those hollow bellowings from the rear, and set the herd again in motion. The head of the column, however, divided; the immovable form of the trapper cutting it, as it were, into two gliding streams of life. Middleton

and Paul instantly profited by his example, and extended the feeble barrier by a similar exhibition of their own persons.

10. For a few moments, the new impulse given to the animals in front served to protect the thicket. But, as the body of the herd pressed more and more upon the open line of its defenders, and the dust thickened so as to obscure their persons, there was, at each instant, a renewed danger of the beasts breaking through. It became necessary for the trapper and his companions to become still more and more alert; and they were gradually yielding before the headlong multitude, when a furious male darted by Middleton, so near as to brush his person, and, at the next instant, swept through the thicket with the velocity of the wind.

11. All their efforts would have proved fruitless, however, against the living torrent, had not Asinus, whose domains had just been so rudely entered, lifted his voice in the midst of the uproar. The most sturdy and furious of the animals trembled at the alarming and unknown cry, and then each individual brute was seen madly pressing from that very thicket, which, the moment before, he had endeavored to reach with the same sort of eagerness as that with which the murderer seeks the sanctuary.

12. As the stream divided, the place became clear; the two dark columns moving obliquely from the copse to unite again at the distance of a mile on its opposite side. The instant the old man saw the sudden effect which the voice of Asinus had produced, he coolly commenced reloading his rifle, indulging, at the same time, in a most heartfelt fit of his silent and peculiar merriment.

13. The uproar which attended the passage of the herd, was now gone, or rather it was heard rolling along the prairie, at the distance of a mile. The clouds of dust were already blown away by the wind, and a clear range was left to the eye, in the place where, ten minutes before, there existed such a strange scene of wildness and confusion.

CXXV. — THE BEE HUNT.

FROM IRVING.

1. THE beautiful forest in which we were encamped, abounded in bee-trees; that is to say, trees, in the decayed trunks of which wild bees had established their hives. It is surprising in what countless swarms the bees have overspread the far west, within but a moderate number of years. The Indians consider them but the harbinger of the white man, as the buffalo is of the red man; and say, that in proportion as the bee advances, the Indian and buffalo retire. They are always accustomed to associate the hum of the beehive with the farmhouse and flower-garden, and to consider those industrious little insects as connected with the busy haunts of man; and I am told, that the wild bee is seldom to be met with at any great distance from the frontier. They have been the heralds of civilization, steadfastly preceding it, as it advanced from the Atlantic borders, and some of the ancient settlers of the West pretend to give the very year when the honey-bee first crossed the Mississippi.

2. The Indians, with surprise, found the moldering trees of their forests suddenly teeming with ambrosial sweets, and nothing, I am told, can exceed the greedy relish with which they banquet, for the first time, upon this unbought luxury of the wilderness. At present, the honey-bee swarms in myriads in the noble groves and forests that skirt and intersect the prairies, and extend along the alluvial bottoms of the rivers. It seems to me as if these beautiful regions answer literally to the description of the land of promise, "a land flowing with milk and honey;" for the rich pasturage of the prairies is calculated to sustain herds of cattle as countless as the sands on the sea-shore, while the flowers with which they are enameled, render them a very paradise for the nectar-seeking bee.

3. We had not been long in the camp, when a party set out in quest of a bee-tree; and, being curious to witness the sport, I gladly accepted an invitation to accompany them.

The party was headed by a veteran bee-hunter, a tall, lank fellow, with a homespun garb, that hung loosely about his limbs, and with a straw hat, shaped not unlike a bee-hive. A comrade, equally uncouth in garb, and without a hat, straddled along at his heels, with a long rifle on his shoulder. To these succeeded half a dozen others, some with axes, and some with rifles; for no one stirs far from the camp without his firearms, so as to be ready either for wild deer or wild Indians.

4. After proceeding for some distance, we came to an open glade on the skirts of the forest. Here our leader halted, and then advanced quietly to a low bush, on the top of which he placed a piece of honey-comb. This, I found, was the bait or lure for the wild bees. Several were soon humming about it, and diving into the cells. When they had laden themselves with honey, they would rise into the air, and dart off in a straight line, almost with the velocity of a bullet. The hunters watched attentively the course they took, and then set off in the same direction, stumbling along over twisted roots and fallen trees, with their eyes turned up to the sky. In this way, they traced the honey-laden bees to their hive, in the hollow trunk of a blasted oak, where, after buzzing about for a moment, they entered a hole, about sixty feet from the ground.

5. Two of the bee-hunters now plied their axes vigorously at the foot of the tree, to level it with the ground. The mere spectators and amateurs, in the meantime, drew off to a cautious distance, to be out of the way of the falling of the tree, and the vengeance of its inmates. The jarring blows of the ax seemed to have no effect in alarming or disturbing this most industrious community. They continued to ply at their usual occupations; some arriving, full freighted, into port, others sallying forth, on new expeditions, like so many merchantmen in a money-making metropolis, little suspicious of impending bankruptcy and downfall. Even a loud crack, which announced the disrupture of the trunk, failed to divert their attention from the intense pursuit of gain. At length, down came the

tree, with a tremendous crash, bursting open from end to end, and displaying all the hoarded treasures of the commonwealth.

6. One of the hunters immediately ran up with a wisp of lighted hay, as a defense against the bees. The latter, however, made no attack, and sought no revenge; they seemed stupefied by the catastrophe and unsuspicious of its cause, and remained crawling and buzzing about the ruins, without offering us any molestation. Every one of the party now fell to, with spoon and hunting-knife, to scoop out the flakes of the honeycomb, with which the hollow trunk was stored. Some of them were of old date, and a deep brown color; others were beautifully white, and the honey in their cells was almost limpid. Such of the combs as were entire were placed in camp-kettles, to be conveyed to the encampment; those which had been shivered in the fall were devoured upon the spot. Every stark bee-hunter was to be seen with a rich morsel in his hand, dripping about his fingers, and disappearing as rapidly as a cream-tart before the holiday appetite of a schoolboy.

7. Nor was it the bee-hunters alone that profited by the downfall of this industrious community. As if the bees would carry through the similitude of their habits with those of laborious and gainful man, I beheld numbers from rival hives, arriving on eager wing, to enrich themselves with the ruin of their neighbors. These busied themselves as eagerly and cheerfully as so many wreckers on an Indiaman that has been driven on shore; plunging into the cells of the broken honey-combs, banqueting greedily on the spoil, and then winging their way, full freighted, to their homes. As to the poor proprietors of the ruin, they seemed to have no heart to do any thing, not even to taste the nectar that flowed around them; but crawled backward and forward, in vacant desolation, as I have seen a poor fellow with his hands in his breeches' pocket, whistling vacantly and despondingly about the ruins of his house that had been burnt.

8. It is difficult to describe the bewilderment and confusion of the bees of the bankrupt hive, who had been

absent at the time of the catastrophe, and who arrived from time to time with full cargoes from abroad. At first they wheeled about in the air, in the place where their fallen tree had once reared its head, astonished at finding it all a vacuum. At length, as if comprehending their disaster, they settled down in clusters, on a dry branch of a neighboring tree, from whence they seemed to contemplate the prostrate ruin, and to buzz forth doleful lamentations over the downfall of their republic. It was a scene on which the "melancholy Jacques" might have moralized by the hour.

9. We now abandoned the place, leaving much honey in the hollow of the tree. "It will all be cleared off by varmint," said one of the rangers. "What vermin?" asked I. "Oh, bears, and skunks, and raccoons, and 'possums," said he; "the bears is the knowingest varmint for finding out a bee-tree in the world. They'll gnaw for days together at the trunk, till they make a hole big enough to get in their paws, and then they'll haul out honey, bees, and all."

CXXVI. — SPRING.

FROM HOWITT.

1. THE Spring! she is a bless-ed thing!
      She is mother of the flowers;
    She is the mate of birds and bees,
    The partner of their revelries,
      Our star of hope through wintry hours.

2. The merry children, when they see
      Her coming, by the budding thorn,
    They leap upon the cottage floor,
    They shout beside the cottage door,
      And run to meet her night and morn.

3. They are soonest with her in the woods,
      Peeping the wither'd leaves among,

To find the earliest fragrant thing
That dares from the cold earth to spring,
    Or catch the earliest wild-bird's song.

4. The little brooks run on in light,
        As if they had a chase of mirth;
    The skies are blue, the air is warm,
    Our very hearts have caught the charm
        That sheds a beauty o'er the earth.

5. The aged man is in the field;
        The maiden 'mong her garden flowers;
    The sons of sorrow and distress
    Are wandering in forgetfulness
        Of wants that fret, and care that lowers.

6. She comes with more than present good,
        With joys to store for future years,
    From which, in striving crowds apart,
    The bow'd in spirit, bruis'd in heart,
        May glean up hope with grateful tears.

7. Up! let us to the fields away,
        And breathe the fresh and balmy air;
    The bird is building in the tree,
    The flower has open'd to the bee,
        And health, and love, and peace, are there.

CXXVII. — APRIL.

FROM WILLIS.

1. I HAVE found violets. April hath come on,
And the cool winds feel softer, and the rain
Falls in the beaded drops of summer-time.
You may hear birds at morning; and at eve
The tame dove lingers till the twilight falls,
Cooing upon the eaves, and drawing in

His beautiful, bright neck; and, from the hills
A murmur, like the hoarseness of the sea,
Tells the release of waters, and the earth
Sends up a pleasant smell, and the dry leaves
Are lifted by the grass; and so I know
That Nature, with her delicate ear, hath heard
The dropping of the velvet foot of Spring.

2. Take of my violets! I found them where
The liquid South stole o'er them, on a bank
That lean'd to running water. There's to me
A daintiness about these early flowers,
That teaches me like poetry. They blow
With such a simple loveliness among
The common herbs of pasture, and breathe out
Their hues so unobtrusively, like hearts
Whose beatings are too gentle for the world.

3. I love to go, in the capricious days
Of April, and hunt violets, when the rain
Is in the blue cups trembling, and they nod
So gracefully to the kisses of the wind.
It may be deem'd too idle, but the young
Read Nature like the manuscript of heaven,
And call the flowers its poetry.

4. Go out,
Ye spirits of habitual unrest,
And read it, when "the fever of the world"
Hath made your hearts impatient; and if life
Hath yet one spring unpoison'd, it will be
Like a beguiling music to its flow,
And you will no more wonder that I love
To hunt for violets in the April time.

CXXVIII. — MAY-DAY.

FROM HEBER.

REGINALD HEBER, a Bishop of the Church of England in one of its provincial dioceses at Calcutta, lived from 1783 to 1826. His prose and poetic writings are distinguished for their beauty and Christian spirit.

1. QUEEN of fresh flowers,
      Whom vernal stars obey,
   Bring the warm showers,
      Bring thy genial ray.
In nature's greenest livery drest,
Descend on earth's expectant breast,
To earth and heaven a welcome guest,
      Thou merry month of May!

2. Mark, how we meet thee
      At dawn of dewy day!
   Hark! how we greet thee
      With our roundelay!
While all the goodly things that be,
In earth, and air, and ample sea,
Are waking up to welcome thee,
      Thou merry month of May!

3. Flocks on the mountains,
      And birds upon their spray,
   Tree, turf, and fountains,
      All hold holiday.
And *love*, the life of living things,
Love waves his torch, *love* claps his wings,
And loud and wide thy praises sings,
      Thou merry month of May!

CXXIX. — THE WIND IN A FROLIC.

FROM HOWITT.

1. THE wind one morning sprung up from sleep,
Saying, "Now for a frolic! now for a leap!
Now for a mad-cap galloping chase!
I'll make a commotion in every place!"
So it swept with a bustle right through a great town,
Creaking the signs, and scattering down
Shutters; and whisking with merciless squalls,
Old women's bonnets and gingerbread stalls;
There never was heard a much lustier shout,
As the apples and oranges tumbled about;
And the urchins, that stand with their thievish eyes
Forever on watch, ran off each with a prize.

2. Then away to the field it went blustering and humming,
And the cattle all wonder'd what ever was coming;
It pluck'd by their tails the grave matronly cows,
And toss'd the colts' manes all about their brows,
'Till offended at such a familiar salute,
They all turn'd their backs and stood silently mute.

3. So on it went, capering, and playing its pranks,
Whistling with reeds on the broad river's banks;
Puffing the birds as they sat on the spray,
Or the traveler grave on the king's highway.
It was not too nice to bustle the bags
Of the beggar, and flutter his dirty rags:
'Twas so bold, that it fear'd not to play its joke
With the doctor's wig, and the gentleman's cloak.
Through the forest it roar'd, and cried, gayly, " Now
You sturdy old oaks, I'll make you bow!"
And it made them bow without more ado,
And crack'd their great branches through and through.

4. Then it rush'd like a monster on cottage and farm,
Striking their dwellers with sudden alarm,
Who ran out like bees in a midsummer swarm.

There were dames with their kerchiefs tied over their caps,
To see if their poultry were free from mishaps.
The turkeys they gobbled, the geese scream'd aloud,
And the hens crept to roost in a terrified crowd :
There was rearing of ladders, and logs laying on,
Where the thatch from the roof threaten'd soon to be gone,
But the wind had pass'd on, and had met in a lane
With a schoolboy, who panted and struggled in vain :
For it toss'd him, and twirl'd him, then pass'd, and he stood
With his hat in the pool, and his shoe in the mud.

CXXX. — DEATH WILL COME.

1. LEAVES have their time to fall,
And flowers to wither at the north wind's breath,
    And stars to set ; but all,
Thou hast *all* seasons for thine own, O Death !

    Thou art where billows foam ;
Thou art where music melts upon the air ;
    Thou art around us in our peaceful home ;
And the world calls us forth, and thou art there.

    Thou art where friend meets friend,
Beneath the shadow of the elm, to rest ;
    Thou art where foe meets foe, and trumpets rend
The skies, and swords beat down the princely crest.

                                        HEMANS.

2. I am in a world of death ; I am amid the dying and
the dead ; I see not a living thing in all my rambles that
will not die ; no man, no woman, no child, no bird, no beast.
no plant, no tree.   The eagle that cuts the air can not fly
over it, the monster of the deep can not dive beneath it ;
the tiny insect cannot make itself so insignificant that
death will not notice it ; Leviathan can not, with his great
strength, struggle against it.   The Christian will die ; the
sinner will die ; yea, the sinner !   Your wealth can not save
you, your accomplishments can not save you.

3. Death cares for none of these things. They are all trifles, gewgaws beneath his notice. He no more loves "a shining mark" than an ignoble one; he has no more pride in cutting down the rich man than the poor man; the daughter of beauty and fashion than the daughter of ugliness and sin. He loves to level the thistle as well as the rose-bud, the bramble as well as the magnolia, the brier as the cedar of Lebanon. He cares as little for the robe of ermine as for the beggar's rags; as little for your richest vestment and gayest apparel as for the blanket of the savage. You will die, and the fear of death will come upon you.

4. Death comes just as he is; pale, solemn, fixed, determined on his work. He hears no cry for pity, he regards no shriek of terror. He comes, steady, certain, unchanged, unchangeable in his purpose, to take you out of your bed of down; to hurry you away from your splendid dwelling; to take you out of the assembly room; calling you away from the companions that will miss you but for a moment, and then resume their dance—that you may die.

5. Death will come. He has been advancing toward you since you began to breathe. He has kept on his way, always advancing to meet you, while you have been asleep or awake; and if you have gone north, or south, or east, or west, he has always put himself in your path; how near or how remote you have never known.

6. Leaves have their time to fall,
And flowers to wither at the north wind's breath,
   And stars to set; but all,
Thou hast all seasons for thine own, O Death!

CXXXI. — INTIMATIONS OF IMMORTALITY.

FROM DANA.

1. O, LISTEN, man!
A voice within us speaks the startling word,
"Man, thou shalt never die!" Celestial voices
Hymn it round our souls; according harps,
By angel fingers touch'd, when the mild stars
Of morning sang together, sound forth still
The song of our great immortality!
Thick clustering orbs, and this our fair domain,
The tall, dark mountains, and the deep-toned seas,
Join in this solemn, universal song.

2. O, listen, ye, our spirits! drink it in
From all the air! 'Tis in the gentle moonlight;
'Tis floating in day's setting glories; night,
Wrapp'd in her sable robe, with silent step,
Comes to our bed, and breathes it in our ears;
Night and the dawn, bright day and thoughtful eve,
All time, all bounds, the limitless expanse,
As one vast mystic instrument, are touch'd
By an unseen, living Hand, and conscious chords
Quiver with joy, in this great jubilee.

3. The dying hear it; and as sounds of earth
Grow dull and distant, wake their passing souls,
To mingle in this heavenly harmony.

CXXXII. — IMMORTALITY OF THE SOUL.

FROM ADDISON.

JOSEPH ADDISON, an English author, whose writings rank among
the best models of style in our language, lived from 1672 to 1719.
He is chiefly known as the principal author of the " *Tatler* " and
" *Spectator*."

1. I WAS yesterday walking alone, in one of my friends'
woods, and lost myself in it very agreeably, as I was

running over, in my mind, the several arguments that established this great point, which is the basis of morality, and the source of all the pleasing hopes and secret joys that can arise in the heart of a reasonable creature. I considered those several proofs drawn,

2. First, from the nature of the soul itself, and particularly its immateriality; which, though not absolutely necessary to the eternity of its duration, has, I think, been evinced to almost a demonstration.

3. Secondly, from its passions and sentiments; as, particularly, from its love of existence, its horror of annihilation, and its hopes of immortality; with that secret satisfaction which it finds in the practice of virtue, and that uneasiness which follows upon the commission of vice.

4. Thirdly, from the nature of the Supreme Being, whose justice, goodness, wisdom, and veracity, are all concerned in this point.

5. But among these, and other excellent arguments for the immortality of the soul, there is one drawn from the perpetual progress of the soul to its perfection, without a possibility of ever arriving at it; which is a hint that I do not remember to have seen opened and improved by others who have written on this subject, though it seems to me to carry a very great weight with it.

6. How can it enter into the thoughts of man, that the soul, which is capable of immense perfections, and of receiving new improvements to all eternity, shall fall away into nothing almost as soon as it is created? Are such abilities made for no purpose? A brute arrives at a point of perfection that he can never pass; in a few years he has all the endowments he is capable of; and were he to live ten thousand more, would be the same thing he is at present.

7. Were a human soul thus at a stand in her accomplishments, were her faculties to be full blown, and incapable of further enlargements, I could imagine she might fall away insensibly, and drop at once in a state of annihilation. But can we believe a thinking being, that is in a perpetual progress of improvement, and traveling on from

perfection to perfection, after having just looked abroad into the works of her Creator, and made a few discoveries of His infinite goodness, wisdom, and power, must perish at her first setting out, and in the very beginning of her inquiries?

8. Man, considered only in his present state, seems sent into the world merely to propagate his kind. He provides himself with a successor, and immediately quits his post to make room for him. He does not seem born to enjoy life, but to deliver it down to others. This is not surprising to consider in animals, which are formed for our use, and which can finish their business in a short life.

9. The silk-worm, after having spun her task, lays her eggs and dies. But a man can not take in his full measure of knowledge, has not time to subdue his passions, establish his soul in virtue, and come to the perfection of his nature, before he is hurried off the stage. Would an infinitely wise Being make such glorious creatures for so mean a purpose? Can he delight in the production of such abortive intelligences, such short-lived reasonable beings? Would he give us talents that are not to be exerted? capacities that are never to be gratified?

10. How can we find that wisdom which shines through all his works, in the formation of man, without looking on this world as only a nursery for the next; and without believing that the several generations of rational creatures, which rise up and disappear in such quick succession, are only to receive their first rudiments of existence here, and afterward to be transplanted into a more friendly climate, where they may spread and flourish to all eternity?

11. There is not, in my opinion, a more pleasing and triumphant consideration in religion, than this of the perpetual progress which the soul makes toward the perfection of its nature, without ever arriving at a period in it. To look upon the soul as going on from strength to strength; to consider that she is to shine forever with new accessions of glory, and brighten to all eternity; that she will be still adding virtue to virtue, and knowledge to knowledge, carries in it something wonderfully agreeable to that am-

bition which is natural to the mind of man. Nay, it must be a prospect pleasing to God himself, to see his creation for ever beautifying in his eyes, and drawing nearer to him by greater degrees of resemblance.

12. Methinks this single consideration of the progress of a finite spirit to perfection, will be sufficient to extinguish all envy in inferior natures, and all contempt in superior. That cherub, which now appears as a god to a human soul, knows very well that the period will come about in eternity when the human soul shall be as perfect as he himself now is; nay, when she shall look down upon that degree of perfection as much as she now falls short of it.

13. It is true, the higher nature still advances, and by that means preserves his distance and superiority in the scale of being; yet he knows that, how high so ever the station is of which he stands possessed at present, the inferior nature will, at length, mount up to it, and shine forth in the same degree of glory.

14. With what astonishment and veneration may we look into our own souls, where there are such hidden stores of virtue and knowledge, such inexhausted sources of perfection! We know not yet what we shall be; nor will it ever enter into the heart of man to conceive the glory that will be always in reserve for him.

15. The soul, considered with its Creator, is like one of those mathematical lines that may draw nearer to another for all eternity, without a possibility of touching it: and can there be a thought so transporting, as to consider ourselves in these perpetual approaches to Him who is the standard not only of perfection, but of happiness!

CXXXIII. — THE GOLDEN CITY.

FROM BUNYAN.

JOHN BUNYAN, an Englishman, the celebrated author of "*The Pilgrim's Progress*," was a tinker, and very dissolute in his early life. He became, however, a religious man, and a preacher; and for his religious opinions was imprisoned twelve years. During his imprisonment, he wrote "The Pilgrim's Progress." He died in 1678.

1. Now, while they were thus drawing toward the gate, behold a company of the heavenly host came out to meet them; to whom it was said, by the other two shining ones, "These are the men who loved our Lord, when they were in the world, and have left all for his holy name; and he hath sent us to fetch them; and we have brought them thus far on their desired journey, that they may go in and look their Redeemer in the face with joy." Then the heavenly host gave a great shout, saying, "Blessed are they that are called to the marriage supper of the Lord." There came, also, out at this time to meet them, several of the king's trumpeters, clothed in white and shining raiment, who, with melodious and loud noises, made even the heavens to echo with their sound. These trumpeters saluted Christian and his fellow with ten thousand welcomes from the world; and this they did with shouting and sound of trumpet.

2. This done, they compassed them round about on every side; some went before, some behind, and some on the right hand, some on the left, as it were, to guard them through the upper regions; continually sounding, as they went, with melodious noise, in notes on high; so that the very sight was to them that could behold it, as if heaven itself was come down to meet them. Thus, therefore, they walked on together; and as they walked, ever and anon these trumpeters, even with joyful sound, would, by mixing their music with looks and gestures, still signify to Christian and his brother how welcome they were into their company, and with what gladness they came to meet them; and now these two men were, as it were, in heaven, before

they came at it, being swallowed up with the sight of angels, and with hearing their melodious notes Here, also, they had the city itself in view, and thought they heard all the bells therein to ring to welcome them thereto. But, above all, were the warm and joyful thoughts that they had about their own dwelling there with such company, and that forever and ever. O! by what tongue or pen can their glorious joy be expressed! Thus they came up to the gate.

3. Now, when they were come up to the gate, there was written over it, in letters of gold, "Blessed are they that do his commandments, that they may have a right to the tree of life, and may enter in through the gates into the city."

4. Then I saw, in my dream, that the shining men bid them call at the gate; the which, when they did, some from above looked over the gate; to wit, Enoch, Moses, Elijah, etc., to whom it was said, "These pilgrims are come from the city of Destruction, for the love that they bear to the king of this place;" and then the pilgrims gave in unto them each man his certificate, which they had received in the beginning; those, therefore, were carried in to the king, who, when he had read them, said, "Where are the men?" To whom it was answered, "They are standing without the gate." The king then commanded to open the gate, "That the righteous nation," said he, "that keepeth truth, may enter in."

5. Now, I saw, in my dream, that these two men went in at the gate; and lo, as they entered, they were transfigured, and they had raiment put on that shone like gold. There were also that met them with harps and crowns, and gave to them the harps to praise withal, and the crowns in token of honor. Then I heard, in my dream, that all the bells in the city rang again for joy, and that it was said unto them, "Enter ye into the joy of your Lord." I also heard the men themselves, that they sang with a loud voice, saying, "Blessing, honor, and glory, and power, be to Him that sitteth upon the throne, and to the Lamb, forever and ever."

6. Now, just as the gates were opened to let in the

H. S. R.—30

men, I looked in after them; and, behold, the city shone like the sun; the streets, also, were paved with gold, and in them walked many men with crowns on their heads, palms in their hands, and golden harps, to sing praises withal.

7. There were also of them that had wings; and they answered one another without intermission, saying, "Holy, holy, holy is the Lord." And after that they shut up the gates; which, when I had seen, I wished myself among them.

CXXXIV. — DROWNED! DROWNED!

FROM HOOD.

1. ONE more unfortunate,
     Weary of breath,
Rashly importunate,
     Gone to her death!
Take her up tenderly,
     Lift her with care;
Fashion'd so slenderly,
     Young, and so fair!

2. Look at her garments
Clinging like cerements;
While the wave constantly
     Drips from her clothing;
Take her up instantly,
     Loving, not loathing.

3. Touch her not scornfully;
Think of her mournfully,
     Gently and humanly;
Not of the stains of her,
All that remains of her
     Now is pure womanly.

4. Loop up her tresses
     Escaped from the comb,

Her fair auburn tresses;
While wonderment guesses
   Where was her home?

5. Who was her father?
      Who was her mother?
   Had she a sister?
      Had she a brother?
   Or was there a dearer one
   Still, and a nearer one
      Yet, than all other?

6. Alas for the rarity
   Of Christian charity
      Under the sun!
   O, it was pitiful!
   Near a whole city full,
      Home she had none.

7. Where the lamps quiver
   So far in the river,
      With many a light
   From window and casement,
   From garret to basement,
   She stood, with amazement,
      Houseless by night.

8. The bleak wind of March
      Made her tremble and shiver;
   But not the dark arch,
      Or the black flowing river:
   Mad from life's history,
   Glad to death's mystery,
      Swift to be hurl'd,
   Any where, any where
      Out of the world!

9. In she plunged boldly,
   No matter how coldly
      The rough river ran;

Over the brink of it,
Picture it, think of it,
　Dissolute man!
Lave in it, drink of it
　Then, if you can!

10. Take her up tenderly,
　　Lift her with care;
　Fashion'd so slenderly,
　　Young, and so fair!

CXXXV. — THE BEAUTIFUL AND GOOD.

1. SOFTLY, peacefully,
　　Lay her to rest;
　Place the turf lightly
　　On her young breast;
　Gently, solemnly,
　　Bend o'er the bed
　Where ye have pillow'd
　　Thus early her head.

2. Plant a young willow
　　Close by her grave;
　Let its long branches
　　Soothingly wave;
　Twine a sweet rose-tree
　　Over the tomb;
　Sprinkle fresh buds there;
　　Beauty and bloom.

3. Let a bright fountain,
　　Limpid and clear,
　Murmur its music,
　　(Smile through a tear,)
　Scatter its diamonds
　　Where the lov'd lies,

Brilliant and starry,
 Like angels' eyes.

4. Then shall the bright birds,
 On golden wing,
Lingering over,
 Murmuring sing;
Then shall the soft breeze
 Pensively sigh,
Bearing rich fragrance
 And melody by.

5. Lay the sod lightly
 Over her breast;
Calm be her slumbers,
 Peaceful her rest!
Beautiful, lovely,
 She was but given,
A fair bud to earth,
 To blossom in heaven.

CXXXVI. — SHE SLEEPS.

FROM HERVEY.

1. SHE sleeps that still and placid sleep
 For which the weary pant in vain;
And where the dews of evening weep,
 I may not weep again;
Oh! never more upon her grave
Shall I behold the wild flower wave!

2. They laid her where the sun and moon
 Look on her tomb with loving eye,
And I have heard the breeze of June
 Sweep o'er it, like a sigh,
And the wild river's wailing song
Grow dirge-like, as it stole along!

3. And I have dream'd, in many dreams,
   Of her who was a dream to me;
And talk'd to her, by summer streams,
   In crowds, and on the sea,
'Till, in my soul she grew enshrined,
A young Egeria of the mind!

4. 'Tis years ago! and other eyes
   Have flung their beauty o'er my youth;
And I have hung on other sighs,
   And sounds that seem'd like truth,
And lov'd the music which they gave,
Like that which perish'd in the grave.

5. And I have left the cold and dead,
   To mingle with the living cold;
There is a weight around my head,
   My heart is growing old;
Oh! for a refuge and a home
With thee, dear Ellen, in thy tomb!

6. Age sits upon my breast and brain,
   My spirit fades before its time;
But they are all thine own again,
   Lost partner of their prime!
And thou art dearer, in thy shroud,
Than all the false and living crowd!

7. Rise, gentle vision of the hours,
   Which go, like birds that come not back!
And fling thy pale and funeral flowers
   On memory's wasted track!
Oh! for the wings that made thee blest,
To "flee away, and be at rest!"

CXXXVII. — WAVERLEY AND MAC-IVOR.

FROM SCOTT.

1. AFTER a sleepless night, the first dawn of morning found Waverley on the esplanade in front of the old Gothic gate of Carlisle castle. But he paced it long in every direction before the hour when, according to the rules of the garrison, the gates were opened, and the drawbridge lowered. He produced his order to the sergeant of the guard, and was admitted. The place of Fergus' confinement was a gloomy and vaulted apartment in the central part of the castle: a huge old tower, supposed to be of great antiquity, and surrounded by out-works seemingly of Henry VIII.'s time, or somewhat later. The grating of the huge oldfashioned bars and bolts, withdrawn for the purpose of admitting Edward, was answered by the clash of chains, as the unfortunate chieftain, strongly and heavily fettered, shuffled along the stone floor of his prison, to fling himself into his friend's arms.

2. "My dear Edward," he said, in a firm and even cheerful voice, "this is truly kind. I heard of your approaching happiness with the highest pleasure; and how does Rose? and how is our old whimsical friend, the baron? Well, I am sure, from your looks; and how will you settle precedence between the three ermines passant, and the bear and boot-jack?" "How, O how, my dear Fergus, can you talk of such things at such a moment?" "Why, we have entered Carlisle with happier auspices, to be sure; on the sixteenth of November last, for example, when we marched in, side by side, and hoisted the white flag on these ancient towers. But I am no boy, to sit down and weep, because the luck has gone against me. I knew the stake which I risked; we played the game boldly, and the forfeit shall be paid manfully.

3. "You are rich," he continued, "Waverley, and you are generous; when you hear of these poor Mac-Ivors being distressed about their miserable possessions by some harsh overseer or agent of government, remember you

have worn their tartan, and are an adopted son of their race. The baron, who knows our manners, and lives near our country, will apprise you of the time and means to be their protector. Will you promise this to the last Vich Ian Vohr?" Edward, as may well be believed, pledged his word; which afterwards he so amply redeemed, that his memory still lives in these glens by the name of the Friend of the Sons of Ivor. "Would to God," continued the chieftain, "I could bequeath to you my rights to the love and obedience of this primitive and brave race: or, at least, as I have striven to do, persuade poor Evan to accept of his life upon their terms; and be to you, what he has been to me, the kindest, the bravest, the most devoted ———"

4. The tears which his own fate could not draw forth, fell fast for that of his foster-brother. "But," said he, drying them, "that can not be. You can not be to them Vich Ian Vohr; "and these three magic words," said he, half smiling, "are the only *open sesame* to their feelings and sympathies; and poor Evan must attend his foster-brother in death, as he has done through his whole life." "And I am sure," said Maccombich, raising himself from the floor, on which, for fear of interrupting their conversation, he had lain so still that, in the obscurity of the apartment, Edward was not aware of his presence, "I am sure Evan never deserved nor desires a better end than just to die with his chieftain."

5. A tap at the door now announced the arrival of the priest; and Edward retired while he administered to both prisoners the last rites of religion, in the mode which' the Church of Rome prescribes. In about an hour he was re-admitted. Soon after, a file of soldiers entered with a blacksmith, who struck the fetters from the legs of the prisoners. "You see the compliment they pay to our Highland strength and courage; we have lain chained here like wild beasts, till our legs are cramped into palsy; and when they free us, they send six soldiers with loaded muskets to prevent our taking the castle by storm."

6. Shortly after, the drums of the garrison beat to arms.

"This is the last turn-out," said Fergus, "that I shall hear and obey. And now, my dear, dear Edward, ere we part, let us speak of Flora, a subject which awakes the tenderest feeling that yet thrills within me." "We part not *here?*" said Waverley. "O yes, we do; you must come no further. Not that I fear what is to follow for myself," he said, proudly; "nature has her tortures as well as art. and how happy should we think the man, who escapes from the throes of a mortal and painful disorder, in the space of a short half-hour! And this matter, spin it out as they will, can not last longer. But what a dying man can suffer firmly, may kill a living friend to look upon.

7. "This same law of high treason," he continued, with astonishing firmness and composure, "is one of the blessings, Edward, with which your free country has accommodated poor old Scotland; her own jurisprudence, as I have heard, was much milder. But, I suppose, one day or other, when there are no longer any wild Highlanders to benefit by its tender mercies, they will blot it from their records, as leveling them with a nation of cannibals. The mummery, too, of exposing the senseless head! they have not the wit to grace mine with a paper coronet; there would be some satire in that, Edward. I hope they will set it on the Scotch gate though, that I may look, even after death, to the blue hills of my own country, that I love so dearly!"

8. A bustle, and the sound of wheels and horses' feet, was now heard in the courtyard of the castle. An officer appeared, and intimated that the high-sheriff and his attendants waited before the gate of the castle, to claim the bodies of Fergus Mac-Ivor and Evan Maccombich. "I come," said Fergus. Accordingly, supporting Edward by the arm, and followed by Evan Dhu and the priest, he moved down the stairs of the tower, the soldiers bringing up the rear. The court was occupied by a squadron of dragoons and a battalion of infantry, drawn up in a hollow square.

9. Within their ranks was the sledge or hurdle, on which the prisoners were to be drawn to the place of execution.

about a mile distant from Carlisle. It was painted black, and drawn by a white horse. At one end of the vehicle sat the executioner, a horrid-looking fellow, as beseemed his trade, with the broad-ax in his hand; at the other end, next the horse, was an empty seat for two persons. Through the deep and dark Gothic archway, that opened on the drawbridge, were seen on horseback the high-sheriff and his attendants, whom the etiquette betwixt the civil and military power did not permit to come further.

10. "This is well GOT UP, for a closing scene," said Fergus, smiling disdainfully, as he gazed around upon the apparatus of terror. Evan Dhu exclaimed, with some eagerness, after looking at the dragoons, "These are the very chields that galloped off at Gladsmuir, ere we could kill a dozen of them. They look bold enough now, however." The priest entreated him to be silent.

11. The sledge now approached, and Fergus, turning round, embraced Waverley, kissed him on each side of the face, and stepped nimbly into his place. Evan sat down by his side. The priest was to follow in a carriage belonging to his patron, the Catholic gentleman at whose house Flora resided. As Fergus waved his hand to Edward, the ranks closed around the sledge, and the whole procession began to move forward.

12. There was a momentary stop at the gateway, while the governor of the castle and the high-sheriff went through a short ceremony, the military officer there delivering over the persons of the criminals to the civil power. "God save King George!" said the high-sheriff. When the formality concluded, Fergus stood erect in the sledge, and, with a firm and steady voice, replied, "God save King *James!*" These were the last words which Waverley heard him speak.

13. The procession resumed its march, and the sledge vanished from beneath the portal, under which it had stopped for an instant. The dead march, as it is called, was instantly heard; and its melancholy sounds were mingled with those of a muffled peal, tolled from the neighboring cathedral. The sound of the military music died

away as the procession moved on; the sullen clang of the bells was soon heard to sound alone.

14. The last of the soldiers had now disappeared from under the vaulted archway, through which they had been filing for several minutes; the courtyard was now totally empty, but Waverley still stood there as if stupefied, his eyes fixed upon the dark pass where he had so lately seen the last glimpse of his friend. At length, a female servant of the governor, struck with surprise and compassion at the stupefied misery which his countenance expressed, asked him if he would not walk into her master's house and sit down? She was obliged to repeat her question twice ere he comprehended her; but, at length, it recalled him to himself. Declining the courtesy by a hasty gesture, he pulled his hat over his eyes, and, leaving the castle, walked as swiftly as he could through the empty streets, till he regained his inn; then threw himself into an apartment and bolted the door.

15. In about an hour and a half, which seemed an age of unutterable suspense, the sound of the drums and fifes, performing a lively air, and the confused murmur of the crowd which now filled the streets, so lately deserted, apprized him that all was over, and that the military and populace were returning from the dreadful scene. I will not attempt to describe his sensations.

CXXXVIII.—THE BURIAL.

FROM WILLIS.

THESE lines were written by Willis on the death of a class-mate in Yale College.

1. YE 'VE gather'd to your place of prayer,
   With slow and measur'd tread:
   Your ranks are full, your mates all there,
   But the soul of one has fled.
   He was the proudest in his strength,
   The manliest of ye all;

Why lies he at that fearful length,
    And ye around his pall?

2. Ye reckon it in days, since he
    Strode up that foot-worn aisle,
With his dark eye flashing gloriously,
    And his lip wreath'd with a smile.
Oh! had it been but told you then,
    To mark whose lamp was dim,
From out yon rank of fresh-lipp'd men,
    Would ye have singled *him?*

3. Whose was the sinewy arm which flung
    Defiance to the ring?
Whose laugh of victory loudest rung,
    Yet not for glorying?
Whose heart, in generous deed and thought,
    No rivalry might brook,
And yet distinction claiming not?
    There lies he; go and look!

4. On, now; his requiem is done;
    The last deep prayer is said;
On to his burial, comrades, on,
    With the *noblest* of the dead!
Slow, for it presses heavily;
    It is a *man* ye bear!
Slow, for our thoughts dwell wearily
    On the noble sleeper there.

5. Tread lightly, comrades! ye have laid
    His dark locks on his brow;
Like life, save deeper light and shade:
    We'll not disturb them now.
Tread lightly, for 'tis beautiful,
    That blue vein'd eyelid's sleep,
Hiding the eye death left so dull;
    Its slumber we will keep.

6. Rest now! his journeying is done;
    Your feet are on his sod;
Death's chain is on your champion,
    He waiteth here his God!
Ay, turn and weep; 'tis manliness
    To be heart-broken here,
For the grave of earth's best nobleness
    Is water'd by the tear.

CXXXIX.—INVASION OF SWITZERLAND.

FROM SIDNEY SMITH.

1. THE vengeance which the French took upon the Swiss, for their determined opposition to the invasion of their country, was decisive and terrible. The history of Europe can afford no parallel to such cruelty. In dark ages, and the most barbarous nations of the east, we must turn for similar scenes of horror, and, perhaps, must turn in vain. The soldiers, dispersed over the country, carried fire, and sword, and robbery into the most tranquil and hidden valleys of Switzerland. From the depth of sweet retreats echoed the shrieks of murdered men, stabbed in their humble dwellings, under the shadow of the high mountains, in the midst of those scenes of nature which make solemn and pure the secret thoughts of man, and appall him with the majesty of God.

2. The flying peasants saw, in the midst of the night, their cottages, their implements of husbandry, and the hopes of the future year, expiring in one cruel conflagration. The men were shot upon the slightest provocation: innumerable women, after being exposed to the most atrocious indignities, were murdered, and their bodies thrown into the woods. In some instances this conduct was resented; and for symptoms of such an honorable spirit, the beautiful town of Altdorf was burnt to the ground, and not a single house left to show where it had stood.

3. The town of Staritz, a town peculiarly dear to the Swiss, as it gave birth to one of the founders of their liberty, was reduced to a heap of cinders. In this town, in the fourteenth century, a Swiss general surprised and took prisoner the Austrian commander who had murdered his father; yet he forgave and released him, upon the simple condition that he would not again serve against the Swiss Cantons. When the French got possession of this place, they burnt it to ashes, not in a barbarous age, but now, yesterday, in an age we call philosophical; they burnt it, because the inhabitants had endeavored to preserve their liberty.

4. The Swiss was a simple peasant; the French, a mighty people, combined for the regeneration of Europe. O, Europe, what dost thou owe to this mighty people? Dead bodies, ruined heaps, broken hearts, waste places, childless mothers, widows, orphans, tears, endless confusion, and unutterable woe. For this mighty nation, we have suffered seven years of unexampled wretchedness, a long period of discord, jealousy, privation, ·and horror, which every reflecting man would almost wish blotted out of his existence. By this mighty people, the Swiss have lost their country; that country which they loved so well, that if they heard but the simple song of their childhood, tears fell down every manly face, and the most intrepid soldiers sobbed with grief.

5. What then? Is all this done with impunity? Are the thunders of God dumb? Are there no lightnings in his right hand? Pause a little, before you decide on the ways of Providence; tarry and see what will come to pass. There is a solemn and awful courage in the human heart, placed there by God himself, to guard man against the tyranny of his fellows, and while this lives, the world is safe. There slumbers even now, perchance, upon the mountains of Switzerland, some youthful peasant, unconscious of the soul he bears, that shall lead down these bold people from their rocks to such deeds of courage as they have heard with their ears, and their fathers have declared unto them; to such as were done in their days, and in the old times

before them, by those magnanimous rustics who first taught foolish ambition to respect the wisdom and the spirit of simple men, righteously and honestly striving for every human blessing.

6. Let me go on a little further in this dreadful enumeration. More than thirty villages were sacked in the canton of Berne alone; not only was all the produce of the present year destroyed, but all the cattle unfit for human food were slaughtered, and the agricultural implements burnt; and thus the certainty of famine was entailed upon them for the ensuing year. At the end of all this military execution, civil exactions, still more cruel and oppressive, were begun; and, under the forms of government and law, the most unprincipled men gave loose to their avarice and rapacity, till Switzerland was sunk at last under the complication of her misfortunes, reduced to the lowest ebb of misery and despair.

CXL. — THE DESTRUCTION OF WAR.

FROM THE BIBLE.

1. BLOW ye the trumpet in Zion;
And sound an alarm in mine holy mountain:
Let all the inhabitants of the land tremble:
For the day of the Lord cometh, for it is near:
A day of darkness and gloom:
A day of clouds, and of thick darkness.
As a dusk spread upon the mountains,
Cometh a numerous people and strong.
Like them, there hath not been of old time,
And after them, there shall not be,
Even to the years of many generations.

2. Before them, a fire devoureth,
And behind, a flame burneth;
The land is as the garden of Eden before them,
And behind them, a desolate wilderness:
Yea, and nothing shall escape them.

Their appearance shall be like the appearance of horses,
And like horsemen shall they run;
Like the sound of chariots, on the tops of the mountain,
    shall they leap;
Like the sound of a flame of fire, which devoureth stubble;
They shall be like a strong people, set in battle array.

3. Before them, shall the people be much pained:
All faces shall gather blackness;
They shall run like mighty men;
Like warriors shall they climb the wall;
And they shall march every one in his way;
Neither shall they turn aside from their paths;
Neither shall one trust another:
They shall march each in his road;
And if they fall upon the sword, they shall not be wounded.
They shall run to and fro in the city,
They shall run upon the wall, they shall climb up into the
    houses;
They shall enter in at the window, like a thief.
Before them, the earth quaketh, the heavens tremble:
The sun and moon are darkened;
And the stars withdraw their shining.

4. And Jehovah shall utter his voice before his army;
For his camp is very great,
And the day of the Lord is very great
And very terrible, and who shall be able to bear it?
Yet, even now, saith Jehovah,
Turn ye unto me with all your heart,
With fasting, and with weeping, and with mourning,
And rend your hearts, and not your garments,
And turn unto Jehovah, your God;
For he is gracious and merciful,
Slow to anger, and of great kindness,
And repenteth him of evil.

CXLI. — THE BURNING OF MOSCOW.

From Headley.

J T. Headley is a living American author, who has written some very popular works, among which are, "Bonaparte and his Marshals," "Washington and his Generals," etc.

1. At length Moscow, with its domes, and towers, and palaces, appeared in sight; and Napoleon, who had joined the advanced guard, gazed long and thoughtfully on that goal of his wishes. Murat went forward, and entered the gates with his splendid cavalry, but as he passed through the streets he was struck by the solitude that surrounded him. Nothing was heard but the heavy tramp of his squadrons as he passed along, for a deserted and abandoned city was the meager prize for which such unparalleled efforts had been made. As night drew its curtain over the splendid capital, Napoleon entered the gates, and immediately appointed Mortier governor. In his directions, he commanded him to abstain from all pillage. "For this," said he, "you shall be answerable with your life. Defend Moscow against all, whether friend or foe."

2. The bright moon rose over the mighty city, tipping with silver the domes of more than two hundred churches, and pouring a flood of light over a thousand palaces and the dwellings of three hundred thousand inhabitants. The weary arm sunk to rest, but there was no sleep for Mortier's eyes. Not the gorgeous and variegated palaces and their rich ornaments, nor the parks and gardens and oriental magnificence that every-where surrounded him, kept him wakeful, but the ominous foreboding that some dire calamity was hanging over the silent capital. When he entered it, scarcely a living soul met his gaze as he looked down the long streets; and when he broke open the buildings, he found parlors, and bedrooms, and chambers, all furnished and in order, but no occupants. This sudden abandonment of their homes betokened some secret purpose yet to be fulfilled. The midnight moon was settling over the city, when the cry of "Fire!" reached the ears of Mor-

tier; and the first light over Napoleon's faltering empire was kindled, and that most wondrous scene of modern times commenced—THE BURNING OF MOSCOW.

3. Mortier, as governor of the city, immediately issued his orders, and was putting forth every exertion, when at daylight Napoleon hastened to him. Affecting to disbelieve the reports that the inhabitants were firing their own city, he put more rigid commands on Mortier, to keep the soldiers from the work of destruction. The Marshal simply pointed to some iron-covered houses that had not yet been opened, from every crevice of which smoke was issuing like steam from the sides of a pent-up volcano. Sad and thoughtful, Napoleon turned towards the Kremlin, the ancient palace of the Czars, whose huge structure rose high above the surrounding edifices.

4. In the morning, Mortier, by great exertions, was enabled to subdue the fire. But the next night, September 15th, at midnight, the sentinels on watch upon the lofty Kremlin saw below them the flames bursting through the houses and palaces, and the cry of "Fire! fire!" passed through the city. The dread scene was now fairly opened. Fiery balloons were seen dropping from the air and lighting on the houses; dull explosions were heard on every side from the shut-up dwellings, and the next moment light burst forth, and the flames were raging through the apartments. All was uproar and confusion. The serene air and moonlight of the night before had given way to driving clouds and a wild tempest, that swept like the roar of the sea over the city. Flames arose on every side, blazing and crackling in the storm; while clouds of smoke and sparks in an incessant shower went driving toward the Kremlin. The clouds themselves seemed turned into fire, rolling wrath over devoted Moscow. Mortier, crushed with the responsibility thrown upon his shoulders, moved with his Young Guard amid this desolation, blowing up the houses and facing the tempest and the flames, struggling nobly to arrest the conflagration.

5. He hastened from place to place amid the ruins, his face blackened with smoke, and his hair and eyebrows

singed with the fierce heat. At length the day dawned, a day of tempest and of flame, and Mortier, who had strained every nerve for thirty-six hours, entered a palace and dropped down from fatigue. The manly form and stalwart arm that had so often carried death into the ranks of the enemy, at length gave way, and the gloomy Marshal lay and panted in utter exhaustion. But the night of tempest had been succeeded by a day of tempest; and when night again enveloped the city, it was one broad flame, waving to and fro in the blast.

6. The wind had increased to a perfect hurricane, and shifted from quarter to quarter, as if on purpose to swell the sea of fire and extinguish the last hope. The fire was approaching the Kremlin, and already the roar of the flames and crash of falling houses, and the crackling of burning timbers, were borne to the ears of the startled Emperor. He arose and walked to and fro, stopping convulsively and gazing on the terrific scene. Murat, Eugene, and Berthier rushed into his presence, and on their knees besought him to flee; but he still clung to that haughty palace as if it were his empire.

7. But at length the shout, "The Kremlin is on fire!" was heard above the roar of the conflagration, and Napoleon reluctantly consented to leave. He descended into the streets with his staff, and looked about for a way of egress, but the flames blocked every passage. At length they discovered a postern gate, leading to the Moskwr, and entered it; but they had entered still further into the danger. As Napoleon cast his eye round the open space, girdled and arched with fire, smoke, and cinders, he saw one single street yet open, but all on fire. Into this he rushed, and amid the crash of falling houses and raging of the flames, over burning ruins, through clouds of rolling smoke, and between walls of fire, he pressed on; and, at length, half suffocated, emerged in safety from the blazing city, and took up his quarters in the imperial palace of Petrowsky, nearly three miles distant.

8. Mortier, relieved from his anxiety for the Emperor, redoubled his efforts to arrest the conflagration. His men

cheerfully rushed into every danger. Breathing nothing
but smoke and ashes, canopied by flame, and smoke, and
cinders, surrounded by walls of fire, that rocked to and
fro, and fell with a crash amid the blazing ruins, carrying
down with them red-hot roofs of iron; he struggled against
an enemy that no boldness could awe or courage overcome.
Those brave troops had heard the tramp of thousands of
cavalry sweeping to battle without fear; but now they stood
in still terror before the march of the conflagration, under
whose burning footsteps was heard the incessant crash of
falling houses, and palaces, and churches. The continuous
roar of the raging hurricane, mingled with that of the
flames, was more terrible than the thunder of artillery; and
before this new foe, in the midst of this battle of the ele-
ments, the awe-struck army stood powerless and affrighted.

9. When night again descended on the city, it presented
a spectacle, the like of which was never seen before, and
which baffles all description. The streets were streets of
fire, the heavens a canopy of fire, and the entire body of
the city a mass of fire, fed by a hurricane that sped the
blazing fragments in a constant stream through the air.
Incessant explosions, from the blowing up of stores of oil,
and tar, and spirits, shook the very foundations of the city,
and sent vast volumes of smoke rolling furiously toward
the sky. Huge sheets of canvas on fire came floating like
messengers of death through the flames; the towers and
domes of the churches and palaces glowing with a red-hot
heat over the wild sea below, then tottering a moment on
their bases, were hurled by the tempest into the common
ruin.

10. Thousands of wretches, before unseen, were driven
by the heat from the cellars and hovels, and streamed in
an incessant throng through the streets. Children were
seen carrying their parents; the strong the weak; while
thousands more were staggering under the loads of plun-
der they had snatched from the flames. This, too, would
frequently take fire in the falling shower, and the miserable
creatures would be compelled to drop it and flee for their
lives. O, it was a scene of woe and fear inconceivable and

indescribable! A mighty and closely-packed city of houses, and churches, and palaces, wrapped from limit to limit in flames, which are fed by a whirling hurricane, is a sight this world will seldom see.

11. But this was within the city. To Napoleon, without, the spectacle was still more sublime and terrific. When the flames had overcome all obstacles, and had wrapped every thing in their red mantle, that great city looked like a sea of rolling fire, swept by a tempest that drove it into billows. Huge domes and towers, throwing off sparks like blazing firebrands, now disappeared in their maddening flow, as they rushed and broke high over their tops, scattering their spray of fire against the clouds. The heavens themselves seemed to have caught the conflagration, and the angry masses that swept it rolled over a bosom of fire.

12. Columns of flame would rise and sink along the surface of this sea, and huge volumes of black smoke suddenly shoot into the air, as if volcanoes were working below. The black form of the Kremlin alone towered above the chaos, now wrapped in flame and smoke, again emerging into view, standing amid this scene of desolation and terror, like Virtue in the midst of a burning world, enveloped but unscathed by the devouring elements. Napoleon stood and gazed on the scene in silent awe. Though nearly three miles distant, the windows and walls of his apartment were so hot that he could scarcely bear his hand against them. Said he, years afterward:

13. "It was the spectacle of a sea and billows of fire, a sky and clouds of flame, mountains of red rolling flames, like immense waves of the sea, alternately bursting forth and elevating themselves to skies of flame below. O! it was the most grand, the most sublime, and the most terrific sight the world ever beheld!"

CXLII.—THE SHIPWRECK.

FROM WILSON.

1. HER giant form,
O'er wrathful surge, through blackening storm,
Majestically calm, would go
Mid the deep darkness, white as snow!
But gently now the white waves glide,
Like playful lambs o'er a mountain's side.

2. So stately her bearing, so proud her array,
The main she will traverse forever and aye.
Many ports will exult at the gleam of her mast!
Hush! hush! thou vain dreamer! this hour is her last!
    Five hundred souls, in one instant of dread,
       Are hurried o'er the deck;
    And fast the miserable ship
       Becomes a lifeless wreck.

3. Her keel hath struck on a hidden rock;
    Her planks are torn asunder;
And down come her masts with a reeling shock,
    And a hideous crash like thunder;
Her sails are draggled in the brine,
    That gladden'd late the skies;
And her pennant that kiss'd the fair moonshine,
    Down many a fathom lies!
Her beauteous sides, whose rainbow hues
    Gleam'd softly from below,
And flung a warm and sunny flush
    O'er the wreaths of murmuring snow,
To the coral rocks are hurrying down,
To sleep amid colors as bright as their own.

4. Oh! many a dream was in the ship
    An hour before her death;
And sights of home with sighs disturb'd
    The sleeper's long-drawn breath.

Instead of the murmur of the sea,
The sailor heard the humming tree,
 Alive through all its leaves;
The hum of the spreading sycamore
That grows before his cottage door,
 And the swallow's song in the eaves.
His arms enclosed a blooming boy,
Who listen'd with tears of sorrow and joy
 To the dangers his father had pass'd;
And his wife, by turns she wept and smiled,
As she look'd on the father of her child
 Return'd to her heart at last.

5. He wakes at the vessel's sudden roll,
And the rush of waters is in his soul.
Astounded, the reeling deck he paces,
'Mid hurrying forms and ghastly faces;
 The whole ship's crew are there:
Wailings around, and overhead,
Brave spirits stupefied or dead,
 And madness and despair!

6. Now is the ocean's bosom bare,
Unbroken as the floating air;
The ship hath melted quite away,
Like a struggling dream at break of day;
No image meets my wandering eye
But the new-risen sun, and the sunny sky.
Though the night shades are gone, yet a vapor dull
Bedims the waves so beautiful;
While a low and melancholy moan
Mourns for the glory that hath flown!

CXLIII.—THE PILOT.

1. THE waves are high, the night is dark,
     Wild roam the foaming tides,
   Dashing around the straining bark,
     As gallantly she rides.
   "Pilot! take heed what course you steer;
     Our bark is tempest driven!"
   "Stranger, be calm, there is no fear
     For him who trusts in Heaven!"

2. "Oh, pilot! mark yon thunder-cloud,
     The lightning's lurid rivers;
   Hark to the wind! 'tis piping loud;
     The mainmast bends and quivers!
   Stay, pilot, stay, and shorten sail,
     Our stormy trysail's riven!"
   "Stranger, what matter's calm or gale
     To him who trusts in Heaven?"

3. Borne by the winds, the vessel flees
     Up to the thundering cloud,
   Now tottering low, the spray-wing'd seas
     Conceal the topmost shroud.
   "Pilot, the waves break o'er us fast,
     Vainly our bark has striven!"
   "Stranger, the Lord can rule the blast;
     Go, put thy trust in Heaven!"

4. Good hope! good hope! one little star
     Gleams o'er the waste of waters;
   'Tis like the light reflected far
     Of beauty's loveliest daughters!
   "Stranger, good hope He giveth thee,
     As He has often given;
   Then learn this truth, whate'er may be,
     To put thy trust in Heaven!"

CXLIV. — THE PRESS ABOVE THE SWORD.

FROM CARLYLE.

THOMAS CARLYLE, a native of Scotland, is a distinguished author of the present day. His principal works are: *Life of Schiller; Sartor Resartus; The French Revolution; Life of Cromwell; Hero Worship;* etc.

1. TAMERLANE was a celebrated Eastern conqueror.
3. FAUST was the inventor of printing.

> "Beneath the rule of men entirely great
> The pen is mightier than the sword.   Behold
> The arch enchanter's wand! itself a nothing!
> But taking sorcery from the master hand
> To paralyze the Cæsars, and to strike
> The loud earth breathless!   Take away the sword,
> States can be saved without it."

1. WHEN Tamerlane had finished building his pyramid of seventy thousand human skulls, and was seen standing at the gate of Damascus, glittering in his steel, with his battle-ax on his shoulder, till his fierce hosts filed out to new victories and carnage, the pale looker-on might have fancied that Nature was in her death-throes; for havoc and despair had taken possession of the earth, and the sun of manhood seemed setting in a sea of blood.

2. Yet it might be on that very gala-day of Tamerlane, that a little boy was playing nine-pins in the streets of Mentz, whose history was more important than that of twenty Tamerlanes. The Khan, with his shaggy demons of the wilderness, "passed away like a whirlwind," to be forgotten forever; and that German artisan has wrought a benefit which is yet immeasurably expanding itself, and will continue to expand itself, through all countries and all times.

3. What are the conquests and the expeditions of the whole corporation of captains, from Walter the Penniless to Napoleon Bonaparte, compared with those movable types of Faust? Truly it is a mortifying thing for your conqueror to reflect how perishable is the metal with which he hammers with such violence; how the kind earth will soon shroud up his bloody footprints; and all that he

achieved and skillfully piled together will be but like his own canvas city of a camp, this evening, loud with life, to-morrow, all struck and vanished, "a few pits and heaps of straw."

4. For here, as always, it continues true, that the deepest force is the stillest; that, as in the fable, the mild shining of the sun shall silently accomplish what the fierce blustering of the tempest in vain essayed. Above all, it is ever to be kept in mind, that not by *material* but by *moral* power are men and their actions to be governed. How noiseless is thought! No rolling of drums, no tramp of squadrons, no tumult of innumerable baggage-wagons, attend its movements.

5. In what obscure and sequestered places may the head be meditating, which is one day to be crowned with more than imperial authority! for kings and emperors will be among its ministering servants; it will rule not *over* but *in* all heads; and with these solitary combinations of ideas, and with magic formulas, bend the world to its will. The time may come when Napoleon himself will be better known for his laws than his battles, and the victory of Waterloo prove less momentous than the opening of the first Mechanics' Institute.

CXLV. — FRANKLIN IN PHILADELPHIA.

From Franklin.

BENJAMIN FRANKLIN, who lived from 1706 to 1790, is well known as the printer's boy, the editor, the philosopher, the statesman, and the patriot. His exertions and influence contributed in no small degree to the success of our Revolutionary contest; and he stands unquestionably at the head of the scientific men of his day. His contributions to literature, serious and comic, are also valuable.

1. I HAVE entered into the particulars of my voyage, and shall, in like manner, describe my first entrance into this city, that you may be able to compare beginnings so little auspicious with the figure I have since made. On my arrival at Philadelphia, I was in my working dress;

my best clothes being to come by sea. I was covered with dirt; my pockets were filled with shirts and stockings; I was unacquainted with a single soul in the place, and knew not where to seek a lodging. Fatigued with walking, rowing, and having passed the night without sleep, I was extremely hungry, and all my money consisted of a Dutch dollar, and about a shilling's worth of coppers, which I gave to the boatmen for my passage. As I had assisted them in rowing, they refused it at first; but I insisted on their taking it.

2. A man is sometimes more generous when he has little than when he has much money; probably because, in the first case, he is desirous of concealing his poverty. I walked toward the top of the street, looking eagerly on both sides, till I came to Market Street, where I met with a child with a loaf of bread. Often had I made my dinner on dry bread. I inquired where he had bought it, and went straight to the baker's shop, which he pointed out to me.

3. I asked for some biscuits, expecting to find such as we had at Boston; but they made, it seems, none of that sort at Philadelphia. I then asked for a three-penny loaf. They made no loaves of that price. Finding myself ignorant of the prices, as well as of the different kinds of bread, I desired him to let me have three penny-worth of bread of some kind or other. He gave me three large rolls. I was surprised at receiving so much. I took them, however, and, having no room in my pockets, I walked on with a roll under each arm, eating a third.

4. In this manner, I went through Market Street to Fourth Street, and passed the house of Mr. Read, the father of my future wife. She was standing at the door, observed me, and thought, with reason, that I made a very singular and grotesque appearance. I then turned the corner, and went through Chestnut Street, eating my roll all the way; and, having made this round, I found myself again on Market Street wharf, near the boat in which I arrived. I stepped into it to take a draught of water; and, finding myself satisfied with my first roll, I gave the other two to

a woman and her child, who had come down with us in the boat, and was waiting to continue her journey.

5. Thus refreshed, I regained the street, which was now full of well dressed people, all going the same way. I joined them, and was thus led to a large Quaker meeting-house near the market-place. I sat down with the rest, and, after looking round me for some time, hearing nothing said, and being drowsy from my last night's labor and want of rest, I fell into a sound sleep. In this state I continued till the assembly dispersed, when one of the congregation had the goodness to wake me. This was, consequently, the first house I entered, or in which I slept, at Philadelphia.

CXLVI. — TURNING THE GRINDSTONE.

FROM FRANKLIN.

1. WHEN I was a little boy, I remember, one cold winter's morning, I was accosted by a smiling man with an ax on his shoulder. "My pretty boy," said he, "has your father a grindstone?" "Yes, sir," said I. "You are a fine little fellow," said he; "will you let me grind my ax on it?" Pleased with the compliment of "fine little fellow," "O yes, sir," I answered. "It is down in the shop." "And will you, my man," said he, patting me on the head, "get me a little hot water?" How could I refuse? I ran, and soon brought a kettle full. "How old are you? and what's your name?" continued he, without waiting for a reply; "I am sure you are one of the finest lads that ever I have seen; will you just turn a few minutes for me?"

2. Tickled with the flattery, like a little fool, I went to work, and bitterly did I rue the day. It was a new ax, and I toiled and tugged till I was almost tired to death. The school-bell rang, and I could not get away; my hands were blistered, and the ax was not half ground. At length, however, it was sharpened; and the man turned to me with, "Now, you little rascal, you 've played truant; scud to the school, or you 'll buy it!" "Alas!" thought I, "it

was hard enough to turn a grindstone, this cold day; but now to be called a little rascal, is too much."

3. It sank deep in my mind; and often have I thought of it since. When I see a merchant over polite to his customers, begging them to take a little brandy, and throwing his goods on the counter, thinks I, That man has an ax to grind. When I see a man flattering the people, making great professions of attachment to liberty, who is in private life a tyrant, methinks, Look out, good people! that fellow would set you turning grindstones. When I see a man hoisted into office by party spirit, without a single qualification to render him either respectable or useful, alas! methinks, deluded people, you are doomed for a season to turn the grindstone for a booby.

CXLVII. — QUOTATIONS FROM SHAKSPEARE.

1. A WRETCHED soul, bruis'd with adversity,
We bid be quiet when we hear it cry;
But were we burden'd with like weight of pain,
As much or more we should ourselves complain.

2. Beauty's a doubtful good, a glass, a flower,
Lost, faded, broken, dead within an hour;
And beauty, blemish'd once, forever's lost,
In spite of physic, painting, pain, and cost.

3. There is a tide in the affairs of men,
That, taken at the flood, leads on to fortune;
Omitted, all the voyage of their life
Is bound in shallows and in miseries.

4. Will fortune never come with both hands full,
But write her fair words still in foulest letters?
She either gives a stomach and no food,
Such are the poor in health; or else a feast,
And takes away the stomach, such are the rich,
That have abundance and enjoy it not.

5. Who steals my purse, steals trash; 'tis something,
        nothing,
'Twas mine, 'tis his, and has been slave to thousands;
But he who filches from me my good name,
Robs me of that which not enriches him,
And makes me poor indeed.

6. Suspicion always haunts the guilty mind;
The thief doth fear each bush an officer.
Thrice is he arm'd that hath his quarrel just;
And he but naked, though lock'd up in steel,
Whose conscience with injustice is corrupted.

7. There is, betwixt that smile we would aspire to,
That sweet aspect of princes, and their ruin,
More pangs and fears than wars or women have;
And when he falls, he falls like Lucifer,
Never to hope again.

8. Friendship is constant in all other things,
Save in the office and the affairs of love:
Therefore, all hearts in love use their own tongues;
Let every eye negotiate for itself,
And trust no agent.

9. This is the state of man: to-day he puts forth
The tender leaves of hope, to-morrow blossoms,
And bears his blushing honors thick upon him,
The third day comes a frost, a killing frost.

10. The man that hath not music in himself,
And is not moved with concord of sweet sounds,
Is fit for treasons, stratagems, and spoils;
Let no man trust him.

11. 'Tis not the many oaths that make the truth;
But the plain single vow that is vow'd true.
It is great sin to swear unto a sin,
But greater sin to keep a sinful oath.

12. The poor beetle that we tread upon,
In corporal suffering feels a pang as great
As when a giant dies.

13. The poet's eye, in a fine frenzy rolling,
Doth glance from heaven to earth, from earth to heaven;
And, as imagination bodies forth
The forms of things unknown, the poet's pen
Turns them to shapes, and gives to airy nothing
A local habitation and a name.

CXLVIII. — THE SEVEN AGES OF MAN.

From Shakspeare.

1. ALL the world's a stage,
And all the men and women merely players:
They have their exits and their entrances;
And one man in his time plays many parts,
His acts being seven ages.

2. At first, the infant,
Mewling and puking in the nurse's arms;
And then, the whining schoolboy, with his sachel,
And shining morning face, creeping like snail
Unwillingly to school. And then, the lover;
Sighing like furnace, with a woeful ballad
Made to his mistress' eyebrow.

3. Then, a soldier;
Full of strange oaths, and bearded like the pard,
Jealous in honor, sudden and quick in quarrel,
Seeking the bubble reputation
Even at the cannon's mouth. And then, the justice;
In fair round belly, with good capon lined,
With eyes severe, and beard of formal cut,
Full of wise saws and modern instances,
And so he plays his part.

4. The sixth age shifts
Into the lean and slipper'd pantaloon;
With spectacles on nose, and pouch on side;
His youthful hose, well saved, a world too wide
For his shrunk shank; and his big manly voice,
Turning again toward childish treble, pipes
And whistles in his sound.

5. Last scene of all,
That ends this strange eventful history,
Is second childishness, and mere oblivion;
Sans teeth, sans eyes, sans taste, sans every thing.

CXLIX.—THE GOUT.

FROM FRANKLIN.

Franklin. EH! O! eh! What have I done to merit these cruel sufferings?

Gout. Many things; you have ate and drank too freely, and too much indulged those legs of yours in their indolence.

Franklin. What is it that accuses me?

Gout. It is I, even I, the Gout.

Franklin. What! my enemy in person?

Gout. No, not your enemy.

Franklin. I repeat it, my enemy: for you would not only torment my body to death, but ruin my good name. You reproach me as a glutton and tippler; now, all the world that knows me will allow that I am neither the one nor the other.

Gout. The world may think as it pleases: it is always very complaisant to itself, and sometimes to its friends; but I very well know that the quantity of meat and drink proper for a man who takes a reasonable degree of exercise, would be too much for another who never takes any.

Franklin. I take—Eh! O!—as much exercise—Eh!—as I can, Madam Gout. You know my sedentary state, and

on that account, it would seem, Madam Gout, as if you might spare me a little, seeing it is not altogether my own fault.

Gout. Not a jot! Your rhetoric and your politeness are thrown away; your apology avails nothing. If your situation in life is a sedentary one, your amusements, your recreations, at least, should be active. But let us examine your course of life. While the mornings are long, and you have leisure to go abroad, what do you? Why, instead of gaining an appetite for breakfast by salutary exercise, you amuse yourself with books, pamphlets, or newspapers; you eat an inordinate breakfast; immediately afterward, you sit down to write at your desk, or converse on business. Thus the time passes till one, without any kind of bodily exercise. What is your practice after dinner? To be fixed down to chess for two or three hours! What can be expected from such a course of living, but a body replete with stagnant humors, ready to fall a prey to all kinds of dangerous maladies, if I, the gout, did not occasionally bring you relief by agitating these humors, and so purifying or dissipating them? Fie, then, Mr. Franklin! But, amidst my instructions, I had almost forgot to administer my wholesome corrections: so take that twinge, and that!

Franklin. O! eh! O!—O-o-o-o! As much instruction as you please, Madam Gout, and as many reproaches, but pray, madam, a truce with your corrections!

Gout. No, sir, no; I will not abate a particle of what is so much for your good,—therefore—

Franklin. O! ch-h-h! It is not fair to say I take no exercise, when I do very often, going out to dine, and return in my carriage.

Gout. That, of all imaginary exercise, is the most slight and insignificant, if you allude to the motion of a carriage suspended on springs. By observing the degree of heat obtained by different kinds of motion, we may form an estimate of the quantity of exercise given by each. Thus, for example, if you turn out to walk in winter with cold feet, in an hour's time you will be in a glow all over;

if you ride on horseback, the same effect will scarcely be perceived by four hours' round trotting; but if you loll in a carriage, such as you have mentioned, you may travel all day, and gladly enter the last inn to warm your feet by a fire. Flatter, yourself, then, no longer, that half an hour's airing in your carriage deserves the name of exercise. Providence has appointed few to roll in carriages, while He has given to all a pair of legs, which are machines infinitely more commodious and serviceable.

Franklin. Your reasonings grow very tiresome.

Gout. I stand corrected. I will be silent, and continue my office; take that, and that!

Franklin. O! O-o! Talk on, I pray you!

Gout. No, no; I have a good number of things for you to-night, and you may be sure of some more to-morrow.

Franklin. What, with such a fever! I shall go distracted. O! eh! Can no one bear it for me?

Gout. Ask that of your horses; they have served you faithfully.

Franklin. How can you so cruelly sport with my torments?

Gout. Sport! I am very serious. I have here a list of your offences against your own health distinctly written, and can justify every stroke inflicted on you.

Franklin. Read it, then!

Gout. It is too long a detail; but I will briefly mention some particulars.

Franklin. Proceed; I am all attention.

Gout. Do you remember how often you have promised yourself, the following morning, a walk in the grove of Boulogne, or in your own garden, and have violated your promise, alleging, at one time, it was too cold, at another, too warm, too windy, too moist, or what else you pleased; when, in truth, it was too nothing, but your insuperable love of ease?

Franklin. That, I confess, may have happened occasionally, probably ten times in a year.

Gout. Your confession is very short of the truth; the gross amount is one hundred and ninety-nine times.

Franklin. Is it possible?

Gout. So possible that it is fact; you may rely on the accuracy of my statement. You know Mr. B.'s gardens, and what fine walks they contain; you know the handsome flight of a hundred steps, which lead from the terrace above to the lawn below. You have been in the practice of visiting this amiable family twice a week after dinner, and, as it is a maxim of your own that "a man may take as much exercise in walking a mile up and down stairs as in ten on level ground," what an opportunity was there for you to have had exercise in both these ways! Did you embrace it, and how often?

Franklin. I can not immediately answer that question.

Gout. I will do it for you; not once.

Franklin. Not once? I am convinced now of the justness of poor Richard's remark, that "our debts and our sins are always greater than we think for."

Gout. So it is! You philosophers are sages in your maxims, and fools in your conduct.

Franklin. Ah! how tiresome you are!

Gout. Well, then, to my office; it should not be forgotten that I am your physician. There!

Franklin. O-o, what a physician!

Gout. How ungrateful are you to say so! Is it not I, who, in the character of your physician, have saved you from the palsy, dropsy, and apoplexy? one or other of which would have done for you long ago, but for me.

Franklin. I submit, and thank you for the past, but entreat the discontinuance of your visits for the future; for, in my mind, one had better die than be cured so dolefully. Permit me just to hint that I have also not been unfriendly to *you.* I never feed physician or quack of any kind, to enter the lists against you; if, then, you do not leave me to repose, it may be said you are ungrateful, too.

Gout. I can scarcely acknowledge that as any objection. As to quacks, I despise them; they may kill *you,* indeed, but can not injure *me.* And as to regular physicians, they are at last convinced that the gout, in such a subject as

you are, is no disease, but a remedy; and wherefore cure a remedy? But to our business. There!

Franklin. O! O! Leave me, and I promise faithfully never more to play at chess, but to take exercise daily, and live temperately.

Gout. I know you too well. You promise fair; but after a few months' good health, you will return to your old habits; your fine promises will be forgotten, like the forms of the last year's clouds. Let us, then, finish the account, and I will go. But I leave you, with an assurance of visiting you again at a proper time and place; for my object is your good, and you are sensible now that I am your real friend.

CL. — THE BRIEFLESS BARRISTER.

FROM SAXE.

1. An attorney was taking a turn,
   In shabby habiliments drest;
   His coat it was shockingly worn,
   And the rust had invested his vest.

2. His breeches had suffer'd a breach,
   His linen and worsted were worse;
   He had scarce a whole crown in his hat,
   And not half a crown in his purse.

3. And thus as he wander'd along,
   A cheerless and comfortless elf,
   He sought for relief in a song,
   Or complainingly talk'd to himself:

4. "Unfortunate man that I am!
   I 've never a client but grief;
   The case is, I 've no case at all,
   And, in brief, I 've ne'er had a brief!

5. "I 've waited and waited in vain,
    Expecting an 'opening' to find,
Where an honest young lawyer might gain
    Some reward for the toil of his mind.

6. "'Tis not that I 'm wanting in law,
    Or lack an intelligent face,
That others have cases to plead,
    While I have to plead for a case.

7. "O, how can a modest young man
    E'er hope for the smallest progression?
The profession 's already so full
    Of lawyers so full of profession!"

8. While thus he was strolling around,
    His eye accidentally fell
On a very deep hole in the ground,
    And he sighed to himself, "It is well!"

9. To curb his emotions, he sat
    On the curb-stone the space of a minute,
Then cried, "Here 's an op'ning at last!"
    And in less than a jiffy was in it!

10. Next morning twelve citizens came,
    ('Twas the coroner bade them attend,)
To the end that it might be determin'd
    How the man had determin'd his end!

11. "The man was a lawyer, I hear,"
    Quoth the foreman who sat on the corse;
"A lawyer? Alas!" said another,
    "Undoubtedly he died of remorse!"

12. A third said, "He knew the deceas'd,
    An attorney well vers'd in the laws,
And as to the cause of his death,
    'Twas no doubt from the want of a cause."

13. The jury decided at length,
    After solemnly weighing the matter,
    "That the lawyer was drown-*d*ed, because
    He could n't keep his head above water!"

CLI. — RULES FOR CONVERSATION.

FROM JOHNSON.

1. THAT conversation may answer the ends for which it was designed, the parties who are to join in it must come together with a determined resolution to please and to be pleased. If a man feels that an east wind has rendered him dull and sulky, he should, by all means, stay at home till the wind changes, and not be troublesome to his friends; for dullness is infectious, and one sour face will make many, as one cheerful countenance is soon productive of others. If two gentlemen desire to quarrel, it should not be done in a company met to enjoy the pleasures of conversation. It is obvious, that he who is about to form a conversation party, should be careful to invite men of congenial minds, and of similar ideas respecting the entertainment of which they are to partake, and to which they must contribute.

2. With gloomy persons, gloomy topics likewise should be (as, indeed, they will be) excluded, such as ill-health, bad weather, bad news, or foreboding of such, etc. To preserve the temper calm and pleasant, it is of unspeakable importance that we always accustom ourselves, through life, to make the best of things: to view them on their bright side, and so represent them to others, for our mutual comfort and encouragement. Few things (especially if, as Christians, we take the other world into account) but have a bright side; diligence and practice will easily find it. Perhaps there is no circumstance better calculated than this to render conversation equally pleasing and profitable.

3. In the conduct of it, be not eager to interrupt others, or uneasy at being yourself interrupted, since you speak either to amuse or instruct the company, or to receive those benefits from it. Give all, therefore, leave to speak

in turn. Hear with patience, and answer with precision. Inattention is ill-manners: it shows contempt, and contempt is never forgiven. Trouble not the company with your own private concerns, as you do not love to be troubled with those of others. Yours are as little to them as theirs are to you. You will need no other rule whereby to judge of this matter.

4. Contrive, but with dexterity and propriety, that each person may have an opportunity of discoursing on the subject with which he is best acquainted. He will be pleased, and you will be informed. By observing this rule, every one has it in his power to assist in rendering conversation agreeable; since, though he may not choose or be qualified to say much himself, he can propose questions to those who are able to answer them.

5. Avoid stories, unless short, pointed, and quite *apropos*. "He who deals in them," says Swift, "must either have a very large stock, or a good memory, or must often change his company." Some have a set of them strung together like onions; they take possession of the conversation by an early introduction of one, and then you must have the whole *rope*, and there is an end of every thing else, perhaps, for that meeting, though you may have heard all, twenty times before.

6. Talk often, but not long. The talent of haranguing in private company is insupportable. Senators and barristers are apt to be guilty of this fault; and members who never harangue in the house, will often do it out of the house. If the majority of the company be naturally silent or cautious, the conversation will flag, unless it be often renewed by one among them, who can start new subjects. Forbear, however, if possible, to broach a second before the first is out, lest your stock should not last, and you should be obliged to come back to the old barrel. There are those that will repeatedly cross upon, and break into, the conversation with a fresh topic, till they have touched upon all and exhausted none. Economy here is necessary for most people.

7. Laugh not at your own wit and humor; leave that

to the company. When the conversation is flowing in a serious and useful channel, never interrupt it by an ill-timed jest. The stream is scattered, and can not be again collected. Discourse not in a whisper, or half-voice, to your next neighbor; it is ill-breeding, and in some degree a fraud; conversation-stock being, as one has well observed, a joint and common property. In reflections on absent people, go no further than you would go if they were present. "I resolve," says Bishop Beveridge, "never to speak of a man's virtues before his face, nor of his faults behind his back." A golden rule! the observation of which would, at one stroke, banish flattery and defamation from the earth.

8. Conversation is affected by circumstances, which, at first sight, may appear trifling, but really are not so. Some who continue dumb while seated, become at once loquacious when they are (as the senatorial phrase is) upon their legs; others, whose powers languish in a close room, recover themselves on putting their heads into fresh air, as a Shrovetide cock does when his head is put into fresh earth; a turn or two in the garden makes them good company. There is a magic sometimes in a large circle, which fascinates those who compose it into silence; and nothing can be done, or rather nothing can be said, till the introduction of a table breaks up the spell, and releases the valiant knights and fair damsels from captivity.

9. A table of any kind, considered as a center of union, is of eminent service to conversation at all times; and never do we more sensibly feel the truth of that old philosophical axiom, that "nature abhors a vacuum," than upon its removal. I have been told that even in the blue-stocking society, formed solely for the purpose of conversation, it was found, after repeated trials, impossible to get on without one card-table. In that same venerable society, when the company is too widely extended to engage in the same conversation, a custom is said to prevail, and a very excellent one it is, that every gentleman, upon his entrance, selects his partner, as he would do at a ball; and when the conversation-dance is gone down, the company change

partners and begin afresh. Whether these things be so or not, most certain it is, that the lady or the gentleman deserves well of the society, who can devise any method whereby so valuable an amusement can be improved.

CLII.—STORY-TELLING.

FROM STEELE.

SIR RICHARD STEELE was an English author, who was born in 1671, and died 1729. He was one of the authors of the *Tatler*, the *Spectator*, and the *Guardian*.

1 TOM LIZARD told us a story, the other day, of some persons which our family know very well, with so much humor and life, that it caused a great deal of mirth at the tea-table. His brother Will, the Templar, was highly delighted with it; and the next day, being with some of his Inns-of-court acquaintance, resolved to entertain them with what he called "a pleasant humor enough." I was in great pain for him when I heard him begin, and was not at all surprised to find the company very little moved by it. Will blushed, looked round the room, and, with a forced laugh, "Faith, gentlemen," said he, "I do not know what makes you look so grave; it was an admirable story when I heard it!"

2. When I came home, I fell into a profound contemplation upon story-telling; and, as I have nothing so much at heart as the good of my country, I resolved to lay down some precautions upon this subject.

3. I have often thought that a story-teller is born, as well as a poet. It is, I think, certain, that some men have such a peculiar cast of mind, that they see things in another light than men of grave dispositions. Men of lively imaginations and a mirthful temper will represent things to their hearers in the same manner as they themselves were affected with them; and whereas serious spirits might, perhaps, have been disgusted at the sight of some odd occurrences in life, yet the very same occurrences shall

please them in a well told story, where the disagreeable parts of the images are concealed, and those only which are pleasing, exhibited to the fancy. Story-telling is, therefore, not an art, but what we call a "knack;" it doth not so much subsist upon wit as upon humor; and, I will add, that it is not perfect without proper gesticulations of the body, which naturally attend such merry emotions of the mind.

4. I would advise all professors of this art never to tell stories, but as they seem to grow out of the subject-matter of the conversation, or as they serve to illustrate or enliven it. Stories that are very common are generally irksome, but may be aptly introduced, provided they be only hinted at, and mentioned by way of allusion. Those that are altogether new should never be ushered in, without a short and pertinent character of the persons concerned. A little circumstance in the complexion or dress of the man you are talking of, sets his image before the hearer, if it be chosen aptly for the story. Besides marking distinct characters, and selecting pertinent circumstances, it is likewise necessary to leave off in time, and end smartly; so that there is a kind of drama in the forming of the story; and the manner of conducting and pointing it is the same as in an epigram. It is a miserable thing, after one has raised the expectation of the company by humorous characters and a pretty conceit, to pursue the matter too far. There is no retreating; and how poor is it for a story-teller to end his relation by saying, "That's all!"

5. As the choosing of pertinent circumstances, is the life of a story, so the collectors of impertinent particulars, are the very bane and opiates of conversation. Poor Ned Pappy—he's gone—was a very honest man, but was so excessively tedious over his pipe, that he was not to be endured. He knew so exactly what they had for dinner; when such a thing happened; in what ditch his bay horse had his sprain at that time; and how his man John—no, it was William—started a hare in the common field, that he never got to the end of his tale. Then he was exceedingly particular in marriages and intermarriages, and

cousins twice or thrice removed; and whether such a thing happened at the latter end of July, or the beginning of August. He had a marvelous tendency, likewise, to digression, insomuch that if a considerable person was mentioned in his story, he would straightway launch out into an episode of him; and, again, if in that person's story he had occasion to remember a third man, he broke off, and gave us his history, and so on.

6. He always put me in mind of what Sir William Temple informs us of the tale-tellers in the north of Ireland, who are hired to tell stories of giants and enchanters, to lull people asleep. These historians are obliged, by their bargain, to go on, without stopping; so that, after the patient hath, by this benefit, enjoyed a long nap, he is sure to find the operator proceeding in his work. Ned procured the like effect in me, the last time I was with him. As he was in the third hour of his story, and very thankful that his memory did not fail him, I fairly nodded in the elbow-chair. He was much affronted at this, till I told him, "Old friend, you have your infirmity, and I have mine."

CLIII. — TRUTH IN PARENTHESIS.

FROM HOOD.

1. I REALLY take it very kind,
    This visit, Mrs. Skinner;
I have not seen you such an age,
    (The wretch has come to dinner!)
Your daughters, too, what loves of girls!
    What heads for painters' easels!
Come here, and kiss the infant, dears!
    (And give it, p'rhaps, the measles!)

2. Your charming boys, I see, are home,
    From Reverend Mr. Russell's;
'Twas very kind to bring them both,
    (What boots for my new Brussels!)

What! little Clara left at home?
　　Well now, I call that shabby!
I should have lov'd to kiss her so,
　　(A flabby, dabby babby!)

3. And Mr. S , I hope he's well;
　　But, though he lives so handy,
He never once drops in to sup,
　　(The better for our brandy!)
Come, take a seat, I long to hear
　　About Matilda's marriage;
You've come, of course, to spend the day,
　　(Thank Heaven! I hear the carriage!)

4. What! must you go? Next time, I hope,
　　You'll give me longer measure.
Nay, I shall see you down the stairs,
　　(With most uncommon pleasure!)
Good by! good by! Remember, all,
　　Next time you'll take your dinners;
(Now, David, mind, I'm not at home,
　　In future, to the Skinners.)

CLIV.—THE POSTMAN.

FROM COWPER.

1. HARK! 'tis the twanging horn o'er yonder bridge,
That, with its wearisome but needful length,
Bestrides the wintry flood; in which the moon
Sees her unwrinkled face reflected bright:
He comes, the herald of a noisy world,
With spatter'd boots, strapp'd waist, and frozen locks,
News from all nations lumbering at his back.

2. True to his charge, the close-pack'd load behind,
Yet careless what he brings, his one concern
Is to conduct it to the destin'd inn:

And having dropp'd the expected bag, pass on.
He whistles as he goes, light-hearted wretch,
Cold and yet cheerful: messenger of grief
Perhaps to thousands, and of joy to some;
To him indiff'rent whether grief or joy.

3. Houses in ashes, and the fall of stocks,
Births, deaths, and marriages, epistles wet
With tears that trickled down the writer's cheeks
Fast as the periods from his fluent quill,
Or charged with am'rous sighs of absent swains,
Or nymphs responsive, equally affect
His horse and him, unconscious of them all.

4. But, O, th' important budget! usher'd in
With such heart-shaking music, who can say
What are its tidings? have our troops awaked?
Or do they still, as if with opium drugg'd,
Snore to the murmurs of th' Alantic wave?
Is India free? and does she wear her plumed
And jewel'd turban with a smile of peace,
Or do we grind her still? The grand debate,
The popular harangue, the tart reply,
The logic, and the wisdom, and the wit,
And the loud laugh; I long to know them all;
I burn to set th' imprison'd wranglers free,
And give them voice and utt'rance once again.

5. Now stir the fire, and close the shutters fast,
Let fall the curtains, wheel the sofa round,
And, while the bubbling and loud-hissing urn
Throws up a steamy column, and the cups,
That cheer but not inebriate, wait on each,
So let us welcome peaceful ev'ning in.

6. Not such his ev'ning who, with shining face,
Sweats in the crowded theater, and, squeez'd
And bored with elbow points through both his sides,
Outscolds the ranting actor on the stage.

This folio of four pages, happy work!
Which not e'en critics criticise; that holds
Inquisitive attention, while I read,
Fast bound in chains of silence, which the fair,
Though eloquent themselves, yet fear to break;
What is it, but a map of busy life,
Its fluctuations, and its vast concerns?

7. Here runs the mountainous and craggy ridge,
That tempts Ambition.   On the summit see
The seals of office glitter in his eyes;
He climbs, he pants, he grasps them!   At his heels
Close at his heels, a demagogue ascends,
And with a dext'rous jerk soon twists him down,
And wins them, but to lose them in his turn.

8. Here rills of oily eloquence, in soft
Meanders, lubricate the course they take;
The modest speaker is ashamed and griev'd,
T' engross a moment's notice; and yet begs,
Begs a propitious ear for his poor thoughts,
However trivial all that he conceives.
Sweet bashfulness; it claims at least this praise:
The dearth of information and good sense
That it foretells us, always comes to pass.

9. Cataracts of declamation thunder here;
There, forests of no meaning spread the page;
The rest appears a wilderness of strange
But gay confusion; roses for the cheeks,
And lilies for the brows of faded age,
Teeth for the toothless, ringlets for the bald,
Heav'n, earth, and ocean, plunder'd of their sweets,
Nectareous essences, Olympian dews,
Sermons, and city feasts, and fav'rite airs,
Ethereal journeys, submarine exploits,
And Katterfelto, with his hair on end
At his own wonders, wond'ring for his bread.

10. 'Tis pleasant, through the loopholes of retreat,
To peep at such a world; to see the stir
Of the great Babel, and not feel the crowd;
To hear the roar she sends through all her gates
At a safe distance, where the dying sound
Falls a soft murmur on th' uninjur'd ear.

CLV. — THE MILLER'S DAUGHTER.

1. TOWARD the close of the last century, there occurred in France one of the most singular political convulsions of which history has any record. The lower orders of the nation, headed by some individuals of influence, rose in arms against their sovereign, and, after a long series of atrocities, succeeded in dethroning and beheading king Louis the Sixteenth, and in completely overturning the power of the nobles and destroying the institutions of the state.

2. Of these scenes of horror, one of the most active agents was Robespierre, who, having raised himself to a situation of power among the disaffected, ruled his country with despotic tyranny. During his temporary elevation, either the secret denunciations of an envious rival, or the false charges preferred by an open enemy, were sufficient to condemn innocence and virtue to a violent death. Any individual who was known, during the *reign of terror*, (as that period of the French revolution has been termed,) to afford the slightest commiseration or assistance to the proscribed victims of tyranny, was almost certain to lose his life as the penalty of his injudicious compassion; and owing to this circumstance, fear seemed to suppress every generous feeling of the heart, and to stifle every sentiment of humanity in the bosoms of the greater part of the unhappy inhabitants of France.

3. There lived, about this time, in one of the northern counties of the kingdom, a miller, in easy circumstances, whose name was Maturin, and who, so far from participating in the alarm and dread which seemed to freeze the

charity of his countrymen, sought every opportunity of conferring acts of kindness on the unfortunate people, who were flying from their homes, to avoid the horrors of prison or of death.

4. During this period, no suspicion had ever attached to him, and, in the opinion of his neighbors, he passed for an excellent *patriot*, as the term was then understood. He contrived, however, to conceal his real feelings under an air of gayety; and on many occasions, in order to avoid suspicion, he had even received into his mill the officers of the tyrant, and entertained them hospitably. Toinette, his daughter, a little girl only ten years of age, was his only confidant and companion. She was the depository of his secrets; and, possessing a great deal of prudence, together with an appearance of childish innocence, she was particularly useful to her father in aiding his efforts to deceive the cruel agents of Robespierre; and she shared in all his rejoicings when they had the good fortune to rescue any innocent sufferer from their snares.

5. One evening, Toinette had gone down to a fountain at some distance from the mill, in order to bring home fresh water for supper, when her father should return from labor. She filled her pitcher, and placing it on the ground, by the side of the well, she seated herself on a mossy bank, under the shade of a beach-tree which grew above it. The sun was just setting; there was not the slightest noise to disturb the calm silence which reigned around her; and leaning her head on her arm, she began to reflect on some melancholy tales of recent suffering which her father had been relating to her that morning. She had not remained in this position more than a few moments, when she fancied that she heard the voice of some one in distress apparently very near her. She started at an incident so unusual; and listening for a moment, heard distinctly a low, faint moan, which seemed to issue from a hovel not far from the well. It had formerly been a comfortable cottage; but having been destroyed by fire about a year before, little more than the four walls and a part of the roof were now remaining.

6. She arose instantly, and proceeding toward the ruined hut, was about to enter the door, when she perceived the figure of a man stretched on the ground, wasted and pale, and apparently in the last struggle of death. She drew near to him without hesitation, attempted to raise his head, and asked him some questions in a voice of pity. The unfortunate man fixed his eyes intently on the little girl, and said, in a low voice, "Give me some bread; I am perishing from hunger."

7. At these words, the tears came into the eyes of Toinette; she knew not what to do; she had no bread with her, and from the exhausted state of the poor sufferer, she feared to leave him to procure any, lest, on her return, she should find that he had breathed his last. For a few moments she hesitated what to do, whether to go, or remain where she was; at length, thinking she had better leave him, and bring some food, than stay with him, and perhaps see him expire before her eyes, she gently laid his head on the floor, and had proceeded a few steps from the door of the hut on her way home, when she remembered that she had a pear and some chestnuts in her pocket. The recollection of these treasures no sooner flashed on her mind than she ran back, and placing the head of the poor man upon her knee, she put a small piece of the pear in his mouth. He had been so long without food, that it was with some difficulty he swallowed the first morsel; but by degrees he seemed to revive, and by the time he had finished the fruit, he was so far recovered as to be able to answer the questions of the little girl.

8. "Tell me," said Toinette, "how long you have been in this horrible place? for your clothes are all ragged, and you can not have been shaved for many weeks. But you shall come with me to my home; it is not far distant, and my father is kind to all who are in distress; and when you are well, he will give you employment in our mill, and every day you shall have abundance to eat, and a comfortable bed to sleep on at night."

9. "Alas! my child," replied Monsieur Passot, (for that was the name of the unhappy man,) "it is impossible for

me to take advantage of the offer which you are so kind as to make me. I am unfortunately obliged to fly, and to conceal myself, far from the haunts of my fellow-creatures; but I should rather prefer to perish here than to end my days on a scaffold. I can only thank you for your kindness, but I can not accept of it; bring me a little bread, it is all that I ask; and promise me faithfully that you will not mention, even to your father, your having seen me."

10. Toinette did all in her power to persuade Monsieur Passot to alter his determination, and to confide in her father; but, finding that she could not succeed, she promised to keep his secret inviolable; and "do not think," said she, "that I will abandon you here without assistance. Oh, no! I will procure you something to eat now, and will find the means to return to you every day, and to bring you some bread. No one shall know of your existence; and, for myself, I will die rather than betray you." When she had gone, Monsieur Passot found himself much more composed and tranquil: he was thankful for the interest which Toinette had taken in his welfare, and he considered it as an especial interference of Providence to preserve his life. He could now keep himself concealed as long as he chose, since his little friend had undertaken to provide him with food; and he hoped to be enabled, by this means, to elude his enemies till his name should be forgotten, or a new order of things in France would permit his return to his home and his family.

11. In a few minutes, Toinette was again by his side, with some bread and a little cup of milk, from which the poor sufferer eagerly drank, and seemed much refreshed. Toinette would have been very glad to learn the particulars of Monsieur Passot's escape; but, fearing that her father would miss her, and inquire the cause of her absence, she took a reluctant leave of her protege; and hastening to the well, she took up her pitcher, and returned to the mill, rejoicing to have had it in her power thus to save the life of a fellow-creature.

12. The little girl, faithful to her promise, continued to supply her pensioner, at stated periods, with bread, to

which she occasionally added some vegetables or cheese. Monsieur Passot took great pleasure in her intelligent and child-like conversation; and, on her part, Toinette was so pleased with her friend, that she was never in a hurry to leave him and return to the mill. At the same time, she was grieved to see that he had no other covering or shelter than the wretched hovel where he lay, and which was, in fact, more fit to be the retreat of a wild beast than that of a human being. In vain she renewed, from time to time, her entreaties that he would confide in the protection of her father, and remove to the mill. He was too generous to endanger, by his presence, the safety of honest Maturin; and preferred enduring all the horrors of his present situation, from a conviction that to their kindness he was chiefly indebted for concealment and security.

13. One morning, when Toinette and he were deeply engaged in conversation, they were alarmed by the approach of a third person, who suddenly started from among the trees, and struck them with terror by his presence. Toinette, however, soon recovered her confidence when she recognized her father; and, turning to Monsieur Passot, she entreated him not to suspect her of having told Maturin of his living in the forest. "Ask himself," said the little girl eagerly, "and he will assure you that I have not." Her father, thus appealed to, replied, "It is very true, my child, that you never have; but how could you suppose that I could be so blind as not to observe your frequent absence, or that I should not feel uneasy when I was at home alone, while you have been here chatting with Monsieur? The quantities of bread, too, which you have been in the habit of carrying off, have excited my suspicions; but, Toinette, how could you think of permitting this gentleman to remain here so long in the midst of so much misery? Had you told me of his being here, I would at once have found him an equally safe, and more commodious retreat."

14. "My good sir," interrupted Monsieur Passot, with great emotion, "it was not the fault of this dear child, for I have uniformly resisted her entreaties to take me to your

home, through my fear of bringing you into difficulty or danger. I have suffered so much, that I would not willingly bring another into similar trouble." "If that be all your fear," replied the miller, with a smile, "you may set your mind at rest. I shall run no risks; and even if I should, I have, at most, but one life to lose, and that I shall gladly endanger to serve my suffering fellow-creatures. No: you must not stay here. This evening, at dusk, Toinette shall come for you. A few days ago, I was obliged to dismiss my assistant, who was an idle fellow. You shall take his place, and do his work when you are able; but we will first rid you of this long beard, which would make you look more like a Capuchin friar than a miller's man; and having arrayed you in one of my dresses, all suspicion will be lulled, and, by the assistance of Providence, all will go on securely and well. But I must leave you now; farewell, Monsieur, for the present, and at night-fall I shall expect to see you at my mill." So saying, Maturin took the hand of his daughter, and both went away together, leaving the heart of Monsieur Passot swelling with gratitude to heaven, and to them as the agents of its bounty.

15. At night Toinette arrived, according to promise, at the forest. She was delighted at the thought of her friend's being no longer exposed to the inclemency of the weather, and deprived of the necessaries of life. They left the ruined cottage together, traversed the paths of the wood in silence, and at last arrived, without having been seen, at the mill. Here Monsieur Passot was immediately shaved, and being dressed in a suit of the miller's clothes, obtained the new name of "Nicholas," and took his seat at the table between Maturin and his daughter. A few glasses of good wine recruited his spirits, and he had soon the pleasure of stretching his weary limbs on a comfortable bed, after lying for six weeks exposed to the dew and the rain, upon the cold, damp floor of the ruined cottage.

16. During the few succeeding days, wholesome and plentiful food, and above all, the tranquillity of his mind, served to recruit the strength of the stranger: and, one

morning, he informed his good host of his previous adventures and his melancholy story. He had been denounced, he said, and condemned to death, without being permitted to speak, or being even asked for a defense, by the revolutionary committee of the town of Bressuiere, where he resided. A friend who knew his danger, and to whom he had once shown a trifling kindness, gave him information of his impending fate, in time to permit him to make his escape, under the disguise of a beggar. During his flight, he traversed each night the high-roads of the department, and during the day, lay concealed in the woods among the lonely hills, where he happened to find himself. By these means he had reached the forest near the mill, and had hid himself in the ruins where Toinette first discovered him. "But even here," continued he, "I should soon have perished from cold and exhaustion, had it not been for the arrival of your dear child; since the terror of falling into the hands of my enemies seldom permitted me to go beyond the walls of my retreat, and I was fast sinking under the pains of hunger, when Toinette came in time to render me assistance, and to save my life."

17. One morning, soon after this conversation had taken place, Toinette came running in, out of breath, to say that four soldiers, armed with sabers and muskets, and of a very ferocious appearance, were approaching the mill from the high-road. Monsieur Passot eagerly inquired where he could hide himself. "That would be impossible," said Maturin, "for if they search the mill, as it is likely they will, they would be sure to find you, and your fate would be inevitable. You must now put a bold face on the matter; summon up all your hardihood, and leave it to me to deceive them."

18. Two minutes after, the soldiers entered the mill. "Good morrow, citizen," said they, striking Maturin on the shoulder, "here we are, four worthy fellows, sadly fatigued with following an aristocrat, (the name given by the revolutionists to those who supported the party of the government and the nobility,) who has unfortunately eluded our pursuit. Come, what can you give us to eat?"

19. "The best in my house, to be sure," replied the miller. "Go, Toinette, put 'a clean napkin on the table, fetch down that piece of ham which was left from yesterday's dinner; and you, Nicholas, off to the cellar, and bring up four bottles of the primest Burgundy for these worthy citizens: quick, blockhead!" he added, pushing him rudely by the shoulder; and Monsieur Passot hastened to do as he was directed. It took some minutes to perform his errand, and on his re-appearance with the wine, Maturin again seemed very angry with Nicholas for presuming to make them wait so long. He appeared, in fact, ready to strike him, and in such a passion, that the soldiers interfered to appease him, and observed that Nicholas seemed really an honest sort of a fellow, though somewhat too much of a simpleton.

20. The miller seated himself at table beside them; pressed them again and again to do honor to his provisions, and supplied them plentifully with wine; and then inquired what was passing in the world, or what news they were charged with. "War," said they, "goes on against all who oppose the progress of the revolution. The prisons are still overflowing with criminals, in spite of the daily execution of thousands, and we are at this moment in pursuit of one of the most decided aristocrats in France, a man called Passot, who lived at Bressuiere, and was condemned by the tribunal; some traitor gave notice of his sentence, and he escaped from the city; but we know that he is at this moment not far distant from the spot where we sit, and we are in hope of soon having him in our custody. There are five hundred crowns proclaimed as a reward for him, which we are determined to earn, if possible." They then asked for another bottle of wine, and when they had finished it, they proposed searching the mill. To this proceeding the miller offered no resistance; but, on the contrary, ordered Nicholas to go for the keys, and to throw open all the doors in the house.

21. When this was done, Toinette took the hand of her father, and accompanied him through the mill; every door was opened, and the soldiers, having inspected every corner,

were about to retire, when one of them recollected that they had not searched the cellar, where, he said, a dozen of traitors might be concealed. Nicholas was accordingly again summoned, and the cellar was visited in due form. On coming up they expressed themselves perfectly satisfied; they then drank another glass of wine to the health of Robespierre, and departed well pleased with the reception they had met with from the miller, his daughter, and the stupid Nicholas.

22. Maturin, however, began to fear that he could not long continue to shelter Monsieur Passot with equal security. He knew that such visits as this would be frequent, and in some of them he might be surprised and discovered. He accordingly pretended that he was going a journey of fifty leagues into the country, and obtained a passport for himself and his servant. He set off in a few days; and the miller conducted his friend in safety to the house of one of his brothers, who lived at some distance from Bressuiere, and leaving him under his protection, returned home to Toinette. Here Monsieur Passot lived securely till the termination of the revolution; when it was not difficult for him to prove his innocence, and reclaim his property.

23. In his prosperity, however, he did not forget his former benefactors. He returned to visit Maturin the miller, and justly regarding Toinette as the preserver of his life, he undertook to have her educated at one of the best schools in Paris; supplied her with masters of every description, and finally, on the sudden death of her father, adopted her as his own child, and took upon himself the charge of establishing her in the world.

CLVI. — HIAWATHA'S WOOING.

FROM LONGFELLOW.

1. AT the doorway of his wigwam
Sat the ancient Arrow-maker,
In the land of the Dacotahs,
Making arrow-heads of jasper,

Arrow-heads of chalcedony.
At his side, in all her beauty,
Sat the lovely Minnehaha,
Sat his daughter, Laughing Water,
Plaiting mats of flags and rushes;
Of the past the old man's thoughts were,
And the maiden's of the future.

2. He was thinking, as he sat there,
Of the days when with such arrows
He had struck the deer and bison,
On the Muskoday, the meadow;
Shot the wild goose, flying southward,
On the wing, the clamorous Wawa;
Thinking of the great war-parties,
How they came to buy his arrows,
Could not fight without his arrows.
Ah, no more such noble warriors
Could be found on earth as they were!
Now the men were all like women,
Only used their tongues for weapons!

3. She was thinking of a hunter,
From another tribe and country,
Young, and tall, and very handsome,
Who, one morning, in the Spring-time,
Came to buy her father's arrows,
Sat and rested in the wigwam,
Linger'd long about the doorway,
Looking back as he departed.
She had heard her father praise him,
Praise his courage and his wisdom;
Would he come again for arrows
To the Falls of Minnehaha?
On the mat her hands lay idle,
And her eyes were very dreamy.

4. Through their thoughts they heard a footstep,
Heard a rustling in the branches,

And with glowing cheek and forehead,
With the deer upon his shoulders,
Suddenly from out the woodlands
Hiawatha stood before them.

5. Straight the ancient Arrow-maker
Look'd up gravely from his labor,
Laid aside the unfinish'd arrow,
Bade him enter at the doorway,
Saying, as he rose to meet him,
"Hiawatha, you are welcome!"
At the feet of Laughing Water
Hiawatha laid his burden,
Threw the red deer from his shoulders;
And the maiden look'd up at him,
Look'd up from her mat of rushes,
Said, with gentle look and accent,
"You are welcome, Hiawatha!"

6. Then uprose the Laughing Water,
From the ground fair Minnehaha,
Laid aside her mat unfinish'd,
Brought forth food and set before them,
Water brought them from the brooklet,
Gave them food in earthen vessels,
Gave them drink in bowls of bass-wood,
Listen'd while the guest was speaking,
Listen'd while her father answer'd,
But not once her lips she open'd,
Not a single word she utter'd.

7. "After many years of warfare,
Many years of strife and bloodshed,
There is peace between the Ojibways
And the tribe of the Dacotahs,"
Thus continued Hiawatha,
And then added, speaking slowly,
"That this peace may last forever,
And our hands be clasp'd more closely,

And our hearts be more united,
Give me as my wife this maiden,
Minnehaha, Laughing Water,
Loveliest of Dacotah women!"

8. And the ancient Arrow-maker
Paus'd a moment ere he answer'd,
Smoked a little while in silence,
Look'd at Hiawatha proudly,
Fondly look'd at Laughing Water,
And made answer very gravely:
"Yes, if Minnehaha wishes;
Let your heart speak, Minnehaha!"

9. And the lovely Laughing Water
Seem'd more lovely, as she stood there,
Neither willing nor reluctant,
As she went to Hiawatha,
Softly took the seat beside him,
While she said, and blush'd to say it,
"I will follow you, my husband!"

10. This was Hiawatha's wooing!
Thus it was he won the daughter
Of the ancient Arrow-maker,
In the land of the Dacotahs!

11. From the wigwam he departed,
Leading with him Laughing Water;
Hand in hand they went together,
Through the woodland and the meadow,
Left the old man standing lonely,
At the doorway of his wigwam,
Heard the Falls of Minnehaha
Calling to them from the distance,
Crying to them from afar off,
"Fare thee well, O Minnehaha!"

12. Pleasant was the journey homeward,
Through interminable forests,

Over meadow, over mountain,
Over river, hill, and hollow.
Short it seem'd to Hiawatha,
Though they journey'd very slowly,
Though his pace he check'd and slacken'd
To the steps of Laughing Water.

13. Pleasant was the journey homeward!
All the birds sang loud and sweetly
Songs of happiness and heart's-ease;
Sang the blue-bird, the Owaissa,
"Happy are you, Hiawatha,
Having such a wife to love you!"
Sang the robin, the Opechee,
"Happy are you, Laughing Water,
Having such a noble husband!"

14. Thus it was they journey'd homeward;
Thus it was that Hiawatha
To the lodge of old Nokomis
Brought the moonlight, starlight, firelight,
Brought the sunshine of his people,
Minnehaha, Laughing Water,
Handsomest of all the women
In the land of the Dacotahs,
In the land of handsome women.

CLVII. — THE LADY OF THE LAKE.

From Scott.

1. NEVER did Grecian chisel trace
A Nymph, a Naiad, or a Grace,
Of finer form or lovelier face!
What though the sun, with ardent frown,
Had slightly tinged her check with brown:
The sportive toil, which, short and light,
Had dyed her glowing hue so bright,

Serv'd too, in hastier swell, to show
Short glimpses of a breast of snow.

2. What though no rule of courtly grace
To measur'd mood had train'd her pace,
A foot more light, a step more true,
Ne'er from the heath-flower dash'd the dew:
E'en the slight hare-bell rais'd its head,
Elastic from her airy tread.

3. What though upon her speech there hung
The accents of the mountain tongue;
Those silver sounds, so soft, so clear,
The list'ner held his breath to hear.
A chieftain's daughter seem'd the maid:
Her satin snood, her silken plaid,
Her golden brooch, such birth betray'd.

4. And seldom was a snood amid
Such wild luxuriant ringlets hid,
Whose glossy black to shame might bring
The plumage of the raven's wing;
And seldom o'er a breast so fair
Mantled a plaid with modest care:
And never brooch the folds combined
Above a heart more good and kind.

5. Her kindness and her worth to spy,
You need but gaze on Ellen's eye:
Not Katrine, in her mirror blue,
Gives back the banks in shapes more true,
Than every free-born glance confess'd
The guileless movements of her breast;
Whether joy danced in her dark eye,
Or woe or pity claim'd a sigh,
Or filial love was glowing there,
Or meek devotion pour'd a prayer,
Or tale of injury call'd forth
The indignant spirit of the North.

6. One only passion, unreveal'd,
With maiden pride the maid conceal'd,
Yet not less purely felt the flame;
O need I tell that passion's name?

CLVIII.—THE DISCONTENTED MILLER.

FROM GOLDSMITH.

1. WHANG, the miller, was naturally avaricious; nobody loved money better than he, or more respected those who had it. When people would talk of a rich man in company, Whang would say, "I know him very well; he and I have been long acquainted; he and I are intimate." But, if ever a poor man was mentioned, he had not the least knowledge of the man; he might be very well, for aught he knew; but he was not fond of making many acquaintances, and loved to choose his company.

2. Whang, however, with all his eagerness for riches, was poor. He had nothing but the profits of his mill to support him; but, though these were small, they were certain; while it stood and went, he was sure of eating; and his frugality was such that he every day laid some money by, which he would at intervals count and contemplate with much satisfaction. Yet still his acquisitions were not equal to his desires; he only found himself above want, whereas he desired to be possessed of affluence.

3. One day, as he was indulging these wishes, he was informed that a neighbor of his had found a pan of money under ground, having dreamed of it three nights running before. These tidings were daggers to the heart of poor Whang. "Here am I," says he, "toiling and moiling from morning till night for a few paltry farthings, while neighbor Thanks only goes quietly to bed and dreams himself into thousands before morning. O, that I could dream like him! With what pleasure would I dig round the pan! How slyly would I carry it home! not even my wife should see me: and then, O, the pleasure of thrusting one's hand into a heap of gold up to the elbow!"

4. Such reflections only served to make the miller un-happy; he discontinued his former assiduity; he was quite disgusted with small gains, and his customers began to forsake him. Every day he repeated the wish, and every night laid himself down in order to dream. Fortune, that was for a long time unkind, at last, however, seemed to smile on his distresses, and indulged him with the wished-for vision. He dreamed that under a certain part of the foundation of his mill there was concealed a monstrous pan of gold and diamonds, buried deep in the ground, and covered with a large flat stone.

5. He concealed his good luck from every person, as is usual in money dreams, in order to have the vision re-peated the two succeeding nights, by which he should be certain of its truth. His wishes in this, also, were answered; he still dreamed of the same pan of money in the very same place. Now, therefore, it was past a doubt; so, get-ting up early the third morning, he repaired alone, with a mattock in his hand, to the mill, and began to undermine that part of the wall to which the vision directed him.

6. The first omen of success that he met was a broken ring; digging still deeper, he turned up a house-tile, quite new and entire. At last, after much digging, he came to a broad flat stone, but then so large that it was beyond man's strength to remove it. "Here!" cried he, in rap-tures, to himself; "here it is; under this stone there is room for a very large pan of diamonds, indeed. I must e'en go home to my wife, and tell her the whole affair, and get her to assist me in turning it up."

7. Away, therefore, he goes, and acquaints his wife with every circumstance of their good fortune. Her raptures on this occasion may easily be imagined. She flew round his neck and embraced him in an ecstasy of joy; but these transports, however, did not allay their eagerness to know the exact sum; returning, therefore, together to the same place where Whang had been digging, there they found—not, indeed, the expected treasure—but the mill, their only support, undermined and fallen.

CLIX.—NUMBER ONE.

FROM HOOD

1. 'Tis very hard, and so it is,
    To live in such a row
   And witness this, that every Miss,
    But me, has got a beau:
   But love goes calling up and down,
    But here he seems to shun;
   I 'm sure he has been ask'd enough
    To call at Number One.

2. I 'm sick of all the double knocks
    That come to Number Four;
   At Number Three, I often see
    A lover at the door.
   And one in blue, at Number Two,
    Calls daily like a dun;
   'Tis very hard they came so near,
    And not to Number One.

3. Miss Bell, I hear, has got a dear
    Exactly to her mind,
   By sitting at the window pane
    Without a bit of blind.
   But *I* go in the balcony,
    Which she has never done,
   Yet arts that thrive at Number Five,
    Don 't *take* at Number One.

4. 'Tis hard with plenty in the street,
    And plenty passing by;
   There 's nice young men at Number Ten,
    But only rather shy.
   And Mrs. Smith, across the way,
    Has got a grown-up son;
   But la, he hardly seems to know
    There *is* a Number One.

5. There's Mr. Wick at Number Nine,
      But he's intent on pelf,
   And though he's pious, will not love
      His neighbor as himself.
   At Number Seven there was a sale,
      The goods had quite a run;
   And here I've got my single lot
      On hand at Number One.

6. My mother often sits at work,
      And talks of props and stays;
   And what a comfort I shall be
      In her declining days.
   The very maids about the house,
      Have set me down a nun;
   The sweethearts all belong to them,
      That call at Number One.

7. Once only, when the flue took fire,
      One Friday afternoon,
   Young Mr. Long came kindly in,
      And told me not to swoon.
   Why can't he come again without
      The Phœnix and the Sun?
   We can not always have a flue
      On fire at Number One.

8. I am not old, I am not plain,
      Nor awkward in my gait;
   I am not crooked like the bride   .
      That went from Number Eight.
   I am sure white satin made her look
      As brown as any bun:
   But even beauty has no chance,
      I think, at Number One.

9. At Number Six, they say Miss Rose
      Has slain a score of hearts:
   And Cupid, for her sake, has been
      Quite prodigal of darts.

The imp that slew, with bended bow,
  I wish he had a gun;
But if he had, he 'd never deign
  To shoot at Number One.

10. 'Tis very hard, and so it is,
  To live in such a row;
And here 's a ballad singer come
  To aggravate my woe.
O take away your foolish song,
  And tones enough to stun,
There is no luck about the house,
  I know, at Number One.

CLX. — MILTON.

FROM CHATEAUBRIAND.

JOHN MILTON, who stands without a rival at the head of English epic poets, lived from 1608 to 1674. His principal work, *Paradise Lost*, was composed after he became blind.

1. MILTON rose at four o'clock in the morning during summer, and at five in the winter. He wore almost invariably a dress of coarse gray cloth; studied till noon, dined frugally, walked with a guide, and, in the evening, sung, accompanying himself on some instrument. He understood harmony, and had a fine voice. He, for a long time, addicted himself to the practice of fencing. To judge by Paradise Lost, he must have been passionately fond of music and the perfume of flowers. He supped off five or six olives and a little water, retired to rest at nine, and composed at night, in bed. When he had made some verses, he sung, and dictated to his wife or daughters.

2. He had been very handsome, and was so even in his age. The portrait of Adam is his own. His hair was admirable, his eyes of extraordinary clearness, no defect could be perceived in them; it would have been impossible to guess that he was blind. If we were not aware what

party rage can do, could we believe that it would make it a crime for a man to be blind? But let us thank this abominable hate; we owe to it some exquisite lines. Milton first replies, that he lost his sight in the defense of liberty, then adds these passages, full of sublimity and tenderness.

3. "In the night that surrounds me, the light of the Divine presence shines the more brightly for me. God beholds me with greater tenderness and compassion because I can see naught but him. The Divine law ought not only to shield me from injury, but render me more sacred; not on account of the loss of sight, but because I am under the shadow of the Divine wings, which seem to produce this darkness in me. To this I attribute the affectionate assiduities of my friends, their soothing attentions, their kind visits, and their respectful behavior."

4. We see to what shifts he was reduced in writing, by a passage in one of his letters to Peter Hiembach: "That virtue of mine which you call political virtue, and which I would rather you would have called devotion to my country, patriotism, enchanting me with her captivating name, almost, I may say, expatriated me. In finishing my letter, let me beg of you this favor, that if you find some parts incorrectly written, you will impute the fault to the boy who writes for me; he is utterly ignorant of Latin, and I am obliged, wretchedly enough, to spell every word I dictate."

5. The miseries of Milton were still more aggravated by domestic griefs. He lost his first wife, Mary Powell, who died suddenly; as, also, after a year's marriage, did his second wife, Catharine Woodcock, of Hackney. His third wife, Elizabeth Minshell, survived him, and had used him well. He appears not to have been loved; his daughters, who played such poetical parts in his life, deceived him, and secretly sold his books. He complains of this. Unfortunately, his character seems to have had the inflexibility of his genius. Johnson has said, with precision and truth, that Milton believed woman only for obedience, and man for rebellion.

6. Milton, in his last days, was forced to sell his library.

He drew near his end. Dr. Wight going to see him, found him confined to the first floor of his small house, in a very small room, to which the visitor ascended by a staircase, carpeted, extempore, with green baize, to deaden the noise of footsteps, and to procure silence for the man who was advancing toward everlasting silence. The author of "Paradise Lost," attired in a black doublet, reclined on an elbow-chair. His head was uncovered, its silver locks fell on his shoulders, his blind, but fine dark eyes, sparkled amid the paleness of his countenance.

7. On the 10th of November, 1674, that God who had discoursed with him by night, came to fetch him; and re-united him in faith with the angels, amid whom he had lived, and whom he knew by their names, their offices, and their beauty. Milton expired so gently that no one perceived the moment when, at the age of 66 years, (within one month,) he rendered back to God one of the mightiest spirits that ever animated human clay. This temporal life, though neither long nor short, served as a foundation for life eternal. This great man had dragged on a sufficient number of days on earth to feel their weariness, but not sufficient to exhaust his genius, which remained entire, even to his latest breath.

CLXI. — ADAM AND EVE.

FROM MILTON.

EVE.

1. My author and disposer, what thou bid'st
Unargued I obey; so God ordains:
God is thy law, thou mine: to know no more
Is woman's happiest knowledge, and her praise.
With thee conversing I forget all time;
All seasons, and their change, all please alike.

2. Sweet is the breath of morn, her rising sweet,
With charm of earliest birds; pleasant the sun,

When first on this delightful land he spreads
His orient beams, on herb, tree, fruit, and flower,
Glistering with dew; fragrant the fertile earth
After soft showers; and sweet the coming on -
Of grateful evening mild; then silent night,
With this her solemn bird, and this fair moon,
And these the gems of heaven, her starry train:
But neither breath of morn, when she ascends
With charm of earliest birds; nor rising sun
On this delightful land; nor herb, fruit, flower,
Glistering with dew; nor fragrance after showers;
Nor grateful evening mild; nor silent night,
With this her solemn bird, nor walk by moon,
Or glittering star-light, without thee, is sweet.
But wherefore all night long shine these? for whom
This glorious sight, when sleep hath shut all eyes?

ADAM.

3. Daughter of God and man, accomplish'd Eve,
These have their course to finish round the earth,
By morrow evening, and from land to land
In order, though to nations yet unborn,
Ministering light prepared, they set and rise;
Lest total darkness should by night regain
Her old possession, and extinguish life
In nature and all things; which these soft fires
Not only enlighten, but with kindly heat
Of various influence foment and warm,
Temper or nourish, or in part shed down
Their stellar virtue on all kinds that grow
On earth, made hereby apter to receive
Perfection from the sun's more potent ray.

4. These then, though unbeheld in deep of night,
Shine not in vain; nor think, though men were none,
That heaven would want spectators, God want praise:
Millions of spiritual creatures walk the earth
Unseen, both when we wake, and when we sleep.

5. All these with ceaseless praise his works behold,
Both day and night: how often from the steep
Of echoing hill or thicket have we heard
Celestial voices to the midnight air,
Sole, or responsive each to other's note,
Singing their great Creator! oft in bands
While they keep watch, or nightly rounding walk,
With heavenly touch of instrumental sounds,
In full harmonic number join'd, their songs
Divide the night, and lift our thoughts to Heaven.

CLXII. — THE LAND OF DREAMS.

FROM BRYANT.

1. A MIGHTY realm is the Land of Dreams,
    With steeps that hang in the twilight sky,
And weltering oceans and trailing streams
    That gleam where the dusky valleys lie.

2. But over its shadowy border flow
    Sweet rays from the world of endless morn,
And the nearer mountains catch the glow,
    And flowers in the nearer fields are born.

3. The souls of the happy dead repair
    From their bowers of light, to that bordering land,
And walk in the fainter glory there,
    With the souls of the living, hand in hand.

4. One calm, sweet smile in that shadowy sphere,
    From eyes that open on earth no more,
One warning word from a voice once dear,
    How they rise in the memory o'er and o'er!

5. Far off from those hills that shine with day,
    And fields that bloom in the heavenly gales,
The Land of Dreams goes stretching away
    To dimmer mountains and darker vales.

6. There lie the shadows of guilty delight,
    There walk the specters of guilty fear,
And soft, low voices, that float through the night
    Are whispering sin in the helpless ear.

7. Dear maid, in thy girlhood's opening flower,
    Scarce wean'd from the love of childish play!
The tears on whose cheeks are but the shower
    That freshens the early blooms of May!

8. Thine eyes are closed, and over thy brow
    Pass thoughtful shadows and joyous gleams,
And I know, by the moving lips, that now
    Thy spirit strays in the Land of Dreams.

9. Light-hearted maiden, O, heed thy feet!
    O keep where that beam of Paradise falls;
And only wander where thou may'st meet
    The bless-ed ones from its shining walls.

10. So shalt thou come from the Land of Dreams,
    With love and peace to this world of strife;
And the light that over that border streams,
    Shall lie on the path of thy daily life.

CLXIII. — MARTYRDOM OF POLYCARP.

FROM MILNER.

1. WHEN he had finished his prayers, having made mention of all whom he had ever known, small and great, noble and vulgar, and of the whole Church throughout the world, the hour of departing being come, they set him on an ass and led him to the city. Herod, and his father Nicetes, met him, who, taking him up into their chariot, began to advise him, asking, "What harm is it to say, Lord Cæsar! and to sacrifice and be safe?" At first he was silent, but being pressed, he said, "I will not follow your

advice." When they could not persuade him, they treated him abusively, and thrust him out of the chariot, so that in falling he bruised his thigh. But he, still unmoved as if he had suffered nothing, went on cheerfully, under the conduct of his guards, to the Stadium. There the tumult being so great, that few could hear any thing, a voice from heaven said to Polycarp, as he entered on the Stadium, "Be strong, Polycarp, and behave yourself like a man." None saw the speaker, but many heard the voice.

2. When he was brought to the tribunal, there was a great tumult, as soon as it was generally understood that Polycarp was apprehended. The proconsul asked him if he was Polycarp; to which he assented. The former then began to exhort him: "Have pity on thy own great age, and the like. Swear by the fortune of Cæsar, repent, say, Take away the atheists." Polycarp, with a grave aspect, beholding all the multitude, waving his hand to them, and looking up to heaven, said, "Take away the atheists." The proconsul urging him, and saying, "Swear, and I will release thee, reproach Christ," Polycarp said, "Eighty-and-six years have I served him, and he hath never wronged me, and how can I blaspheme my King who hath saved me?"

CLXIV. — ABIDE WITH ME.

1. I will lift up mine eyes unto the hills, from whence cometh my help. My help cometh from the Lord, who made heaven and earth.

2. The Lord is thy keeper. The Lord is thy shade upon thy right hand. He that keepeth thee will not slumber nor sleep.

3. ABIDE with me, fast falls the eventide;
   The darkness thickens, Lord, with me abide;
   When other helpers fail, and comforts flee,
   Help of the helpless, oh! abide with me.

4. Swift to its close ebbs out life's little day;
   Earth's joys grow dim, its glories pass away;
   Change and decay on all around I see;
   O Thou who changest not, abide with me.

5. Come not in terrors, as the King of kings,
   But kind and good, with healing on thy wings;
   Tears for all woes, a heart for every plea;
   Come, Friend of sinners! thus abide with me.

6. I need thy presence every passing hour;
   What but thy grace can foil the Tempter's power?
   Who like thyself my guide and stay can be?
   Thro' cloud and sunshine, oh! abide with me.

7. I fear no foe with thee at hand to bless;
   Ills have no weight, and tears no bitterness:
   Where is Death's sting? where, Grave, thy victory?
   I triumph still, if thou abide with me.

8. Reveal thyself before my closing eyes;
   Shine thro' the gloom, and point me to the skies:
   Heaven's morning breaks, and earth's vain shadows flee:
   In life, in death, O Lord! abide with me.

CLXV.— THE CANT OF CRITICISM.

FROM STERNE.

LAURENCE STERNE, who lived from 1713 to 1768, was an English author, of wit and pathos, but of very eccentric character. His writings abound in beauties, but are disgraced by indelicacies.

The names in the 5th paragraph are those of celebrated painters. *Corregiescity* is a word made for the idea.

1. AND how did Garrick speak the soliloquy last night?
O, against all rule, my lord; most ungrammatically! Betwixt the substantive and adjective, (which should agree together, in number, case, and gender,) he made a breach,

thus, —, stopping as if the point wanted settling. And after the nominative case, (which, your lordship knows, should govern the verb,) he suspended his voice in the epilogue a dozen times, three seconds and three-fifths, by a stop-watch, my lord, each time.

2. Admirable grammarian! But in suspending his voice, was the sense suspended likewise? Did no expression of attitude or countenance fill up the chasm? Was the eye silent? Did you narrowly look?

I looked only at the stop-watch, my lord.

3. Excellent observer! And what of this new book the whole world makes such a rout about?

Oh! 'tis out of all plumb, my lord, quite an irregular thing! not one of the angles at the four corners was a right angle. I had my rule and compasses, my lord, in my pocket.

Excellent critic!

4. And, for the epic poem your lordship bid me look at, upon taking the length, breadth, highth, and depth of it, and trying them at home upon an exact scale of Bossu's, 'tis out, my lord, in every one of its dimensions.

5. Admirable connoisseur! And did you step in to take a look at the grand picture, in your way back?

'Tis a melancholy daub, my lord; not one principle of the pyramid in any one group! And what a price, for there is nothing of the coloring of Titian, the expression of Rubens, the grace of Raphael, the purity of Dominichino, the corregiescity of Corregio, the learning of Poussin, the airs of Guido, the taste of the Garrichis, or the grand contour of Angelo.

6. Grant me patience! Of all the cants which are canted in this canting world, the cant of criticism is the most tormenting. I would go fifty miles on foot, to kiss the hand of that man whose generous heart will give up the reins of his imagination into his author's hands, be pleased, he knows not why and cares not wherefore.

CLXVI.—OLD JACOB STOCK.

1. OLD Jacob Stock! The chimes of the clock were not more punctual in proclaiming the progress of time, than in marking the regularity of his visits at the temples of Plutus in Threadneedle-street and Bartholomew-lane. His devotion to them was exemplary. In vain the wind and the rain, the hail and the sleet, battled against his rugged front. Not the slippery ice, nor the thick-falling snow, nor the whole artillery of elementary warfare, could check the plodding perseverance of the man of the world, or tempt him to lose the chance, which the morning, however unpropitious it seemed, in its external aspect, might yield him of profiting by the turn of a fraction.

2. He was a stout-built, round-shouldered, squab-looking man, of a bearish aspect. His features were hard, and his heart was harder. You could read the interest-table in the wrinkles of his brow, trace the rise and fall of stocks by the look of his countenance; while avarice, selfishness, and money-getting, glared from his gray, glassy eye. Nature had poured no balm into *his* breast; nor was his "gross and earthly mold" susceptible of pity. A single look of his would daunt the most importunate petitioner, that ever attempted to extract hard coin by the soft rhetoric of a heart-moving tale.

3. The wife of one, whom he had known in better days, pleaded before him for her sick husband and famishing infants. Jacob, on occasions like these, was a man of few words. He was as chary of them as of his money, and he let her come to the end of her tale without interruption. She paused for a reply; but he gave none. "Indeed, he is very ill, sir." "Can't help it." "We are very distressed." "Can't help it." "Our poor children, too——" "Can't help that, neither."

4. The petitioner's eye looked a mournful reproach, which would have interpreted itself to any other heart but his, "Indeed, you can;" but she was silent. Jacob felt more awkwardly than he had ever done in his life. His

hand involuntarily scrambled about in his breeches' pocket. There was something like the weakness of human nature stirring within him. Some coin had unconsciously worked its way into his hand; his fingers insensibly closed; but the effort to draw them forth, and the impossibility of effecting it without unclosing them, roused the dormant selfishness of his nature, and restored his self-possession.

5. "He has been very extravagant." "Ah, sir, he has been very unfortunate, not extravagant." "Unfortunate! Ah, 'tis the very same thing. Little odds, I fancy. For my part, I wonder how folks *can* be unfortunate. *I* was never unfortunate. Nobody need be unfortunate, if they look after the main chance. *I* always looked after the main chance." "He has had a large family to maintain." "Ah! married foolishly; no offense to you, ma'am. But when poor folks marry poor folks, what are they to look for? you know. Besides, he was so foolishly fond of assisting others. If a friend was sick, or in jail, out came his purse, and then his creditors might go whistle. Now if he had married a woman with money, you know, why then ——."

6. The supplicant turned pale, and would have fainted. Jacob was alarmed; not that he sympathized, but a woman's fainting was a scene that he had not been used to: besides, there was an awkwardness about it; for Jacob was a bachelor.

7. Sixty summers had passed over his head without imparting a ray of warmth to his heart; without exciting one tender feeling for the sex, deprived of whose cheering presence, the paradise of the world were a wilderness of weeds. So he desperately extracted a crown piece from the depth profound, and thrust it hastily into her hand. The action recalled her wandering senses. She blushed; it was the honest blush of pride at the meanness of the gift. She courtesied; staggered toward the door; opened it; closed it: raised her hand to her forehead, and burst into tears.

CLXVII. — THE QUARREL.

FRO﹥ SHERIDAN.

SIR PETER TEAZLE AND LADY TEAZLE.

Sir Peter Teazle. When an old bachelor marries a young wife, what is he to expect? 'Tis not above six months since my Lady Teazle made me the happiest of men, and I have been the most miserable dog ever since. We tifted a little going to church, and fairly quarreled before the bells were done ringing. In less than a month I was nearly choked with gall, and had lost every satisfaction in life, before my friends had done wishing me joy. I am laughed at by her, and the jest of all my acquaintance. And yet, the worst of it is, I am afraid I love her, or I should never bear all this; but I am determined never to be weak enough to let her know it. But here she comes; apparently in a mighty good humor; I wish I could teaze her into loving me a little.

[*Enter Lady Teazle.*]

Lady Teazle. What's the matter, Sir Peter? You seem to be out of humor.

Sir P. Ah! Lady Teazle, it is in your power to put me in a good humor at any time.

L. Teaz. Is it? I'm glad of it, for I want you to be in a monstrous good humor now. Come, do be good-humored and let me have a hundred pounds.

Sir P. What the plague! Can't I be in good-humor without paying for it? But look always thus, and you shall have two hundred pounds. Be satisfied with that sum now, and you shall not much longer have it in your power to reproach me for not making you a proper settlement. I intend shortly to surprise you.

L. Teaz. Do you? You can't think, Sir Peter, how good-humor becomes you. Now you look just as you did before I married you.

Sir P. Do I, indeed.

L. Teaz. Do n't you remember when you used to walk with me under the elms, and tell me stories of what a

gallant you were in your youth, and asked me if I could like an old fellow who could deny me nothing?

Sir P. Ay, and you were so attentive and obliging to me then.

L Teaz. To be sure I was, and used to take your part against all my acquaintance; and when my cousin Mary used to laugh at me for thinking of marrying a man old enough to be my father, and call you an ugly, stiff, formal old bachelor, I contradicted her, and said, I did not think you so ugly by any means, and that I dared say you would make a good sort of a husband.

Sir P. That was very kind of you. Well, and you were not mistaken; you have found it so, have not you? But shall we always live thus happy?

L. Teaz. With all my heart. I don't care how soon we leave off quarreling, provided you will own you are tired first.

Sir P. With all my heart.

L. Teaz. Then we shall be as happy as the day is long, and never, never, never quarrel more.

Sir P. Never, never, never; and let our future contest be, who shall be most obliging.

L. Teaz. Ay!

Sir P. But, my dear Lady Teazle, my love, indeed you must keep a strict watch over your temper; for you know, my dear, that in all our disputes and quarrels, you always begin first.

L. Teaz. No, no, my dear Sir Peter, 'tis always *you* that begin.

Sir P. No, no, no such thing.

L. Teaz. Have a care; this is not the way to live happy, if you fly out thus.

Sir P. No, no, 'tis you.

L. Teaz. No, 'tis you.

Sir P. Zounds, I say 'tis you.

L. Teaz. Law! I never saw such a man in my life; just what my cousin Mary told me.

Sir P. Your cousin Mary is a forward, saucy, impertinent minx.

L. Teaz. You are a very great bear to abuse my relations.

Sir P. But I am well enough served for marrying you, a pert, forward, rural coquette, who had refused half the honest squires in the country.

L. Teaz. I am sure I was a great fool for marrying you, a stiff old bachelor, who was unmarried at fifty, because nobody would have you.

Sir P. You were very glad to have me; you never had such an offer before.

L. Teaz. O, yes I had; there was Sir Tivey Terrier, whose estate was full as good as yours, and he has broken his neck since we were married.

Sir P. Very well, very well, madam; you're an ungrateful woman: and many plagues light on me if 1 ever try to be friends with you again; you shall have a separate maintenance.

L. Teaz. By all means a separate maintenance.

Sir P. Very well, madam, oh, very well. Ah, madam, you shall rue this. I'll have a divorce.

L. Teaz. A divorce!

Sir P. Ay, zounds, I'll make an example of myself for the benefit of all old bachelors.

L. Teaz. Well, well, Sir Peter, be it so. I see you are going to be in a passion, so I'll leave you; and when you come properly to your temper, we shall be the happiest couple in the world, and never, never, never quarrel more.

CLXVIII.—THE POND.

1. ONCE on a time, a certain man was found,
That had a pond of water in his ground:
A fine, large pond of water, fresh and clear,
Enough to serve his turn for many a year;
Yet so it was, a strange unhappy dread
Of wanting water, seiz'd the fellow's head.
When he was dry he was afraid to drink
Too much at once, for fear his pond should sink.

Perpetually tormented with this thought,
He never ventur'd on a hearty draught;
Still dry, still fearing to exhaust his store,
When half refresh'd he frugally gave o'er;
Reviving of himself revived his fright,
" Better," quoth he, " to be *half* choked than *quite*."

2. Upon this pond continually intent,
In cares and pains his anxious life he spent;
Consuming all his time and strength away,
To make his pond rise higher every day ;
He work'd and slaved, and, oh how slow it fills!
Pour'd in by pailfuls, and took out by gills.
In a wet season he would skip about,
Placing his buckets under every spout;
From falling showers collected fresh supply
And grudging every cloud that pass-ed by;
Cursing the dryness of the times each hour,
Although it rain'd as fast as it could pour.
Then he would wade through every dirty spot,
Where any little moisture could be got,
And when he had done draining of a bog
He kept himself as dirty as a hog;
And cried, whene'er folks blamed him, "What d'ye mean?"
" It costs a world of water to be clean !"

3. If some poor neighbor craved to slake his thirst,
What! rob my pond! I'll see the rogue hang'd first;
A burning shame, these vermin of the poor
Should creep unpunish'd thus about my door!
As though I had not frogs and toads enow'
That suck my pond, whatever I can do.

4. The sun still found him, as he rose or set,
Always in quest of matters that were wet:
Betime he rose to sweep the morning dew,
And rested late to catch the evening's, too.
With soughs and troughs he labored to enrich
The rising pond from every neighboring ditch:

With soughs, and troughs, and pipes, and cuts, and sluices,
From growing plants he drain'd the very juices;
Made every stick and twig upon the hedges,
Of good behavior to deposit pledges;
By some conveyance or another, still
Devised recruits from each declining hill:
He left, in short, for his belov-ed plunder
No stone unturn'd that could have water under.

5. Sometimes, when forced to quit his awkward toil,
And, sore against his will, to rest awhile:
Then straight he took his book and down he sat
To calculate the expenses he was at;
How much he suffer'd, at a moderate guess,
From all those ways by which the pond grew less;
For as to those by which it still grew bigger
For them he reckon'd not a single figure;
He knew a wise old saying, which maintain'd,
That t'was bad luck to count what one had gain'd.

6. "First for myself, my daily charges here
Cost a prodigious quantity a year:
Although, thank Heaven, I never boil my meat,
Nor am I such a sinner as to sweat:
But things are come to such a pass indeed,
We spend ten times the water that we need:
People are grown, with washing, cleansing, rinsing,
So finical and nice, past all convincing;
So many proud, fantastic modes, in short,
Are introduced, that my poor pond pays for 't.
Not but I could be well enough content
With what upon my own account is spent,
But those large articles from whence I reap
No kind of profit, strike me on a heap.

7. "What a vast deal each moment at a sup
This ever thirsty earth itself drinks up!
Such holes! and gaps! Alas! my pond provides
Scarce for its own unconscionable sides:

Nay, how can one imagine it should thrive,
So many creatures as it keeps alive!
That creep from every nook and corner, marry!
Filching as much as ever they can carry:
Then all the birds that fly along the air
Light at my pond, and come in for a share:
Item, at every puff of wind that blows,
Away, at once, the surface of it goes:
The rest, in exhalations to the sun:
One month's fair weather, and I am undone."

8. This life he led for many a year together;
Grew old and gray in watching of the weather:
Meager as Death itself, till this same Death
Stopp'd, as the saying is, his vital breath,
For as the old fool was carrying to his field
A heavier burden than he well could wield,
He miss'd his footing, or somehow he fumbled
In tumbling of it in; but in *he* tumbled:
Mighty desirous to get out again,
He scream'd and scrambled, but t'was all in vain;
The place was grown so very deep and wide,
Nor bottom of it could he feel, nor side,
And so, in the middle of his pond, he died.

9. What think ye now, from this imperfect sketch,
My friends, of such a miserable wretch?
"Why, 'tis a wretch, we think, of your own making,
No fool can be supposed in such a taking;
Your own warm fancy." Nay, but warm or cool,
The world abounds with many such a fool:
The choicest ills, the greatest torments, sure
Are those, which numbers *labor* to endure.
"What! for a pond?" Why, call it an *estate*:
You change the name, but realize the fate.

H. S. R.—37

CLXIX. — LIFE AND DEATH.

1. THERE went a man through Syrian land,
Leading a camel by the hand.
The beast, made wild by some alarm,
Began to threaten sudden harm,
So fiercely snorting, that the man
With all his speed, escaping, ran;
He ran, and saw a well that lay,
As chance would have it, by the way.

2. He heard the camel snort so near,
As almost madden'd him with fear,
And crawl'd into the well; yet there
Fell not, but dangled in mid air;
For from a fissure in the stone
Which lined its sides, a bush had grown;
To this he clung with all his might,
From thence lamenting his sad plight.

3. He saw, what time he look'd on high,
The beast's head perilously nigh,
Ready to drag him back again;
He look'd into the bottom, then
And there a dragon he espied,
Whose horrid jaws were yawning wide
Agape to swallow him alive,
As soon as he should there arrive.

4. But as he hung two fears between,
A third by that poor wretch was seen;
For, where the bush by which he clung
Had from the broken wall outsprung,
He saw too mice precisely there,
One black, one white, a stealthy pair;
He saw the black one and the white,
How at the root by turns they bite,
They gnaw, they pull, they dig; and still
The earth that held its fibres spill,

Which, as its rustling downward ran,
The dragon to look up began,
Watching how soon the shrub and all
Its burden would together fall.

5. The man in anguish, fear, despair,
Beleaguer'd, ·threaten'd every-where,
In state of miserable doubt,
In vain for safety gazed about.
But as he look'd around him so,
A twig he spied, and on it grow
Ripe berries from their laden stalk;
Then his desire he could not balk.
When these did once his eye engage,
He saw no more the camel's rage,
Nor dragon in the underground,
Nor game the busy mice had found.

6. The beast above might snort and blow,
The Dragon watch his prey below,
The mice gnaw near him as they pleas'd.
The berries eagerly he seiz'd;
They seem'd to him right good to eat;
A dainty mouthful, welcome treat,
They brought him such a keen delight,
His danger was forgotten quite.

7. But who, you ask, is this vain man,
Who thus forget his terror can?
Then learn, O friend, that man art thou!
Listen, and I will tell thee how.

8. The dragon in the well beneath,
That is the yawning gulf of death.
The camel threatening overhead
Is life's perplexity and dread.
'Tis thou who, life and death between,
Hangest on this world's sapling green;
And they who gnaw the root, the twain
Who thee and thy support would fain

Deliver unto death a prey,
These names the mice have, Night and Day.·

9. From morn to evening gnaws the white,
And would the root unfasten quite;
From evening till the morn comes back,
In deepest stillness gnaws the black;
And yet, in·midst of these alarms,
The berry, Pleasure, has such charms,
That thou, the camel of life's woe,
That thou, the dragon death below,
That thou, the two mice, Night and Day,
And all forgettest, save the way
To get most berries in thy power,
And on the grave's cleft side devour.

CLXX. — AN INDIAN FIGHT.

THIS description, though found in one of Scott's Novels, is a very accurate account of a historical fact. The deliverer was one of the judges of Charles I. and an exile. He was concealed many years at the village here referred to.

1. AMONG my wanderings, the transatlantic settlements have not escaped me; more especially the country of New England, into which our native land has shaken from her lap, as a drunkard flings from him his treasures, so much that is precious in the eyes of God and of his children. There thousands of our best and most godly men; such whose righteousness might come between the Almighty and his wrath, and prevent the ruin of cities; are content to be the inhabitants of the desert, rather encountering the unenlightened savages than stooping to extinguish, under the oppression practiced in Britain, the light that is within their own minds. There I remained for a time, during the wars which the colony maintained with Philip, a great Indian chief, or Sachem, as they were called, who seemed a messenger sent from Satan to buffet them. His cruelty was great, his dissimulation profound. and the skill

and promptitude with which he maintained a destructive and desultory warfare, inflicted many dreadful calamities on the settlement.

2. I was, by chance, at a small village in the woods, more than thirty miles from Boston, and in its situation exceedingly lonely, and surrounded with thickets. Nevertheless, there was no idea of any danger from the Indians at that time, for men trusted to the protection of a considerable body of troops, who had taken the field for the protection of the frontiers, and who lay, or were supposed to lie, betwixt the hamlet and the enemy's country. But they had to do with a foe, whom the evil one himself had inspired at once with cunning and cruelty.

3. It was on a sabbath morning, when we had assembled to take sweet counsel together in the Lord's house. Our temple was but constructed of wooden logs; but when shall the chant of trained hirelings, or the sounding of tin and brass tubes amid the aisles of a minster, arise so sweetly to heaven as did the psalm in which we united at once our voices and our hearts! An excellent worthy, who now sleeps in the Lord, Nehemiah Solsgrace, long the companion of my pilgrimage, had just begun to wrestle in prayer, when a woman, with disordered looks and disheveled hair, entered our chapel in a distracted manner, screaming incessantly, "The Indians! The Indians!"

4. In that land, no man dares separate himself from his means of defense; and whether in the city or in the field, in the plowed land or the forest, men keep beside them their weapons, as did the Jews at the rebuilding of the Temple. So we sallied forth with our guns and pikes, and heard the whoop of these incarnate demons, already in possession of a part of the town, and exercising their cruelty on the few whom weighty causes or indisposition had withheld from public worship; and it was remarked as a judgment, that, upon that bloody sabbath, Adrian Hanson, a Dutchman, a man well enough disposed toward man, but whose mind was altogether given to worldly gain, was shot and scalped as he was summing his weekly gains in his warehouse. In fine, there was much damage done;

and although our arrival and entrance into combat did, in some sort, put them back, yet being surprised and confused, and having no appointed leader of our band, the cruel enemy shot hard at us, and had some advantage.

5. It was pitiful to hear the screams of women and children amid the report of guns and the whistling of bullets, mixed with the ferocious yells of these savages, which they term their war-whoop. Several houses in the upper part of the village were soon on fire; and the roaring of the flames, and crackling of the great beams as they blazed, added to the horrible confusion; while the smoke which the wind drove against us gave further advantage to the enemy, who fought, as it were, invisible, and under cover, while we fell fast by their unerring fire. In this state of confusion, and while we were about to adopt the desperate project of evacuating the village, and, placing the women and children in the center, of attempting a retreat to the nearest settlement, it pleased Heaven to send us unexpected assistance.

6. A tall man, of a reverend appearance, whom no one of us had ever seen before, suddenly was in the midst of us, as we hastily agitated the resolution of retreating. His garments were of the skin of the elk, and he wore sword and carried gun. I never saw any thing more august than his features, overshadowed by locks of gray hair, which mingled with a long beard of the same color. "Men and brethren," he said, in a voice like that which turns back the flight, "why sink your hearts? and why are you thus disquieted? Fear ye that the God we serve will give you up to yonder heathen dogs? Follow me, and you shall see this day that there is a captain in Israel." He uttered a few brief but distinct orders, in the tone of one who was accustomed to command; and such was the influence of his appearance, his mien, his language, and his presence of mind, that he was implicitly obeyed by men who had never seen him until that moment.

7. We were hastily divided, by his orders, into two bodies; one of which maintained the defense of the village with more courage than ever, convinced that the unknown

was sent by God to our rescue. At his command, they assumed the best and most sheltered positions for exchanging their deadly fire with the Indians; while, under cover of the smoke, the stranger sallied from the town at the head of the other division of the New England men, and, fetching a circuit, attacked the red warriors in the rear. The surprise, as is usual among savages, had complete effect; for they doubted not that they were assailed in their turn, and placed betwixt two hostile parties by the return of a detachment from the provincial army. The heathens fled in confusion, abandoning the half-won village, and leaving behind them such a number of their warriors, that the tribe hath never recovered its loss.

8. Never shall I forget the figure of our venerable leader, when our men, and not they only, but the women and children of the village, rescued from the tomahawk and scalping knife, stood crowded around him, yet scarce venturing to approach his person, and more minded, perhaps, to worship him as a descended angel than to thank him as a fellow-mortal. "Not unto me be the glory," he said; "I am but an implement, frail as yourselves, in the hand of Him who is strong to deliver. Bring me a cup of water, that I may allay my parched throat ere I essay the task of offering thanks where they are most due."

9. I was nearest to him as he spoke, and I gave into his hand the water he requested. At that moment we exchanged glances, and it seemed to me that I recognized a noble friend, whom I had long since deemed in glory; but he gave me no time to speak, had speech been prudent. Sinking on his knees, and signing us to obey him, he poured forth a strong and energetic thanksgiving for the turning back of the battle, which, pronounced with a voice clear as a war trumpet, thrilled through the joints and marrow of the hearers.

10. I have heard many an act of devotion in my life, had Heaven vouchsafed me grace to profit by them; but such a prayer as this, uttered amid the dead and the dying, with a rich tone of mingled triumph and adoration, was beyond them all; it was like the song of the inspired

prophetess, who dwelt beneath the palm tree between Ramah and Bethel. He was silent; and for a brief space we remained with our faces bent to the earth, no man daring to lift his head. At length we looked up, but our deliverer was no longer among us; nor was he ever again seen in the land which he had rescued.

CLXXI. — THE INDIAN CHIEF.

1. DURING the war in America, a company of Indians attacked a small body of the British troops, and defeated them. As the Indians had greatly the advantage in swiftness of foot, and were eager in the pursuit, very few of the British escaped; and those who fell into their hands were treated with a cruelty, of which there are not many examples, even in that country. Two of the Indians came up to a young officer, and attacked him with great fury. As they were armed with battle-axes, he had no hope of escaping. But, just at this crisis, another Indian came up, who was advanced in years, and was armed with a bow and arrows.

2. The old man instantly drew his bow, but after having taken his aim at the officer, he suddenly dropped the point of his arrow, and interposed between him and his pursuers, who were about to cut him to pieces. They retired with respect. The old man then took the officer by the hand, soothed him into confidence by caresses; and having conducted him to his hut, treated him with a kindness which did honor to his professions.

3. He made him less a slave than a companion; taught him the language of the country; and instructed him in the rude arts that are practiced by the inhabitants. They lived together in the most perfect harmony; and the young officer, in the treatment he met with, found nothing to regret, but that sometimes the old man fixed his eyes upon him, and having regarded him for some minutes with a steady and silent attention, burst into tears.

4. In the mean time the spring returned, and the Indians again took the field. The old man, who was still vigorous, and able to bear the fatigues of war, set out with them, and was accompanied by his prisoner. They marched above two hundred leagues across the forest, and came at length to a plain, where the British forces were encamped. The old man showed his prisoner the tents at a distance." "There," says he, "are thy countrymen. There is the enemy who wait to give us battle. Remember that I have saved thy life, that I have taught thee to conduct a canoe, to arm thyself with a bow and arrows, and to surprise the beaver in the forest. What wast thou when I first took thee to my hut? Thy hands were those of an infant. They could neither procure thee sustenance nor safety. Thy soul was in utter darkness. Thou wast ignorant of every thing. Thou owest all things to me. Wilt thou then go over to thy nation, and take up the hatchet against us?"

5. The officer replied, that he would rather lose his own life than take away that of his deliverer. The Indian then bending down his head, and covering his face with both his hands, stood some time silent. Then looking earnestly at his prisoner, he said, in a voice that was at once softened by tenderness and grief, "Hast thou a father?" "My father," said the young man, "was alive when I left my country." "Alas!" said the Indian, "how wretched must he be!" He paused a moment, and then added, "Dost thou know that I have been a father? I am a father no more. I saw my son fall in battle. He fought at my side. I saw him expire! He was covered with wounds, when he fell dead at my feet!"

6. He pronounced these words with the utmost vehemence. His body shook with a universal tremor. He was almost stifled with sighs, which he would not suffer to escape him. There was a keen restlessness in his eyes, but no tears flowed to his relief. At length, he became calm by degrees; and turning toward the east, where the sun had just risen, "Dost thou see," said he to the young officer, "the beauty of that sky, which sparkles with pre-

vailing day? and hast thou pleasure in the sight?" "Yes," replied the young officer, "I have pleasure in the beauty of so fine a sky.' "I have none!" said the Indian, and his tears then found their way.

7. A few minutes after, he showed the young man a magnolia in full bloom. "Dost thou see that beautiful tree?" said he, "and dost thou look upon it with pleasure?" "Yes," replied the officer, "I look with pleasure upon that beautiful tree." "I have no longer any pleasure in look-ing upon it," said the Indian, hastily; and immediately added, "Go, return to thy father, that he may still have pleasure, when he sees the sun rise in the morning, and the trees blossom in the spring!"

CLXXII.—GLENARA.

FROM CAMPBELL.

1. O, HEARD ye yon pibroch sound sad in the gale,
Where a band cometh slowly with weeping and wail?
'Tis the chief of Glenara laments for his dear;
And her sire and her people are call'd to the bier.

2. Glenara came first, with the mourners and shroud;
Her kinsmen, they follow'd, but mourn'd not aloud;
Their plaids all their bosoms were folded around;
They march'd all in silence, they look'd on the ground.

3. In silence they reach'd, over mountain and moor,
To a heath where the oak-tree grew lonely and hoar;
"Now here let us place the gray stone of her cairn;
Why speak ye no word?" said Glenara the stern.

4. "And tell me, I charge ye, ye clan of my spouse,
Why fold ye your mantles, why cloud ye your brows?"
So spake the rude chieftain; no answer is made,
But each mantle, unfolding, a dagger display'd.

5. "I dreamt of my lady, I dreamt of her shroud,"
Cried a voice from the kinsmen, all wrathful and loud;
"And empty that shroud and that coffin did seem;
Glenara! Glenara! now read me my dream!"

6. O, pale grew the cheek of that chieftain, I ween,
When the shroud was unclosed and no lady was seen;
When a voice from the kinsmen spoke louder in scorn,
'Twas the youth who had lov'd the fair Ellen of Lorn.

7. "I dreamt of my lady, I dreamt of her grief,
I dreamt that her lord was a barbarous chief;
On a rock of the ocean fair Ellen did seem;
Glenara! Glenara! now read me my dream!"

8. In dust low the traitor has knelt to the ground,
And the desert reveal'd where his lady was found;
From a rock of the ocean that lady is borne;
Now joy to the house of fair Ellen of Lorn.

CLXXIII.—THE LITTLE WOMAN.

FROM DICKENS.

CHARLES DICKENS is one of the most popular English authors of
the present day. He has written much, and is distinguished, per-
haps chiefly, by his graphic delineation of character.

1. THERE was a little woman on board, with a little
child; and both little woman and little child were cheer-
ful, good-looking, bright-eyed, and fair to see. The little
woman had been passing a long time with her sick mother
in New York. The child was born in her mother's house,
and she had not seen her husband, to whom she was now
returning, for twelve months, having left him a month or
two after their marriage. Well, to be sure, there never
was a little woman so full of hope, and tenderness, and
love, and anxiety, as this little woman was; and all day
long she wondered whether "he" would be at the wharf;

and whether "he" had got her letter; and whether, if she sent the child ashore by somebody else, "he" would know it, meeting it in the street; which, seeing that he had never set eyes upon it in his life, was not very likely in the abstract, but was probable enough to the young mother.

2. She was such an artless little creature, and was in such a sunny, beaming, hopeful state, and let out all the matter clinging closely about her heart so freely, that all the other lady passengers entered into the spirit of it as much as she; and the captain, who heard all about it from his wife, was wondrous sly, I promise you, inquiring, every time we met at table, as if in forgetfulness, whether she expected any body to meet her at St. Louis, and cutting many other dry jokes of that nature. There was one little weazen, dried-apple-faced old woman, who took occasion to doubt the constancy of husbands, in such circumstances of bereavement; and there was another lady, with a lap-dog, old enough to moralize on the lightness of human affections, and yet not so old that she could help nursing the child now and then, or laughing with the rest, when the little woman called it by its father's name, and asked it all manner of fantastic questions concerning him, in the joy of her heart.

3. It was something of a blow to the little woman, that, when we were within twenty miles of our destination, it became clearly necessary to put this child to bed. But she got over it with the same good-humor, tied a handkerchief round her head, and came out into the little gallery with the rest. Then such an oracle as she became in reference to the localities! and such facetiousness as was displayed by the married ladies, and such sympathy as was shown by the single ones, and such peals of laughter as the little woman herself, who would just as soon have cried, greeted every jest with!

4. At last, there were the lights of St. Louis, and here was the wharf, and those were the steps; and the little woman, covering her face with her hands, and laughing, or seeming to laugh, more than ever, ran into her own cabin, and shut herself up. I have no doubt but, in the charming

inconsistency of such excitement, she stopped her ears, lest she should hear "him" asking for her; but I did not see her do it. Then a great crowd of people rushed on board, though the boat was not yet made fast, but was wandering about among the other boats, to find a landing-place; and every body looked for the husband, and nobody saw him, when, in the midst of us all, Heaven knows how she ever got there, there was the little woman, clinging with both arms tight round the neck of a fine, good-looking, sturdy young fellow; and clapping her little hands for joy as she dragged him through the small door of her small cabin, to look at the child, as he lay asleep.

CLXXIV. — HOME.

1. THERE is a land, of every land the pride,
Belov'd by heaven o'er all the world beside;
Where brighter suns dispense serener light,
And milder moons emparadise the night;
A land of beauty, virtue, valor, truth,
Time-tutor'd age, and love-exalted youth.

2. The wandering mariner, whose eye explores
The wealthiest isles, the most enchanting shores,
Views not a realm so bountiful and fair,
Nor breathes the spirit of a purer air;
In every clime the magnet of his soul,
Touch'd by remembrance, trembles to that pole;
For in this land of heaven's peculiar grace,
The heritage of nature's noblest race,
There is a spot of earth supremely blest,
A dearer, sweeter spot than all the rest,
Where man, creation's tyrant, casts aside
His sword and scepter, pageantry and pride,
While in his soften'd looks benignly blend
The sire, the son, the husband, brother, friend.

3. Here woman reigns; the mother, daughter, wife,
Strew with fresh flowers the narrow way of life!
In the clear heaven of her delightful eye,
An angel-guard of love and graces lie;
Around her knees domestic duties meet,
And fire-side pleasures gambol at her feet.

4. Where shall that land, that spot of earth be found?
Art thou a man? a patriot? look around
O, thou shalt find, howe'er thy footsteps roam,
That land *thy* country, and that spot *thy* home!

CLXXV.—THE CONTRAST.

FROM PLUMMER.

1. In the parlor, singing, playing,
Round me like a sunbeam straying,
All her life with joy o'erladen,
Is a radiant little maiden.
Constant love, her cares beguiling,
Shields her from sin's dread defiling;
Shelter'd safe from worldly rudeness,
Grows she in her native goodness.
Every morn brings fond caressing,
Every night brings earnest blessing;
So her heart gets sweeter, purer,
And her steps in virtue surer.

2. In the street, where storms are sighing,
Is a child deserted, crying;
Poor lost lamb! with plaintive bleating
All my sympathy entreating.
No home's holy loves enfold her,
No protecting arms uphold her:
And the voices that should guide her
Utter only tones that chide her.
O'er her spirit's waste and blindness
Falls no ray of saving kindness;

Wandering thus in earth's dark places,
Sin her tender soul embraces.

3. Then I know, that radiant maiden,
All whose life with love is laden,
Only *love* saves from the danger
And the fate of this lost stranger!

CLXXVI. — ASTRONOMY.

FROM WIRT.

1. MILKY WAY; a bright belt encompassing the heavens, supposed to be composed of stars.
3. PY-THAG'O-RAS; a Grecian philosopher.

1. IT was a pleasant evening in the month of May, and my sweet child and I had sauntered up to the castle's top, to enjoy the breeze that played around it, and to admire the unclouded firmament, that glowed and sparkled with unusual luster from pole to pole. The atmosphere was in its purest and finest state for vision; the Milky Way was distinctly developed throughout its whole extent; every planet and every star above the horizon, however near and brilliant, or distant and faint, lent its lambent light or twinkling ray to give variety and beauty to the bemisphere; while the round, bright moon seemed to hang off from the azure vault, suspended in midway air; or stooping forward from the firmament her fair and radiant face, as if to court and return our gaze.

2. We amused ourselves for some time in observing, through a telescope, the planet Jupiter, sailing in silent majesty with his squadron of satellites, along the vast ocean of space between us and the fixed stars; and admired the felicity of that design by which those distant bodies have been parceled out and arranged into constellations, so as to have served not only for beacons to the ancient navigators, but, as it were, for landmarks to astronomers at this day; enabling them, though in different countries,

to indicate to each other with ease the place and motion of those planets, comets, and magnificent meteors, which inhabit, revolve, and play in the intermediate space. We recalled and dwelt with delight on the rise and progress of the science of astronomy; on that series of astonishing discoveries through successive ages, which display in so strong a light the force and reach of the human mind; and on those bold conjectures and sublime reveries, which seem to tower even to the confines of divinity, and denote the high destiny to which mortals tend.

3. We dwelt on that thought, which is said to have been first started by Pythagoras, and which modern astronomers approve, that the stars which we call fixed, although they appear to us to be nothing more than large spangles, of various sizes, glittering on the same concave surface, are, nevertheless, bodies as large as our sun, shining, like him, with original and not reflected light, placed at incalculable distances asunder, and each star the solar center of a system of planets which revolve around it, as the planets belonging to our system do around the sun:

4. That this is not only the case with all the stars which our eyes discern in the firmament, or which the telescope has brought within the sphere of our vision, but according to the modern improvements of this thought, that there are probably other stars whose light has not yet reached us, although light moves with a velocity a million times greater than that of a cannon ball: that those luminous appearances, which we observe in the firmament, like flakes of thin, white cloud, are windows, as it were, which open to other firmaments, far, far beyond the ken of human eye or the power of optical instruments, lighted up, like ours, with hosts of stars or suns.

5. We dwelt on the thought that this scheme goes on through infinite space, which is filled with those suns, attended by ten thousand times ten thousand worlds, all in rapid motion, yet calm, regular, and harmonious, invariably keeping the paths prescribed to them; and these worlds peopled with myriads of intelligent beings. One would think that this conception, thus extended, would be

bold enough to satisfy the whole enterprise of the human imagination.

6. But what an accession of glory and magnificence does Dr. Herschel superadd to it, when, instead of supposing all those suns fixed, and the motion confined to their respective planets, he loosens those multitudinous suns themselves from their stations, sets them all into motion with their splendid retinue of planets and satellites, and imagines them, thus attended, to perform a stupendous revolution, system above system, around some grander, unknown center, somewhere in the boundless abyss of space!

7. And when carrying on the process, you suppose even that center itself not stationary, but also counterpoised by other masses in the immensity of space, with which, attended by their accumulated trains of

> "Planets, suns, and adamantine spheres,
> Wheeling unshaken through the void immense,"

it maintains harmonious concert, surrounding, in its vast career, some other center, still more remote and stupendous, which in its turn ———— "You overwhelm me," cried my daughter, as I was laboring to pursue the immense concatenation; "my mind is bewildered and lost in the effort to follow you, and finds no point on which to rest its weary wing."

8. "Yet there is a point, my dear, the throne of the Most High. Imagine *that* the ultimate center, to which this vast and inconceivably magnificent and august apparatus is attached, and around which it is continually revolving. Oh! what a spectacle for the cherubim and seraphim, and the spirits of the just made perfect, who dwell on the right hand of that throne, if, as may be, and probably is the case, their eyes are permitted to pierce through the whole, and take in, at one glance, all its order, beauty, sublimity, and glory, and their ears to distinguish that celestial harmony, unheard by us, in which those vast globes, as they roll on in their respective orbits, continually hymn their great Creator's praise!"

CLXXVII. — APOSTROPHE TO THE SUN.

FROM PERCIVAL.

JAMES G. PERCIVAL, a native of Connecticut, was a distinguished Poet, Geologist, Botanist, and Philologist. He died a few years since.

1. CENTER of light and energy! thy way
    Is through the unknown void; thou hast thy throne,
Morning, and evening, and at noon of day,
    Far in the blue, untended and alone:
    Ere the first waken'd airs of earth had blown,
On didst thou march, triumphant in thy light;
    Then didst thou send thy glance, which still hath flown
Wide through the never-ending worlds of night,
And yet, thy full orb burns with flash unquench'd and
    bright.

2. Thy path is high in heaven; we can not gaze
    On the intense of light that girds thy car;
There is a crown of glory in thy rays,
    Which bears their pure divinity afar,
    To mingle with the equal light of star;
For thou, so vast to us, art, in the whole,
    One of the sparks of night that fire the air;
And, as around thy center planets roll,
So thou too, hast thy path around the central soul.

3. Thou lookest on the earth, and then it smiles;
    Thy light is hid, and all things droop and mourn;
Laughs the wide sea around her budding isles,
    When through their heaven thy changing car is borne;
    Thou wheel'st away thy flight, the woods are shorn
Of all their waving locks, and storms awake;
    All, that was once so beautiful, is torn
By the wild winds which plow the lonely lake,
And, in their maddening rush, the crested mountains shake.

4. The earth lies buried in a shroud of snow;
    Life lingers, and would die, but thy return

Gives to their gladden'd hearts an overflow
  Of all the power, that brooded in the urn
  Of their chill'd frames, and then they proudly spurn
All bands that would confine, and give to air
  Hues, fragrance, shapes of beauty, till they burn,
When, on a dewy morn, thou dartest there
Rich waves of gold, to wreath with fairer light the fair.

5. The vales are thine: and when the touch of Spring
  Thrills them, and gives them gladness, in thy light
They glitter, as the glancing swallow's wing
  Dashes the water in his winding flight,
  And leaves behind a wave, that crinkles bright,
And widens outward to the pebbled shore:
  The vales are thine; and when they wake from night,
The dews that bend the grass tips, twinkling o'er
Their soft and oozy beds, look upward and adore.

6. The hills are thine: they catch the newest beam,
  And gladden in thy parting, where the wood
Flames out in every leaf and drinks the stream,
  That flows from out thy fullness, as a flood
  Bursts from an unknown land, and rolls the food
Of nations in its waters; so thy rays
  Flow and give brighter tints than ever bud,
When a clear sheet of ice reflects a blaze
Of many twinkling gems, as every gloss'd bough plays.

7. Thine are the mountains, where they purely lift
  Snows that have never wasted, in a sky
Which hath no stain; below, the storm may drift
  Its darkness, and the thunder-gust roar by;
  Aloft in thy eternal smile they lie
Dazzling, but cold; thy farewell glance looks there,
  And when below thy hues of beauty die,
Girt round them, as a rosy belt, they bear
Into the high, dark vault, a brow that still is fair.

8. The clouds are thine; and all their magic hues
  Are pencil'd by thee; when thou bendest low

Or comest in thy strength, thy hand imbues
   Their waving folds with such a perfect glow
   Of all pure tints, the fairy pictures throw
Shame on the proudest art.

9. These are thy trophies, and thou bend'st thy arch,
   The sign of triumph, in a sevenfold twine,
Where the spent storm is hasting on its march;
   And there the glories of thy light combine,
   And form, with perfect curve, a lifted line,
Striding the earth and air; man looks and tells
   How Peace and Mercy in its beauty shine,
And how the heavenly messenger impels
Her glad wings on the path, that thus in ether swells.

10. The ocean is thy vassal; thou dost sway
   His waves to thy dominion, and they go
Where thou, in heaven, dost guide them on their way,
   Rising and falling in eternal flow:
   Thou lookest on the waters, and they glow,
And take them wings, and spring aloft in air,
   And change to clouds, and then dissolving, throw
Their treasures back to earth, and, rushing, tear
The mountain and the vale, as proudly on they bear.

11. In thee, first light, the bounding ocean smiles,
   When the quick winds uprear it in a swell,
That rolls in glittering green around the isles,
   Where ever-springing fruits and blossoms dwell.
   Oh! with a gifted joy no tongue can tell,
I hurry o'er the waters when the sail
   Swells tensely, and the light keel glances well
Over the curling billow, and the gale
Comes off from spicy groves to tell its winning tale.

CLXXVIII. — WATCHMAN, WHAT OF THE NIGHT?

FROM DENNIE.

1. To this query of Isaiah, the watchman replies, that "The morning cometh, and also the night." The brevity of this answer has left it involved in something of the obscurity of the season in which it was given. I think that night, however sooty and ill-favored it may be pronounced by those who were born under a day-star, merits a more particular description. I feel peculiarly disposed to arrange some ideas in favor of this season. I know that the majority are literally *blind* to its merits; they must be prominent, indeed, to be discerned by the *closed* eyes of the snorer, who thinks that night was made for nothing but sleep. But the student and the sage are willing to believe that it was formed for higher purposes; and that it not only recruits exhausted spirits, but sometimes informs inquisitive and mends wicked ones.

2. Duty, as well as inclination, urges the Lay Preacher to sermonize while others slumber. To read numerous volumes in the morning, and to observe various characters at noon, will leave but little time, except the night, to digest the one or speculate upon the other. The night, therefore, is often dedicated to composition, and, while the light of the paly planets discovers at his desk the Preacher, more wan than they, he may be heard repeating emphatically, with Dr. Young,

"Darkness has much divinity for me."

He is then alone; he is then at peace. No companions near, but the silent volumes on his shelf; no noise abroad, but the click of the village clock or the bark of the village dog. The deacon has then smoked his sixth, and *last* pipe, and asks not a question more concerning Josephus or the church. Stillness aids study, and the sermon proceeds. Such being the obligations to night, it would be ungrateful not to acknowledge them. As my watchful eyes can discern its dim beauties, my warm heart shall feel.

and my prompt pen shall describe, the uses and pleasures of the nocturnal hour.

3. "Watchman, what of the night?" I can with propriety imagine this question addressed to myself; I am a professed lucubrator; and who so well qualified to delineate the sable hours as

"A meager, muse-rid mope, adust and thin?"

However injuriously night is treated by the sleepy moderns, the vigilance of the ancients could not overlook its benefits and joys. In as early a record as the book of Genesis, I find that Isaac, though he devoted his assiduous days to action, reserved speculation till night. "He went out to meditate in the field at eventide." He chose that sad, that solemn hour, to reflect upon the virtues of a beloved and departed mother. The tumult and glare of the day suited not with the sorrow of his soul. He had lost his most amiable, most genuine friend, and his unostentatious grief was eager for privacy and shade. Sincere sorrow rarely suffers its tears to be seen. It was natural for Isaac to select a season to weep in, that should resemble "the color of his fate." The darkness, the solemnity, the stillness of the eve, were favorable to his melancholy purpose. He forsook, therefore, the bustling tents of his father, the pleasant "south country," and "well of Lahairoi;" he went out and pensively meditated at eventide.

4. The Grecian and Roman philosophers firmly believed that the "dead of midnight is the noon of thought." One of them is beautifully described by the poet as soliciting knowledge from the skies in private and nightly audience, and that neither his theme, nor his nightly walks, were forsaken till the sun appeared, and dimmed his "nobler intellectual beam." We undoubtedly owe to the studious nights of the ancients most of their elaborate and immortal productions. Among them it was necessary that every man of letters should trim the midnight lamp. The day might be given to the forum or the circus, but the night was the season for the statesman to project his schemes, and for the poet to pour his verse.

5. Night has, likewise, with great reason, been considered, in every age, as the astronomer's day. Young observes, with energy, that .

"An undevout astronomer is mad."

The privilege of contemplating those brilliant and numerous myriads of planets which bedeck our skies is peculiar to night, and it is our duty, both as lovers of moral and natural beauty, to bless that season, when we are indulged with such a gorgeous display of glittering and useful light. It must be confessed, that the seclusion, calmness, and tranquillity of midnight, are most friendly to serious, and even airy contemplations.

6. I think it treason to this sable Power, who holds divided empire with Day, constantly to shut our eyes at her approach. To long sleep I am decidedly a foe. As it is expressed by a quaint writer, we shall all have enough of it in the grave. Those who can not break the silence of the night by vocal throat, or eloquent tongue, may be permitted to disturb it by a snore. But he among my readers who possesses the power of fancy and strong thought, should be vigilant as a watchman. Let him sleep abundantly for health, but sparingly for sloth. It is better, sometimes, to consult a page of philosophy than the pillow.

CLXXIX. — WONDERS OF A FEATHER.

1. EVERY single feather is a mechanical wonder. If we look at the quill, we find properties not easily brought together, strength and lightness. I know few things more remarkable, than the strength and lightness of the very pen with which I am now writing. If we cast our eye toward the upper part of the stem, we see a material made for the purpose, used in no other class of animals, and in no other part of birds; tough, light, pliant, elastic. The pith, also, which feeds the feathers, is neither bone, flesh, membrane, nor tendon.

2. But the most artificial part of the feather is the beard, or, as it is sometimes called, the vane, which we usually

strip off from one side, or both, when we make a pen. The separate pieces of which this is composed are called threads, filaments, or rays. Now, the first thing which an attentive observer will remark is, how much stronger the beard of the feather shows itself to be when pressed in a direction perpendicular to its plane, than when rubbed either up or down in the line of the stem. He will soon discover, that the threads of which these beards are composed, are flat, and placed with their flat sides toward each other; by which means, while they easily bend for the approaching of each other, as any one may perceive by drawing his finger ever so lightly upward, they are much harder to bend out of their plane, which is the direction in which they have to encounter the impulse and pressure of the air, and in which their strength is wanted.

3. It is also to be observed, that when two threads, separated by accident or force, are brought together again, they immediately reclasp. Draw your finger down the feather which is against the grain, and you break, probably, the junction of some of the contiguous threads; draw your finger up the feather, and you restore all things to their former state. It is no common mechanism by which this contrivance is effected. The threads or laminæ above mentioned, are interlaced with one another; and the interlacing is performed by means of a vast number of fibers or teeth, which the threads shoot forth on each side, and which hook and grapple together.

4. Fifty of these fibers have been counted in one twentieth of an inch. They are crooked, but curved after a different manner: for those which proceed from the thread on the side toward the extremity, are longer, more flexible, and bent downward; whereas, those which proceed from the side toward the beginning or quill-end of the feather, are shorter, firmer, and turned upward. When two laminæ, therefore, are pressed together, the crooked parts of the long fibers fall into the cavity made by the crooked parts of the others; just as the latch, which is fastened to a door, enters into the cavity of the catch fixed to the door-post, and there hooking itself, fastens the door.

CLXXX. — THE PAUPER'S DEATH-BED.

1. TREAD softly! bow the head!
   In reverent silence bow!
No passing bell doth toll,
Yet an immortal soul
   Is passing now.

2. Stranger! however great,
   With lowly reverence bow!
There's one in that poor shed,
One by that paltry bed,
   Greater than thou.

3. Beneath that beggar's roof,
   Lo! Death does keep his state
Enter! no crowds attend,
Enter! no guards defend
   This palace gate.

4. That pavement damp and cold,
   No smiling courtiers tread;
One silent woman stands,
Lifting with meager hands   .
   A dying head.

5. No mingling voices sound;
   An infant wail alone;
A sob suppress'd; again
That short deep gasp, and then
   The parting groan.

6. O, change! O, wondrous change!
   Burst are the prison bars;
This moment there, so low,
So agonized, and now,
   Beyond the stars!

7. O, change! Stupendous change!
   There lies the soulless clod:
The sun eternal breaks;
The new immortal wakes;
   Wakes with his God.

---

8. Alas! we think not that we daily see
About our hearths, angels that *are to be*,
Or *may* be, if they will, so we prepare
Their souls and ours to meet in happy air;
A child, a friend, a sister, whose heart sings
In unison with ours, breeding its future wings.

CLXXXI. — OUR SAVIOR'S MORAL COURAGE.

FROM ABBOTT.

1. THE delivery of the Sermon on the Mount is probably the most striking example of moral courage which the world has ever seen. There are two circumstances, which render the occasion on which it was delivered extraordinary. First, it was a very public occasion. A vast multitude from almost every part of the country were assembled. Judea, the southern province, and Galilee, the northern, were represented; so were the eastern and western shores of the river Jordan, and many distant cities and towns.

2. From all this wide extent of country a vast multitude, attracted by the fame of our Savior's miracles, had assembled to hear what this professed messenger from heaven had to say. Again, it was probably, though not certainly, a very early occasion; perhaps the first on which the great principles of the gospel were to be announced to men by this discourse, containing, as it does, so plain and specific an exposition of the false notions of religion then prevailing. The Savior must have known, that he

was laying the foundation of that enmity which was to result in his destruction.

3. But did he shrink? Did he hold back? Did he conceal or cover over one single obnoxious feature of the truth? He knew that the report of that meeting must be spread to every part of the country. As he looked around upon his auditory, he must have seen, here one from Galilee, there another from beyond the Jordan, and again a third, who would carry his report to distant Jerusalem; and yet, thus completely exposed, instead of attempting to soften or conceal, he brought out all the distinctive features of prevailing error, and contrasted them with the pure principles of his spiritual religion, with a plainness and a point, which was exactly calculated to fix them in memory, and to circulate them most widely throughout the land.

4. It was always so. The plainness, the point, the undaunted boldness, with which he exposed hypocrisy and sin, and the clear simplicity with which he held up to view the principles of real piety, have no parallel. And yet he knew perfectly well that, in direct consequence of these things, a dark storm was gathering, which must burst in all its fury upon his unsheltered head.

5. But the enterprising and determined spirit with which Christ entered into his work, was not satisfied with his own personal exertions. He formed the extraordinary plan of sending out, simultaneously, a number of his most cordial friends and followers, to assist in making the most extensive and powerful impression possible on the community.

6. At first he sent twelve, then seventy, who went everywhere, presenting to men the simple duties of repentance for the past, and of pure and holy lives for the future. There could not have been measures more admirably adapted to accomplish the work he had to do. And they succeeded. In two or three years it was done. And every Christian, who has work to do for his Master here, should learn a lesson from the enterprise, and system, and energy, which Jesus Christ exhibited in doing his great work.

CLXXXII. — THE WIDOW OF NAIN.

FROM WILLIS.

1. THE Roman sentinel stood helm'd and tall
Beside the gate of Nain.   The busy tread
Of comers to the city mart was done;
For it was almost noon, and a dead heat
Quiver'd upon the fine and sleeping dust,
And the cold snake crept panting from the wall,
And bask'd his scaly circles in the sun.

2. Upon his spear the soldier leau'd, and kept
His idle watch, and, as his drowsy dream
Was broken by the solitary foot
Of some poor mendicant, he rais'd his head
To curse him for a tributary Jew,
And slumberously dozed on.

3. 'Twas now high noon.
The dull, low murmur of a funeral
Went through the city; the sad sound of feet,
Unmix'd with voices; and the sentinel
Shook off his slumber, and gazed earnestly
Up the wide streets, along whose pa-ved way
The silent throng crept slowly.   They came on,
Bearing a body heavily on its bier,
And, by the crowd that in the burning sun
Walk'd with forgetful sadness, 'twas of one
Mourn'd with uncommon sorrow.   The broad gate
Swung on its hinges, and the Roman bent
His spear-point downward, as the bearers pass'd,
Bending beneath their burden.

4. There was one,
Only *one* mourner.   Close behind the bier,
Crumpling the pall up in her wither'd hands,
Follow'd an aged woman.   Her short steps
Falter'd with weakness, and a broken moan

Fell from her lips, thicken'd convulsively,
As her heart bled afresh. The pitying crowd
Follow'd apart, but no one spoke to her.
She had no kinsmen. She had liv'd alone,
A widow, with one son. He was her all,
The only tie she had in the wide world,
And *he* was dead. They could not comfort her.

5. Jesus drew near to Nain, as from the gate
The funeral came forth. His lips were pale
With the noon's sultry heat. The beaded sweat
Stood thickly on his brow, and on the worn
And simple latchets of his sandals lay,
Thick, the white dust of travel.

6. He had come,
Since sunrise, from Capernaum, staying not
To wet his lips by green Bethsaida's pool,
Nor wash his feet in Kishon's silver springs,
To catch Gilboa's light and spicy breeze.

7. Genesareth stood cool upon the east,
Fast by the Sea of Galilee, and there
The weary traveler might bide till eve;
And on the alders of Bethulia's plains
The grapes of Palestine hung ripe and wild;
Yet turn'd he not aside, but, gazing on,
From every swelling mount, he saw afar,
Amid the hills, the humble spires of Nain,
The place of his next errand; and the path
Touch'd not Bethulia, and a league away
Upon the east, lay pleasant Galilee.

8. Forth from the city-gate the pitying crowd
Follow'd the stricken mourner. They came near
The place of burial, and, with straining hands,
Closer upon her breast she clasp'd the pall,
And, with a gasping sob, quick as a child's,
And an inquiring wildness flashing through

The thin, gray lashes of her fever'd eyes,
She came where Jesus stood beside the way.

9. He look'd upon her, and his heart was moved.
"Weep not!" he said; and as they stay'd the bier,
And, at his bidding, laid it at his feet,
He gently drew the pall from out her grasp,
And laid it back in silence from the dead.
With troubled wonder the mute throng drew near,
And gazed on his calm looks. A minute's space
He stood and pray'd. Then, taking the cold hand,
He said, "Arise!" and instantly the breast
Heav'd in its cerements, and a sudden flush
Ran through the lines of the divided lips,
And with a murmur of his mother's name,
He trembled and sat upright in his shroud.
And while the mourner hung upon his neck,
Jesus went calmly on his way to Nain.

CLXXXIII.—FALSE ESTIMATE OF WEALTH.

1. I once saw a poor fellow, keen and clever,
 Witty and wise: he paid a man a visit,
And no one noticed him, and no one ever
 Gave him a welcome. "Strange!" cried I; "whence is it?"
He walk'd on this side, then on that,
He tried to introduce a social chat;
Now here, now there, in vain he tried;
Some formally and freezingly replied,
 And some
Said, by their silence, "Better stay at home."

2. A rich man burst the door,
As Crœsus rich, I'm sure!
He could not pride himself upon his wit;
And as for wisdom, he had none of it;
He had what some think better; he had wealth.
 What a confusion! all stand up erect;

These crowd around to ask him of his health;
  These bow in equal duty and respect;
And these arrange a sofa or a chair,
And these conduct him there.
"Allow me, sir, the honor!" then a bow
Down to the earth. Is 't possible to show
  Meet gratitude for such kind condescension?

3. The poor man hung his head,
And to himself he said,
  "This is, indeed, beyond my comprehension!"
      Then looking round,
      One friendly face he found,
And said, "Pray tell me, why is wealth preferr'd
  To wisdom?" "That's a silly question, friend!"
Replied the other: "Have you never heard
      A man may lend his store
      Of gold or silver ore,
But wisdom none can borrow, none can lend!"

CLXXXIV.—CHANGE.

1. AND this is what is left of youth!
There were two boys, who were bred up together,
Shared the same bed, and fed at the same board;
Each shared the other's sport, from their first chase,
Young hunters of the butterfly and bee,
To when they follow'd the fleet hare, and tried
The swiftness of the bird. They lay beside
The silver trout-stream, watching as the sun
Play'd on the bubbles; shared each in the store
Of cither's garden; and together read
Of him, the master of the desert isle,
Till a low hut, a gun, and a canoe,
Bounded their wishes. Or if ever came
A thought of future days, 'twas but to say
That they would share each other's lot, and do
Wonders, no doubt.

2. But this was vain: they parted
With promises of long remembrance, words
Whose kindness was the heart's, and those warm tears
Hidden like shame by the young eyes which shed them,
But which are thought upon in after years,
As what we would give worlds to shed once more.

3. They met again, but different from themselves,
At least what each remember'd of themselves:
The one, proud as a soldier of his rank
And of his many battles; and the other,
Proud of his Indian wealth, and of the skill
And toil which gather'd it; each with a brow
And heart alike darken'd by years and care.
They met with cold words, and yet colder looks:
Each was changed in himself, and yet each thought
The other only changed, himself the same.

4. And coldness bred dislike; and rivalry
Came like the pestilence o'er some sweet thoughts,
That linger'd yet, healthy and beautiful,
Amid dark and unkindly ones. And they,
Whose boyhood had not known one jarring word,
Were strangers in their age: if their eyes met,
'Twas but to look contempt, and when they spoke,
Their speech was wormwood!
    And this, this is life!

CLXXXV. — EXTRAVAGANT WISHES.

FROM JOHNSON.

1. WHEN the plains of India were burned up by a long
continuance of drought, Hamet and Raschid, two neigh-
boring shepherds, faint with thirst, stood at the common
boundary of their grounds, with their flocks and herds
panting round them, and in the extremity of their distress
prayed for water. On a sudden, the air was becalmed,
the birds ceased to chirp, and the flocks to bleat. They

turned their eyes every way, and saw a being of mighty stature advancing through the valley, whom they knew, upon his nearer approach, to be the Genius of Distribution. In one hand, he held the sheaves of plenty, and in the other, the saber of destruction.

2. The shepherds stood trembling, and would have retired before him; but he called to them with a voice gentle as the breeze that plays in the evening among the spices of Sabæa: "Fly not from your benefactor, children of the dust! I am come to offer you gifts which only your own folly can make vain. You here pray for water, and water I will bestow; let me know with how much you will be satisfied; speak not rashly; consider that, of whatever can be enjoyed by the body, excess is no less dangerous than scarcity. When you remember the pain of thirst, do not forget the danger of suffocation. Now, Hamet, tell me your request."

3. "O, being kind and beneficent," says Hamet, "let thine eye pardon my confusion. I entreat a little brook, which in summer shall never be dry, and in winter never overflow." "It is granted," replied the genius; and immediately he opened the ground with his saber, and a fountain, bubbling up under their feet, scattered its rills over the meadows; the flowers renewed their fragrance, the trees spread a greener foliage, and the flocks and herds quenched their thirst.

4. Then turning to Raschid, the genius invited him likewise to offer his petition. "I request," says Raschid, "that thou wilt turn the Ganges through my grounds, with all his waters, and all their inhabitants." Hamet was struck with the greatness of his neighbor's sentiments, and secretly repined in his heart that he had not made the same petition before him; when the genius spoke: "Rash man, be not insatiable! Remember, to thee that is nothing which thou canst not use; and how are thy wants greater than those of Hamet?" Raschid repeated his desire, and pleased himself with the mean appearance that Hamet would make in the presence of the proprietor of the Ganges.

5. The genius then retired toward the river, and the two shepherds stood waiting the event. As Raschid was looking with contempt upon his neighbor, on a sudden was heard the roar of torrents, and they found by the mighty stream, that the mounds of the Ganges were broken. The flood rolled forward into the lands of Raschid, his plantations were torn up, his flocks overwhelmed; he was swept away before it, and a crocodile devoured him.

CLXXXVI.— COMPLAINTS OF THE POOR.

I.

"And wherefore do the poor complain?" the rich man ask'd of
    me.
"Come, walk abroad with me," I said, "and I will answer thee."
'Twas evening, and the frozen streets were cheerless to behold,
And we were wrapt and coated well, and yet we were a-cold.

II.

We met an old bareheaded man, his locks were few and white;
I ask'd him what he did abroad in that cold winter's night.
'Twas bitter keen, indeed, he said, but at home no fire had he,
And therefore he had come abroad to ask for charity.

III.

We met a young barefooted child, and she begg'd loud and bold;
I ask'd her what she did abroad when the wind it blew so cold.
She said her father was at home, and he lay sick abed;
And therefore was it she was sent abroad to beg for bread.

IV.

We saw a woman sitting down upon a stone to rest;
She had a baby at her back, and another at her breast.
I ask'd her why she loiter'd there, when the night-wind was so
    chill;
She turn'd her head, and bade the child that scream'd behind
    be still.

V.

She told us that her husband serv'd, a soldier, far away,
And therefore to her parish she was begging back her way.
I turn'd me to the rich man then, for silently stood he;
"You ask'd me why the poor complain, and these have answer'd
    thee."

CLXXXVII. — CHILDREN OF THE POOR.

FROM LAMB.

CHARLES LAMB is an English author, who lived from 1775 to 1834.
His writings in prose and verse are distinguished by good taste,
gentle pathos, and exquisite humor.

1. THE innocent prattle of his children takes out the
sting of a man's poverty. But the children of the very
poor do not prattle. It is none of the least frightful fea-
tures in that condition, that there is no childishness in its
dwellings. "Poor people," said a sensible old nurse to us
once, "do not bring up their children; they drag them
up." The little careless darling of the wealthier nursery,
in their hovel, is transformed betimes into a premature,
reflecting person. No one has time to dandle it, no one
thinks it worth while to coax it, to soothe it, to toss it up
and down, to humor it. There is none to kiss away its
tears. If it cries, it can only be beaten. It has been
prettily said, that "a babe is fed with milk and praise."

2. But the aliment of this poor babe was thin, unnour-
ishing; the return to its little baby tricks, and efforts to
engage attention, was bitter, ceaseless objurgation. It never
had a toy, or knew what a coral meant. It grew up
without the lullaby of nurses; it was a stranger to the
patient fondle, the hushing caress, the attracting novelty,
the costlier plaything or the cheaper off-hand contrivance
to divert the child, the prattled nonsense, (best sense to
it,) the wise impertinences, the wholesome fictions, the apt
story interposed, that puts a stop to present sufferings, and
awakens the passions of young wonder.

3. It was never sung to; no one ever told to it a tale of

the nursery. It was dragged up, to live or die, as it happened. It had no young dreams. It broke at once into the iron realities of life. A child exists not for the very poor as any object of dalliance: it is only another mouth to be fed, a pair of little hands to be betimes inured to labor. It is the rival, till it can be the co-operator, for food with the parent. It is never his mirth, his diversion, his solace; it never makes him young again, with recalling his young times.

4. The children of the very poor have no young times. It makes the very heart to bleed to overhear the casual street talk between a poor woman and her little girl, a woman of the better sort of poor, in a condition rather above the squalid beings which we have been contemplating. It is not of toys, of nursery books, of summer holidays, (fitting that age,) of the promised sight or play, of praised sufficiency at school. It is of mangling and clear-starching, of the price of coals, or of potatoes. The questions of the child, that should be the very outpourings of curiosity in idleness, are marked with forecast and melancholy providence. It has come to be a woman, before it was a child. It has learned to go to market; it chaffers, it haggles, it envies, it murmurs; it is knowing, acute, sharpened; it never prattles. Had we not reason to say, that the home of the very poor is no home?

CLXXXVIII. — I REMEMBER.

FROM HOOD.

1. I REMEMBER, I remember,
   The house where I was born,
The little window where the sun
   Came peeping in at morn:
He never came a wink too soon,
   Nor brought too long a day;
But now, I often wish the night
   Had borne my breath away!

2. I remember, I remember,
   The roses, red and white;
The violets and the lily-cups,
   Those flowers made of light!
The lilacs where the robin built,
   And where my brother set
The laburnum on his birth-day;
   The tree is living yet!

3. I remember, I remember,
   Where I was used to swing;
And thought the air must rush as fresh
   To swallows on the wing:
My spirit flew in feathers then,
   That is so heavy now,
And summer pools could hardly cool
   The fever on my brow!

4. I remember, I remember,
   The fir-trees dark and high;
I used to think their slender tops
   Were close against the sky:
It was a childish ignorance,
   But now 'tis little joy
To know I 'm further off from heav'n
   Than when I was a boy.

CLXXXIX. — I 'M PLEASED, AND YET I 'M SAD.

FROM WHITE.

HENRY KIRKE WHITE was an English poet of great promise, who died in 1806, at the age of 21. His death was the result of excessive study.

1. WHEN twilight steals along the ground,
And all the bells are ringing round,
   One, two, three, four, and five,

I at my study window sit,
And, wrapp'd in many a musing fit,
　　To bliss am all alive.

2. But though impressions calm and sweet
Thrill round my heart a holy heat,
　　And I am inly glad,
The tear-drop stands in either eye,
And yet I can not tell thee why,
　　I 'm pleas'd, and yet I 'm sad.

3. The silvery rack that flies away
Like mortal life or pleasure's ray,
　　Does *that* disturb my breast?
Nay, what have I, a studious man,
To do with life's unstable plan,
　　Or pleasure's fading vest?

4. Is it that here I must not stop,
But o'er yon blue hill's woody top
　　Must bend my lonely way?
No, surely no! for give but me
My own fire-side, and I shall be
　　At home, where'er I stray.

5. Then is it that yon steeple there,
With music sweet shall fill the air,
　　When *thou* no more canst hear!
Oh, no! oh, no! for then forgiven,
I shall be with my God in heaven,
　　Releas'd from every fear.

6. Then whence it is I can not tell,
But there *is* some mysterious spell
　　That holds me when I 'm glad;
And so the tear-drop fills my eye,
When yet, in truth, I know not why,
　　Or wherefore, I am sad.

CXC. — CASTLE-BUILDING.

FROM ADDISON.

1. DRACHMA; (drak'ma), a silver coin worth about 18 cents.
3. VIZIER; (viz'yer), chief minister or ruler.

1. ALNASCHAR, says the fable, was a very idle fellow, who never would set his hand to any business during his father's life. His father, dying, left to him the value of a hundred drachmas in Persian money. Alnaschar, in order to make the best of it, laid it out in glasses, bottles, and the finest earthenware. These he piled up in a large open basket, and having made choice of a very little shop, placed the basket at his feet, and leaned his back upon the wall, in expectation of customers. As he sat in this posture, with his eyes upon the basket, he fell into a most amusing train of thought, and was overheard by one of his neighbors, as he talked to himself. "This basket," says he, "cost me at the wholesale merchant's a hundred drachmas, which is all I have in the world.

2. "I shall quickly make two hundred of it, by selling it in retail. These two hundred drachmas will in a little while rise to four hundred, which, of course, will amount in time to four thousand. Four thousand drachmas can not fail of making eight thousand. As soon as by this means I am master of ten thousand, I will lay aside my trade of a glass-man, and turn jeweler. I shall then deal in diamonds, pearls, and all sorts of rich stones. When I have got together as much wealth as I can well desire, I will make a purchase of the finest house I can find. I shall then begin to enjoy myself and make a noise in the world. I will not, however, stop there, but still continue my traffic, till I have got together a hundred thousand drachmas.

3. "When I have thus made myself master of a hundred thousand drachmas, I shall naturally set myself on the footing of a prince, and will demand the Grand Vizier's daughter in marriage, after having represented to that minister the information which I have received of the

beauty, wit, discretion, and other high qualities, which his daughter possesses. I will let him know, at the same time, that it is my intention to make him a present of a thousand pieces of gold on our marriage night. As soon as I have married the Grand Vizier's daughter, I will make my father-in-law a visit with a grand train and equipage; and when I am placed at his right hand, where I shall be, of course, if it be only to honor his daughter, I will give him the thousand pieces of gold which I promised him, and afterward, to his great surprise, will present him another purse of the same value, with some short speech, as, 'Sir, you see I am a man of my word; I always give more than I promise.'

4. "When I have brought the princess to my house, I shall take particular care to cause her duly to respect me. To this end, I shall confine her to her own apartment, make her a short visit, and talk but little to her. Her women will represent to me that she is inconsolable by reason of my unkindness, and beg me with tears to notice her, and let her sit down by me; but I shall still remain inexorable; and will turn my back upon her. Her mother will then come and bring her daughter to me, as I am seated upon my sofa. The daughter, with tears in her eyes, will fling herself at my feet, and beg of me to receive her into my favor. Then will I, to imprint in her a thorough veneration for my person, draw up my legs and spurn her from me with my foot, in such a manner that she shall fall down several paces from the sofa."

5. Alnaschar was entirely swallowed up in this chimerical vision, and could not forbear acting with his foot what he had in his thoughts. So that, unluckily striking his basket of brittle ware, which was the foundation of all his grandeur, he kicked his glasses to a 'great distance from him into the street, and broke them into ten thousand pieces.

CXCI. — THE FOUR WISHES.

CHARLES.

I ASK for power, that 'neath my sway
Nations might tremble and obey;
Over the sea to stretch my hand,
And sway my scepter o'er the land;
That the proudest monarch should lay down,
At will of mine, his jewel'd crown;
That rich and poor should bend the knee,
And pay due homage unto me;
That the sun's eye should never shine
On kingdoms that I call'd not mine;
Thus seated on my lofty throne,
The whole wide world my sway should own.

MOTHER.

Thirst not for power! for, rightly used,
'Twill make some foes; but, if abused,
Nations will rise and curses shed,
Long, loud, deep curses on thy head!
Thirst not for power! thy life will be
A life of splendid misery;
And thou wilt be the slave of all,
Though at thy feet the world should fall.
Thirst not for power! for though to-day
Nations thy slightest will obey,
Perchance to-morrow thou 'lt lay down,
Before the king of death, thy crown!

ALBERT.

I ask for riches, wealth untold;
For coffers fill'd with glittering gold;
For pearls which in the ocean shine,
As gems that sparkle in the mine;
Upon the treasures of each zone
I 'd lay my hands and call my own.
H. S. R.—40

I would each star that decks the sky
A diamond at my feet might lie;
That every leaf on every tree,
Would fall in precious stones for me.
Yes, wealth into my coffers pour,
Till mortal would not wish for more.

MOTHER.

Oh, ask not gold! 'twill melt away,
Like dew drops in the early day;
Oh, ask not gold! for it will fling
A fetter o'er the spirit's wing,
And bind it when it fain would rise
To seek true riches in the skies.
Oh, ask not gold! for it will prove
A snare, and cause thy feet to rove
Far from the straight and narrow way,
Which leads to realms of endless day.

MARY.

I ask for beauty; for an eye
Bright as the stars in yonder sky;
For tresses on the air to fling,
And put to shame the raven's wing;
Cheeks where the lily and the rose
Are blended in a sweet repose;
For pearly teeth, and coral lip,
Tempting the honey-bee to sip;
And for a fairy foot as light
As is the young gazelle's in flight;
And then a small, white, tapering hand:
I'd reign a beauty in the land.

MOTHER.

Sigh not for beauty! like the flower,
That opes its petals for an hour,
And droops beneath the noontide ray,
So will thy beauty fade away.

The brightest eye at last must close,
And on the cheek where blooms the rose
The hand of death will set his seal;
O'er it the canker-worm will steal.
Those tresses rich and glossy now,
Clustering round the snowy brow,
Will turn to dust; yes, beauty's bloom
Must wither in the silent tomb.

ELIZA.

I ask the poet's gift; the lyre,
With skillful hand to sweep each wire;
I 'd pour my burning thoughts in song,
In lays deep, passionate, and strong,
Till hearts should thrill at every word,
As mine is thrill'd at song of bird.
Oh! I would die and leave some trace
That earth has been my dwelling-place;
Would live in hearts for evermore,
When my frail, fitful life is o'er.
Oh! for the gifted poet's power,
This is my wish, be this my dower!

MOTHER.

A glorious gift! yet it will be
A source of 'sorrow unto thee,
In this cold, selfish world of ours,
Where piercing thorns grow 'mid the flowers.
'Twill fill that gentle breast of thine
With thirst for something too divine;
And, like a young, caged bird, whose eye
Looks out upon the free blue sky,
Thy spirit's wing will long to soar
To seek some far-off peaceful shore.
It may not be a happy lot:
Then, gentle maiden, ask it not.

ALL.

What shall we ask? If power will shed
So many curses on the head;

And if the gift of wealth will fling
A fetter o'er the spirit's wing;
If beauty blooms but for a day,
Then, like the spring-flower, fades away;
And if the poet's thrilling lyre
Will waken such a restless fire
Within the soul, and make it pine
With thirst for something too divine;
What shall we ask, fain would we know,
To make us happy here below?

MOTHER.

Oh! ask for things of nobler worth
Than the poor cankering gifts of earth;
Ask for the treasures of the mind,
A heart all generous, true, and kind;
Ask virtue a green wreath to twine,
To deck these young, fair brows of thine,
A wreath of fadeless buds and flowers,
Destin'd to bloom in heaven's own bowers;
Ask for *religion;* it will be
Worth beauty, fame, and power to thee,
And when this fleeting life is o'er,
'Twill give thee life for evermore.

CXCII. — SABBATH IN THE COUNTRY.

FROM MRS. SIGOURNEY.

MRS. SIGOURNEY is a living authoress, distinguished for the high character, intellectual, moral, and religious, of her numerous productions in prose and poetry. She resides in Hartford, Conn.

1. THE churches that spring up on every village green, are pleasing and peculiar features of the scenery of New England. They are often seen side by side with the small school-house, in loving brotherhood, teachers for this life and the next. The simplicity of the appearance of many of their congregations might be an object of curious observation to those accustomed only to the fashionably dressed

throngs of city worshipers. I once attended divine service, many years since, with some friends, in an exceedingly secluded village, at the distance of a few miles from the spot where we were spending a part of the summer. The church was small and antique, and remote from other buildings.

2. The audience was almost entirely composed of practical agriculturists and their families. They were attired with perfect neatness, though with little conformity to the reigning modes. Their bronzed cheeks and toil-hardened hands showed that the physical comfort of a day of rest might be appreciated, while their intelligent and serious countenances evinced that they aspired to its higher privileges.

3. The weather being warm, many of the farmers removed their coats, depositing them on the back of their seats, and seemed much to enjoy the additional coolness, while they thus disclosed the snowy whiteness of their coarse, home-made linen, that now almost obsolete branch of manufacture, which had such close affinity with habits of domestic industry and comfort. Their wives were evidently inured to toil, nor of that toil ashamed. A few of the mothers bore in their arms healthful and ruddy infants, leaving probably no person at home with whom they could safely intrust so precious a charge. They seemed to make no trouble, or if any was anticipated, the mother withdrew with them. The guileless spirit of the babe need not be counted an unfitting, though an unwonted guest, in the temple of the God of truth.

4. The form of the aged pastor was bent with time, and his thin hair of a silvery whiteness. For more than fifty years he had been the guide and friend of his people;

"And ne'er had changed, nor wish'd to change, his place."

The affection was reciprocal, and it was touching to see with what attention they listened to every word that fell from his lips. His voice was tremulous, and the involuntary movement of his hand paralytic; but he spoke to them of sacred themes, and they loved them the better

because he uttered them, and him the better because his life had so long been in harmony with what he taught. For two generations he had been with them, at bridal and at burial, at the christening-carol and at the death-wail. He had rejoiced in their prosperity, and at their last conflict with the Spoiler, had armed himself with prayer, and stood by, until there was no more breath. He had shed the baptismal dew on infant brows, that, now mottled with gray, bent over their children's children. His flock had not been so numerous but that every part of their history was familiar to him, and kept its place in his memory.

5. Such an intercourse had created, as it ought, no common attachment. They saw that his step was feeble, and that time had taken from him somewhat of manhood's glory; but they remembered that he had grown old in their service, that his eye had become dim while he cared for their souls, and every infirmity was a new bond of sympathy. If there were any of the young who might have taken pride in a modern preacher, one less prolix, or more after the fashion of the day, they checked the thought ere it was spoken, for they had learned to venerate their faithful pastor from the patriarchs who had gone to rest.

6. The intermission between the services was short, as most of the congregation, coming from quite a distance, did not return home at noon. Their horses were sheltered by sheds, constructed for that purpose, while they, seated in groups, amid clumps of lofty forest trees, partook of such refreshments as they had brought for the occasion. It was pleasant to see families gathering together, with their healthful children, upon the green turf, beneath canopies of shade. In an interesting group near us, the hoary grandsire, with lifted hands, besought the divine blessing on their simple repast. Here and there, the young walked by themselves, on the margin of the fair stream; but there seemed in their deportment or conversation nothing unworthy of the consecrated day. We returned home from the little village church, cheered, and I hope edified, by its devotion, and the beautiful and time-tried love of the white-haired shepherd and his confiding flock.

CXCIII. — CHARITY.

FROM THE BIBLE.

CHARITY, in this extract, is the old English for *love*. It would be well for the reader, occasionally at least, to substitute the latter.

1. THOUGH I speak with the tongues of men and of angels, and have not charity, I am become as sounding brass, or a tinkling cymbal. And though I have the gift of prophecy, and understand all mysteries and all knowledge; and though I have all faith, so that I could remove mountains, and have not charity, I am nothing. And though I bestow all my goods to feed the poor, and though I give my body to be burned, and have not charity, it profiteth me nothing.

2. Charity suffereth long, and is kind; charity envieth not; charity vaunteth not itself, is not puffed up, doth not behave itself unseemly, seeketh not her own, is not easily provoked, thinketh no evil; rejoiceth not in iniquity, but rejoiceth in the truth; beareth all things, believeth all things, hopeth all things, endureth all things.

3. Charity never faileth; but whether there be prophecies, they shall fail; whether there be tongues, they shall cease; whether there be knowledge, it shall vanish away. For we know in part, and we prophesy in part. But when that which is perfect is come, then that which is in part shall be done away.

4. When I was a child, I spake as a child, I understood as a child, I thought as a child: but when I became a man, I put away childish things. For now we see through a glass, darkly; but then face to face: now I know in part; but then shall I know even as also I am known.

And now abideth faith, hope, charity, these three; but the greatest of these is charity.

CXCIV. — EARTH'S ANGELS.

1. EARTH has angels, though their forms are molded
 But of such clay as fashions all below;
Though harps are wanting, and bright pinions folded,
 We know them by the love-light on their brow.

2. I have seen angels by the sick one's pillow;
 Theirs was the soft tone and the soundless tread,
When smitten hearts were drooping like the willow,
 They stood "between the living and the dead."

3. And if my sight, by earthly dimness hinder'd,
 Beheld no hovering cherubim in air,
I doubted not, for spirits know their kindred,
 They smiled upon the viewless watchers there.

4. There have been angels in the gloomy prison;
 In crowded halls; by the lone widow's hearth;
And where they pass'd, the fallen have uprisen,
 The giddy paus'd, the mourner's hope had birth.

5. I have seen one whose eloquence commanding,
 Rous'd the rich echoes of the human breast;
The blandishments of wealth and ease withstanding,
 That hope might reach the suffering and opprest.

6. And by his side there moved a form of beauty,
 Strewing sweet flowers along his path of life,
And looking up with meek and love-blent duty:
 I call'd her angel, but *he* call'd her wife.

7. O! many a spirit walks the world unheeded,
 That, when its vail of sadness is laid down,
Shall soar aloft with pinions unimpeded,
 And wear its glory like a starry crown.

THE END.

English
Français
Deutsche
Italiano
Español
Português

www.forgottenbooks.com

Mythology Photography **Fiction**
Fishing Christianity **Art** Cooking
Essays Buddhism Freemasonry
Medicine **Biology** Music **Ancient
Egypt** Evolution Carpentry Physics
Dance Geology **Mathematics** Fitness
Shakespeare **Folklore** Yoga Marketing
Confidence Immortality Biographies
Poetry **Psychology** Witchcraft
Electronics Chemistry History **Law**
Accounting **Philosophy** Anthropology
Alchemy Drama Quantum Mechanics
Atheism Sexual Health **Ancient History**
Entrepreneurship Languages Sport
Paleontology Needlework Islam
Metaphysics Investment Archaeology
Parenting Statistics Criminology
Motivational

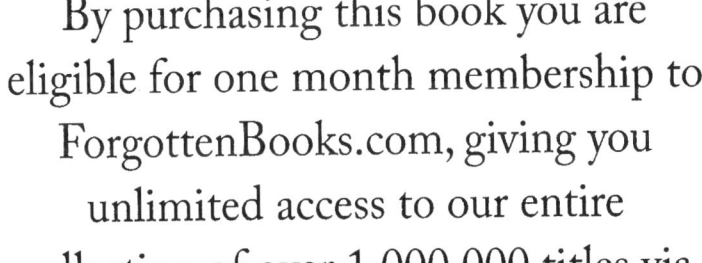

ISBN 978-1-333-77961-0
PIBN 10547165